The Ethics of Parenthood

Norvin Richards

OXFORD
UNIVERSITY PRESS

2010

OXFORD
UNIVERSITY PRESS

Oxford University Press, Inc., publishes works that further
Oxford University's objective of excellence
in research, scholarship, and education.

Oxford   New York
Auckland   Cape Town   Dar es Salaam   Hong Kong   Karachi
Kuala Lumpur   Madrid   Melbourne   Mexico City   Nairobi
New Delhi   Shanghai   Taipei   Toronto

With offices in
Argentina   Austria   Brazil   Chile   Czech Republic   France   Greece
Guatemala   Hungary   Italy   Japan   Poland   Portugal   Singapore
South Korea   Switzerland   Thailand   Turkey   Ukraine   Vietnam

Published by Oxford University Press, Inc.
198 Madison Avenue, New York, New York 10016

www.oup.com

Oxford is a registered trademark of Oxford University Press.

Library of Congress Cataloging-in-Publication Data
Richards, Norvin, 1943–
The ethics of parenthood / Norvin Richards.
     p. cm.
Includes bibliographical references and index.
ISBN 978-0-19-973174-9
1. Parenting—Moral and ethical aspects.   I. Title.
HQ755.85.R515 2010
173—dc22   2009032507

9 8 7 6 5 4 3 2 1

Printed in the United States of America
on acid-free paper

For Norvin and Genevieve,
apples of their parents' eyes,
and for Janet,
my fellow fruiter

Acknowledgments

Many friends and colleagues read my efforts at various chapters, as did my son. Their comments were invaluable. I owe debts of this kind to Torin Alter, Andrew Brien, W. R. Carter, Russell Daw, Scott Hestevold, Terry McConnell, James Otteson, Stuart Rachels, George Rainbolt and Norvin Richards, and I am grateful to them all. I want also to thank three anonymous reviewers for Oxford University Press for suggestions that greatly improved the final version. I am also grateful to the late Douglas Lanford, who employed me to teach seminars to judges of the juvenile court under the auspices of the American Academy of Judicial Education, and to the judges who endured my early thoughts about how the legal system should treat juveniles and who gave me the wisdom of their experience.

My greatest debts are to James Montmarquet and Robert Young, who read everything that is here and much that is not. They managed both to save me from error and to encourage me to believe I had ideas worth pursuing. Writing with their help was rich in its own rewards, and the pages that follow are incomparably better for it.

Contents

The Ethics of Parenthood

Introduction

When we are young, our parents have our lives in their hands, to an extraordinary extent. They have enormous influence on what our lives are like, and more to do with the kind of person we become than anyone except us. As we grow up, we grow away from our parents, increasing our forays into the larger world and doing ever more of what they once did for us. Still, it is hard to think of any other extended human relationships in which one party is as deeply affected by what the other party does or does not do.

Our relationship with our parents changes when we become adults and take up whatever our culture expects of adults, but it does not ordinarily end. Our parents are still our parents, not just people who were our parents once upon a time. Often parents and their grown children are deeply fond of one another, and even when the relationship is strained and distant, each retains a remarkable power to affect the other.

This is a book about how parents and children ought to treat each other at the different stages of this uncommonly long and uncommonly powerful relationship. I try to say what the parental obligations are while a child is young and under the parent's care, and also what obligations the child has to them during this period. Then I analyze the moral relationship between a parent and a grown child, including what obligations each has to the other and why they have these.

Of course, it would be a rare child who wanted only to be a figure of obligation to his parents, and an unfortunate child whose parents thought of him only in that way. It would also be a rare parent who wanted her children to take her only as someone to whom there were certain duties to be kept. Instead, children ordinarily want their parents to love them, and parents ordinarily want their sons and daughters to love them as well. This is true not only while the child is young but also when he or she has become an adult. So an account that spoke only of the obligations of parenthood and only of the obligations children have would miss what we hope to have at the heart of it all, and what can make it so sweet and so rich. There is one chapter below on loving one another, and points about love between parent and child are also central to the accounts of filial obligations and of a parent's decisions about how her life is to end.

The chapters fall into three categories. The first group concerns the significance of being the biological parent of a child. Presumably that ought to matter, but *why* should it matter? What is it about being the biological parent that ought to give a person special standing where a child is concerned? Chapter 1 argues for an answer to that question. That answer shapes the answer to the further question of how much the biological relationship ought to matter, relative to other considerations.

Sometimes the biological relationship shouldn't matter at all. Imagine a rapist who impregnates his victim. He is the biological father of the child, but surely that fact gives him no rights at all where the child is concerned. Chapter 2 considers whether the same is true in a range of other cases. For example, there are cultures that do not allow women to decline to have children. When men impregnate women in such cultures, should that action always be regarded as akin to rape? I argue against this view. There are also biological parents who employ surrogates to carry their child to term, or who use eggs donated by others, or both. Do these ways of creating a child forfeit the significance that the biological connection would have had? I argue that they do not. I also argue against the view that homosexuals ought not to be allowed to be parents, and I explore the important idea that someone can be too young to be a parent despite having had a baby. In all of these contexts, being the biological parent of a child might be taken not to entail a right to be a parent to that child in the years to come. My view is that this is true only when a person is incapable of performing adequately as a parent, and I explore when we are entitled to conclude that and when we are not.

How much the biological connection should matter comes up in a different way when parents have been absent from the lives of their children for a time and then wish to return. The reason for the absence is crucial, and there are many possibilities. In some leading legal cases it is the biological father who eventually comes forward, claiming that he was deceived, was told the child was not his, that he has come forward promptly upon learning the truth, and that he should now be allowed to be a father to his child. In the meanwhile others have served as parents to the child they think of as theirs, and they want desperately to continue. There are several factors to weigh in resolving these disputes, in my opinion. Chapter 3 identifies those factors and offers a way to give them the importance that they ought to have, relative to each other.

The chapter also applies this approach to cases in which the parent's absence has a different explanation. For example, the biological father may not have been told lies but simply took no interest in whether a sexual partner had become pregnant. It was a one-night stand, he never looked back, and now he has learned that there was a child, to whom he says he wants to be a father. Does he have any claims? It can also happen that babies are switched at birth and sent home with the wrong parents. When the mistake is discovered, what should happen? Or a family may be ripped asunder by war or natural disaster, none of them even knowing who survived. Suppose the children are taken in by others, who raise them as their own, and years later the biological parents are able to find their children—and they want them back. What should happen then? Chapter 3 argues for a way of answering these and other questions.

Whoever serves as a parent to a child must not abuse or neglect that child, we would all agree. But what should count as abuse and neglect, given that all parents make mistakes, and given also the intuition that parents ought to have some latitude in the way they raise their children? Chapter 4 addresses these matters and offers a view about when the state should intervene on behalf of a child and what form that intervention should take.

That discussion serves as a transition to the second group of chapters, which concerns not who is to serve as parents to a young child but what that role *amounts* to. What are parents to do during this time, beyond being careful not to abuse or neglect their children? Here it was necessary to restrict the discussion to families in which the children should be expected to become adults. Of course, there are also children for whom the reasonable expectation is that they will die while still very young, or that they will not develop the capacities of an adult regardless of how long they live. There are important moral questions about how to be a good parent to such children, and about how this differs from being a parent to a child who will grow up—and how it does not. Doing those questions justice would require a book of its own, however, and here I have only been able to allude to them.

I have focused instead on parents whose child, if all goes as expected, will become an adult. One question is what is required of such parents; another concerns what responsibilities the children have toward their parents, during their childhood. Both are discussed mainly in Chapter 5, on the autonomy of children, Chapter 6, on raising a child, and Chapter 7, on providing a child with a moral education. The line taken is that children have certain obligations of obedience and also have further obligations to participate both in their own moral education and in developing what I call selves of their own. Raising a child ought not to be something the parent does to the child, as if she were a crop in the field, but something the two of them do together. What that process amounts to is spelled out in the account of the obligations parents and children have to one another while the child is growing up.

Chapter 8 turns to this: although parents must certainly be concerned to do right by their child, they must also be concerned about what the child does to others. No child is perfect in that respect, of course. When one of them treats someone badly, should it matter that she is "only a child"? That seems to be the standard view. As Tamar Schapiro puts it, "the knowledge that an agent is a child rather than an adult often prompts us to modify our 'reactive attitudes' toward her. An adult who laughs at your bald spot is to be resented; a child who does the same is to be disciplined—at least insofar as you decide to treat her as a child. In this sense, we do not take child action as seriously as adult action, or, rather, we do not take it seriously in the same way."[1]

Unfortunately, children can do much worse things than laugh at someone's bald spot. What, if anything, should remain of the idea that the person who did wrong is just a child? Quite a lot, I argue, both for wrongs that call the criminal justice system into play and for bad behavior of the kinds that every parent encounters. I explain why being a child should matter in both of these contexts, how it should matter, and when it should not matter enough to preserve the child from very harsh punishment. The answers draw on an account of "reactive attitudes" such as hatred and resentment. They also use the ideas developed in Chapter 5 "The Autonomy of Children," to explain the relevance of the child's age.

Chapter 9 considers the place that love has in the moral relationship between a parent and a child. Certainly parents ordinarily do love their children very much, especially when the children are young and under their care. Is that just the way we are, or do we have a moral obligation to love our children? If we do, is this our obligation only while our children are still children, or do we also have an obligation to love them after they have become grown men and women?

I argue against dismissing these questions on the ground that love can never be a matter of obligation, and then argue for a set of answers to them. My claim is that we do have an obligation to love our children while they are young and under our care, and that there is no parental obligation to love them after they are grown. Rather, there are only ways in which particular parents can incur an obligation to love their grown sons or daughters, Chapter 9 suggests what those are.

When the children reach adulthood, there are significant differences in the moral relationship between them and their parents. Chapters 10, 11, and 12 are about being a good parent to an adult son or daughter and about being good sons or daughters to our parents after we are no longer children. I offer arguments concerning what a parent's obligations are at this stage of life, and I also suggest how these might be fulfilled without treating the son or daughter as if he or she were still a child.

I offer as well a view about what grown children owe their parents. Others have argued that adults do not owe their parents debts of gratitude. I disagree, but I also argue that there are filial obligations over and above these: an idea I adopt from Simon Keller's important work.[2] With certain restrictions, I argue that what we owe by way of filial obligations is a place in our affections that roughly corresponds to the one we had in our parents' affections when we were under their care. I then try to indicate what that would entail, and what it would not.

Chapter 12 offers a view about a question that might arise toward the end of a parent's life: namely, whether there are sacrifices that parents should not allow their grown children to make for their sake, even if the children want to make them. I argue against taking a cost/benefit approach to these questions, and I develop a different way of thinking about what parents should permit their children to do for them. It allows mutual devotion between parent and child to be significant in a way that the cost/benefit approach does not, and it requires us to be willing to honor the debts we incur when we accept a sacrifice made for our sake. This certainly doesn't mean that a parent can do no wrong at such times. However, it also leaves considerable room for the parties to shape the final stage of their relationship in ways that express both who they are and what they have had together.

The ethics of parenthood offered in this book leaves the parties at considerable liberty to shape their relationship, not only at the end of their lives together, but at many earlier junctures as well. For example, although parents are certainly not free to raise their children in any way they like, or to provide whatever they wish by way of a moral education, there are a variety of ways for them to carry out their obligations along these lines. If those demands of parenthood were rigid and required exactly the same actions from all parents, then being a parent would be nowhere near the rich opportunity it is to put oneself into play in the world.

On the view offered here, parents acquire the right to that opportunity when they create a child, or adopt one, or assume the role informally, so long as they were free to take this first step. Of course, once they have the opportunity, they are certainly not free to make whatever use of it they wish. In large part, the limitations on what they may do derive from the fact that this is a *child* they have in their charge. Children are sentient beings, with a right not to suffer. They also have developing selves of their own, with corresponding rights to put those selves into action and rights to a parent's help in continuing to become someone of their own. Moreover, children don't live only with their parents, but function in society with others throughout their lives. These considerations impose important constraints on the way a parent may treat his or her child—but they do not constrain so severely that there can be nothing *personal* about being a parent. There is similar latitude in being a good son or a good daughter, on the view I offer.

As was noted, many of us want our grown children to love us, not just to respect us and to have a strong sense of duty where we are concerned. Similarly, we want our parents to love us, not just to regard us as continuing sources of obligations, and certainly not only as people who are greatly in their debt. Parents have no obligation to love us just because we are still their children, nor do we have an obligation to love them just because they are still our parents. Any obligations here will be particular to the relationship, deriving from ways in which the individuals have been parents and child to one another. That is yet another way in which the moral relationship is our own joint creation, rather than something that will take the same form for all.

In all of these ways, parenthood is an opportunity to try to shape something that is enormously powerful, not only in what sorts of people our children become but also in what sorts of people we become ourselves, and in whether our lives and theirs are sweet or bitter. This book tries to say what that opportunity is, if we act as we should, and to bring to light some ways in which to take advantage of it.

1

The Rights of Biological Parents

Early on the morning of February 8, 1991, a young woman named Cara Clausen gave birth to a baby girl. Some 40 hours later Ms. Clausen signed papers waiving her parental rights and giving the child up for adoption. The adoptive couple, Jan and Robbie DeBoer, took the baby home, named her "Jessica DeBoer," and immersed themselves in the delighted doting that is so typical of new parents.

Within the next two months, though, Clausen had sued to get Baby Jessica back. So had the child's biological father, Daniel Schmidt. Clausen's initial claim was that she had waived her parental rights only because of coercion by an attorney for the adoptive parents. That assertion went nowhere, but Schmidt's was a different story. His claim was that he had never waived his rights at all. Initially, Cara Clausen had named a different man as the child's father. That man had signed a release of paternal rights, but Schmidt had not; according to him, at the time of his daughter's adoption he hadn't known she was his daughter.

The DeBoers did not yield readily but made every legal effort they could to retain Jessica as their daughter. Public sympathy was very much on their side, even after Schmidt and Clausen married. However, it was Daniel Schmidt who prevailed in court; eventually, the adoption was voided and his parental rights were restored. Once the legal struggles were over, he and Cara Clausen came to collect a "Baby Jessica" who was then two and a half years old. The scene was a media event, featuring "a terrified little girl, screaming and crying as she was carried away from the only home she had ever known."[1]

The story of Baby Richard is similar, if somewhat more colorful. The baby's mother, Daniella Janikova, was eight months pregnant when his father, Otakar Kirchner, returned to Czechoslovakia to visit his own dying grandmother. A relative in Prague told Daniella that Otakar had resumed a relationship there with a former girlfriend. This information appears to have been false, but Daniella certainly believed it. She tore up their marriage license, moved from the apartment they had shared to a women's shelter, and arranged privately to have the child adopted as soon as he was born.

Upon Otakar's return the two reconciled to some degree, but not sufficiently to change Daniella's plans. When the baby arrived, she gave birth in a different hospital than the couple had planned and she had her uncle tell Otakar that the child was born dead. Otakar appears never to have believed this story; he visited several hospitals in search of records of the birth and then rooted through Daniella's garbage cans in search of diapers or other physical evidence. He found nothing, and she stuck to her story for nearly two months. Then she told him what had actually happened, and he immediately took legal action to regain custody from the adoptive couple. That couple did everything they could to retain the boy they thought of as their son, just as the DeBoers had resisted surrendering Baby Jessica.

By the time this second case became public, Baby Richard had spent the first two and a half years of his life with his adoptive parents. Public sympathies favored leaving him with them, just as they had favored leaving Baby Jessica with the DeBoers. Once again, however, it was the biological father who prevailed in court. By the time the legal battles ended and Otakar came to collect the child, Baby Richard was four and a half. This time the scene was played in front of television cameras, and it featured a sizable crowd of vocal adults who made it very plain how strongly they disapproved of Otakar and of what he was doing.

The adoptive couples in these cases had wanted the court to think in terms of which course would be in the best interests of the disputed child. It is not hard to see why they sought that ruling, and the only court that did reason in this way required only thirty minutes' reflection before finding for the DeBoers instead of Daniel Schmidt.[2] Another court eventually rejected that approach but felt its pull:

> The argument that the best interests of the baby are best served by allowing her to stay with R.D. and J.D. is a very alluring argument. Daniel has had a poor performance record as a parent. He fathered two children prior to this child, a son, age fourteen, and a daughter born out of wedlock, now age twelve. The record shows that Daniel has largely failed to support these children financially and has failed to maintain meaningful contact with either of them. In contrast…the DeBoers "have provided exemplary care for the child [and] view themselves as the parents of the child in every respect."[3]

The courts did not reach the conclusion the adoptive couples sought, though, because they found it improper to reason in this way. Here is Justice Larson, to that effect:

> While cognizant of the heartache which this decision will ultimately cause, this court is presented with no other option than that dictated by the law in this state. Purely equitable principles cannot be substituted for well-established principles of law.
> The parental rights of this father may not be dismissed without compliance with our termination statute.[4]

As he also notes,

> The district court found that Daniel was in fact the real father, that he had not released his parental rights, and that he had not abandoned the baby. The court denied the adoption and ordered the baby to be surrendered to Daniel….We agree with the district court…that Daniel proved he was the father, that he had not abandoned the baby, and that the adoption proceeding was therefore fatally flawed. Custody of the baby is ordered to be transferred to Daniel.[5]

The grounds on which the Supreme Court of Illinois found for Otakar Kirchner are much the same:

In vacating the adoption, this court noted that a child is not available for adoption until it has been validly determined that the rights of his parents have been properly terminated....Though we note that the best-interests-of-the-child standard is not to be denigrated, we reiterate that this standard is never triggered until after it has been validly determined that a child is available for adoption.

Under Illinois law, parents may be divested of parental rights either through their voluntary consent or involuntarily due to a finding of abuse, abandonment, neglect, or unfitness by clear and convincing evidence.[6]

Since Otakar Kirchner had neither waived his rights nor forfeited them and had not been shown to be unfit to be a parent, Baby Richard was not available for adoption. Under the law, therefore, he was Otakar Kirchner's child to raise, the reasoning went, and for the court to turn to considerations of the child's best interest would have violated Otakar's legal rights as his biological parent.

Both rulings take it to be a well-established principle of law that biological parents have a right to raise their children, which they can waive or can forfeit by being clearly incompetent or by abusing, neglecting, or abandoning their child, but which is otherwise dispositive. In particular, Justice Larson tells us, "[c]ourts are not free to take children from parents simply by deciding another home offers more advantages."[7] Instead, when biological parenthood has been neither waived nor forfeited, the court cannot even consider where the child would be better off. This is true even when the child has lived virtually all of his or her young life with someone else, who now wishes to adopt.

That was the structure of American law at the time these cases were heard, and it remains so. I believe it is also correct, and I will offer arguments for that view. The first step is to explain what is wrong with the leading alternative, according to which such cases shouldn't be decided in terms of the rights of the adults involved, but in terms of the best interests of the child.

1.

Here is a passage in which Justice Larson seeks to explain why judges within the American system cannot reason in that way.

As tempting as it is to resolve this highly emotional issue with one's heart, we do not have the unbridled discretion of a Solomon. Ours is a system of law...without established procedures to guide courts in such matters, they would 'be engaged in uncontrolled social engineering.' This is not permitted under our law.[8]

His point is that in a system of law, judges who are deciding cases are required to apply the rules that have been established in statutes and in precedents, rather than consulting their own sense of what might be most just. Justice Larson isn't trying to justify that understanding of life under the rule of law, but only asserting that he is bound by it. However, his remarks do suggest the following way to try to justify it where these cases are concerned.

Unless cases of this kind are decided by granting biological parents the right to raise their children, we will have a system of uncontrolled social engineering.

Biological parents would lose control not to a Big Brother with a Master Plan but to a raft of independent social engineers wearing judicial robes, each implementing his or her personal theory about what life would be best for the child and about who would be the best people to provide it. This is objectionable in so many ways that our own way of life is bound to be far superior, even if it has sad outcomes where the Baby Jessicas and Baby Richards are concerned.

Notice, though, that it is not appealing to reject *all* "uncontrolled social engineering" involving newborns. For example, it is uncontrolled social engineering when people see to it that abandoned babies are looked after instead of letting nature take its course. It is also uncontrolled social engineering when friends or relatives assist a parent who needs information about nutrition, or who needs help with his temper. None of that is objectionable. So to say only that the alternative to our system is one of uncontrolled social engineering leaves the argument incomplete. We must also be told what is objectionable about this particular kind of social engineering, or it remains unclear why we should not engage in it.

One difference, of course, is that judges are agents of the state, whereas friends, relatives, and people who find abandoned babies are not, and the state need not be involved in what they do. So let us consider an actual effort by a state to do some social engineering in this area. From the 1930s to the 1970s the governments of several Australian states sought to improve the lives of children born out of wedlock.[9] Their theory was that those children would have a hard time of it, given cultural attitudes: "Post-war Australia was conservative and intolerant. The stigma of an illegitimate baby was hard-shaken by either mother or child…adoption was seen as the answer."[10] It was thought far better for such children to be placed with married couples who yearned to have children but had not been able to conceive. So, the babies were placed with such couples—but not by anything resembling the free choice of the child's mother. Often the procedure was to tell the birth mother that her baby had been stillborn or had died immediately after being born, then provide the child to the chosen couple to raise as their own.[11] Sometimes instead, the women were "drugged and bullied into surrendering their babies at the very time they were in no state to decide anything."[12] One of these women "recalls the chloroform-soaked nappy that was held firmly over her face as she began to push during the final stage of labor at a Melbourne clinic in 1961. When she awoke, there was no baby. Somewhere from the fog she remembers someone putting a fountain pen in her hand."[13]

What comes to mind first isn't that these officials might have been wrong about which life would be the best one for the children. The *first* thought is that the women in these stories were done a terrible wrong: the officials had no right to act as they did. The women should have had a chance to raise their children themselves or to decide that someone else was to do it instead, rather than having the state take their babies from them.

If that strong intuition is correct, it tells us what would also be most objectionable about assigning Baby Jessica and Baby Richard according to a judge's sense of where these children would be best off. It isn't that the judges might not get this right, nor is it that judges' deciding special cases in that way will lead to their doing it wholesale. Rather, the deepest wrong is that a judge who did this would ignore the right that biological parents have to raise their children themselves or to decide that it would be better if someone else did. That idea also fits our ready acceptance of the two undistressing examples of "uncontrolled social engineering," since strangers who see to it that an abandoned baby is looked after are certainly not violating the biological parents' right to raise their child as they see fit, and neither are friends and relatives who provide a beleaguered parent some help, at least so long as the help is needed and is kept within certain limits. In short, if we regard biological parents as having this right, that view rationalizes our very different reactions to these cases.

Still, it hasn't emerged why social engineering by the *state* should be especially objectionable, and it would be the state in action if judges decided where children were to go. Martin Guggenheim says this about having the state make such decisions: "If government played a significant role in choosing parents for children at birth, government would likely have entered the prohibited arena of participating in value inculcation in children. In a polity committed to the ideal of government serving the people's will, it is unimaginable to conceive of children as belonging to the government. Quite the opposite."[14]

Since Guggenheim speaks of values inculcation as a prohibited arena, it sounds as if he thinks it is wrong for the state to have anything at all to do with providing children their values. That can't be what he means. It would then be improper for the state to erect monuments to soldiers who fell valorously in the service of their country, since that act speaks to children of values, or to hold public ceremonies or have national holidays honoring individuals for their accomplishments, or to have a pledge of allegiance in a public school or performance of a national anthem at any of the state's events. None of that is outrageous, surely. Moreover, it seems to be part of the very idea of a state in modern times that there are *laws*. Some of these laws define which behavior is criminal, and some govern civil transactions between individuals and structure the economy. Both bodies of law include many messages about how people are to act, and some of those messages are certainly conveyed to children. So if it really were objectionable for the state to "enter the arena" of giving children their values, it appears that any modern version of a state would be objectionable as such. That is certainly not Guggenheim's view.

His point would be better put by saying that the state shouldn't venture as far into this arena as it would if it decided which adults were parents to which children, according to its judgment of who would do this best. A child's parents have the opportunity to have more to do with what sort of person that child becomes than anyone else, aside from the child himself or herself (and, on some views, even more to do with it than the child does.) The parents are in a position to play a more central role than others in what the child comes to value, in the sense the child comes to have of himself or herself and of the place the world has for someone like him or her, and in which talents the child develops and which are unrecognized or undeveloped. That is the heart of who the child becomes, and it greatly shapes what sort of life he or she comes to have. To be the child's *parent* is to have the opportunity to have more to do with all of that than anyone else has, except for the child himself or herself.

Of course, to have this opportunity is very far from having the power to ensure that the child turns out just as you plan. There are many competing external influences. There is also the material itself: the child is a person, with both a mind and a body of his or her own.[15] Even so, however, a parent can be central to who the child becomes, whether by attending to this opportunity or by ignoring it. I think Guggenheim's point is that this is not a power we should want to centralize, if we believe individuality is important.

That is surely correct. It is also reasonable to believe that politicians who had this power would eventually put it to some appalling use. Both are reasons not to want the state to have this role, and we can add another. As was noted, it seems inevitable that the state will make forays of its own into "value inculcation in children." Those appear to be part of our living together under a government, and any view that said they must be prohibited would be untenable. The reason they are no great cause for concern is precisely because parents are a powerful counterweight. If we were to allow the state to choose who the parents are to be, we would lose that balance.

We would also empower the state to choose which adults are to have the great goods of parenthood. With any luck at all, parents and children come to love each other, often deeply and fiercely. That is a rare good in a person's life. Moreover, to quote William Galston, "As Eamonn Callan rightly suggests, parenting is typically undertaken as one of the central-meaning giving tasks of our lives. We cannot detach our aspirations for our children from our under-standing of what is good and virtuous."[16] Ferdinand Schoeman adds that the relationship between a parent and a child is an intimate one, and that: "an intimate relationship [is] one in which one shares one's self.…For most people, not only are such unions central to defining who one is, but human existence would have little or no meaning if cut off from all possibility of maintaining or reestablishing such relationships."[17] Perhaps there are instances in which the state should prevent a person from pursuing these goods by having a child, but that case surely that would be a special one. It might suffice that this person's child would be in great peril, for example, but it certainly *shouldn't* suffice that the child could have what the larger society agrees is a better life with a different parent.

These points might sound a bit overheated, as if they applied only to social engineering on a grand scale, but even more limited programs would give the state power it shouldn't have. That is a reason not to want even cases of the kind we have been considering to be decided by a judge's conclusions about whether the child will be better off with the would-be adoptive parents or with the biological ones. Still, it is greatly distressing for our system to tear a Baby Jessica from the arms of the people who have been parents to her and make her live instead with others who are strangers to her. Perhaps the social engineering would be the lesser evil at a time like that? The next section considers this response but argues that it is mistaken.

2.

Assuming we agree that the state should not ordinarily enforce its judgment of what is best for a child by deciding who her parents are to be, why should it do so in the Baby Jessica case? The answer can't be that children have a right to whatever arrangement is best for them and that the state should enforce that right. That would justify too much, since it wouldn't restrict the social engineering to cases of Baby Jessica's kind.

Nor can the answer be that children have a right to a decent minimum in life and that the state should enforce that. This would justify too little, since the worry really isn't that Daniel Schmidt wouldn't be a good enough parent to provide his daughter a decent life. Rather, the worry is that he is a stranger to the girl, whereas she has been with the DeBoers long enough to become attached to them. As the authors of one important text would put it, Robbie and Jan DeBoer had each become Baby Jessica's "'psychological parent,' in whose care the child can feel secure, valued, and 'wanted.'"[18] To take her from them would do her whatever harm a child suffers when this tie is severed.

That wouldn't happen in social engineering that separated babies from their biological parents at birth, as in the Australian example. The psychological attachment on which Goldstein *et al.* place such importance comes later, out of being looked after, and it takes time to become established: "For the infant…attachment to her parents results from their day-to-day attention to her needs for physical care, nourishment, comfort, affection, and stimulation. A parent who satisfies these needs builds a psychological relationship with the child…and will become her 'psychological parent.'"[19] No exact timetable can be provided, but when Goldstein *et al.* are discussing the Baby Richard case, they say that when he was "*not yet three months old,* [he] might not have been with the Does long enough for a firm psychological tie to have developed."[20] If three months is a good approximation, then there would be quite a long period during which the state could place babies with the parents it thought best without severing this "firm psychological tie." Whereas the state *would* sever that tie, it is urged, if it were to return children such as Baby Jessica and Baby Richard to their biological parents, because it would do this after a longer period with a would-be adoptive parent who had been conscientious in the role.

That is a difference between the two kinds of social engineering, but it does not restrict the practice in the way sought. The reason is that it allows for two ways to avoid doing children the harm of severing their tie with their psychological parent. One is to leave them with those with whom such a tie exists, but another is to place them where the state thinks best only during their first three months of life. So if our rule were not to do any child the harm of severing his psychological tie with his parents, we wouldn't have restricted social engineering to cases of the Baby Jessica kind, which was what we sought to do.

Let us try again. Suppose we say two things. One, if there is an established psychological tie with other parents, that connection justifies denying biological parents their child. Two, there is no other consideration that can justify doing so when the child is a newborn: not the fact that the child will be raised by an unwed mother in a culture that would disapprove of both mother and child, as in the Australian example, and not that the child will be raised below the poverty line. In fact, there is *nothing* else that could call for the state to ensure that a newborn is to be raised by different parents than the ones who created her—except, perhaps, such clear and utter incompetence that no one will object. If both these claims are true, social engineering is improper where newborns are concerned but called for in cases of Baby Jessica's kind.

Should we agree that both claims are true, though? Is it right that nothing could be as good a reason against separating a newborn from her parents as the one against separating a very young child from the people she identifies as her parents? Goldstein *et al.* do say that "At birth the interests of a child are and should be presumed to coincide with the interests of her biological parents"[21]—but that is a declaration rather than an argument. They also observe that when it comes to "who, among alternatives, holds the most promise for meeting the child's psychological needs....Psychoanalytic theory confirms the substantial limitation of our ability to make such a prediction."[22] In other words, we don't know enough to predict such things—except for where severing psychological ties is concerned. In that case alone, the view is, we do know enough to predict that life with the current psychological parent "holds the most promise for meeting the child's psychological needs."

That statement relies on the current state of psychoanalytic theory, though. At most, it supports the conclusion that the state shouldn't go in for social engineering of a broader kind *now*, at a time when psychoanalytic theory tells us we don't know enough to do it. This leaves open the possibility that the matter could change. The bar is not permanent, but exactly the kind that invites declarations of new discoveries—including new psychological theories that we should embrace instead of the psychoanalytic one. In short, if we let our concern for the harm to Baby Jessica in severing her psychological tie to the DeBoers be decisive, we open the door to eventual social engineering of a broader kind in the future. This is a reason not to want the judgments in our cases made solely on the basis of the best interests of the child.

It might be replied that we have at least justified restraining the social engineering we might do at the present time. We can say that to the best of our current knowledge, the harm done in separating a very young child from her psychological parents is unique in its gravity and it alone ought to determine that she is not to be returned to her biological ones. So, for the present, that is all we should do along these lines, and we can deal with other possibilities when they are proposed. At least we will be doing the right thing now, rather than letting fear of a slippery slope keep us from doing it.

But is that an argument we should accept? For Goldstein *et al.*, the harm clearly is serious enough to justify refusing to restore a child to his or her biological parents. As they say in their introduction, "we believe that the law should make the child's needs paramount" (p. 7). If this statement is taken literally, to take the child's needs as paramount would mean that no other consideration is more important than an improvement in serving the child's needs, no matter how minor that improvement and how major the other consideration. There are indications that Goldstein *et al.* mean exactly that, as when they use the following italics to indicate the ways in which they believe Justice Rizzi's appellate opinion was exactly right: "*A child's best interest is not part of an equation. It is not to be balanced against any other interest.* In adoption cases, like custody and abuse cases, a child's best interest is and must remain impregnable from all other factors, including the interests of the parents."[23] See also this later passage, (the italics my own): "Had Justice Rizzi said no more in his opinion, we would be persuaded that in Illinois the best-interests-of-the-child standard had come a long way toward accepting that the child's interests are to be paramount, *and are not to be weighed against the interests of competing adults.*"[24] On this view, what would be best for the child isn't something to be weighed in a balance—it's the only thing to consider. The wrangling adults in these cases might find it hard to accept what it costs them to do that, but they are wrong to put themselves ahead of the child.

But why, exactly? Well, they are adults, and the child is a *child*. Indeed, there are senses in which the child is *their* child—their biological child, or their psychological child. It is appealing to say that parents should put their children ahead of themselves. But here that would have to mean more than just that parents should be willing to sacrifice for their children, as they certainly should. Saying only that parents should be willing to sacrifice for their children leaves open the possibility that *some* sacrifices would be beyond the call of duty, or even troubling in their self-abnegation. It assumes that the parent and the child both matter, and simply asserts that parents should sometimes regard their children as mattering more than they do themselves. That's right, but it isn't the view in question, according to which it is *only* the child who matters, and parents are to make *every* sacrifice. The child's interests aren't to be weighed against those of the parent, remember: only what is best for the child matters. I don't see a reason to take the child to be the only person with interests in play, or to say that what is best for the child must outweigh any other interest (which I think comes to the same thing).

However, perhaps the reason Goldstein *et al.* believe that the child's interests should be paramount in cases such as that of Baby Richard is not that they believe children should *always* come first. Perhaps they think the child's interests should be paramount only in cases of this special kind, because what is at stake here is the child's need for continuity with his or her psychological parent, and they think that factor is more important than any right or interest the biological parent could have. In support of this belief, they might note the more or less immediate costs to the child if this continuity is broken. There is the distress that is clearly visible in the pictures of the child clinging to those she considers her parents. Moreover, "For infants and toddlers, changes in routine may lead to food refusals, digestive upsets, sleeping difficulties, crying, or withdrawal states....Being moved from the familiar to the unfamiliar person is often associated with discomfort and distress, and affects the infant's orientation and adaptation to her surroundings."[25] That sounds miserable, and we should certainly avoid inflicting it on a child—but surely it isn't so terrible that nothing can be more important than to prevent it.

Suppose, for example, that the toddler had been kidnapped from the hospital nursery by the person who had become his psychological parent, and this had now been found out. No one would think the child had to be left with the kidnapper because nothing could be more important than to avoid subjecting him to the distress of being moved. However, the immediate harms in separation are only one thing. There are also said to be serious long-term costs to the toddler who is separated from his psychological parent. Perhaps it is *those* that are uniquely severe, so severe that the law should treat them as more important than the right of a biological parent to have the child back. But whatever these long-term costs will be, I doubt they would change your mind about the case in which the child was kidnapped from the hospital nursery. You would still think that child should be taken from the person with whom she had this firm psychological tie and returned to her biological parents. If the cases of Baby Jessica and Baby Richard are different, the reason can't be that the long-term harm is different. It will have to be because their biological parents don't have the same standing as the victims of the kidnapping, and the would-be adoptive parents haven't done a wrong of the same kind as the kidnapper.

To put this differently, what calls for these cases to be handled differently will have to be a difference in the claims that the adults have. The view that the focus should be entirely on serving the best interests of the child assumes that the rights of *these* biological parents aren't as impressive as the rights of the parents whose child was kidnapped. That stance calls for an argument. We don't provide that argument if we simply insist that the rights of adults are irrelevant to what really matters in these cases, which is how best to serve the interests of the children.

However, let us return to the long-term harms of separation from a psychological parent, to see whether we ought at least to think them uniquely significant and important enough to call for the rights of the biological parents to be overridden. Goldstein *et al.* say this about the infant's attachment to his or her psychological parent: "Such primitive and tenuous first attachments form the base from which further relationships develop"; "Continuity of relationships is essential for a child's healthy development.... The attachments of infants and toddlers are as upset by separations as they are promoted by the constant, unrationed, consistent presence of a familiar adult. When these children feel themselves abandoned by their parent, their distress leads to weakening their next attachments"; "...emotional attachments are tenuous and vulnerable in early life, and children need stability of relationships for their healthy growth and development."[26]

However, keep in mind that the question in our cases isn't whether there would be great harm of these kinds done to a child who was bounced from one foster parent or group home to another. The question is whether that would also be true of a very young child who was moved, once, from one place of loving care to another, since the argument is only that her biological parents are not *currently* her psychological parents, not that they wouldn't be good to her and wouldn't become a new set of psychological parents. Perhaps the answer is that she too would be done grave harm, but the reasons to think so would rest on arguments that psychoanalytic theory has the correct way of understanding human development and human psychology, at least in this respect. This wouldn't be the place to explore such arguments even if I were capable of doing so. It seems fair to say, however, that this is not so obviously the truth of the matter that we ought to think in these terms rather than in terms of respecting a person's right to be a parent to a child he or she helped to create, if there is such a right.

That is not to insist that rights must be absolute. There can be a threshold at which rights give way to other concerns. I will have more to say in Chapter 3 about when that might happen. For now, let me observe only that this has to be a *high* threshold, or else saying that we had to override a right in order to avoid bad consequences will just be solemn hypocrisy. I've argued that it is quite uncertain how severely infants such as Baby Jessica and Baby Richard are harmed when they are transferred from one psychological parent to another. If so, we don't have as powerful a reason to refrain from transferring them as Goldstein *et al.* take us to have. This means that even if we could restrict the state's social engineering to cases such as these, we would be treating rights as if they were not so great a moral barrier to producing good consequences after all, and we would be wrong to do so. Either that, or we would have to say *these* biological parents have no rights to raise their child.[27]

Since I believe they do have the right to raise their children, I think the better way to avoid harming a child by severing her ties to her psychological parents is to decide such cases before the ties are developed: before the child is three months old, if we go by our authors' observation concerning Baby Richard. As Guggenheim urges, if the courts were also to take psychological ties to be decisive in cases of *our* kind, "Both parties would devote their entire effort in these cases to securing 'temporary' custody as quickly as possible and holding on for dear life. Even worse, the custodial party's litigation tactics would be crystal clear: Figure out a way to stretch the lawsuit long enough, any way will do, and it will be impossible to lose."[28]

Guggenheim believes the process could be constructed to move much more quickly. He offers the analogy of disputes over challenges to elections—for example, over whether a candidate is entitled to appear on a ballot. "... [C]ourts routinely handle these claims in a highly efficient manner: within weeks if not days, in plenty of time for the election to take place on time, even leaving time to appeal to the state's highest court for final review before the election process."[29] In contrast, disputes of the kind we are considering drag on for years, allowing the child to reach an age at which it is painful to be separated from "the only parents he has ever known." According to Guggenheim, "What can work for candidates for elected office can work for children, if we have the will."[30] If so, we should revise our procedures so that they have this efficiency.

3.

The previous section identified a number of problems with using the best-interests standard as the sole consideration. Those problems provide one kind of reason to think of biological parents as having a right to raise their children, but no reason of another kind has been offered. Nothing has been said to explain what there is about being a biological parent that ought to put a person in this position. I will discuss two efforts along those lines and will argue that one of them has the matter right.

Our children are "our own flesh and blood," we sometimes say. Perhaps that is where the argument for our right to raise them lies. Here is an effort to spell it out:

> Parents should have the legal right to raise their children because they created those children, out of their own bodies. A cake the parents made out of ingredients that belonged to them would be their cake, surely, and an apple tree they planted in their garden would be their apple tree. So a baby they made should also belong to them, and since it belongs to them they have a right to raise it. Any judge who dealt their child to other parents would be practicing theft, of a particularly painful kind.

Those who reject this argument might think it easy to dismiss, on the ground that we cannot have *people* as our property, as we can cakes and apple trees. After all, if a cake or an apple tree belongs to me, I may do pretty much as I like with it. As its owner, I may consume the cake or cut the tree down for firewood; as their owner, I may sell either of these to someone else, or mark them with my initials. That is simply part of what it is for this to be my cake, or my tree. Clearly, it would be highly immoral to treat another person in these ways. So, the argument would be, we cannot own people, even very small ones, because we are not free to treat them as we would if we did own them.

This dismissal is too quick, however. Essentially, it construes all ownership on the model of owning inanimate objects that are of no particular importance to others. It is true that there are few limitations on the rights of ownership when what one owns is a cake, or an apple tree, or an article of clothing. But it is also possible to own a *horse*, for example, and then the owner is not so free to do with it as she will. There are things her ownership does not entitle her to do, because it is a horse she owns, and (for example) horses suffer, unlike cakes and trees and shirts. The horse does belong to her; it's just that the rights of ownership vary according to the sort of item one owns.

Just so with the children who belong to their parents, the arguer might urge. For a child to belong to you won't mean you have the right to destroy it, sell it, or brand it with your initials. But we shouldn't conclude that the child cannot belong to you, the claim would be, any more than the limits on what you may do to your horse mean that a horse cannot belong to you. Your rights are simply more limited than they would be if what belonged to you were an inanimate object of no particular importance to anyone else. Here, they are limited by this particular item's being a person. The fact remains that the two of you created this child, out of your bodies. Shouldn't that fact put you in some version of the position it would if you had created something else out of your own ingredients?

Well, no. To see why not, it will be useful to consider briefly two of John Locke's arguments about gaining ownership through one's labor. I hasten to note that Locke himself rejected extending these arguments to the case of parents and their children. His reason appears to have been a conviction that we don't make our babies: he thought God made them, using us as his instruments.[31] He also thought the children thus made belonged to God. So he might actually have been amenable to the idea that labor confers ownership of the product even when the product is a child.

Be that as it may, it will be useful to refer to two of Locke's accounts of why making something makes it yours, and consider how well they would serve at showing why making babies makes them yours. The first of these accounts emphasizes that the labor we expend belongs to us. In Locke's words,

> Though the earth and all inferior creatures be common to all men, yet every man has a property in his own person; this nobody has any right to but himself. The labor of his body and the work of his hands we may say are properly his. Whatsoever, then, he removes out of the state that nature hath provided and left it in, he hath mixed his labor with, and joined to it something that is his own, and thereby makes it his property.…For this labor being the unquestionable property of the laborer, no man but he can have a right to what that is once joined to, at least where there is enough, and as good left in common for others.[32]

The parallel argument for parents and their children would be somewhat simpler. Since parents don't fashion their children out of materials they find in nature, there is no need to worry about whether they have left enough and as good for others to use in fashioning their own babies. Nor need we worry that others had a prior claim to the materials the parents used to make their baby and so might have a claim to the baby the two of them made. Rather, the two parents contributed all the ingredients: not only were the actions by which the baby was made theirs, so were all the physical ingredients. So the resulting baby must be theirs, the argument would conclude: there simply are no other candidates.

Could we not say the baby belongs neither to the parents nor to any other individuals but to the community as a whole, who may owe the couple gratitude for their contribution to the common store? Certainly some are inclined to say this about the farm someone has made out of the common land. Here that would be more awkward, however, since the couple has not been working on something that had been in the common store. We would be obliged to explain why making something new out of materials they already owned should cost them their ownership: not an easy explanation to give. It is also not the conclusion we want if we want the child not to belong to anyone, since now he or she would belong to the larger community.

Let us turn instead to the second Lockean argument of interest. Here Locke's idea is that when someone's labor produces a thing of value, it is the labor that is responsible for most of the value, not the materials. Locke thought that labor transformed the worthless or nearly worthless into something worth having, and he thought it only fair that the laborer should have this newly valuable item:

> …it is labor indeed that puts the difference of value in everything…the improvement of labor makes the far greater part of the value. I think it will be but a very modest computation to say that of the products of the earth useful to the life of

man nine-tenths are the effects of labor; nay, if we will rightly estimate…we shall find that in most of them ninety-nine hundredths are wholly to be put to the account of labor.[33]

Again, the parallel argument for parents and their children would be simpler. Parents make babies out of their own bodies, not out of something held in common by the community and already having some little value of its own. No need, then, to sort out how much more valuable the child is than the materials from which the parents made it. Since the parents contributed everything, it is even clearer that the child should be theirs, on this line of reasoning.

Perhaps it is because these arguments are simpler than Locke's originals that they are so clearly unappealing. For example, Locke's argument about labor making worthless land into something valuable takes seriously only one sort of value that land might have: as a source of comestibles or income. If that is a somewhat dubious way to think about land, it is an even more dubious way to think about a person. Not that a person cannot be a source of value to others, of course, but to think of someone as *primarily* a resource for the use of others loses sight of something many have tried to formulate. It makes the person an object; it fails to treat others as ends in themselves; it endorses *using* people; and so on.

This objection can't be disarmed by the earlier notion that since a child is a *person* who belongs to the parents rather than something inanimate, there simply are limits to what they may do in making use of him or her. The problem is that to own something is to be entitled to control it and to reap the benefits of that control. That concept is thoroughly objectionable as a relationship to another person, and it has particular drawbacks as an orientation toward one's children. A great deal of parenthood consists in doing things for the child, not all of which are likely to pay off in his or her being more valuable to the parent. You read him his favorite story for example, or you teach her to hit a ball even though she clearly does not have the sort of athletic ability that will later bring you prestige; you go to yet another ballet recital, and so on. If the child is supposed to be your resource, this part of parenthood seems only something about which to be impatient: it doesn't even come under the heading of sensible maintenance. More particularly, to think of your child as primarily something you are entitled to control and to enjoy does not encourage you to take especially seriously what the child's life will be like for her once she is an adult. And surely that is at least as important, morally, as the quality of life *you* have during her childhood.

I do not mean to suggest that someone who thought of his child as his property could not be concerned about the child in these other ways. My point is only that such concerns are foreign to thinking of the child as one's property, and so are easily omitted from that frame of mind. Those omissions are likely to go uncorrected, as well. The child has no defense against them. And others ought not to intervene on the child's behalf except under extreme circumstances, if we are true to the ownership model—how I treat my resources is mostly none of your business, after all, and we raise our children in private as well.

It is also interesting to consider what happens when the child becomes an adult, if we think of children as belonging to the parents in the way that property does, even property of a special kind. Presumably, on any view the passage into adulthood is a time of emancipation: we won't want to say the child is still her parents' to control. It looks as if the special relationship as parent simply ends: as if you would have no obligation to help this person who is now an adult just because she is your daughter, and no right to any different standing toward her just because you are her father or mother, now that the ownership that gave you those rights and obligations has come to an end. It seems to me, though, that there are still rights and obligations of parenthood after the child has become an adult. These do change, as they do at other stages of life, but they remain as part of a different moral relationship than you have to other adults of your grown child's current age. If so, this is another aspect of parenthood that goes missing, if we think of parenthood as a special variety of property right.

Finally: there are cultures that handle the raising of children differently than we do, so that the biological parents do not play the role that the property-rights argument asserts that they should. Children in such cultures may fare at least as well as children in our own. If we accept the property-rights argument, we ought still to object very strongly to those ways of life, it seems, since we would then regard them as depriving parents of their natural rights to their property. So much the worse for the property-rights view: we should have a way of thinking that is less presumptuous. It should also be a way of thinking that promotes taking one's children to be persons in their own right, rather than demoting that to a restraint one must remember, and a way that takes continuing the project of parenthood as seriously as it takes beginning it. I want next to offer an account of parenthood that I believe has these features.

4.

There is a principle of broad appeal, usually traced to John Stuart Mill, according to which we have a right to act as we choose if our actions are suitably innocent with regard to others. The restriction means in part that we were free to perform these actions, as opposed to beginning in violation of someone else's rights. In the standard formulation, the restriction also means that the actions we have a right to continue must do no one any harm once they are underway, or at least no one who did not consent to risk being harmed. I am going to suggest that we take the rights of parenthood as an instance of this more general right to continue with whatever we have underway.

Of course, parenthood is not a single action, but a continuing role in the life of the child. But if we do have a right to act in harmless ways, this right should also extend to continuing roles and projects. That is, once someone who is free to begin a project or to play a role has done so, that person has a right to carry on with it, if it does others no harm. The rights of parenthood come out as rights to continue to play such a role in its various aspects.

In simple cases, those who begin as parents to a child were free to do so. That is, there was nothing standing in the way of their creating a child, or there was nothing standing in the way of their adopting one or taking over informally as parents to one. All such parents would have a right to continue to raise and look after the child in the way of their choosing, limited only by their obligation to neither abuse the child nor neglect her.

I have also been putting this as a right to continue what we have underway *so long as we are doing no one else harm*, however, and although that is a standard usage it has certainly drawn fire. "Harm" has proven difficult to define. Indeed, on some definitions of harm virtually everything we do causes harm and, accordingly, our right to be at liberty comes to virtually nothing. To anyone who believes in the right, this means either that harm must be defined differently or that the line must be drawn not in terms of actions that harm and actions that are harmless, but in some other terms.

There have been several efforts along these lines. I need not attempt to solve the problem here, however, because parenthood turns out to be an easy case. If there is anything at all to the idea that we have a right to carry on with what we have underway, parents who are not abusing or neglecting their children have a right to carry on with what *they* have underway. The reason is not that there will be no negative effects on others, if two people act as parents—no harm they will do, regardless how we define "harm." Instead, the reason is that the negative effects parenting has in the normal case are all of kinds that cannot be taken seriously, if the right to be at liberty is to have any significant content. Regardless of whether the right is taken to protect harmless behavior (under some interpretation of "harm") or is put in a different way altogether, it extends to normal parenting, if there is anything to the right at all. And I think we would all agree that there *is* something to the right to be at liberty.

In defense of this contention, here are what seem to be the candidates for harms done in normal parenting. First, since all normal parenting is imperfectly done, it always includes some selection of mishaps for the child. If those were enough to mean one had no right to continue, no parent would have this right for long. We could accept that, but then we would have to say something similar about any lengthy project that involves human interaction, since all of those also expose others to some selection of mishaps. This doesn't quite reduce to saying that we have no right to do anything, but it does limit any meaningful right to interact with others to brief interchanges. Rather than reduce so sharply what we may freely do with others, it is better to allow some imperfections in our performance. The imperfections in ordinary parenting shouldn't make us think again about this activity, as if its routine imperfections were terribly damaging.

What about harm to those outside the relationship between parent and child, though? Someone else might disapprove of the way in which a particular pair of parents raised their child—the fact that they were raising the child as a vegetarian, for instance (or the fact that they were not), or the fact that their child was to have no lessons in music or the arts. That disapproval might be a source of unhappiness for this third person when she saw the parents in action, or even when she thought about the child she was convinced was being raised badly. But although that unhappiness is a bad consequence for her, it cannot be enough for us to conclude that the child's parents have no right to act as they are. If it were enough, the right to act as one chooses would only be a right to act in ways others approve. That would leave too little of liberty, surely.

Similarly, suppose that because two people are raising their daughter, a couple on the list to adopt must remain childless, and their childlessness is a source of deep unhappiness for them. We could say that the first couple causes the second great pain by continuing as parents, but that possibility cannot suffice for us to conclude that they have no right to do so. The same reasoning would mean that you and your wife would have no right to continue to be married if I fell deeply in love with her, since your marriage would be a source of deep unhappiness for me. Nor would you have a right to continue in your job if I wanted it very badly. The pain I would suffer in these cases would be genuine, but causing this kind of pain doesn't undercut the right to carry on with what you are doing. If it did, you would have the right only to do what no one else badly wants to do in your stead.

Finally, it could certainly be true that others would do a better job than the present parents, if they were to replace them, and that this would be of some benefit to the child. That fact cannot be sufficient for the parents to have no right to continue either. If it were, a person would also have no right to continue preparing dinner for his guests if one of them were a better cook than he, and a pianist would have no right to carry on with her performance if the audience contained a superior musician. Admittedly, there is something to be said for deferring on such occasions to the person who would do better at what one is doing, but to defer would be a *courtesy*. You would have the right to carry on yourself; that is why it would be outrageous for the superior musician to demand that the pianist leave the stage, or for the better cook to expel his host from the kitchen. In short, the fact that someone could do a better job at what you are doing does not entail that you have no right to continue to do it, if there is anything to the right to act as you choose.

Those are the "harms" routinely done in parenting, it seems to me. Our children suffer some range of mishaps, we provoke disapproval in those who would act differently, we contribute to the sometimes very deep disappointment of those who want to adopt but haven't yet been permitted to do so, and there are others who would do a better job as parents than we would. None of those are harms we can take seriously if we value liberty, *however* liberty is to be understood. For present purposes, then, it is not necessary to formulate very precisely the right we have to continue innocent behavior. It will include a right to continue as parents, in the normal case.

Of course, anyone who is doing his or her child *damage* would not have this right to carry on in that way. Not all parental inefficiencies are so drastic, however, fortunately for all of us who are parents. The limitation simply tracks what we have in mind when we say that parental rights don't permit us to abuse or neglect our children. Parents who are not doing that badly have a right to continue to act as parents, assuming they haven't gotten started in a way that simply violated someone's rights. In the usual case, in short, anyone who is acting as a parent has a right to continue, not because the children belong to them as property of a special sort, and not because they made these children, but simply because they are already doing so and they have a right to continue any action that is harmless to others (to revert to the standard usage).

There must be more to it than that, you may be thinking. At least the property-rights approach acknowledges that there is something momentous about "having a baby." Surely this momentous event is more than merely something you were doing before being so rudely interrupted, so to speak. Biological parents put themselves into their work, or at least they put their genes into it, and only someone who had never carried a baby to term and given birth to it could think of this event as no more than *starting* something. So, to reduce the claim of biological parents just to a right to carry on with whatever they have underway is far too tepid, isn't it?

I think it will seem so only if what come to mind as illustrations of the right to carry on are relatively trivial bits of behavior, of no particular importance to the person engaged in them. Those do fall under the right, but so do actions of the deepest importance to us: actions in which we invest our sense of ourselves, and which we expect others to take with an equal seriousness in their own lives. Parenthood is like that. As was noted earlier, with any luck at all, the parent and the child come to love each other, often deeply and fiercely, and that is a rare good in a person's life. For that reason alone, a right to continue to be a parent would be no small thing after all, precisely because it is *parenthood* that one would have underway.

But what *counts* as continuing with parenthood, it is reasonable to ask. Which actions are a part of playing that role and are thus to be regarded as a parental right? The answer will vary somewhat from culture to culture, since to serve as a child's parent is not the same thing everywhere. In the America of Baby Jessica and Baby Richard, it is roughly this. To play the role of a child's parents is to be the ones who see to it that this child's physical and emotional needs are met; who decide where the child is to live and how he or she is to be disciplined; who define and look after the child's moral and religious education; who determine what education in factual matters and in skills the child is to have, beyond a certain minimum; and who raise the child to become someone who functions acceptably as an adult. There are many ways of carrying out those actions. Those who act as the child's parents have the choice among them, including the choice of which variety of acceptably functioning adult to try to influence the child to become.

In cultures where that is what parenthood is, those are the actions that biological parents have the right to perform by virtue of having performed the first act or acts of parenthood, and that adoptive parents may acquire the right to perform. There are also cultures that do not manage the raising of children in a way that gives any particular individuals the role just described. In those cultures, those who create or adopt a child have not taken a first step in the same project, since their culture does not expect the same things of them, or accord them the same privileges. Since they have not begun the same course of action, what they have a right to do next as part of that course of action is not the same. So, if they are not permitted to act in ways that our culture makes part of parenthood but theirs does not, that does not violate their rights as parents, on the account of those rights that I am offering.[34]

That means this account of parental rights is not automatically critical of ways of life that differ by not affording biological parents the same role we afford them, in the way it seems we should be critical if we pictured those ways of life as denying the people who created a valuable product their natural right to control it and profit from it. Of course, if we think instead as I've urged and take parental rights to be rights to continue doing something begun with no violation of rights and harmless to others, we are still free to object to ways of life that do great damage to the children or that impose great uncompensated burdens on others. That is a point of a different kind, however.

This perspective on other ways of life strikes me as an advantage of the recommended way of thinking. It has a second advantage, I believe, exactly where the property-rights view may be most troubling. On the property-rights view, a child is essentially his or her parents' resource to develop and enjoy. Whatever obligations they have as parents enter only as reminders that this particular resource is also a person. That view does not lend itself to paying any great attention to the effects that one's behavior might have on the child's life when she is an adult and no longer one's property. Nor does it lend itself to taking an interest in her present experiences beyond one roughly analogous to concern that the oil in an engine is changed regularly. By contrast, suppose that what is fundamental is not that you created this resource, who happens also to be a person. Rather, what is fundamental is the project you have underway, which amounts to looking after her and ensuring that she grows into a responsible adult who functions happily without your control. That approach takes the child seriously in a way we must be reminded to do, if the fundamental thought is that he or she belongs to us.

This chapter has argued that we ought to construe the rights of parenthood in this way, as an instance of the right to continue whatever we have underway so long as it is innocent with regard to others. The next chapter further develops that idea by considering more closely who would have these rights: in particular, who would count as having begun parenthood innocently, and who would have begun instead in a way that meant he had no right to continue, as (for example) there is no right to continue on my merry way with goods that I have shoplifted. We can then return in Chapter 3 to the question with which we began: whether biological fathers such as Daniel Schmidt and Otakar Kirchner should be taken to have the right they assert to be fathers to the children they helped conceive.

2

Who Has Parental Rights?

Every child's first parents are the ones who create him, and their first act as his parents is to do so. On one view, that act is completed at the moment of conception. Carrying the child to term and giving birth are later acts of parenthood that are performed after the creating is done. On a different view, creating a child takes a good deal longer.

Clearly this is an important disagreement where some issues are concerned. However, it doesn't matter with regard to the rights of biological parents, if we take those to be rights to continue what one has underway. The reason is that a right to continue would surely entitle one both to complete the first action in a project and to go on with any subsequent actions. Thus, on either view of conception a child belongs to his or her biological parents, at the beginning, if they violated no rights in creating that child. Again, this wouldn't be due to anything about manufacturing and ownership. It would be because they had parenthood underway and had the usual right to continue with what one is doing.

A second way to become the parent of a child is by adoption. That confers the same rights and responsibilities as creating the child, as long as no one's rights are violated in the process. The child must be "available for adoption," to use a phrase from our earlier cases, and must be given up without coercion. When that restriction is satisfied, the adoptive parents are in exactly the same position as the biological ones were where their moral standing in the child's life is concerned. They differ only in the way in which they came to have that standing.

It is also possible to become the parent of a child informally, by joining the child's other parent in this role. As with biological parenthood and adoption, the "joining" can't be achieved through coercion or some other violation of rights, but when the other parent freely gives permission it is a third way to obtain the same rights and obligations that a biological parent has. Martin Guggenheim draws our attention to a variety of legal cases in which this issue has been contested as a matter of law.[1] Some of these involve step-parents who never formally adopted the child or children of their spouse, some involve men who never married the single women whose families they joined, and some involve same-sex couples who separated after a period in which they had jointly raised the biological child of one of them. The story is the same for all of these people, on the view I am offering. What matters is whether they became parents to the child without violating anyone's rights. If they did, they have the same moral standing as they would have if they were biological or adoptive parents.

Let us now consider instead the ways in which the first act of parenthood might go wrong, so that (on my view) parental rights are not acquired after all. The first section below deals with the easiest case of that kind, in which a child is conceived as the result of a rape. The second section turns to the fact that many women conceive children under cultural conditions that leave them little choice but to agree to do so. The question is whether having children under those conditions is a way of being raped or has the same implications as rape. If it does, then no biological father who impregnates a woman under those conditions has a right to be a parent to his child, on the view I am offering about the source of such rights. The same would hold if such women were always *exploited* in becoming pregnant, since those conditions too would violate their rights. The third section addresses that position. I argue against both of these positions, urging that they rest on mistaken conceptions of coercion and exploitation. Of course, such oppressive conditions are highly objectionable and go hand in glove with coercing and exploiting women. My contention is only that not every pregnancy in such places occurs though coercion or exploitation, and thus some men in those cultures would have the right to continue as fathers to their biological children.

The fourth section turns to the use of what are called "assisted reproductive technologies" to create children; in particular, the use of donor eggs and of commercial surrogates. The question is whether those who use these procedures have thereby violated the rights of the women who are paid to provide the eggs or to serve as "gestational mothers." If so, they would be in the same position as the rapist, with no right to be parents to those children. I argue that this idea too is mistaken. Commercial surrogates and egg donors certainly can be victims of coercion and exploitation, but that isn't essential to employing them.

The fifth section turns from the circumstances under which a child is created to a different matter: whether those who created her are *able* to continue as her parents. If we are not capable of doing something, then we also have no right to do it, and under some conditions we also have no right to try. I offer a criterion for when a parent should be regarded as incapable of going on. I also explore the idea that there are some people who *could* perform what parenthood required but *wouldn't* do so, and that this is a different reason to deny their right to try. I discuss that reasoning in connection with cases commonly described as "children having children."

The sixth section turns to the contention that parenthood should be reserved for heterosexuals. The reasons to think so are far too weak, I argue. Sexual orientation is no barrier to acquiring the rights of parenthood, on my account of the source of those rights. Neither is the fact that the biological parents procreated under conditions that are ripe for coercion and exploitation, or that they used technology and the assistance of third parties to create the child, or that the continuing parent is unmarried, or even that he or she is both unmarried and quite young, so long as this person is still capable of playing the role. None of those circumstances mean either that rights have been violated in creating the child, as they are in the case of pregnancy following a rape, or that the parent should be considered incapable of playing the continuing role, or that he or she should be prevented from trying for the sake for the child. In short, on the view I am offering, the rights of parenthood are available very broadly indeed.

1.

Whatever account we give of parental rights, it certainly ought to entail that if the victim of a rape conceives, her rapist has no right to be a father to the child. It does turn out that way on the view I am offering, because no one who uses force or fraud to gain the other party's participation in a joint endeavor acquires a right to continue. He acquires no right to continue with the other party's forced cooperation, since that would amount to a right to go on coercing others. Nor does he acquire a right to continue on his own the project thus begun, or to do so with a different partner. That would amount to a right to use others for his own benefit, discard them, and retain the benefits. He *does* incur an obligation to ensure that the child is looked after, since he created the need for that to be done, but he would have no right to do so himself.

His victim's story is a very different one, of course. She violated no one's rights in "helping" to create this child, so this argument would not disqualify her from continuing to be a parent to the child, if she wished to do so. To speak generally again, we have the right to continue not only what we freely began, but also what we were forced to begin but which it now pleases us to continue, so long as our continuing violates no one's rights. To say otherwise would carry a step further the control of our behavior that began when we were coerced into the first act.

What constitutes rape is a disputed topic, once we are beyond the obvious cases.[2] In contrast, it ought to be very clear who has the right to raise a child who was conceived in this terrible way. That is clear, on the view I am offering. The next sections take up some more complex cases.

2.

> For a great many women around the world, decisions about whether to have children, how many children to have, and under what conditions are controlled by the husband and his family or are made in the context of overwhelming cultural pressures.[3]

If a man were to use those conditions to coerce a woman to have a child against her will, his behavior would differ from rape by force or threat of force only in the means by which he had imposed his will. His actions would have undercut his right to continue as a father to a child conceived in this way. However, I have described him as someone who used the coercive power that his culture gave him. I think it is also possible for a man who has that power not to use it when he and a woman create a child. Others hold that his having this power is enough: that every woman who has a child under those circumstances is in the same position as a woman who has been raped. If that were true, no biological father in such a culture would have a right to continue, any more than a rapist who used force would have that right.

The crucial premise in the argument for that view is that every pregnancy that occurs under these oppressive circumstances begins in violation of the woman's rights. I will argue that this notion is mistaken. The circumstances certainly make it exceedingly easy for a woman to be coerced, and they also make it easy for a man to coerce without being aware that he is doing so. Those are reasons to find the circumstances highly objectionable, but that is a different point. My contention is that the circumstances don't convert every sexual encounter into one in which the woman has been coerced. Rather, rights are violated only when this power is put to coercive use. So, men whose culture puts them in this position can have the right to continue as fathers to their biological children, even if a great many of them do not.

There are two lines of argument for the more radical position. The first is that wherever there is a great differential in power, it is impossible for the relatively powerless person to give free and voluntary consent to anything that the far more powerful person asks of her. When she complies, what happens is never consensual, on this view, but always a violation of her right not to be coerced.

This reasoning is sometimes offered in a different context, in support of the contention that sex between a professor and a student cannot be consensual, because the professor is vastly more powerful than the student. It holds that no detail can alter the difference in their power, or its implications. If the student is a 26-year-old graduate student rather than a teenager, that fact doesn't make the sex consensual, because it doesn't change the power differential. Nor does the sex become consensual if it is the student rather than the professor who initiates the relationship and seems to control it, or because the student *believes* that he or she is acting freely. Rather, in every case of sex between a professor and a student, the power differential between them means this has been a violation of the student's right not to be coerced in such matters.[4]

If so, the same would hold for our cases, in which there is a great power differential between the woman and the man in regard to having children (and most likely in many other matters). That is, the woman could never *freely* consent to have a child under those circumstances, because the man would always have the power to make her agree. It would also follow that all sexual activity between males and females in these cultural settings is akin to rape, just as all sexual activity between the professor and the 26-year-old graduate student is said to be. Some would regard that implication as a reason to reject the argument; others might regard it as the truth of the matter.[5]

On behalf of the view that a great power differential does invalidate consent, we might observe that circumstances certainly can transform behavior that would not be coercive in other contexts into behavior that is. A sharp glance from your boss can have the force of an order to stop what you are doing, unlike the same glance from a co-worker. The reason is surely that your boss has power over you that your co-worker does not, The boss's sharp glance has the standing of an order, and it can function to coerce you even if she didn't mean it to do that.

Because the co-worker doesn't have the boss's power to make you pay in any way, however, *his* sharp glance has neither standing nor psychological force.

So far, so good, but the view we are considering claims a good deal more than this. It isn't just that what is otherwise noncoercive behavior can become coercive if the person who engages in it has the power to compel compliance. It's that *anything the powerful person does* is coercive, if the end result is "compliance": in the earlier illustration, if the end result is that the professor and the student have sex. Anything the professor does is coercive, because on this view sex between them is *always* coerced, by virtue of the power differential. So it wouldn't only be the professor's meaningful glances that would be coercive in this context, or his singling the student out as special, or whatever else he might use—none of which would coerce her but for his power, but any of which could do so in this context. Rather, if there is *always* coercion in these encounters, it will also have to count as coercing her if (as professors sometimes claim) he did nothing that she could even interpret as an overture and the whole thing was her idea. Here his coercion would be in his responding enthusiastically to her efforts, or his allowing them to succeed—those would be what compelled her to have sex with him, since this sex too is said to be coerced.

The trouble is that to say the circumstances are such that *anything this person does* is coercive means that it is really the circumstances that coerce, not the individual. The circumstances have the power to compel by virtue of the victim's susceptibility to them, not what the other party does. We do speak of being compelled by our circumstances—the boss says he "had to" fire the secretary, or the miscreant says he had no alternative but to take the money he needed to cover his gambling debt, and so on. All are examples in which the circumstances might have left a person with only one reasonable alternative, in the light of his beliefs and desires, just as an armed robber might do so by pointing a gun at him and demanding his money. However, hard circumstances and armed robbers also differ in ways that mean our talk of being compelled by our circumstances is only a metaphor.

One such difference is that when one *person* coerces another, he violates her right not to have her actions controlled by someone else. That is not the case when it is the circumstances that leave her only one reasonable choice. This matters, because a right not to have your *circumstances* severely limit your options would not have the same implications as a right not to have another person do so. Suppose that B has done something that would give A certain entitlements, if B had done this freely. For example, given the papers that B signed, A would now own B's car; or, given the ceremony B went through, A would now be B's spouse. That is true if B has done these things freely, at any rate. Next, suppose that B signed the papers or made the vows only because A held a gun to her head or used some other means to make her do what she did. If so, A would have forfeited the rights he would otherwise have gained from B's actions.

That reasoning seems straightforward. But now imagine that it hadn't been A who coerced B, but the circumstances in which B found herself. That is, it wasn't A who left B no reasonable alternative to selling him her car, or to marrying him, but other difficulties in her life. They made it necessary for her to sell her car, and his was easily the best offer; or they made marrying someone a necessity, and he was easily the best of her options. The crucial question is why that too should mean that he cannot be the new owner of her car, or that he cannot be her husband.

The answer can't be that through his actions he has forfeited those rights, as it was when it was he who coerced her. Nor can the answer be that he shouldn't gain the usual rights because someone else coerced her and no one should gain rights regarding another through the misconduct of a third party. No individual coerced her, in our story—her circumstances did. So it would have to be the hard circumstances themselves that meant she could not sell him her car and that she could not marry him.

There is no good reason to say this, and there are many other contexts in which we regard hard circumstances very differently. For example, suppose that a patient's health left her no reasonable alternative to surgery. We wouldn't take this to mean she could not validly consent to the operation and that any surgeon who had her "consent" was no different than someone who assaulted her with a knife. Hard circumstances can make for a bitter life, and no one's life ought to be bitter, but that is a different misfortune than being forced to act under the control of another, and it does not have the same implications. Accordingly, it isn't true that every pregnancy that occurs under conditions that leave the woman in no position to refuse violates her right not to be coerced and therefore means that the man involved had no right to continue as a father to the child.

That is a point worth making, but let me emphasize that it is only a narrow one. The idea is that we shouldn't think it is a necessary truth that every man who impregnates a woman under these oppressive circumstances has coerced her. It remains true that many would have done exactly that, and also that threats can be subtle and unstated, so that it will often be unclear whether what happened should be regarded as equivalent to a rape. The only claim so far is that it shouldn't always be so regarded.

A different thought is that the male might still have violated her rights in a different way, by taking unfair advantage of her situation. Similarly, to reject the view that there is always coercion when professors have sex with their students isn't to say that when there has been no coercion the professor has done nothing wrong. The professor might still have taken unfair advantage of the student's vulnerability. In fact, surely that often happens when professors have sex with their students. So far, I've argued only that it is wrong to think there is always *coercion* when there is a great power differential and the weaker party agrees to do what the stronger party wants.[6]

Just to say that there is "almost always" misuse of a different kind when professors and students have sex might sound as if nothing all that bad has happened, but it isn't meant to minimize. Abusing a trust and taking advantage of someone who is vulnerable are hardly minor misdeeds. This issue leads us to the second argument for saying that if a woman became pregnant under cultural conditions that vested such choices in men, the biological father would have no right to continue as a father to the child. The second argument, developed in the next section, is that this circumstance is always exploitation, and that exploitation should be regarded in the same way as coercion.

3.

We have a right not to be exploited. Therefore if it's true that to impregnate a woman under conditions of great disparity of power is always to exploit her, then doing so always violates her rights. It would follow that in the societies we are considering, no biological father would have a right to continue as a father to the child, on the view I am offering, any more than he would if he were a rapist.[7]

I will argue, though, that a great disparity in power does not entail that the more powerful person exploits the less powerful one whenever they interact within the sphere of his greater power, any more than it entails that he coerces her. It does put him in a position to exploit her, but exploiting her is more than that: it's a matter of taking advantage of this position. As an analogy, consider a merchant who owns much of the bottled water available in an area that has been ravaged by a storm. The merchant is certainly in a position to exploit those who want to buy the water, but it isn't true that she will be exploiting them regardless of what she requires them to pay for it; the price would have to be one they should not have to pay for what they are getting.

Laws against gouging seek to identify such prices and impose sanctions that limit this abuse of power, while still permitting legitimate commerce. They acknowledge that the commerce can be legitimate: that some prices won't be too high, and thus that it is possible for the merchant not to exploit those who are in her power where buying water is concerned. Notice that the same would have been true if there had been no laws against gouging: it isn't the laws that make some prices fair and others exploitive.

Now let us return to the man and woman who create a child under circumstances that would allow him to exploit her. Here too, it won't be true that whatever he does is bound to be a case of exploiting her. There must also be something wrong with what he gets her to do in return for whatever she gets out of doing as he wants, just as the merchant takes improper advantage only if there is something wrong with what she gets the desperate customers to do. With the bottled water, this is a matter of getting them to pay a price they shouldn't have to pay. With the man and woman who have a child, there is a good deal more we can say about when there is something wrong with what he has gotten her to do.[8]

In particular, there is something wrong with her having a child either because she must or because she believes she must. Bringing a child into the world requires an act of intimacy, followed by nine months of pregnancy, followed by childbirth. Moreover, in the cultures we are considering, once the child is born, he will require a great deal of his mother, and how she feels about him will affect both his life and her own. (If instead the child were handed over to others, so that the mother had been used as a type of breeding stock, this would be terrible in a different way.) These are all reasons why there is a great deal wrong with a woman's having a child because she must or because she believes she must.

Accordingly, to use a position of power to get a woman to do exactly that is to abuse this power, just as it would be an abuse of power for the merchant to get others to do something they shouldn't have to do in order to buy her water.[9]

Anyone who did it would forfeit the right to be a father to the child, on the view I am offering. However, it also seems clear that not every man who is in a position to do these things actually does them, any more than every merchant who is in a position to gouge the customers does that. As with coercion, it isn't the oppressive circumstances that undercut the parental rights of biological fathers, and we would be wrong to think that no man who fathered a child under those circumstances would have a right to be a father to that child. What matters is what individuals do under those circumstances.

We should also return to the case in which a woman *is* misused in this way, and note a second terrible wrong that this behavior does to her. It derives from the fact that in these cultural settings, she might be in no position to part with the man who did this to her. It's obvious that no one should have to remain with her rapist. To remain with him as parents to their child has horrors of its own, which are worth drawing out. An analogy will be useful.

As cooks know, even when there is a recipe to follow, the cook is at considerable liberty. The measurements might say "one cup," but that amount is really only approximate. Using a little more or a little less will make no difference at all, and when deviating from the recipe *would* make a difference, it isn't always a difference between success and failure: sometimes it only changes the dish. In short, in cooking there is a great deal of space for doing it your way, even when you are given a book that tells you how it is to be done. My guess is that a good many beginners think that cooking is more precise, and that some retain this anxious thought for a good while.

There are also books about how to be a parent, and plenty of anxiety at the start and sometimes thereafter, but parenthood is even more imprecise than cooking. How else could parents have the latitude to raise their children *as they choose*? If raising children required precision, there would be no latitude of this kind, whereas parents are actually at considerable liberty to do this in their own way.

For single parents, what that way amounts to represents the choices of one person. That changes when parenthood is shared. Then the choices become *our* choices, rather than *my* choices. That means there has to be an *us*, so to speak. The union can take many forms, including those in which A leaves "all of that" to B, or all of some parts of it, but there has to be agreement of some kind as to how we are to proceed, since it is *we* who are proceeding.

When the joint endeavor is looking after and raising a child rather than cooking a dinner, some of the choices to be made will draw upon deep truths about the people who are making them. Sharing the choices reveals those truths, making the activity an intimate one. Moreover, how it is going with the children is likely to be given far more importance than how the meals are going. Ordinarily, there is emotional investment of a different order, and the level of emotional investment that is both needed and natural where your children are concerned is considerable.

It is obvious that no one should even have to cook dinner with a man who raped her. It is even more obvious that she shouldn't have to share with her rapist an intimate project of many years' duration and much emotional investment, as parenthood would be. In fact, that is so terrible a prospect that she could be right to refuse it even if her child could be better off if she were to agree.

Of course, there is also plenty of room to argue that the child would *not* be better off if she allowed a rapist to help her raise him—not even if events had left the child psychologically attached to the rapist as "the only father he had ever known," I would say, despite the importance of not disrupting psychological parenthood. But now suppose that the woman lived in a culture that took it for granted that husbands were to say when wives had children, and that her particular husband took advantage of this policy to impose a child upon her against her will. Suppose further that this culture had no place for "single mothers," or at least none for women who had made single mothers of themselves. I think it would then be much harder to argue that her child *could not* be better off if she stayed with her husband and allowed him to be a father to the child.

If so, and if I was right to take what happened to her to be equivalent to being raped by a different means, then the husband did her a terrible wrong of a second kind. The earlier point was that he got her to have a child because she believed she had no alternative, and that no one should have to do that. The current point is that he also forces her to choose between sharing the intimate and emotional project of parenthood with her rapist so that her child will have a better life, and refusing to do so at great cost to her child and to herself. That is a terrible position even if it is clear which is the better choice, since whatever she does will cost someone dearly. It is also a terrible position when it isn't clear what she should do, since then she has a version of Sophie's Choice: she must impose a high cost on someone without whatever solace there would be in thinking she was morally obligated to do as she did.

So there are two ways in which the men we have been imagining do the women a great wrong, when they exploit them or coerce them. Again, however, it also seems clear that not every man who is in a position to do these things actually does them. So although we have two reasons why some men in cultures of this kind have no right to be fathers to the children they "help" create, we have no reason to say this is true of every man who has a child in such a culture.

4.

The biological parents with whom we began in Chapter 1 created their children the old-fashioned way, by having sex, and so did the ones we have just been considering. There are now alternatives, known collectively as "assisted reproduction technologies." These are employed mostly by couples who are using their own eggs and sperm to cope with fertility problems: in 2003 in the United States 86 percent of the cases were of that kind.[10] However, we will be interested in two other methods. One is the use of donor eggs or donor embryos, as occurred in 12 percent of the U.S. cases in 2003.[11] The other is the use of a commercial surrogate to carry the fetus to term. That is far less common, and a handful of U.S. states have laws prohibiting the enforcement of such agreements.[12] It is also the practice that has drawn the most opposition.

One question is, when donor eggs or surrogate mothers are employed, who has the rights of biological mother to the child, assuming for the moment that someone does? It will be a mistake to try to answer this question by saying who the biological mother would *be* in such cases. The biological concept of parenthood developed long before a mother's part in bringing a child into the world could be shared, and it provides no way to choose among candidates who make different biological contributions.

That does not matter, however, if we think of parental rights as deriving not from biology as such but from a right to continue something that one has underway. The important question then is which woman has parenthood underway, rather than which of them is properly called the "biological mother." The answer will depend on who takes the actions that start matters biologically.

For example, suppose that a woman arranges to have her fertilized egg carried to term by someone else, or agrees to have this arrangement made on her behalf, with the understanding that the child is to be hers after birth. Then it is she who has begun a project of parenthood, one in which she gives the second woman a role, and it is she who has a right to continue as the child's parent. In a different case, the arrangement a woman made (or agreed to have made on her behalf) could be for someone else to provide a fertilized egg, which she herself would then carry to term, again with the understanding that the child is to be hers from that point. This is still her project, even though her biological part in it is the opposite one. Therefore it is still she who has the right to continue as a parent to the child. In yet another case, two women might embark upon this procedure mutually, with one of them providing the eggs that are fertilized and the other one carrying the fetus to term and giving birth. Here both would have the right to continue as parents to the child, since both have begun in this role.

All of this would hold only if no rights were violated in creating the child, however. Some have argued that rights always *are* violated when a woman is paid to carry the child to term and give birth. If that is true, then arranging to create a child in this way wouldn't deliver a right to continue as parents to the child, on my view about the source of such rights, any more than abducting someone and impregnating her would deliver that right. However, I am going to argue that commercial surrogacy *doesn't* necessarily violate the rights of the woman who serves as a surrogate, and thus that making this arrangement can be yet another way to "have a child."

One argument for the opposite view is that to be paid to be a "gestational mother" is to be exploited. According to Uma Narayan, the reasoning is that

> Commercial surrogacy...involves the economic and gender-role exploitation of women.... That commercial surrogacy involves the *economic* exploitation of women is a plausible claim, since the average commercial surrogate is paid $10,000—not very generous payment for all the effort and inconvenience involved...[As for] gender-role exploitation...Aspects of "femininity" that glorify motherhood and portray women as loving, nurturing, and self-sacrificing seem deeply involved in motivating women to become commercial surrogates....The motivations frequently expressed by commercial surrogacy included a desire to help infertile

couples, a love of being pregnant, a sense that having children was one of women's most important accomplishments, and a desire to resolve the guilt of having had an abortion.[13]

Let us consider economic exploitation first. If a surrogate who carried a baby to term were paid the U.S. federal minimum wage as of 2006, her 270 days of work would earn her $44,085.60.[14] Even if the going rate for surrogacy is now up to $15,000, that is certainly very poor pay in comparison. The argument is that no form of employment should pay this badly.

Laura Purdy has argued that actually it isn't such bad pay for being a surrogate gestational mother, since that kind of work leaves one unusually free to pursue other activities while one's body carries the child.[15] Even if the poor-pay argument is granted, however, it only identifies a problem with the current pay scale, not a respect in which this way of having a baby *necessarily* exploits the woman who carries the fetus to term and gives birth. For that, the exploitation would have to lie at a deeper level, one that wouldn't be remedied by requiring that she be paid at least a minimum wage. To find that deeper exploitation, we might turn to the complaint that surrogacy isn't only economic exploitation but also gender-role exploitation. Here is Narayan, again: "Aspects of 'femininity' that glorify motherhood and portray women as loving, nurturing, and self-sacrificing seem deeply involved in motivating women to become commercial surrogates."[16] The claim would be that women have a right not to have *those* buttons pushed, so they are motivated to be surrogates even partly for *those* reasons, for when they are they have been exploited.

The idea of a right not to be presented with certain motivations does have application. For example, you have a right not to have someone present you with a reasonable fear that you will be shot unless you act in a certain way. But the reasoning in our case can't be that a woman's being told that her actions would be "loving, nurturing, and self-sacrificing" is just like having a gun pointed at her, in its power to make complying her only reasonable choice. Appeals to these aspects of femininity leave a person too free to do otherwise to be plausibly described as coercive.

So, it will be better to understand the complaint that surrogacy involves gender-role exploitation in a different way. Its point would be that this makes use of an objectionable conception of femininity, taking it to be significantly defined as "loving, nurturing, and self-sacrificing." But suppose we were to grant that this is an objectionable conception of womanhood. Should we draw the conclusion that no one who employs a surrogate so as to create a child has a right to be a parent to that child? That would be appealing only if employing this objectionable conception were just as objectionable as violating someone's rights. That claim is badly in need of supporting argument, however.[17]

We might try again by adapting a second line of argument Narayan mentions: "such commercial transactions permit serious intrusions into women's reproductive autonomy and privacy... [they amount to] an *enforceable surrogacy contract* whereby women may be *contractually* bound to refrain from abortion; to undergo various intrusive medical procedures, such as amniocentesis; to be vulnerable to surveillance regarding matters of diet, exercise, and lifestyle; and to be subject in a variety of ways to serious intrusions on their autonomy and privacy and regarding their own bodies."[18] Those particulars seem negotiable, though—whether she is free to have an abortion, for example, and what is required of her in diet, exercise, and "lifestyle." As Laura Purdy puts it, "certain conditions [in such a contract] are unacceptable. Among them are clauses in a contract that subordinate a woman's reasonable desires and judgments to the will of another contracting party, clauses legitimating inadequate pay for the risks and discomforts involved, and clauses that penalize her for the birth of a handicapped or dead baby through no fault of her own."[19] But since extremely confining and intrusive contracts are no more an inherent part of commercial surrogacy than poor pay, they go no further toward showing that this practice *must* exploit the surrogate. They do help us to see when it would exploit her and so would not bring those who employed it the rights of parenthood, but they aren't ways in which the practice must always exploit.

Perhaps the argument can be salvaged, though. Surely the surrogate inevitably surrenders a great deal by way of autonomy and privacy. After all, the contract entitles the other party to raise the child whom she has carried and given birth. That other party will want to ensure that the woman has proper prenatal care, both for the sake of the child they think of as theirs and for their own sake as parents to that child. Any contract they will want to sign will reflect those concerns by imposing significant limits on what the woman is free to do while pregnant and on her liberty to keep what she does to herself. If that means every such contract exploits the person who signs it by violating her right to autonomy and privacy, then it is true that this way of having a baby always exploits the surrogate.

This reasoning would be compelling if the surrogate's surrenders of autonomy and privacy were akin to contracting oneself into slavery—but they are far from that. I think Purdy is right about them, as well: "The oft-asserted objection that women lose autonomy by demands for medical care and abstention from smoking, drinking, and drugs is troubling...such provisions...are no more than is morally required of any pregnant woman. Do we really want to assert women's right to behave in ways known to harm the persons the fetuses will become? If the principle of autonomy supports rights of this sort, then...so much the worse for autonomy."[20] Indeed, Purdy suggests that commercial surrogacy might actually improve the autonomy of some women who chose to engage in it: "Not only might contracted pregnancy be less risky and more enjoyable than other jobs women are forced to take, but there are other advantages as well. Since being pregnant is not usually a full-time occupation, 'surrogate mothering' could buy time for women to significantly improve their lot: students, aspiring writers, and social activists could make real progress toward their goals."[21]

It might be replied that Purdy is assuming that the women who sign these contracts do so voluntarily, when actually they sign them only because they are in desperate circumstances. Why women sign the contracts is an empirical question, but two earlier points are also important. First, even if the contracts are signed because of hard circumstances, it does not follow that those who sign them have been the victims of coercion, if my earlier arguments are correct. At their worst, what circumstances do is to leave a person with very bad alternatives. To have her sign a contract in which she takes one of those alternatives is not the same as to coerce her. Second, it isn't the same as to exploit her either, that is, to take advantage of her in her hard times. Exploiting occurs only if there is something wrong with her having to do what she agrees to do. So far, what has been said to be wrong with such an arrangement is that it sacrifices autonomy and privacy, and that contention seems to have failed.

Here is a different candidate for what is wrong with what every surrogate must do, offered by Elizabeth Anderson. I will argue that it fails as well, completing my argument that those who employ surrogates have not necessarily begun their parenthood in a corrupted way. Rather, in and of itself this is just as legitimate a way to acquire the rights of a biological parenthood as creating a child through coitus. Here is Anderson's thesis to the contrary, however.

> Commercial surrogacy attempts to transform what is specifically women's labor—the work of bringing forth children into the world—into a commodity. It does so by replacing the parental norms which usually govern the practice of gestating children with the economic norms which govern ordinary production processes. The application of commercial norms to women's labor reduces the surrogate mothers from persons worthy of respect and consideration to objects of mere use.[22]

Since this is only one passage from Anderson's article, it's important to add her explanation of her key ideas.

On the one hand, there are the norms that properly govern our treatment of persons, particularly respect and consideration: "To respect a person is to treat her in accordance with principles she rationally accepts—principles consistent with the protection of her autonomy and her rational interests. To treat a person with consideration is to respond with sensitivity to her and to her emotional relations with others, refraining from manipulating these for one's own purposes."[23] On the other hand, there are also "the economic norms which govern ordinary production processes." In particular, there is "the market norm that owners may use commodities to satisfy their own interests without regard for the interests of the commodities themselves."[24]

To treat a person as a commodity is degrading, since such treatment is "a lower mode of valuation than is proper to" persons.[25] Anderson contends that women are degraded in this way if they are paid a fee in return for doing what a surrogate mother does: for becoming pregnant, carrying the fetus to term, giving birth, and then allowing the other party to be the child's parent. If it were urged that this is something to which the women freely agree, presumably Anderson's answer would be that even if they did freely agree to it, they would be agreeing to be treated in a way they should not be treated. Thus there would still be something very wrong with having gotten them to do it.

Anderson offers some horrific illustrations of ways in which the norm that persons are to be treated with respect is violated in surrogacy. For example, "The commercial promoters of surrogacy commonly describe the surrogate mothers as inanimate objects: mere 'hatcheries,' 'plumbing,' or 'rented property'—things without emotions which could make claims on others. They also refuse to acknowledge any responsibility for the consequences of the mother's emotional labor. Should she suffer psychologically from being forced to give up her child, the father is not liable to pay for therapy."[26] Those practices are disrespectful. However, surely they are not essential to the practice, any more than inadequate pay or unreasonable restrictions on the woman's conduct while pregnant are essential. So they don't go to show that commercial surrogacy is immoral *as such*, which is Anderson's contention, but only show us some of what has to be avoided in an acceptable version.

She also believes that the practice degrades the surrogate in a second way, however, by failing to treat her with the consideration that persons merit. The lack of consideration is in failure to treat the surrogate's emotions as they should be treated.

> In the surrogate contract, she agrees not to form or to attempt to form a parent-child relationship with her offspring. Her labor is alienated, because she must divert it from the end which the social practices of pregnancy rightly promote—an emotional bond with her child. The surrogate contract thus replaces a norm of parenthood, that during pregnancy one create a loving attachment to one's child, with a norm of commercial production, that the producer shall not form any special emotional ties to her product.[27]

Actually, though, the surrogate is perfectly free to form special emotional ties to her "product," including maternal love. What she is not free to do is "to form or to attempt to form a parent-child relationship" with the child after he or she is born. In other words, the surrogate doesn't agree that she will not love the child; she agrees that she will not be the child's mother as the years go by. The question is whether agreeing to *those* terms, in return for pay, is agreeing to be degraded, treated as if one were not a person but an object for use. That's far from clear.

For example, a number of writers share Anderson's conviction that the emotions of a woman who has given birth must be given their proper due, but they believe this can be done by requiring that surrogate mothers have a period of time after the child is born during which they may choose to keep the baby for their own.[28] That arrangement gives the woman a chance to decide for herself whether to do as her maternal love urges her after she appreciates the strength of these feelings. Anderson's argument requires us to say that if a surrogate who had this second chance were to decide against continuing as a mother to the child, she would collude in her own degradation, or that she colludes in this if she even agrees to be put in a position to make this choice after she gives birth to the child.

A different understanding is at least as plausible. Although powerful emotions are one aspect of being a person, rationality is another. Treating someone as a person therefore requires respecting her rationality. Allowing her to make a rational decision about what place to give her love for the child does exactly that. Therefore it doesn't degrade her to a commodity, after all, and to agree to it isn't to fail to respect oneself as a person. It isn't the essence of surrogacy to wrong the surrogate in *this* way either.

I have been arguing that those who employ surrogate mothers are not thereby akin to rapists, having begun their biological parenthood in a way that violates the rights of another and so forfeiting the rights they would ordinarily have to continue as the child's parents. Paying a donor to contribute eggs has not drawn the same opposition and does not need as thorough a defense. It too requires the donor to surrender some privacy and some autonomy, but not remotely as much as a surrogate mother would. It too commercializes part of "what is specifically women's labor—the work of bringing forth children into the world," to use Anderson's phrase, but a far smaller part of it. Moreover, since Anderson says a "semen donor sells only a product of his body"[29] and she does not regard doing this as a degrading reduction to market-norms, presumably she ought to say the same of selling an egg that one's body had produced.

In sum, whether we are speaking of the use of donor eggs or the employment of a commercial surrogate, there is nothing in the nature of creating a child in this way that undercuts the parental rights of those who employ it, if those rights have the source I am claiming they have. The next section turns to a different argument about the right to be the parent of a child one has created: an argument that concerns the *ability* to be one.

5.

We can have a right to do something only if we are capable of doing it. If you cannot leap tall buildings in a single bound, it makes no sense to say that you have a right to leap them. Less fancifully, if you could not close the door to your room, it would be wrong to say that you had a right to close it. That isn't to say you would have no right to privacy if you couldn't close your door. You would, but others would have to protect your right to privacy for you, where closing the door is concerned. The point is that you would have no right to close your door yourself, if that were not within your capabilities, any more than you would have the right to leap over the Empire State Building.

The same would hold for a right to be a mother or a father to your child. Suppose that were impossible for a child's biological parent, because he or she was in a persistent vegetative state. Someone in that state would have had a right to be a parent to the child if things had been different, and others might honor this right by undertaking to look after the child in the ways they think this person would have done it. However, being a parent to the child is not something the person in a vegetative state would have a right to do himself or herself while lying there so severely disconnected from the world.

Presumably there are other conditions in which parenthood is beyond a person's capabilities. Imagine someone who is greatly delusional and is thus disconnected from the world in a different way. Or imagine someone who suffers mental defects so severe that tasks of any complexity are beyond him—someone you think should be looked after himself for his own good. Assume further that there is no medication or medical treatment that can render these conditions manageable. These are not people who would just be imperfect as parents to a child, or who would only fall very short of perfection. Rather, they could not be parents *at all*—despite being able to impregnate someone (if a male) or to become pregnant (if a female).

Here is a test for that: if the child were under this person's care, then what happened would quickly amount to levels of abuse or neglect that would call for the state to take the child into protective custody. Thus acceptable performance as a parent would be beyond this person. It would follow that he or she would have no right to be a parent, since we can have a right to do something only if we are capable of doing it.

Might we have a right at least to *try*, though, even if we are bound to fail? To try to leap over the tall building, or to try to close a door even if we can't manage it—or to try to be a parent to our child even though we can't meet even this minimal criterion for success? One problem here is that often the people we are imagining can't even *try* to be parents. That is certainly true of someone in a persistent vegetative state, and it could also be true of someone who was highly delusional or severely disabled mentally. Another problem derives from a point in common between the right to do something and the right to try to do it. In both cases, you have the right only when you can do this without violating the rights of others. The person we are imagining can't even try to be a parent to his or her child without violating the child's own right to be free of abuse and neglect. So, nothing changes even if there is a right to try what we can't succeed in doing. It remains true that someone entirely incompetent to be a parent does not have a biological parent's usual rights upon creating a child, on the view I am offering about those rights.

Let me repeat that this applies only to very extreme cases, not to the far more common case in which the biological parent would not be expected to be very *good* at looking after her child and raising him or her to be an adult. Even if that expectation were both correct and well-grounded, she would still have a right to try to do it. If her performance were to fall short in certain serious ways, that is when the state would intervene on behalf of the child. At what point that intervention should happen and in what ways is discussed in chapter 4, "Abuse, Neglect and the State." For now, the idea is that poor prospects don't amount to inability and similarly don't entail that no right is intruded upon if the child is taken from the biological parent and given to others to raise.

The difference between poor prospects and inability is not a very sharp one, and my suggested way of distinguishing them doesn't solve this problem. It says we should regard the task as beyond someone if we have very good reason to believe that what would happen if he were permitted to try would quickly amount to levels of abuse or neglect that would call for the state to take the child into protective custody. That isn't going to settle every case, but it still seems to indicate what matters. I think it also represents the proper view to take of Hugh LaFollette's important idea that the state should require a license before allowing someone to be a parent, just as it requires a license before allowing someone to drive a motor vehicle.[30] His idea is to protect children from abuse and neglect *before* it happens rather than after it does, and that prospect is very appealing. The crucial question would be which prospective parents should be considered too dangerous to be allowed to create a child and should be denied the license to do so. There are obvious dangers in allowing the state to decide who will be "good enough." LaFollette's proposal "is designed to exclude only the very bad [parents]...those who will abuse or neglect their children,"[31] and that is surely the right tack to take. My own proposal regarding parents of children who are newly born is not all that different. It denies the right to continue as a parent to one's child only to those whose conduct "would quickly amount to levels of abuse or neglect that would call for the state to take the child into protective custody." I would call that incompetence to be a parent at all, rather than a way of being a very bad one.

That description might be contested. What if our belief were not that a certain person *couldn't* be an acceptable parent to the child he had helped create, but that he just *wouldn't* do this despite being perfectly capable of it? We think he would be so bad a parent to this child that he would soon forfeit his right to be one, even though behaving differently wouldn't have been beyond his capacity. If we knew that about him in advance, shouldn't we say for the sake of the child that he has no right to try?

This idea is appealing in theory and very dangerous in practice. Its appeal is in the importance of protecting children from harm, and in the fact that there is a right to be a parent to your child only as long as you don't abuse or neglect the child. If we knew someone would fail at this task, it wouldn't seem to matter whether the reason was that he *couldn't* succeed or that he *wouldn't* succeed. Either way, his right to try despite our knowing he would fail doesn't seem to merit much weight in comparison to the costs to the child. The danger in practice, of course, is in our ability to know such things. We would be claiming to know that although someone could perform acceptably as a parent, he would not do so. That supposition invites us to indulge biases, as adoption laws invite us to do when they say the adoptive parent can be "Any *proper* adult person" (Hawaii, Paragraph 578.1, emphasis added) or "Any *reputable* person of legal age" (Illinois, 750 ILCS 50/1, emphasis added). In our case, the power to say who is proper or reputable and thus may be a parent would be employed with regard to the person's own biological child, with the state proposing to take the child.

Exactly when the state ought to wield that power is a question I can't pursue very far, but it would be possible to see my proposal as just a very conservative one in this regard. Clearly it would be the state that had the burden of argument, and the burden ought to be a very heavy one, since the proposal would be to preempt what would have been a right. The logic is the same as that regarding our laws on abuse and neglect. There too, although it should certainly be possible for the state to take a child for his or her own protection, there should be very good reasons to think it necessary. What I've offered can be taken to extend this same idea to cases in which the child is newborn.

In contrast, there could be no compelling argument that a mother shouldn't be allowed to raise her child just because she is unmarried, for example. (In 2003, 34.6% of all births in the United States were to unmarried women.)[32] William Galston has argued that life is *better* for children in nuclear families than for children who live with single parents. "Some 80 percent of children growing up in two-parent families experienced no poverty during the first ten years of their lives, whereas only 27 percent of the children in single-parent families were so fortunate. Only 2 percent of children in two-parent families experienced persistent poverty (seven years or more), whereas a full 22 percent of children in single-parent households literally grew up poor."[33] However, even if we agree that an impoverished life is a worse one, this is certainly not to say that single parents cannot or will not function capably as parents, a point Galston is careful to emphasize.[34]

There is a greater basis for concern if we add that the child's single parent is a teenager. According to one study, more than half a million teenagers give birth every year in the United States, 72 percent of them out of wedlock.[35] Seventy percent of these new mothers drop out of high school, and during the first thirteen years of parenthood they earn an average of about $5,600 annually, less than half of poverty level.[36] In addition, the chances are that their children will have special problems: "The children of adolescents are more likely to be born prematurely and 50% more likely to be low birth-weight babies of less than 5.5 pounds. Low birth-weight raises the probabilities of a variety of adverse conditions such as…blindness, deafness, chronic respiratory problems, mental retardation, mental illness and cerebral palsy. It also doubles the chance the child will later be diagnosed as having dyslexia, hyperactivity, or another disability."[37] It follows that many unwed teenaged mothers have especially difficult lives ahead as parents.

I would still resist seeing this circumstance as sufficient to decide in advance that unwed teenaged mothers cannot succeed as parents and have no right to try. It would be better to intervene only if they cannot be parents *at all*, since otherwise we are deciding who will be good enough at it to be allowed to raise her child, and there are many reasons not to take that upon ourselves. The test, again, should be whether we knew that what was going to happen to the child would quickly amount to levels of abuse or neglect that would call for the state to take him into protective custody. We certainly *don't* know that, given just the fact that his mother is an unwed teenager.

There is also this to consider. Suppose that these mothers would be capable of looking after their children adequately if they had a great deal of help but would not be capable of doing so without help of that magnitude. Of course, there are levels of "help" that are better described as someone else carrying out the task. It might often be like that when the mother was very young. According to the U.S. Bureau of Census figures for 2003, there were 6,661 babies born to girls between the ages of 10 and 14; about one girl that age out of every 2,000 gave birth.[38] Surely when a girl that young keeps her baby, it is often her own mother or grandmother who must function as a mother to the child.

If a girl this young were incapable of being the mother herself, that fact would mean she did not have a biological mother's usual right to be a mother, according to the arguments offered earlier. So her parental rights wouldn't be violated by this arrangement. Nor would her parental rights be violated if her baby were taken from her custody to be adopted by others—because she would have no parental rights. Both for the girl's own sake and for that of her child, by far the highest priority is to protect girls this young from becoming pregnant in the first place. When they do, however, our highest priority should be to help both them and their babies. To regard a biological parent's right to raise her child as a barrier to this solution would be a terrible mistake. This is one respect in which it matters that she is still a child, if she were of such tender years as actually to be incapable of doing what she would otherwise have a right to do.

Imagine next a case of a different kind, in which the new mother is 17 rather than 10. Suppose that if she were helped very extensively she would be able to be a mother to her child, but that she would not be able to do this without that help. One question is whether she would have a right to have that help from the state. Another is whether the state ought to provide this help even if she has no right to it. The answers to both turn on political philosophy issues that are too deep to contemplate here. However, it is certainly possible that where *some* rights are concerned, the state should provide its citizens what they need if they are to have these rights. If such an argument can be made in this case, it would support the conclusion that the 17-year-old should be allowed to keep her child if she wishes to do so.

A different question is whether she would have a right to very extensive help from her own mother. There are certainly mothers who wouldn't have it any other way. To allow their grandchild to be adopted, or to allow him to go into a system from which he might or might not be adopted, isn't something they would even contemplate. Our question is a different one: whether the girl has a right to have her mother do this much to help her raise her baby. I think that is true of some but not every such situation.

I can see only two arguments for saying instead that every grandmother would have this obligation. One would be that the alternative is for the young mother to give up her child, that this would be very painful to her, and that children have a right to have their parents protect them from great pain. The other would be that parents are responsible for what their children do while the children are under their care, and that this responsibility requires the parent to accept any obligations the child incurs to others, if the child cannot fulfill these obligations herself. I don't believe either of these arguments succeeds.

First, it may not be true that every girl who is too young to be a mother will suffer great pain if *her* mother does not take the child into her own care. That possibility alone would be enough to undercut a claim that every child has this right because of a broader right to be protected from great pain. Second, even if a particular girl would suffer great pain if her mother didn't take her baby in, she might also suffer great pain if her mother did do so. It could be far from clear which of these courses would better meet a parent's obligation to protect her child: the argument oversimplifies such situations. Third, the obligation to protect your child from great pain has limits, some of them deriving from other obligations to the child: an obligation to help her to have a good and happy life once she is an adult, for example. That obligation could call for the girl's mother to inflict the pain of separation despite wanting to protect her daughter from misery. It is also obvious that the costs to the mother who keeps her daughter's child could be very high. The argument assumes that this issue is irrelevant: that no cost could be so high that the parent might properly allow her child to suffer great pain instead of paying it. I don't believe this is true.

Those are all reasons not to hold that a parent's obligation to protect her children from great pain would always require being a mother to a baby that her very young daughter had. The alternative argument correctly asserts that to create a child is to incur obligations, and that if a child incurs obligations she cannot fulfill, then those pass to the child's parents. In principle, however, there is almost never only one way of fulfilling an obligation. The obligations the daughter incurred in creating a child have to do with providing for the child and raising him. The daughter could meet those obligations by doing these things herself, if she were capable of doing so, or by allowing someone else to do them. Her parents are in that same position. They could discharge her obligations themselves, but they could also discharge them by allowing her child to be adopted. They have no additional obligation to discharge her obligations in the way that she prefers.[39]

In sum, it isn't true that those who have children while too young to perform acceptably as parents have a right to have their own parents do this until they are able to assume the role themselves. At least, this isn't true in every case, by virtue of the fact that the baby has been born while the new parent is still a child herself, under the parental care of another. It *can* be true in a particular case. Recall the earlier point that the babies we are speaking of are likely to have a range of special needs:"blindness, deafness, chronic respiratory problems, mental retardation, mental illness and cerebral palsy...[and a doubled] chance the child will later be diagnosed as having dyslexia, hyperactivity, or another disability."[40] The truth is that such children are not readily adopted. So the alternative of allowing someone else to raise their daughter's baby might be somewhat hypothetical. The greater likelihood is that they would be allowing the child to pass into "the system," with a very uncertain future indeed.

Indeed, if the child who goes into the system is not adopted, that future is worse than uncertain. According to a study conducted by the School of Social Work at the University of Wisconsin, "After aging out of foster care, 27% of males and 10% of females were incarcerated within 12 to 18 months. 50% were unemployed, 37% had not finished high school and 19% of females had given birth to children. 47% had been receiving some kind of counseling or medication for mental health problems."[41] The report adds that the number receiving help with mental health problems dropped from 47% to 21% after they had left foster care—not, assuredly, because these young people all got better. To consign a child to such a life would be to fail him. The obligation to take up your child's obligations *would* oblige you to raise her child yourself. The grandmother's sense that it is shameful to do otherwise is perfectly right.

This discussion of "children having children" has focused exclusively on young girls who give birth. But of course there has been a male involved too, and he might well have been a young boy. What if, contrary to many cultural practices, we were interested in whether he had a right to be a father to the child, rather than whether she had a right to be a mother to it? The answer is that our reasoning ought to be the same. He would have no right to be a father to the child if he were incapable of performing acceptably as its father, and we ought not to allow him to try if we have good reasons to believe that the state would quickly have to take the child into protective custody. Perhaps, like the young girl, he could perform acceptably as a father if he had a great deal of help. As with the young girl, there are degrees of help that would demand too much of others for him to have a right to it, though of course they might choose to provide him that help. Where young parents of either gender are concerned, what matters is capacity: boys who are too young to be fathers have no right to continue as fathers to children they have helped create, just as girls who are too young to be mothers have no right to continue in that role.

6.

Although virtually everyone approves of adoption as a social institution, state laws vary greatly in their restrictions on who may adopt. As of 2005, at least five states in the United States had wholly prohibited homosexuals from adopting, and in February 2006 sixteen more states had ballot initiatives underway to prohibit it.[42] Presumably this same animus toward allowing gays to be parents would extend to their use of assisted reproductive technologies. That is, presumably there would be opposition to a gay person hiring a commercial surrogate, and also to gay women using donated sperm to conceive fetuses that they then carried to term themselves. The objection would be to homosexuals being parents at all.

There is nothing whatsoever to support this objection, in the view I have offered about parental rights. First, anyone who begins parenthood without violating the rights of another has a right to continue. There is no plausible argument that rights must be violated if the person who does this is homosexual. The second line of argument permitted in my view draws on the principle that no parent is permitted to abuse or neglect a child. That principle justifies terminating parental rights. If we could know in advance that someone was incapable of being a parent to his or her child, there would also be justification in terminating those rights before the abuse and neglect occurred. Presumably, the same reasoning would justify refusing to allow such a person to become a parent to begin with, at least if this process were through adoption or the use of assisted reproductive technologies. But it should be very plain that no such argument could be made to exclude gays from parenthood. Although the judicial record in cases of contested custody is mixed, as Sharon Rush observes:

> [Some] judges see that the parent's sexual orientation has little if anything to do with the parent–child relationship and place a child with his or her homosexual parent because the quality of the parent–child relationship compels that decision. Those judges find, consistent with many leading authorities, that good parenting depends, for example, on the person's ability to care, listen, and empathize.... How "good" someone might be at relating to others, including a child, depends on the social and psychological influences that shaped that person's personality. Clearly, homosexuals are as capable and as likely as heterosexuals to have good affective skills.[43]

There are a number of other arguments against permitting homosexuals to be parents, all of which fall woefully short. Rush refers us to some of these: "For example, many members of society believe that homosexuals should be kept away from children because, by definition, homosexuals abuse children. A second common fear supporting a ban on gay parenting is that a child raised by a homosexual parent also will learn to be homosexual."[44] If the belief that it is true *by definition* that homosexuals will abuse children seems like something from the lunatic fringe, consider that it is far more commonly believed that *most* homosexuals are *likely* to do this, especially gay men. Here are some figures to that effect from a 2002 study of public opinion. The survey item was: "Now I'll read a few statements that people sometimes use to describe [men/women] who are homosexual, that is [gay men/lesbians]. As I read each one, please tell me for how many [gay men/lesbians] you think each statement is true—whether you think it is true for all of them, most of them, about half of them, less than half of them, or hardly any of them.

1. How about "They are mentally ill"?
2. How about "They tend to act like [women/men]"?
3. How about "They are likely to molest or abuse children?"[45]

Of the male respondents to this item, *19.1%*—nearly one-fifth—said that *most* gay men are likely to molest or abuse children, and 8.5% said that most gay women are likely to do so;[46] 9.6% of the female respondents said this was true of most gay men, 5.8% that it was true of most gay women."[47]

Actually, statistical studies of children who have been sexually abused indicate that the risk of being molested by a heterosexual parent is far higher. For example, a 1994 study in the medical journal *Pediatrics* reported that "in this sample, a child's risk of being molested by his or her relative's heterosexual partner is over 100 times greater than by someone who might be identifiable as being homosexual, lesbian, or bisexual."[48] In a 1995 survey done for the American Psychological Association, Charlotte Patterson reports that empirical research on child abuse finds "the great majority of adults who perpetrate sexual abuse are male...the overwhelming majority of child sexual abuse cases involve an adult male abusing a young female...[and that] Available evidence reveals that gay men are no more likely than heterosexual men to perpetrate child sexual abuse....Fears that children in custody of gay or lesbian parents might be at heightened risk for sexual abuse are thus without basis in the research literature."[49]

Perhaps a true believer would reply that these statistics show only that we have sharply limited the opportunities homosexuals have to molest children by preventing them from having children of their own, a practice we must therefore continue. The conviction that many homosexuals are child molesters in waiting could certainly be this strong, but anyone who relied upon it would have to show reasons for believing it was true. Evidently the reasons can't be statistics showing that gay men and women do molest children, since those figures indicate that they are only a small percentage. It appears just to be an article of faith, and a premise of that kind certainly can't justify the conclusion that homosexuals should be denied the opportunity to be parents.

The other argument Sharon Rush reports invokes concern that living with gay parents will teach a child to be gay. This assumes sexual orientation is learned, obviously, and that is certainly a matter on which there is much disagreement. Even if we granted that it is learned, there would be empirical research of interest here as well. Patterson reports that "In all studies, the great majority of offspring of both gay fathers and lesbian mothers described themselves as hetero-sexual.... Taken together, the data do not suggest elevated rates of homosexu-ality among the offspring of lesbian or gay parents."[50]

There is also a different concern that children raised by gay parents will grow up *confused* about their sexuality: in their identification of themselves as male or female, or in whether they are happy with their gender or wish they were a member of the opposite sex, or in the extent to which their activities, occupa-tions, and the like match the culture's expectations for their gender. Here the empirical research has been on children of lesbian mothers—and, again, it indi-cates that these worries are without foundation. Patterson's survey found that "There was no evidence in any of the studies of gender identity difficulties among children of lesbian mothers," and that gender-role behavior "among chil-dren of lesbian mothers fell within typical limits for conventional sex roles."[51]

Those findings raise serious problems for the view that the state should deny homosexuals the right to be parents *for the sake of the children*. There is also something truly remarkable about assuming that growing up to be gay is so dreadful that the state should protect children from environments in which this is likely to happen, as perhaps it should remove a child from a family in which he is being taught that the weak are *prey*, properly robbed of whatever they have and used in whatever way one wishes. It is hard to imagine how an argument that being gay is a defect of that order would even go, assuming we agree that it won't suffice just to identify biblical text.[52]

A broader concern is that if homosexuals are permitted to have children, this entitlement will undermine the traditional family, an institution taken to be of great social value. Aside from extremely strained contentions that the undermin-ing will occur as part of an organized program—for these, see the writings of the Reverend James Dobson—it is difficult to see how this is supposed to work. Presumably the idea isn't that if there were a competing institution of families in which the parents are gay this trend would *catch on*, with the traditional mom-and-pop version becoming as out-of-date as a preference for old-fashioned clothes. The reasoning is more likely to be that our laws ought to preserve our way of life, and that our way of life is one in which families must take the tradi-tional form.[53]

However, even enthusiasts for the majority's right to have things their way must agree that this is limited to cases in which the majority's way does not include violating anyone else's rights. So this idea would need to be supple-mented by an argument that homosexuals have no right to be parents, unlike heterosexuals. I've argued that they have exactly the same right, since (1) the ways in which they might become parents violate no one's rights and (2) it cer-tainly can't be shown that homosexuals *couldn't* function acceptably as parents, or that they *wouldn't* do so despite being capable of it. Thus, a majority that disapproved of allowing gays to be parents would have no more right to have the laws reflect its view than one that disapproved of allowing members of a certain race or a certain religion to be parents.

There is one further point worth making. As was noted earlier, a high percentage of children are not born into traditional families, but to unmarried women: in 1998 in the United States the figure was 32.8%.[54] That is a far higher number of babies than would be born or adopted into a family of gay parents. To those inclined to think in such terms, this should suggest that allowing unmarried women to raise their children poses a far greater threat to the traditional family than allowing homosexuals to adopt or to employ assisted reproduction technologies. Yet surely this inclines almost no one to favor laws prohibiting unmarried women from keeping their children, or laws making it illegal for them to use assisted reproductive technologies to become mothers. This suggests that the operative idea isn't really concern for the traditional family, but a deep conviction that homosexuals in particular should not be allowed to be parents. That conviction lacks the supporting argument it would need, I have argued. Homosexuals should be as free as heterosexuals to gain the right to be the parent of a child, whether by creating the child through coitus or through the use of assisted reproductive technologies, or by adopting a child, or informally by living as a parent to one.

7.

The question for this chapter was who would have the rights of parenthood, on the view I am offering about the source of such rights. In the abstract, the answer is: anyone who has begun being a parent to a child, whether this beginning is biological or through adoption or informal, so long as (1) he or she violated no one's rights in doing so, (2) he or she is capable of continuing as a parent, and (3) we do not have the very compelling evidence we would need to conclude that this person would not function capably as a parent. In particular, this approach does not limit parenthood to those who are married, or to heterosexuals, or (in the case of biological parents) to those who conceive through coitus rather than with the use of donor eggs or surrogate mothers. Nor does it exclude teenagers, with the lone exception of boys and girls who are so young that they cannot function as parents.

The next chapter turns to cases in which there is a dispute over who has parental rights with regard to a particular child, and who does not. Such disputes arise in a variety of circumstances; the question is how they are to be settled. Later chapters turn from who ought to have the standing of a parent to what that standing amounts to. They take up the very rich subject of what the rights and obligations of parenthood are, and what the rights and obligations of a child are as well.

3

Whose Child Is This?

Daniel Schmidt and Otakar Kirchner were the biological fathers of Baby Jessica and Baby Richard, respectively, and the biological mothers with whom they created those children acted of their own free will. On the view I've offered, it follows that all of these adults were entitled to continue to be parents to their children. However, very soon after playing their biological part in creating the child, Schmidt and Kirchner were absent from the scene. What follows from their absence, if parental rights are rights to continue something we have underway?

More generally, when should someone whose parenthood has been interrupted for some reason be allowed to begin again, and when should this not be permitted? When the answer is that this person is *not* to regain full parenthood, when should he or she be allowed some lesser role in the child's life, and what should that role be? These questions arise in a rich array of cases. The cases differ in the reason the interruption occurred, which can include everything from the parent's deserting the child to the child's being kidnapped. They also differ in how long the interruption lasts before the missing parent reappears and seeks to have the child back. They differ yet again in whether those who acted as parents to the child during this period were complicit in bringing the interruption about. Finally, there are differences in where the best interests of the child now lie, and in what respect we owe the child's own preference in how the matter is resolved.

In the next section, I argue that all of these factors are relevant, and offer a way in which to try to give them their proper weight. Later sections apply the recommended approach to the cases of Baby Jessica and Baby Richard, as well as to cases of several other kinds.

1.

When a parent has been absent from the life of his or her child, the first question of interest is why this has happened.[1] At one end of the spectrum there are men (and, less frequently, women) who simply desert their families, in pursuit of a life they find more appealing. I take that to forfeit their right to parenthood.

This would be true even if the return of the prodigal father or mother would actually improve things for the child. Of course, that prospect could motivate someone who had served as the child's parent during the interim to step aside for the child's sake, just as advantages to a child could motivate someone to give her up for adoption. In extreme cases there might even be an obligation to step aside. However, that would apply only when those who had been serving as parents could not provide an acceptable life for her, not just when the child would have a better one with someone else. So even if the parent who wanted to return could give the child a better life, that fact alone would not give him the right to do so.

This situation does not change if we add that the prodigal parent is the child's biological father or mother. A biological parent is the child's parent at the start and ordinarily has a right to continue, but a free choice to stop forfeits that right, and it leaves no residual right to resume at some time of one's choosing. The same would be true of leaving a job to which one later wanted to return, for example, or ending a marriage one later wished one could resume. There is no reason to think that being a parent must be different.[2]

For a simple case of a different kind, imagine that someone kidnaps a baby in order to have a child of her own. Kidnappers of this kind are seriously disturbed psychologically, and perhaps it is typical for them to be immediately disillusioned once they have the baby in their possession. However, let us imagine a kidnapper who is neither disturbed nor disillusioned. She performs the tasks of early parenthood perfectly adequately, she is eager to continue, and she is competent to do so. It certainly wouldn't follow that she is entitled to keep the child, because her otherwise exemplary parenthood began with a theft. Of course, the theft did interrupt what the child's parents had underway, but it's obvious that this interruption was the kidnapper's doing, not a free choice of theirs. It can't cost them their right to be the child's parents, if there is to be any sense at all in speaking of their having had that right.

None of this would change if the kidnapper had not taken the child for herself but for someone who had hired her for the purpose. Nor would it change if a would-be adoptive couple had not commissioned the kidnapping but were aware that the child they were receiving had been stolen, or even that this might very well be the case. Perhaps it could be argued that couples of these last kinds are less blameworthy than someone who kidnaps the child herself, or someone who commissions the kidnapping, but this would be irrelevant to some very elementary truths about rights. In all such cases, the parents from whom the child was taken have a right to have her back, and those who took her or were at all complicit in her taking have no claim at all to keep her or to play any significant part in her life.

What makes these cases such easy ones is that some of the people in them have acted in ways that forfeit any claim they might have had to be a parent to the child. The harder cases are different. In them, the original parent didn't abandon the child. Instead, the separation occurred through the wrongdoing of others, or through circumstances beyond the parent's control. In addition, those who served as parents during this person's absence didn't kidnap her and were in no way complicit in the kidnapping, but had every reason to think they were simply adopting a child who was available for adoption. None of these people can be dismissed as having acted in a way that cannot rightfully be rewarded with the relationship they seek, or with some other special role in the child's life. What then?

There are good reasons not to reply that we should have the child make the decision. We couldn't do that at all if the child were a babe in arms, and few would find it appealing if she were very young. We *could* let the child decide if she were an adolescent, but even an adolescent is someone we think needs a parent—that is why there is a choice to be made at all about who her parent is to be. In part, to need a parent is to need someone to help you avoid making great mistakes about what would be in your best interests. But obviously there could be just such a mistake in the choice of who is to help you avoid such mistakes. To allow the child to choose that person is to act as if there could be no great mistake in it, or as if this were one decision in which the child's vision would be unusually clear and her thinking unusually mature. It is more plausible to expect that some children who were asked to make the choice would exaggerate what bothered them about their current family life and romanticize the new life with their "real" parents, and that others would cling to what was familiar even though they would be wiser not to do so. The child would be in extraordinary circumstances, of course, but that fact shouldn't change our assessment of her ability to make good decisions when matters are highly emotional and facts are uncertain.

A different proposal is that the cases should be decided in whatever way best serves the interests of the child, with the child's own preference serving only as one of the factors. That resolution resembles a common way of deciding which of two divorcing parents is to have custody, and what relationship (if any) the other parent is to have with the child.[3] As in the divorce cases, it would sometimes be very clear that the child would be better off with one potential parent than with the other. However, also as in divorce cases, often each alternative would have its own set of advantages and disadvantages, with neither clearly the better choice on balance. This problem makes the best-interests standard an uncertain tool—but I think there is uncertainty in any plausible approach to these difficult cases.

A more fundamental question is why the test of best interests of the child should be the only tool that we use at such times. Why should we attend only to what is best for the child, rather than also considering whatever claims the adults have to be her parents? The reason can't be that adults simply have no claims when the question is who should serve as parent, or that the claims of adults are always irrelevant at such times. Those positions would commit us to a system in which special authorities were always in charge of who raised the children, on the basis of where they believed the child would fare best. Assuming we reject such systems, our idea must be that *in these special cases* all that matters is what is best for the child.

That idea is most likely to take the following form: when a former parent reappears and wants a child back, the potential damage to the child if this is done is so great that no adult could have a claim of comparable importance, and that is why the child should be our sole focus at such times. However, it can't be taken for granted that the potential damage is that significant. That claim is best assessed after careful thought about what the damage would be and about what claims the adults in these cases could have; I also believe it turns out to be false.

Finally, it might be urged that the reason we should attend only to the interests of the child in these cases is that none of the contending adults has a stronger
claim than the others. Instead, there is a kind of a tie where their claims to be the
parents are concerned, but not where what is best for the child is concerned.
Therefore, the reasoning is, we should attend only to what is best for the child.
This alternative too is best assessed after it is clear what claims the adults could
have, and I believe it too is wrong about them: the differences can be quite
substantial. On the approach I will offer, both the best interests of the child and
the child's preference have weight, but neither of these is the sole factor to be
considered. Instead, they are both weighed together with the claims that the
adults have in the matter.

To some extent, the approach I have in mind is present in the thinking that
seemed so obviously correct when a child had been kidnapped. In particular, it
seemed obvious that someone whose child has been kidnapped has a very strong
claim to have him back. Suppose it were proposed that when a kidnapped child
is located we should consider whether the child's life prospects would be better
if he were raised by a different set of parents, and return him to his parents only
if that proves untrue. I take that to be something we shouldn't even consider.
But why is the parents' claim to have their kidnapped child returned so
strong?

I think the (very) short answer is that their child was *kidnapped*. They were
done a terrible wrong, as was the child. To decline to return him and ensure
instead that he becomes the child of others is to be complicit in those wrongs.
Of course, it isn't the kind of complicity in which we help the kidnappers take
the child—they have already taken him. Nor would our complicity be a matter
of helping them escape justice. Rather, what we would be doing if we didn't
return the child to his parents is to ensure that their nightmare continues, when
we could bring it to an end. We would see to it that they did not recover what
was wrongly taken from them.

As a pale analogy, suppose that someone had stolen a great deal of money, and
we found this sum in his off-shore accounts. No doubt the person from whom
the money was stolen would expect it to be returned. Suppose instead that we
thought carefully about whether the money would do more good if someone else
had it, and returned it only if the person from whom it was taken was the best
person to have it. Surely this solution is unappealing?

Admittedly, it differs from the kidnapping case in important ways. A child is
not a *possession*, and whereas what the parent wants is the actual child who was
taken, the person whose money was stolen doesn't ordinarily want exactly those
bills back. However, there are also central similarities between these cases. In
both, it's clear that if someone has suffered a loss through the wrongdoing of
others, she has an important claim to have this loss brought to an end. In both,
if we choose instead to ensure that the loss continues, there is at least a risk that
we are playing an improper role in what happened to her. I've characterized
that role as a kind of complicity in the wrong she was done. I will later argue that
it can be right for us to be complicit in this way under certain circumstances, but
I want first to show how very strong a consideration it is.

There are three ways we might try to defend against the charge that we are being complicit. We might argue (1) that if we did as the biological parents asked, we would be complicit in a different wrong that someone else had suffered, or (2) that although the child's parents do have an important claim to his return, someone else has a stronger claim that outweighs this, or (3) that although no individual has a stronger claim than the parents have, ethical considerations of other kinds outweigh it. None of these is at all promising as a defense for choosing not to return a kidnapped child because his life prospects would be better with a different set of parents. We are right to think doing that is indefensible. It will be more useful to see the above defenses in play with regard to the following example.

Suppose that a baby is kidnapped from her biological parents in the first week of her life. The kidnappers immediately pass her on to a couple who have no reason to suspect anything is amiss. That couple think they are adopting a newborn, and they are good parents to her. When the child is only two months old, it is learned that she had been kidnapped, and from whom. Her biological parents are eager to have her returned to them, but the couple who have been parents to her for nearly all of her two months of life are equally eager to keep her. Neither couple wants to embark upon a venture of joint parenthood, or even to allow the other couple a significant role in the life of the child they regard as theirs.

According to the earlier reasoning, the parents from whom the child was kidnapped would have a strong claim to have her back, because if we kept her from them we would be complicit in the wrong they were done. We would be complicit in a lesser way if we returned her to them but only with conditions, because that too would prevent them from resuming the life they had before their child was taken. It would require them now to allow others a place in their child's life. Thus even this arrangement falls short of bringing what happened to them to an end, and it continues some aspects of their loss. It is complicity of a lesser order.

The first form of defense against the charge of complicity asserts that if we return the child to the biological parents, we will just be complicit in a different wrong that someone else suffered. The proposed victims of that other wrong would be the couple who took the child in. They were deceived about the child's history—that is the wrong they were done. If the child is now taken from them, that wrong will cause them the same misery that anyone would suffer if their two-month-old daughter were taken from them and given to others. The idea is that to cause them this misery is to be complicit in the wrong they were done, not by declining to bring it to an end but by ensuring that it has these terrible consequences that we could prevent. The further contention is that this means the couple would have exactly the same kind of claim as the parents from whom she was originally taken, namely, that we should not be complicit in the wrongdoing of others.

Actually, however, it would be a mistake to regard these two claims as equivalent. The reason is that the wrong suffered by the couple who were deceived is subsequent to the one suffered by the couple from whom the child was kidnapped. The kidnapping made the deception possible. Moreover, the deception the second couple suffered isn't an independent event, but part of the history of what happened when the baby was taken from the first couple. Here is why that matters.

If it did not, our practice would be to treat a claim for relief from an initial wrong as no more significant than a claim to be protected from the costs of a subsequent one—including costs that would result from our providing relief to the initial victims. For example, consider a case in which a stolen vehicle was purchased by someone who had every reason to believe it was properly for sale. The car is finally located, but returning it to its original owner would impose a hardship on the innocent purchaser. The innocent purchaser has a claim to be protected from this hardship—but surely it shouldn't be equated to the original owner's claim to have his car back, so that we are at a loss to say what we should do. Rather, the original owner should be taken to have a claim of a higher order. The same is true when it isn't a car we are talking about but a child. There too, a claim to have the wrong redressed should take priority over someone else's claim not to suffer the consequences that will befall him if it is redressed. This is true even though the person who unwittingly bought the car or adopted the child has "done nothing to deserve this."

We would give that position up if we took complicity in the subsequent wrong to be just as significant as complicity in the original one. Since we'd be wrong to do that, we can't defend leaving the child with the second couple on the ground that otherwise we would just be complicit in the wrong that *they* were done.

The second defense against that charge grants that the child's parents have an important claim to her return but asserts that someone else has a stronger claim. Here the people said to have the stronger claim would be the couple who had served as parents to the child since shortly after her birth. By hypothesis, the couple have been very good parents to her in every way. It might be urged that this behavior has made the couple *deserve* to keep her.

However, it would then have to be explained why they deserve that, exactly, rather than a reward of some other kind. This is especially hard to support if being a parent to a child whom you cherish is the marvelous good that we ordinarily take it to be. There may be *nothing* we can do to deserve a good that is supposed to be precious beyond price, and here the claim would be that we would deserve it if we were good parents to a child for less than two months. Taking the two months to suffice is implausible, at least for ordinary cases, in which being a parent to a baby is not extraordinarily difficult, and the baby would not otherwise have perished or languished without a parent. Of course, there are also extraordinary cases of those kinds; in them,: we might want to say that the two months of being a parent to the child were so heroic or so saintly or so hugely valuable to the child that the person who did this does deserve what is commonly pictured as a good beyond price. But even if that's right, those descriptions would rarely apply. To put it differently, at most it would only rarely be right to say that the would-be adoptive parents deserved to keep the two-month-old because of all that they had done for her.

A somewhat different thought is that they would have *earned* the right to be the ones who continue. That position should arouse similar misgivings, however. That is, if we regard being a parent to a child as the marvelous good that we ordinarily take it to be, we should think that it is too handsome a wage to have been earned by what they did. Notice too that this case is very unlike those in which it is appealing to speak of "sweat equity." In those, one party to a mutual project has been much more assiduous in work that both had the opportunity to do and thereby has earned greater standing than the other party. In contrast, in our cases, the original parents had no opportunity to do the good and important work that the child's current parents did. Moreover, the reason they lacked that opportunity is that the kidnappers put it out of their reach, and the current parents had it only because the kidnappers wrongly made it available to them. Those facts rule out regarding this case as one in which one party simply worked harder than the other and so has earned pride of place.

I take these points to defeat the contention that the couple who have been serving as parents to the baby have a stronger claim to keep her than those from whom she was kidnapped have to her return. That was the second defense against the argument that if we do not return her, we will be complicit in the wrong that they were done. The third defense grants that no individual has a stronger claim to be a child's parent than the couple from whom he was taken, but it asserts that ethical considerations of another kind outweigh that claim.

What could those considerations be? One thought is that we ought to avoid causing great suffering to those who have done nothing to deserve it and, in fact, have acted in a way we ought to value. Surely that is important, morally. The argument would be that we should take it to be more important than honoring the first couple's claim to have their kidnapped child returned to them, and thus that we should leave the child with the second couple.

A problem here is that although it is true that we should want to avoid causing great suffering to those who have done nothing to deserve it, that description also applies to preventing those from whom the child was taken from recovering him. That too would cause innocent and presumably worthy people to suffer—it would just be different ones. Moreover, there are times when the right course of action just does cause misery to innocent people, as when a family will suffer if we send to jail someone who has egregiously violated just laws. This could be another such time, in which the suffering of the second couple is only a deeply regrettable consequence of acting as we should.

But shouldn't we avoid letting life be unfair, as it so often seems to be? It just isn't right for virtuous activity to bring great unhappiness, especially when that activity was of great benefit to someone else, and perhaps even more so when the person it greatly benefited was a child. Naturally, what the second couple did for the baby gave them a deep emotional tie to her, they did it in all innocence, and it was just as valuable to the baby as loving parenthood is to any baby. It would be terribly unfair for those actions to cause the couple any pain at all, let alone the misery they will suffer if we take the baby from them. We should try to prevent that sort of thing.

This is true, but there are also restrictions on what it is right to do in order to prevent life from being unfair to someone. For example, no one would favor a Robin Hood, who took a child or two from those with large families and gave them to childless couples who yearned to be parents, even if their childlessness were a way in which life had been unfair to them. We should have the same reaction to declining to return a kidnapped child so as to prevent life from being unfair to the couple who had thought of her as their own. There are the same reasons to say that we would only be deciding the people to whom life is unfair, not preventing it from being unfair to anyone.

A different argument for overriding the original parents' claim would be that returning the child would not be best for the child. I argued earlier that this consideration alone should not be decisive, but surely the effects on the child are not simply irrelevant either. Suppose that all of the considerations just discussed were to converge in a way that supported leaving the child with the second couple. The new argument would be that even if each of the considerations fails when it stands alone, if they are taken collectively they outweigh a parent's claim to the return of her kidnapped child. That is, if the child would be better off if she were to stay with her current parents, and they would suffer greatly and unfairly if she were taken from them, and what they did for her calls at least for something better than to be cast aside, then these factors outweigh the claim of those from whom she was kidnapped, even though no individual has a stronger claim than they.

We should reject this argument as well. First, it's plausible to say that the worse the wrong that someone suffers, the worse it would be to be complicit in that wrong. To have your newborn child kidnapped is to suffer a terrible wrong indeed. That makes the claim that others should not be complicit especially strong, as such claims go. This means it cannot be outweighed unless the case on the other side is itself extremely strong. Second, it wouldn't *be* extremely strong, in this instance. So, it wouldn't be true that the child we have imagined should remain with those who have been parents to her.

Here is why the case for leaving her with her current parents is not the especially strong one it would need to be: her time with them has been very brief and occurred when she was very young. I assume here that we agree with Goldstein, Solnit, Goldstein and Freud that the great risk of harm in relocating a child is in separating her from her psychological parents. That risk is at a minimum for the child we are imagining, since she had been kidnapped within days of her birth and rediscovered within a month or two. In speaking of the case of Baby Richard, Goldstein et. al. said that when he was "*not yet three months old*, [he] might not have been with the Does long enough for a firm psychological tie to have developed."[4] If there is no psychological tie at this age, the kidnapped baby might be done no harm at all if she were returned promptly to her original parents. At most, the harm would be minimal.

In addition, since she is a babe-in-arms, this is not a case in which the child tells us she prefers to stay with her current parents. The other reasons to override the claim of those from whom she was kidnapped derive from concern for those who had (in all innocence) been parents to her during this time. Those concerns are not to be trivialized, but they are nearly at their weakest in our case. These people did something of great value when they took the baby in and treated her as their own—but they did it only for a month or so, not for years. The other point was that if they lose her, they will be miserable. After all, just as children become psychologically attached to the adults who are parents to them, the adults become deeply attached to the children as well—and this attachment doesn't take three months. The pain these good people would suffer if they were to lose the child might be the best of the reasons to let them keep her.

But there is pain in the other alternative too, of course—for the parents who lost her to a kidnapper and did not get her back. There is certainly no reason to hold that if their miseries were compared, the balance must favor leaving the child where she is. Moreover, terrible as this is to contemplate, imagine that your newborn appeared to be healthy but died suddenly within a month or two. That would be devastating. Even so, I think it would be even worse if the child who suddenly died had lived a good deal longer than a month or two. Then he would have developed more of a personality than he had had in his first months of life. There would also have been more between you: more moments in which you felt intense connection, and a longer time in which he was the part of your life that our children are. Perhaps that thought would provide solace of a kind, in that you would have more of the person he was becoming to remember, and would have more to recall. My thought is that it would also make your loss more substantial, in a way that is difficult to capture—one that would make it more terrible to endure.

It certainly wouldn't follow that the unhappiness of someone who must give up a very young baby is of little consequence. What *would* follow is that it would be on the low end of the scale, where suffering from the loss of a child is concerned. That might seem unimportant, since *anything* on this list is terrible. But recall the earlier conclusion that, by itself, the misery in having to give up a child cannot override the claims that those from whom she was kidnapped would have to her return, which include their claim that we not be complicit in this wrong. We could put that by saying that those from whom she was kidnapped have a claim of a stronger kind. Moreover, since the kidnapping of a newborn child is so terrible a wrong to suffer their claim is especially impressive, as such claims go. That means it cannot be outweighed by combinations of weaker claims that feature relatively unimpressive versions of those. When the child is this young and the time the other couple have looked after her is this brief, the case is not pressing in these dimensions.

This completes the discussion of defenses against the argument that if we do not return the kidnapped child to her parents, we will be complicit in the wrong that they were done. We will be complicit in that wrong, and more so the more completely our actions sustain their loss. To allow the second couple just to keep her, with the usual authority that parents have to choose whom to allow any extensive contact with their child, would sustain the first couple's loss to a maximum degree. But although that might very well be the arrangement the second couple sought, let us next consider a different proposal: that the two couples share parenthood.

To impose this solution would still prevent the original parents from regaining what they had lost, because having to share the parenthood of your child is very far from simply having the child returned to you. However, the contention would no longer be that the second couple deserves to have the child to themselves, but only to have a parental role. Suppose that they did have a claim to share parenthood, and also that this claim should be given greater weight than one the biological parents have. That would mean imposing the shared parent-hood was not wrongful complicity in the initial wrong done, but a proper response to the competing claims.

An important point in deciding whether this reasoning is compelling is where the burden of argument lies. What we should require are good arguments that the second couple ought to share parenthood, rather than imposing this situation on the original parents unless there are good arguments not to do so. Otherwise, we would be requiring that those who had been done a wrong prove that it ought to be relieved before we were willing to do so. Surely it should fall to others to show that it *shouldn't* be done.

If so, it will be necessary to show that the couple described do indeed deserve equal standing for their service as parents to the child, or have earned it. Doing that faces the same problems as showing that they deserve full parenthood, or have earned it. It is still arguable that co-parenthood is *more* than they deserve for their brief time with the child. As to their having earned it, what they would be said to have earned is still something the original parents would be required to relinquish: namely, all the aspects of parenthood that would now belong to the second couple. We would still be taking the second couple to have earned these by what they made of an opportunity that was provided by a wrong done to the original parents—a wrong that prevented the first couple from doing this same work themselves. We ought to have the same misgivings about that situation as we had about saying they had earned the standing of exclusive parents to the child.

It is more plausible to say only that this second couple deserves *something*: that is, that they shouldn't be treated as if they had never done what they did and were the same as anyone else where the child was concerned. But what is it that they deserve, if it isn't to be the child's parents or at least to share in her parent-hood? The alternative seems to be *access* of some kind. Ordinarily, parents choose who spends time with their child, and in what ways. The proposal would be that the couple to whom she had been returned would not have this authority in full. They wouldn't be free to exclude the couple who had been parents to their child, because that couple deserves not to have the child be entirely lost to them.

The particulars could take many forms. These would vary in how deeply they compromised the authority that a parent ordinarily has. For example, to be required to allow your child to live with others for part of every year is to lose a great deal of control over her associations, whereas to be required only to allow weekend visits is to lose much less control. To be required only to allow visits in your presence is to lose very little. And to have the choice of what form the contact takes and whether the arrangement is to continue is to lose even less.

A great deal more would have to be said, but it is obvious that the interests of the child should in some way guide what arrangement is made, whether it con-tinues, and in what ways it changes. That solution would exclude some arrange-ments, but it would also leave many choices from among alternatives that served the child well enough though in different ways. The child's original parents would make those choices, since under such arrangements they are the child's parents, except with the limitation that they must allow the second couple access, rather than these being arrangements in which the parenthood is shared.

The original parents still would not have gotten what they sought—the full return of their child. Therefore the complaint could still be raised that we had been complicit in the wrong that was done to them, albeit in a far lesser way. The reply is that what we would have done should be understood instead as an appropriate response to a claim that others have in the matter. Specifically, although the other couple does not have a stronger claim to be parents to the child, they do deserve not to be strangers to her, and this factor outweighs the original couple's claim to be restored to full and exclusive parenthood of their child. That is a defense of the second kind against the charge of complicity, offered here on behalf of arrangements in which the second couple has access to the child.

This defense wouldn't assert claims rejected earlier, such as the claim that the second couple deserve to be the exclusive parents of the child themselves, or that they deserve to share parenthood with the original couple. The claim would be the more modest one that they deserve to have access to the child, as opposed to being no different where she is concerned than a stranger. I think that impinges as modestly as possible on the full parenthood that the original parents seek to have restored, and that this element makes it the appropriate compromise.

Still, it might be asked why there should be a compromise of any kind. To return to an earlier illustration, suppose that what had been taken from the first couple hadn't been their child, but only their car. Suppose further that the second couple bought that car in all innocence, looked after it, and grew attached to it in the way the some people do grow attached to motor vehicles. Once it was learned that the car had been stolen, it would simply be returned to its original owners. No one would think (for example) that the second couple ought to be allowed to drive it on weekends as a compromise. Why should the situation be different with regard to the child?

The reason is that the cases differ in two important ways. First, it is of no importance to the car whether the second couple has anything further to do with it, whereas that can be of importance to the child. Similarly, the car has no preference in the matter, and the child certainly can. Those considerations give us something important to which to attend when we decide how to resolve the case involving the child—something that played no part in resolving the case of the stolen car. Second, the relationship that the second couple has with the child they took to their hearts is morally significant in ways that can't be attributed to the relationship between an owner and his car. It's appropriate to recognize that difference by (1) taking the couple who took in the child to have acquired claims worthy of weight when we consider how to look after the child and (2) taking the couple who took in the stolen car to have acquired no such claims.

The discussion in this section also suggests the following ideas for use in thinking about cases of other kinds.

1. Parents who are separated from their children by the wrongdoing of others begin with a priority over the other candidates. Theirs is a claim that we should not be complicit in the wrong they were done by ensuring that their loss continues. No other party has an equally significant claim to full parenthood of the child.

2. There are reasons to override that priority and allow full parenthood to someone else instead, although they did not prevail in our example. Those reasons would be that

   (a) it would be better for the child if someone else raised her;
   (b) the child prefers not to go to her original parents;
   (c) to take the child from those who have served as parents during this period would be devastating for them;
   (d) what they have done as the child's parents during this time deserves our respect.

3. All four of these potentially overriding considerations are at their weakest when the child is very young and the time of separation from the original parents and life with the second parents was correspondingly brief. If the child is older and the period she is with the second couple is longer, the reasons to leave her where she is are stronger.

4. Although the original parents have a stronger claim to full parenthood than anyone else, the resolution need not be zero-sum, and there are times when it shouldn't be.

The next section adds to these ideas, and applies them to the cases of Baby Richard and Baby Jessica. Later sections take up several other kinds of cases.

2.

In the cases of Baby Richard and Baby Jessica, it is fathers who have been apart from the children. If they had simply deserted those children, they would have forfeited their parental rights and would not have an original parent's strong claim to have full parenthood restored. So the first question is whether these men did simply desert their children.

It is clear that Otakar Kirchner did not desert Baby Richard. The initial period during which Kirchner was absent included the last month of Daniella Janikova's pregnancy, the birth of the baby, and the first days of the baby's life. Apparently, his original reason for leaving was to attend to his dying grandmother, he made it clear that his absence would be temporary, and he left with the intention of returning. There is no indication that Ms. Janikova was unaware of any of these facts, or took issue with them. In short, the absence did not begin as a desertion.

There are indications that she later believed his absence had become a desertion, when she believed the report that he had taken up with a former girlfriend in Prague. Apparently that report was not true, however. On this understanding of the facts, then, Kirchner was not a man who simply forfeited his rights by abandoning his fatherhood.

Upon his return from Prague, Kirchner made immediate and sustained efforts to find the child that Janikova told him had been stillborn. In doing so, he acted exactly as a father whose child had been taken from him would have been expected to act. She prevented him from acting as Richard's father in the more conventional ways, and she put the adoptive father in a position to do so. She did this by seeing to it that Kirchner wasn't present when she gave birth and then giving the baby to a couple who had arranged to take it.

These events have much in common with a conventional kidnapping. The child Janikova took to others was one that Kirchner knew he had helped create, and he had a right to serve as the child's father. On the view I have offered, that fact would give him a very strong claim to full parenthood of the child. In addition, the couple who served as parents to Baby Richard acted in a way that disqualified them from continuing in that role. According to the majority opinion, "At all relevant times, both the Does' lawyer and the Does were fully aware that Daniella knew who the father was and that she intended to tell the father that the child had died at birth."[5] In addition, "The majority suggests that the Does, intending to advance Daniella's scheme to keep the birth of the child a secret from Kirchner, prevailed upon Daniella...to give birth to the child in a hospital different from the one originally selected by her and Kirchner."[6] This is complicity, and it means they have no claim to continue as parents to Baby Richard or to have some lesser place in his life. The case turns out to be an easy one.

The one involving Daniel Schmidt, Baby Jessica, and the DeBoers is far less straightforward. What Cara Clausen did was not a kidnapping or a quasikidnapping of a child that Daniel Schmidt knew was his. Cara Clausen simply told some lies. She told Schmidt he was not the father of the child, naming a different man whom Schmidt knew to be at least a rival for Cara's affections. She told the other man *he* was the father. Both men believed her. We may assume it was *because* Schmidt believed her that he was absent from his child's life for the period in question. One question is whether her behavior did him a wrong at all.

I would say it did. Schmidt had the same right that all biological parents have to help raise the children they help create. Lies that deprive us of our rights require very strong justification, and Clausen didn't have one. What *can* be said against Schmidt as a prospective father is that he has a bad temper, he has had two other children with two other women, and he hasn't been a responsible father to those children. Cara would have been right to find all of that history worrying, and she couldn't have been faulted if it had led her to decide she didn't want him to raise their child. If that was her thinking, what she did wrong was to act as if the child with whom she was pregnant were not his child, but hers alone. She did that when she excluded him from any role in what happened after she became pregnant, including any discussion of what arrangement was to be made if he were not to do anything further as the father. He had a right to that role, and she denied him this right by lying to him.

A different thought would be that this was a lie Schmidt believed only because he wanted it to be true. We do sometimes participate in our own deception, happily accepting what we should know better than to believe. That doesn't mean the person who deceived us is blameless, of course, but it does mean we haven't simply been this person's victim. Suppose a man should have known better than to believe he was not the father of a child. Unlike someone who had been taken in by a compelling lie, the wishful thinker would resemble a man who abandoned his child for reasons of his own. Perhaps he needed help from his deceiver to put those reasons into action, but they would play a part in his accepting the lie and thus in his subsequent absence from the child's life.

In short, not all lies are alike. This fact doesn't alter the proper conclusion about this particular case, however, because Cara Clausen's lies were not lies that Daniel Schmidt should have seen through. He did know that the timing of his sexual relationship with her was such that the child could have been his, and that would be a reason to think she wasn't telling the truth, but he also knew that he had a rival. In addition, Clausen told him this other man was the father and the other man agreed that he was, and that amounts to a believable alternative to the child's being Schmidt's own. Nor was this a story Clausen told only once. She told it to everyone with whom she discussed the matter, and she stuck with it through the whole pregnancy, childbirth, and surrendering for adoption. In sum, it was a very plausible lie, rather than one that we should blame Schmidt for believing.

Since her lie was also unjustified, this is a case in which wrongdoing by another person separated a biological father from his child. That fact gives him priority over other candidates to be parents to her, on the view I have offered. Unlike the case of Baby Richard, the other candidates include the couple who have been acting as parents to the child, since they were not complicit in the wrong done to Schmidt but acted in all innocence when they took her in. However, the case for allowing them to keep her is weak, for the same reasons that there was only a weak case for allowing a couple to keep a child who had been kidnapped. In both cases, the couple has the child only for the first two months of her life. That means the reasons for leaving her with them are relatively weak versions of those kinds of reasons. Since they are also reasons of a lower order than the ones that call for us not to ensure that parents are separated from their children by the wrongdoing of others, weak versions of them can't override the parent's higher-order claim to have his kidnapped child returned.[7]

As was noted, what happened to Schmidt was not the kidnapping of his child but was wrongdoing of a different kind. I think a weak case to override his claim not to have *that* wrong bought to an end also fails to be strong enough. The reason is that to be deceived as he was is still a very considerable wrong. Consider what the lie would cost him if it were allowed to succeed: the opportunity to be a father to his child. Since that opportunity is greatly to be valued, a lie that would deprive someone of it is no minor wrong, but a very serious one. As a result, Daniel Schmidt's claim that we should not be complicit in this wrong is an especially strong one, as opposed to a claim that we not be complicit in a deception about something less important. Since the DeBoers have no claim at all of this order, his priority over them is substantial. To override it would require an impressive set of considerations. They don't have one: as considerations of this kind go, their case is at the weak end rather than the strong. It can't be good enough to show that they ought to retain full parenthood of the child, since a claim not to have a wrong prolonged is of a higher order than these other considerations.

However, like the couple who had unwittingly taken in a kidnapped child, the DeBoers deserve to be more than strangers to the child, in return for the loving care they gave her. So although Daniel Schmidt should "have her back," the arrangement should also allow the DeBoers access to her. What form that access should take would be guided by concern for the interests of the child, with Schmidt allowed to choose from among the many possible arrangements that would serve her acceptably well. He would otherwise have a father's standing and role.

Further points emerge if we imagine an example of a different sort, in which the biological father doesn't come forward within the child's first months of life but not for *years*: not until the child is fifteen years old, let us say. If this man had simply been dilatory, it would be appropriate to treat him in the same way as someone who had abandoned his child. That is, he would have forfeited his claims where his biological daughter was concerned. Those who had acted as parents to her would continue and would have the authority to decide whether he was to have any role in her life.

Suppose, though, that the man hasn't simply delayed his appearance for reasons of his own. Instead, this is the earliest he could have come forward: until now she was lost to him. So he hasn't done anything to forfeit the claim that Daniel Schmidt had to be a father to his child, and he seeks to be her father. The first question is whether the matter should be resolved in the same way as the one involving Daniel Schmidt. If it were, the man would be declared the legal father of the girl who is now fifteen, with the only limitation being that those who had served as parents to her must now be given some form of access.

It would seldom work out this way, on the approach I am offering. The key reason is that although the claim of the man we are imagining is just as strong as it would have been if he had come forward in the first months of his daughter's life, the case for overriding that claim is now much stronger. One difference is that the girl herself should now have a say in what happens. I imagine that typically she would want to stay where she was. I've argued that this shouldn't settle such matters, but it isn't irrelevant either. It is a reason not to give him the custody that he seeks, a reason we wouldn't have had if he had reappeared in her infancy.

The other child-centered reason not to award him custody is also much stronger. Here is an observation by a Florida court.

> It is conceivable that a man who has established a loving, caring relationship of some years' duration with his legal child later will prove not to be the biological father. Where this is so, it seldom will be in the children's best interests to wrench them away from their legal fathers and judicially declare that they must now regard strangers as their fathers. The law does not require such cruelty toward children.[8]

The distress that would be inflicted on a child who had been in a "loving, caring relationship of some years' duration" is in a different league than the experiences of a Baby Jessica who is returned promptly to her biological father. The costs to the adolescent would be higher, and although these costs aren't the only issue that matters, they certainly aren't irrelevant. They are a second respect in which there is a better case for overriding the biological father's strong claim to simply "have her back" when the child is fifteen.

The same is true in regard to those who have been parents to her during his absence. If the loving care they have given her ought to mean something, it ought to mean much more when it is given for fifteen years than when it is given for two months. The other thought was that we should save people from suffering great pain that they don't deserve. No one should regard the pain of losing a two-month-old as a minor matter, but it seems to me that to lose a fifteen-year-old would be to enter a new dimension of grief. There would be more from which to want to protect the couple who would lose the girl they think of as their own.

I take these to be such substantial differences in the case for overriding the biological father's claim that they ought to make a difference in how we resolve the dispute. The biological father who didn't appear until she was fifteen wouldn't get as close to full parenthood as someone who reappeared when the child was only months old. The next question is what should happen instead.

I am going to argue that this depends on a fuller description of the wrong he was done when he was separated from his child. That is always a very serious wrong, because of what it costs the person who suffers it. However, there are also differences within this category, and they can make what was done more or less grievous. The worse it was, the stronger the claim to the relief of having the child returned. That consideration affects what we should do when the concerns that urge us to override this claim are themselves so strong that the proper course is more of a compromise. The more even the competition between the claims that the adults have, the more equal the standing they should have in the child's life.

Of course, the child's own preference plays an important role, and I will return to that. At present, the idea is to characterize the role that should be played by her biological father's claim to have her back. I am claiming that this depends on how nearly his claim is matched by the considerations urging that he not prevail, which depend partly on how strong his claim is. I want now to elaborate upon the earlier suggestion that the strength of his claim depends on a fuller description of the wrong he was done when he was separated from his child.

For example, I think it is one thing to lose the opportunity to be a father to your child because you are lied to in the way Cara Clausen lied to Daniel Schmidt, and quite another to lose this opportunity because your child is kidnapped in her first days of life. That isn't meant to trivialize what happened to Schmidt. It was a great wrong—but it isn't one from which he *suffered* in the same way as someone whose infant daughter is kidnapped. That man loses a daughter he *knows*, and what he has to endure in the fifteen years before she is found must strain human capacity. This is not true for someone who is told lies that keep him from knowing that a woman is carrying his daughter. He hasn't lost someone he knew, and the worst that the years have in store for him are regrets that this child had not been his.

There are contexts in which a man who was deceived is done a worse wrong than Schmidt was when he was deceived. Suppose a couple are married and have long had a relationship that the man believed was both exclusive and permanent. The woman becomes pregnant with what he happily assumes is his child. He is unaware that the woman also has a lover. Although she knows the child is her husband's, she decides that she would prefer to make a break and raise the child with her lover, so she tells both men that the lover is the father of the child, and both men accept this story.

Her lie has far greater power to devastate her husband than the one Cara Clausen told to a man who knew perfectly well that theirs was not an exclusive relationship. It is a betrayal of trust in a way that Cara's lie was not because there was no trust to betray. In that respect the wife's lie to her husband is a worse wrong than the one Cara did to Daniel, and we could expect the husband's reflections to be bitter in a way Daniel's might not be. I'm not inclined to equate this situation with having your infant daughter kidnapped, but let us put that issue aside. In the case with which we began, the lie wasn't a great wrong of that kind, because it was told within the kind of relationship that Daniel Schmidt had with Cara Clausen. My claim is that this was not as grievous a wrong as the one done to someone whose child is kidnapped in the first days of her life, even though both of these men have been badly used. My inference is that this distinction should affect the compromise to be made between the man's claim to have his child back and the counterconsiderations that are now so strong because the child has been looked after for so long by others.

Consider first the man whose daughter was kidnapped fifteen years earlier and now wants to stay with the people she regards as her mother and father. Both they and her biological father ought to have important places in her life. He should have one because he was done so terrible a wrong when she was kidnapped. They should have one because (1) the fifteen-year-old child herself wishes it; (2) to separate her from them completely should be expected to cost her dearly; (3) they have given her loving care for fifteen years; and (4) for them to lose her would be as devastating as it would be for anyone to lose their fifteen-year-old child.

Exactly what the arrangement would be would have to be negotiated, at least at the start, with the help of a mediator appointed by the court. Unless there are powerful reasons to deny the girl's wishes, she should live with the set of parents with whom she prefers to live. Since her home would be with them, they would have a parent's usual role and authority where matters within the home are concerned. Her biological father couldn't insist that life in that house must be as it would be in his house. Of course, "life in that house" couldn't include abuse or neglect, any more than that would be permissible under more conventional circumstances.

That is a relatively generous restriction, and I think it is the right one to apply to other features of the arrangement as well. That is, the arrangement could take any form that neither abused the child nor neglected her. That differs from saying an arrangement should be rejected if there is another under which the child would have fared better, which would be one way to understand a requirement that the arrangement must be "in the best interests of the child." It preserves us from imposing on this unconventional set of parents and child a requirement that we know better than to ask of conventional families.

The goal would be to find an arrangement that respects the fifteen-year-old's claim to autonomy, the effects that what is done will have on her, and the fact that the adults are nearly equal as candidates to be her parents. There is no formula for what that arrangement would be. That's a reason to settle it by a negotiation rather than by a judicial decree. Another reason to settle it by negotiation is that what is settled upon is something that these people will have to make work. If they are its authors, they will have that added stake in it and that understanding of why it has the features it does. Both should be a help.

Still, for either the negotiation or the resultant arrangement to work well would require good will on the part of all. From the adults it might also require great flexibility and resistance to jealousy, since there would be other adults deeply embedded in the child's life whose ways would not be theirs and whom they could easily regard as rivals. None of the adults would have gotten exactly what they might have wanted most, because none of them would have exactly the same standing in the girl's life that a parent would normally have. I think the compromise and the opportunity it offers them is the right response to their history. Let me emphasize that it is meant to be the initial response to the situation; it would be subject to change by a court if it went badly for the child. How badly it would have to go is an important question about which I have nothing to say, except that it certainly could be too detrimental to the child to continue and that efforts should be made during a "period of adjustment" to make it work. I also contend that a different compromise would be in order if what had separated the biological father from the girl who is now fifteen hadn't been a kidnapping, but a lie of the kind that Cara Clausen told Daniel Schmidt. For the reasons mentioned, that man would not have been done as great a wrong as the one whose baby was kidnapped, and so his claim to be a father to the girl would not be as strong. It would be strong enough that he should have a place in her life, but that place should not so nearly approach equality.

3.

Daniel Schmidt and Cara Clausen had an ongoing relationship when Baby Jessica was conceived, as did Otakar Kirshner and Daniela Janikova when she became pregnant with Baby Richard. Imagine next a couple who have a one-night stand and then go their separate ways. The woman later learns that she is pregnant, and there is no other plausible candidate for the father of the child. However, their one night together was enough for her not to want to see him again, let alone raise a child with him, so she decides to handle the matter herself. She carries the child to term, gives birth, and then gives the child up for adoption. She enters "father unknown" in the appropriate blanks on various documents. Later, the man in our story somehow learns that he "has a child somewhere." He is able to find this child, and he sues for custody, just as Daniel Schmidt sued for custody of Baby Jessica.

On the approach I have offered, the first question is whether he was done a wrong when the woman didn't tell him she had become pregnant. If so, he would have a stronger claim than anyone else to the full parenthood he seeks, just as Schmidt and Kirchner did. On a different view, his actions are the moral equivalent of abandoning the child he helped create, and he has no claims at all where she is concerned. Let me first try to resolve that issue.

Arguments for saying that this man was done a wrong are likely to begin from a premise that he had a right to know that he had fathered a child. The next premise would be that when someone has a right to know something, it is wrong not to tell him. This is plausible, but it also invites the reply that we are responsible for finding out certain things for ourselves, including some that we have a right to know. On this view others shouldn't mislead us about these matters, as Cara Clausen misled Daniel Schmidt. Nor should they make it unreasonably difficult for us to find out what we have a right to know, as Daniela Janikova made it for Otakar Kirchner. However, they have no obligation to inform us if we haven't done what we should have done to inform ourselves.

The idea would be that this is how we should picture a man who takes no interest in whether a woman with whom he had sex got pregnant. That is, the woman would have been wrong to mislead him if he had asked, but she was perfectly free not to inform him when he didn't bother to ask. And since he was done no wrong when he lost the opportunity to be a father to his child but lost it through his own poor conduct, he has no claim that he can later assert.

Here it is worth drawing a further distinction. Suppose first that the couple had used a reliable method of contraception so that it was reasonable for them to believe the woman would not become pregnant. Then it would also be reasonable for the man to continue to assume that, and to act as anyone would who should regard himself as having acted safely: that is, not to ask whether the safe behavior had had undesired consequences but to assume it had not. Therefore, not to ask later whether a child had been conceived wouldn't be cavalier or irresponsible, so that he would deserve no consideration, but would be a perfectly legitimate way to act. He would be like someone who had taken all the precautions that made it safe to have a campfire, including the ones that made it reasonable to believe the fire had gone out, and then left. That man would have a right to be told that the fire had restarted despite his steps and given the opportunity to do what he could about it, rather than taken to have no such right because "he didn't ask." I think the same would be true of the man in the one-night stand. He too makes no moral error in failing to see whether the precautions failed, and he has a right to be told that they did fail and to do what he should about this.

Things are different when we have acted in ways we should know are not safe. Then failure to ask about the consequences of our behavior is irresponsible, more so the more significant those consequences could be. If we don't ask, others are entitled either to call us to account or to choose not to do so, dealing with what has happened on their own rather than enabling us to deal with it. The application to one-night stands in which no care is taken to avoid pregnancy will be obvious. If the woman became pregnant and the man never asked whether she had, it would not be wrong for her to leave him uninformed.

To some that position will seem correct, while others might take it to be ignoring a responsibility to help others avoid making mistakes. Here is how the latter thinking might go.

1. To create a child is an act of profound importance—little else that we do compares. It incurs obligations of such significance that how well we have acted with regard to our child goes a long way toward defining whether ours was a life well-lived.
2. It follows that when our actions might have helped to create a child, we should take a great interest in whether they did so. To be cavalier about it is a serious moral failure.
3. That's what we should say of the man who has a one-night stand in which no precautions are taken and who never looks back.
4. However, it is also possible for the woman to try to rescue him, by giving him a second opportunity to act as he should with regard to this matter that bears so importantly on whether he has lived as he should.
5. We owe each other that much help in life. Just as we should try to stop someone from stepping into traffic because he hasn't paid the attention he should, we should also try to rescue people from enormous moral errors that they have begun to make.
6. The woman in our story fails to do that when she does not tell the man that she is pregnant, and in this she does him a wrong.

Not everyone would grant that we do have a general obligation to try to rescue others from serious moral errors. It could be held instead that we have this obligation only with regard to people with whom we are in what can loosely be called relationships of *concern*. On this view we are wrong not to help our loved ones in this way, as well as our friends, but we don't owe this same help to strangers or near-strangers. The point would be that people who have one-night stands in which no protection is used and then have no more to do with one another are closer to strangers than they are to loved ones. If this is the case, the woman had no obligation to rescue the man from the mistake he was making. Thus, she did him no wrong when she didn't tell him she was pregnant. Thus, he has no claim later to be a part of the child's life.

Actually, I think the implications are very nearly the same if we think she does have an obligation to tell him. This is so because the wrong done in *not* telling him would be one of not trying to rescue him from his own error. That does not seem to be on a par with deceiving someone into making this same error, as when falsely convincing him that a baby is not his leads him not to do whatever he should about a child that is his. If it isn't as great a wrong, someone who suffers it wouldn't be in the same position as a Daniel Schmidt.

So, unlike Schmidt and certainly also unlike the father whose child has been kidnapped, if the matter comes to light very soon, then the man who had the one-night stand without precautions would not receive anything approaching full parenthood, with those who had been parents to his child allowed only some form of access to her. What if the matter comes to light only years later? Again, he would receive less than Schmidt and the father whose child was kidnapped, because his claim is weaker.

Indeed, there are good reasons to say that regardless of how soon he comes forward he should have no special standing at all in the life of the child he helped create. In terms of the earlier argument, what he seeks is to be rescued from his error because he wasn't rescued earlier by the woman who could have told him she was pregnant with his child. There are limits to how far others must go to try to save a person from his mistakes and his ignorance. Of particular importance are costs that the effort to rescue him would inflict on innocent parties. In our cases, it would be easy to argue that there would be costs to the child and costs to those who had served as parents to the child. If those costs were at all considerable, as they would be after a separation of many years, we would be wrong to impose them in order to try to rescue him.

In sum, on the approach offered here, men who have one-night stands and never look back have a right to be informed if it was reasonable for them to believe no pregnancy would occur, but not if their behavior left such a pregnancy a distinct possibility. In the latter case they are certainly not entitled to custody of their biological children, and it is plausible to argue that they are entitled to nothing at all.

4.

Headlines reporting cases of our next kind often employ the phrase "babies switched at birth." In the United States the best-known case of this kind involved a girl named Kimberly Mays. The facts are as follows.[9]

In 1978 Kimberly was born to Ernest and Regina Twigg. At about the same time and in the same hospital, another baby girl was born to Robert and Barbara Mays. Somehow, the tags identifying the babies were reversed, and each couple went home with the girl born to the other.

The Twiggs named the girl they thought of as their daughter "Arlena." This poor child died during heart surgery at the age of ten. Tests taken at that time revealed that she was not genetically related to the Twiggs. The Twiggs concluded that the hospital had sent them home with the wrong baby and began a nationwide search for their biological daughter.

She was Kimberly Mays, who (of course) was then also ten years old. By then, Mrs. Mays had died of cancer, and Robert Mays was raising Kimberly alone. When the Twiggs located Kimberly, they were eventually able to persuade Mr. Mays to undergo genetic testing. In return for his agreement to do that, they agreed that if Kimberly proved to be their biological daughter they would not seek custody but only visitation rights. The tests proved that Kimberly was the Twiggs' biological daughter, and in 1990 their visits began. The girl was then twelve.

After five such visits, Robert Mays refused to allow them to continue. His assertion was that they were too disruptive to the girl's schoolwork and to her attitude. Legal battles ensued. They ended with a suit in which Kimberly, now fifteen years old, sought to sever all relations with the Twiggs so as to be legally adopted by Robert Mays. The rulings were in her favor, with the judge asserting that Kimberly had the legal right to cease any further contact with her biological parents.[10]

On the approach I have offered, we should ask first whether it was wrongdoing by others that initially separated the Twiggs from their biological daughter.

It clearly was—most plausibly, the wrongdoing was negligence at the hospital.[11] That means the Twiggs had a claim to have their child returned to them that was stronger than the claim Robert Mays had to continue in full parenthood. However, there is also more to say about the Twiggs' claim. Its strength, and thus its vulnerability to counterconsiderations, depends on how grievously they were wronged when they were separated from their child shortly after her birth.

A first point is that they were not wronged as grievously as someone whose baby is kidnapped. Like Daniel Schmidt, the Twiggs were not deprived of a child that they knew they had, with the almost unimaginable distress that would bring. Rather, they were unaware of the wrong they had been done.

Second, unlike Schmidt, the Twiggs were also led to believe that a different child was theirs, and they were given that child to raise as their own. There is a separate wrong in that. However, it is also a wrong that reduces the psychic costs of the first wrong. Unlike Schmidt, the Twiggs had a child to cherish, one they had every reason to think of as their own biological daughter. No one would infer that they were done no wrong after all, but this fact does change what it was like to suffer that wrong. In the ten years before it came to light, they didn't suffer from it at all, and they had joys of parenthood that Schmidt did not.

On the other hand, they were doubly misled. There is no clear way to conclude either that they were done a worse wrong than Schmidt (and so have a stronger claim to full parenthood of Kimberly Mays) or were done a lesser wrong (and so have a weaker claim). However, even if it is a lesser wrong, it still seems serious enough to merit return of the child if the switch had been discovered promptly.

Suppose next that it is a greater wrong than was done to Schmidt, though closer to the wrong of being deceived about having had a child than to that of having your child kidnapped. If (as in the case of Kimberly Mays) the wrong isn't discovered until the child is ten years old, the claim for relief from it faces the same stiff competition as we discussed earlier: in the importance of the child's own preference in the matter, the costs to her of the disruption, the costs to those who have been parents to her this whole time, and their years of loving service in that role. At best, the parent who had been given the wrong child would have a claim to a negotiated place in the life of her biological child, but not one that approaches equal parenthood. It was perfectly appropriate for the Twiggs to have visitation rights, and it was also perfectly appropriate for the man who had been a father to her to have the authority to cancel those for good reasons.

We should also note that in this case, the biological daughter of the Mays, who was also taken from them shortly after her birth, was no longer alive. As a result there was no question of each girl leaving those who had raised her and returning to her biological parents. There are such cases, and in some the mistake is discovered while the children are still very young. On the reasoning I've sketched, both sets of parents in cases of that kind would have the same strong claim to have their children returned to them, and neither would have a stronger claim to keep the other child. Suppose, though, that the adults preferred to leave things as they were, each continuing to raise the child they had always regarded as their own.

One such case involved two Czech couples. "The two families whose daughters were switched at birth and have spent the last ten months being raised by a wrong mother have several plans how to solve this situation without risking severe psychological problems of the girls.... One of the plans is to build houses next to each other so that the families would live close to one another and so that the girls would grow up together."[12] Since that would be done by agreement, neither set of parents would have a complaint that the wrong done to them in the switching of the babies was being allowed to continue. Moreover, this arrangement would be meant to be in the interest of the girls, and in the short term that would be the case, since neither girl would be separated from her psychological parents. It would certainly have to be made clear to the girls what had happened and what the arrangement was, rather than this being a secret the parents kept. Presumably it would be at least unsettling to learn that your biological parents had chosen not to reclaim you. However, it isn't clear that this information means such arrangements should be prohibited for the sake of the children, any more than it is clear that adoption should be prohibited because of the distress that might be in store for the child when he learned that his biological parents had chosen not to keep him.

How stable the Czech couples' arrangement would be is a different question. It's easy to imagine the adults coming to lose their enthusiasm for the arrangement before the girls reached adulthood. There could also be economic reasons for one of the families to move elsewhere and the other to remain. What then?

First, there would be no more reason to insist that this unconventional group must remain a unit than to insist that a conventional family cannot come apart. Second, if they did part ways, the adults would have no special claim to end up with their biological child rather than the one they had been raising. They would have given up the claim they once had of that kind when they chose not to end the wrong done to them originally. At this later point, their own strongest claims would be to continue to be parents to the children they had been raising. That solution could be expected to be in the interests of the children as well, and to be what the children would prefer. All of these considerations would be stronger the longer the arrangement had lasted before coming apart.

Suppose, though, that these considerations did not neatly cohere, with all of them pulling toward leaving the children with those who had been parents to them. Suppose the children wanted to switch parents, or that both children wanted to be with one set of them and neither wanted to be with the other. I think this situation would be the same as a divorce in a conventional family that included more than one child, this time with contesting couples rather than contesting former spouses. Not that this possibility makes the proper resolution easy to see, but it does mean that the chance of this problem arising is not a reason to prohibit such arrangements.

5.

On the approach I have offered, the first question to ask when parents have been substantially absent from the lives of their children is why this has occurred. Sometimes the cause has been conduct of their own that forfeited their parental rights, as when someone simply abandons his family. Then the later desire to return would carry no moral weight, though of course those who had been parents to the child during this person's absence would be free to grant it. Assuming they had performed acceptably as parents to the child, they ought to be allowed to continue.

At other times, it was wrongdoing by others rather than the parent's own misconduct that separated parent from child. Then the parent has not forfeited his rights but has been deprived of them. His claim to have the child returned is a claim to have this wrong brought to an end. Any other arrangement continues it, since any other arrangement prevents the parent from regaining the relationship he lost when the wrong was done. I take the claim to relief from that wrong to be a stronger claim to what we might call full parenthood than any other candidate would have, including those who were parents to the child during this time.

Since it is a claim for relief from a wrong, it is stronger the worse the wrong that was done. I argued that it is a worse wrong to have your child kidnapped than to be deceived in the way that Daniel Schmidt was deceived when he was separated from his child because he was led to believe she was not his. Even at its weakest, no one else will have a stronger claim to full parenthood than the parent who was separated from his or her child by the wrongdoing of others.

Even so, however, there are almost always reasons not to allow that claim to prevail. There can be negative effects on the child if she is taken from those currently serving as parents to her. The child may prefer to stay where she is. Other factors are what her current parents have done for her and what it would cost them emotionally to have to give her up. Those considerations also vary in strength. Generally speaking, they are stronger the longer the others have served as parents to the child.

There are cases in which these counterconsiderations shouldn't affect the outcome. Then full parenthood should be restored to those who were wrongly separated from the child. However, there are also cases in which this is not true: those who were wrongly separated from the child may have a stronger claim than anyone else to full parenthood, but they may have a relatively weak version of that claim, and the reasons not to grant it may be strong. Then the proper outcome is a compromise rather than a winner-take-all.

Such compromises are to be negotiated by the parties, but not without restriction. Sometimes one disputant is to be the parent but must allow the others contact with the child, something that full parenthood would entitle her to deny. Then what is up for negotiation is only the form that contact is to take. Or the parties are to be more equal in their standing with regard to the child but what must be settled is more complicated. Those restrictions are set by the relative strength of the reasons to restore the absent parent and the reasons not to do so.

As was noted, the reasons not to restore full parenthood can include the belief that the child would fare better if this were not done, the child's own preference to remain where she is, and the claim that those who have served as parents to her ought not to be as strangers to the child they took to their hearts. Those are not always equally good reasons to override the claims of the parent who was wrongly separated from the child, but when they are strong and the version of the claim to restoration is weak, they can call for a compromise. When they do, that compromise should recognize the relative strength of the claims.

Those are the positions I've taken on what should happen when the parent's absence is caused by his own wrongdoing and on what should happen when the cause is wrongdoing by others. I've said nothing about what should happen when it wasn't *anyone's* wrongdoing that separated parent from child. Sometimes it is a natural disaster that rips a family asunder. When that happens, it may be that no one knows who the parents are, or whether they are still alive. We would hope that others would take those children in. Moreover, if the prospects of ever finding the original parents were dim, we would want the child's new parents to regard the child as their own, not as a temporary charge in whom they ought not to invest too much.

But now suppose that the parents who had lost these children managed to reappear, to everyone's surprise, and wanted their children back. What then? The reasoning can't be as before, because that reasoning took a parent's claim to reunion to be that the wrong done to her should not be continued. The parents we are imagining were not done a wrong. They were separated from their children by larger events.

I believe what happened to them should be taken just as seriously as if it were the work of a wrongdoer. The natural disaster took their children, as effectively as a kidnapper could have done. It was a terrible loss to suffer in the same way that the kidnapping of a child would be. Moreover, it too deprived them of something to which they had a right, namely their continuing life as parents to their child. I think the claim to redress when natural events deprive one of something to which one has a right is on a par with the claim to redress when a wrongdoer does so.

If so, the parents we are describing are in the same moral position as they would be if their child were kidnapped, and their claim to have full parenthood restored is as strong. This means that if they are able to reappear very quickly, they should have their child back, and those who had served as parents to the child should be allowed some negotiated form of contact with him. It also means that if years pass before the parents are able to reappear, the roles that the sets of adults negotiate should be more equal. Again as in the kidnapping case, a prior condition is that if the child is old enough for his preference to merit respect, he should get to choose the parents with whom he lives. The situation we are imagining is all the more difficult in that the child is likely to have left one country and culture for another. The compromise that would have to be made would be truly daunting, but it ought to be tried.

In all these cases it's clear that a child's original parent or parents have been absent for a time. There might also be a question whether a child's biological father had *been* absent, and I want to close with a proposal about that situation. In particular, consider that a man can abandon his child before the child is born. This is certainly the way to describe someone who knows perfectly well that his sexual partner is pregnant with his child and simply vanishes. He would have no more claim to be a father to the child than he would have if he vanished after the child was born. The interesting question is whether there are other ways of behaving while a woman is pregnant that should be regarded in this same way. A Florida court took the following plausible position in this regard:

> Because prenatal care of the pregnant mother and unborn child is critical to the well-being of the child and of society, the biological father, wed or unwed, has a responsibility to *provide support* during the prebirth period. Respondent natural father's argument that he has no parental responsibility prior to birth and that his failure to *provide prebirth support* is irrelevant to the issue of abandonment is not a norm the society is prepared to recognize. Such an argument is legally, morally, and socially indefensible.[13]

However, in later cases the court allowed the required support to extend beyond the financial to the emotional. Here they quote with approval a passage from *In re Adoption of Baby E.A.W.*

> We conclude that a trial court, in making a determination of abandonment, may consider the lack of emotional support and/or emotional abuse by the father of the mother during her pregnancy...Although *Doe* primarily concerned the father's ability to provide financial support for the mother, the Court also noted:
>
> A finding of abandonment under chapter 63 means, for whatever reason, the parent or parents have not provided the child with *emotional* and financial sustenance.
>
> *Id.* at 744 (emphasis added).[14]

The assertion is that if the biological father does not provide sufficient emotional support to the child's mother, this fact can at least help to show that he has abandoned that child. But what is the required emotional support? How significant is failure to provide it? Suppose the man has provided the financial support but has been insufficiently supportive emotionally. Will that be enough to say he has abandoned the child, or will the fact that he continued to pay the bills block that conclusion? The Court leaves such questions to be answered case by case:

> G.W.B. urges this Court to quantify how much weight a court may give to a father's lack of emotional support during the mother's pregnancy. We are not in a position to assign weight in this manner. The determination of abandonment is fact-specific and, absent direction from the Legislature, we cannot dictate to trial courts precisely how to evaluate the factors that go into making this decision.[15]

That decision leaves a great deal undefined, obviously. Views about what even constitutes emotional support and failure to provide it will vary with the judge, presumably, as will views about what men owe pregnant women along these lines and views about how much importance to place upon it relative to other forms of support. Biological fathers are left somewhat in the dark. Moreover, suppose there were substantial commonality to the views that judges took of such matters, or that a legislature formulated such views by statute. That would provide advance notice, but surely we don't want the state to define the proper emotional life for couples to lead when a woman is pregnant. Couples should be left to define this for themselves.

We can do better by shifting Florida's questions slightly, so that we are not asking about abandoning one's child before the child is born, but about abandoning fatherhood itself during this period, as a father later does if he simply deserts his family. The question will be what (if anything) constitutes discontinuing the project while a woman is pregnant. Assuming there was nothing to justify abandoning it, this behavior ought to forfeit the right to be a parent to the child.

To get further, we will need to decide what (if anything) the acts of fatherhood would be while one's child was still a fetus, since it is failure to act in those ways that will count as letting the project lapse. A first answer might be that there are none: once the woman is pregnant all the work of parenthood is hers until the baby is born. While she is pregnant, her role as a mother is to act in ways that help ensure that she gives birth to a healthy baby, but there is nothing for a man to do as father of the child until there is a baby in the world. If there is nothing for him to do, there is no *failure* to act that can forfeit his right to continue as the child's father. The position excoriated by the court in *Doe* as "legally, morally, and socially indefensible" actually turns out to be the truth of the matter: men really do have no "*parental* responsibility prior to birth."

This argument has fatal flaws. Although it is true that parenthood requires nothing of men biologically during pregnancy, it doesn't follow that it requires nothing of any kind. After all, nothing biological is required of fathers *after* a child is born; why couldn't the same could be true at this stage? A different thought is that a man cannot act *directly* with regard to a child that is not yet born, but only by way of actions toward the pregnant woman. However, this too would provide no reason to think there is nothing for him to do as a father, since there is no reason to think fatherhood can involve *only* direct actions. Again, compare his position after a child has been born. For example, it is certainly part of being a father to intercede on your child's behalf if someone else is mistreating her, even if doing so affects the child only indirectly, through its effects on the other party. Since indirect actions are part of fatherhood after the child is born, they might also be part of it before then.

I can see no other potential reason to claim that men have nothing at all to do as fathers during the period of pregnancy, once we set aside their being unnecessary biologically during this time and their being unable to act toward the child except indirectly. Let us turn, then, to what there might be for them to do while their children are as yet unborn. The question is whether some failures to do it should be regarded as abandoning the role, and thus as forfeiting the right to be a father to the child.

Since we are considering cases in which the sex was consensual, on the view I've offered the child has two parents, at this stage: two people with a right to continue in that role. Although parenthood can certainly become a solo act, at this point it is supposed to be a mutual project. This does not mean each party must be active in the project at all times, of course, any more than musicians who are performing a piece together must each be playing at all times. One of the musicians might very well be doing all of the playing at some point, even though the performance that is underway is a performance by the group. Similarly, one of two parents could be doing all the specific acts of parenting at some point, even though parenthood is their mutual project rather than the mother's alone. Moreover, where parenthood is concerned there is no score for the musicians to follow, dictating who is to play which notes at which times. Similarly, we need not find that there are any specific acts of fatherhood that all fathers are called upon to perform while their children are *in utero*. In particular, it will be open to couples to define their roles, including arrangements under which one of them is to do nothing at all for a period. That system is preferable to a court's determining what is sufficiently supportive and requiring all couples to follow this.

Still, the leeway couples have isn't absolute. There are still requirements that derive from the parenthood being a mutual project, and these would apply to every such relationship. For example, one part of participating in a mutual project is permitting the others to play their parts. Anyone who doesn't do so either converts what was supposed to be done together into his exclusive project or prevents it from being carried out at all. In either case, he prevents the mutual project from taking place.

Here is a related point. Participation in a mutual project requires coordinating your own behavior with what others are doing as part of the project. That can take a variety of forms. At a minimum, it involves refraining from behaving in ways that you know, or should know, will make it more difficult for the others to play their parts (assuming the project itself is not designed so as to require one to behave in exactly those ways). Coordination of this minimal kind is part of working together with the others, as opposed to working separately or at cross-purposes. And the idea of a mutual project, of course, is that the parties are carrying it out together, so one part of participating is to refrain from acting in ways that one knows (or ought to know) would make it more difficult for others to play their parts.

Where the mutual project of parenthood is concerned, then, one way for a man to fail to act as a father while a woman is pregnant with his child is to behave in ways he knows (or ought to know) would make it difficult for her to play *her* part. One cautionary note: there has to be a difference between participating in a project but doing so rather uncooperatively, on the one hand, and being so uncooperative that one is not really participating at all, on the other. The occasional lapse is not particularly interesting for our purposes. It is thoroughgoing obstructionism sustained over time that constitutes this person's no longer participating in the project at all.

Suppose someone withdrew from this project of his own free will and not under special circumstances that justified this course of action. That action should have the same implications as abandoning fatherhood after the child is born, I suggest. It too should forfeit the right to be a father to one's biological child. The only difference is that he would have done so before the child was born.

Since the central idea is one of withdrawing by substantially obstructing the efforts of the other parent to play her role, to get any further we will need a sense of what a pregnant woman is to do as a mother during this time. I would say she is to do whatever is needed to carry a healthy baby to term. What that amounts to more specifically would depend on the woman, the fetus, and their circumstances. It is obvious, however, that it will ordinarily be more difficult for the woman to carry out those various actions if she is impoverished. Thus, withdrawing financial support on which she had relied would ordinarily be one way for a man to act substantially in ways he knew (or should know) would make it difficult for the woman to play her part in what is supposed to be their mutual project. Arguably, then, men who stop paying the bills in such cases have stopped being fathers, because they are not even minimally coordinating their behavior with that of the other party to the mutual project of parenthood. The same would be true of a man who regularly acted in ways likely to induce a miscarriage.

The second point about participating in a mutual project is that this entails accepting that one has a role in it, however grudging that acceptance might be. It is possible to work under protest, of course, or to do so while wishing heartily that one were not, or with a hope that the project fails, and certainly to regard it as not yet time to play the role one must. It is also possible to try to get the mutual project halted while pledging to play one's part if it is not. That would happen if a biological father encouraged the biological mother to have an abortion but made it clear that he would be a father to the child if she did not. It would be importantly different from all of these if someone were to deny that there would ever be anything for him to do where this project was concerned. To deny that would be to opt out of the project, if certain further conditions are met.

Identifying those further conditions requires making the same sorts of distinctions that we made earlier. There might be passing episodes in tempestuous relationships, in which the person who "breaks it off" means the break to be permanent even though the fact is that the relationship survives this episode. There might also be refusals to accept some aspects of a role that one agrees one must play, just as someone who is part of a project can occasionally obstruct the work of others. Neither of those instances would be the disassociation I am trying to characterize. Rather, the refusal to accept that one has a role in the project must be thorough, and it must be sustained over a substantial period of time. If it is, it has the effect of eliminating the person as a participant in the project, by his own doing.

That too is something a biological father can do before the child is born, just as he can do it afterwards. In either case, his behavior has the effect of forfeiting his right to be the father of his child. This right is not regained by a change of heart at a later time. At best, that situation would leave him a contender to be judged by the criterion of the best interests of the child. At worst, he would be excluded by parental rights that someone else has established. Here is one example of the latter kind.

> In July 1992, J.M. was conceived by fifteen-year-old E.M. during a two-day relationship with eighteen-year-old R.S. When E.M was about two months pregnant, she told R.S. she was carrying his child. In September 1992, E.M.'s grandfather confronted R.S. regarding R.S.'s responsibility for the pregnancy. From time to time during the pregnancy, R.S. heard rumors from acquaintances that E.M. was pregnant with his child...
>
> J.M. was born on April 15, 1993. E.M and her father paid all expenses related to the birth. When J.M. was about three months old, E.M. brought J.M. to meet R.S. In response, R.S. turned his back and walked away.[16]

By the time the baby was two years old, he had been taken into custody by Utah Division of Family Services in order to protect him from being "severely abused" by his stepfather, and then was assigned to a foster family.

At this point, the state served his biological father, R.S., with a paternity petition, ordering tests to determine whether he was indeed the biological father. When
those tests were positive, R.S. acknowledged paternity and filed a motion for custody. The juvenile court then ordered a gradual visitation schedule. The visits did
not go well: "...visitation sessions between R.S. and J.M. were 'extremely trauma-
tizing' to J.M;"[17] "...documentary evidence showed that J.M. experienced increasing
stress before and emotional and behavioral difficulties after visiting R.S..."[18] In the
end, the Court found against awarding R.S. custody of his biological child.

This was exactly the right course to follow, on the view I have offered. First,
R.S. had no right to the custody, because his behavior when E.M was pregnant
with the child amounted to abandoning the project of parenthood. He had a
change of heart, after the first two years of the boy's life, a period during which
he might himself have greatly matured. Still, he had earlier forfeited his right to
parenthood by denying that he had any parental role to play—a denial he
sustained for a sufficient length of time. When he was drawn back into his son's
life, the boy had been placed with foster parents but had not been adopted.
Whether R.S. was to be allowed to provide something more permanent was
rightly evaluated in terms of how best to serve the interests of the child. It was
also right that R.S. did not prevail under that test, given the information gathered by allowing visitation. So he first forfeited his right to parenthood, then lost
again when circumstances provided a second opportunity.

Here the forfeit was in his behavior when E.M. was pregnant with his child.
There is also a forfeit of that kind when the biological father accepts the role for a
time but then rejects it, if the rejection is sustained and thorough. As an illustration, here is one version of the facts in an Alabama case, *C.V. v. J.M.J. and T.F.J.*

> C.V. is the biological father of Baby Boy G, a child born out of wedlock. J.M.J. and
> T.F.J. are the prospective adoptive parents of Baby Boy G, who was born March
> 19, 1996...both C.V. and the birth mother testified to the following: in February,
> 1995, they began a sexual relationship; in July 1995, they discovered that she was
> pregnant; and in August 1995, they moved into an apartment together...
>
> C.V. moved out in November 1995 and, when he left, took even the dishes,
> the eating utensils, the food and the Christmas tree...C.V. had very little contact
> with her after he moved out of the apartment...C.V. contributed no money
> toward their living expenses, and...the electricity and telephone service in the
> apartment were disconnected and...there were times when she went without
> food because there was none...It is undisputed that C.V. took no financial
> responsibility for his unborn child—he did not pay any of the birth mother's pre-
> natal medial bills or the hospital bill, and he was not listed as the father when the
> birth mother applied for Medicaid benefits. The birth mother said that he had
> asked her not to list him on the application because he did not want anyone com-
> ing after him for reimbursement.[19]

C.V. differs from the biological father in the preceding example in that he had
been living with the woman who became pregnant, and for a time he did accept
the role of father to his biological child. However, it's clear that he stopped
accepting that role when he moved out and ceased to contribute financially. This
was no temporary measure on his part. He left and stopped paying the bills, he

never returned, and he never went back to contributing financially. That was a clean and sustained break, and it was a refusal to accept (any longer) that he had a part in their nascent project of parents to Baby Boy G. On the view I am offering, that meant he was no longer participating in that mutual project, any more than a father who refused the role from the outset, and it meant he therefore had no right to continue it or to resume it.

Once this birth mother gave up on the biological father of her unborn child, she began efforts to arrange for that child to be adopted. Those efforts came to C.V.'s notice as early as February, three months after he had moved out and a month before the child was born. He refused his consent to the adoption. She went to a second adoption agency, told them she did not know who the father was, and relinquished her parental rights to them on March 12. The baby was born on March 19, the adoption was arranged on March 22, and on March 25 the adoptive couple left the state with Baby Boy G. The story continues:

> After she was discharged from the hospital, the birth mother telephoned the father, who went to the birth mother's apartment. The birth mother informed the father that their child had been stillborn. The father was very upset.... In late March, the father asked the birth mother for a death certificate or documents to prove that their child had been stillborn. The birth mother did not have and could not produce any documents....On April 10, 1996...the father filed a paternity and custody action against the birth mother. He asserted paternity of Baby Boy G. and sought custody.[20]

Clearly, C.V. began his legal efforts to regain custody very promptly, only 22 days after the boy was born. Had he not forfeited his parental rights by his earlier conduct, his situation would have been the same as that of Otakar Kirchner and Daniel Schmidt. Like them, he would have been a man who was displaced from the fatherhood of his child by misbehavior on the part of the birth mother, and therefore entitled to resume that role. The crucial difference is that C.V. had displaced himself voluntarily. That action forfeited his rights before she acted, and it meant that what she did was within her own rights as the child's remaining parent.

6.

This chapter has offered a general approach to cases in which a parent who has been apart from a child seeks to return. Those cases vary in many ways. The chapter explores what differences should matter, and in what ways they should matter, when we try to decide what form the child's life is now to take where her parents are concerned. If the answers reached in the cases discussed here are appealing, that is a reason to think this approach is on the right track, though of course cases I have not discussed could call for it to be modified.

The next chapter turns to a different context in which the state might play a role in the lives of parents and children. Here the problem is not what to do when there are rival claimants to the role of parent. The issue instead is whether the state should intervene in a family's life on behalf of the child and, if so, what form this intervention should take.

4

Abuse, Neglect, and the State

Although parents have a right to raise their children as they see fit, their latitude certainly has limits. Moreover, when they exceed these limits the person they mistreat is a child, and that means there are especially good reasons for the state to intervene on the victim's behalf. Children who are mistreated have relatively little ability to cope with the aftermath of what has happened to them, and they remain vulnerable to more of the same. Those are important considerations in their own right, and they also combine to make the mental state of a child who is abused or neglected similar in some ways to that of a captive who is subjected to torture. The victims of both child abuse and torture have the same uncertainty and dread—or, the same certainty and despair—and are vulnerable to the same feelings of worthlessness.

Abuse or neglect is certainly not the ordinary rough-and-tumble of life, which a person ought just to handle on his own, but a misery that calls for us to help the person who suffers it. We intervene in such cases in order to make it stop, to ease the child's sense that this is what life will be like in the days to come, and to protect him from being harmed again. We also have reason to want to deal appropriately with the person who treated the child in this way, whether through punishment or through therapy.

But given that abuse and neglect ought to trigger intervention by the state, the next question is what ought to count as these. Clearly not every parental failure should, since no parent is perfect. If we set the point at which the state should intervene very low, the system that is meant to protect children will simply be overwhelmed. Nor are the state's interventions bound to do more good than harm, since they have costs of their own. Those can be as high as you'd care to imagine, since terrible things can happen to children who are "in care," at the hands of foster parents or in institutions. Even if we put those tragedies aside, every intervention by the state brings strangers who are not of the child's choosing to play some more or less intimate role in the child's life, at least temporarily. The most extensive interventions remove the child permanently to another place entirely, and he loses the life he knew and whatever broader community he had. Even the less extensive interventions are something the child must fit into his view of the world, including whether what happened was his fault and perhaps what to do about those who are now angry at him for having "made so much trouble." Finally, the more readily the state is authorized to intervene on behalf of the child, the less there is to a parent's right to raise her child as she chooses.

It certainly doesn't follow that it would always be better not to try to protect a child, but it does seem that only relatively serious parental failures ought to count as abuse or neglect (at least to a point that calls for the state to intervene.) David Archard represents that belief in this way:

> "Abuse' [and neglect] must thus be serious enough to warrant such intervention. We might call this 'the threshold requirement." Many things can be done to children which are not condoned or encouraged. But when a parent exceeds to a certain point in their ill-treatment of the child the State may step over the family's threshold and protect the child. That point serves to separate bad parenting from parental "abuse" [and neglect].[1]

Archard himself regards this view as naïve in taking the family to be a separate, private realm with the state outside of it (the truth being that the state defines what even counts as a family), and also as naïve in supposing that the state can be a neutral enforcer of impartial law.[2] Even if his points are granted, however, it remains true that when a state enforces its statutes concerning the abuse and neglect of children, this action is costly to the children in the ways mentioned, and is an intrusion by an impersonal collective into the lives of individuals whom the state has allowed to constitute a family. It also remains true that the system would be overwhelmed if substantial intervention were easily triggered. So it remains plausible to want the state to regard what parents have done as abuse or neglect only if their behavior is rather *badly* wrong. If that were all we could say, however, we would not have gotten very far. My effort to get further focuses first on neglect, rather than on abuse.

1.

To neglect a child is to neglect obligations one has where the child is concerned. I have said little about what a parent's obligations are, though, and this omission might invite the thought that it would also be neglectful never to go beyond your obligations and do something special for your child. Thus it isn't only the child who isn't adequately fed whose parents are neglecting her, but also the one who never gets a treat.

I think this amendment makes a valid point, but one better put by saying that a parent's obligations include doing enough of what is special for his or her child, as well as doing the more mundane. So the parent who fails in this regard does fail in a duty and does count as neglecting the child, though in a different way than the one who neglects his child's health or physical well-being. As a different route to that same conclusion, it might be argued that parents have a duty to love their children and to communicate this love to the child.[3] The parent we are imagining would do poorly where that obligation is concerned, so again, he would have failed in a duty and would count as having neglected his child.

The broader point is that a neglected child is one who either does not matter to her parents as much as she should, or who is treated as if she didn't. Other concerns occupy her parents too greatly. In a common form of neglect this conduct happens not just on a single occasion, but over a longer period of time. It isn't just that her parents didn't feed her adequately last night, or didn't see to it that she went to school today: this is their fairly regular pattern. Neglect of that kind takes time. It certainly calls for the state to intervene on the child's behalf, at least when there is no reason to expect it to change.

Here is an example of a different kind, however. One Saturday night a man named Leroy Iverson drove from Los Angeles to Primm, Nevada, where he stopped at about midnight to play the slots. He had his two children with him, and children can be distracting, but Leroy also had great concentration. It probably helped that Sherrice, his seven-year-old daughter, eventually began a game of her own. Sherrice played hide-and-seek with another gambler, a young man of 18. Their game is on the tape of the casino's security camera, including the point a little before 4:00 A.M. when she darted into the women's rest room—and the young man followed her in.

The casino's cameras do not film what happens in the rest rooms, of course, but what happened this time did come to light. The young man took Sherrice into one of the stalls, raped her, and strangled her to death. Her father was unaware of all this. He was playing the slots.[4]

His behavior isn't on a par with what the young man did to Sherrice, but surely it is still a way in which he badly failed his daughter. He didn't harm her himself; rather, he was inattentive in ways that brought her to harm through other agencies. In that respect, his behavior is like neglect that happens over a period of time so that, for example, the child finally contracts a disease or suffers the cumulative effects of continuing poor nutrition. But what Leroy Iverson did is also different from neglecting a child's health or failing to see that she eats properly. We don't need to learn that what he did that night at the casino was a pattern with him: it is distressing even if this was the only occasion. It invites us to consider what ought to count as neglecting one's child on a particular occasion as opposed to doing so over time.

The episode is so horrific that there is a strong inclination to focus on what happened to the little girl: it seems almost disrespectful not to do so. It will be important not to stop there, however, if we are to capture what was wrong with Leroy's behavior. The fact that a child comes to great harm doesn't mean the parents have neglected her well-being, since the world is dangerous enough that terrible things can happen to children whose parents are doing everything they should. By the same token, a child might come to no harm at all even though his parents were absolutely reckless with his well-being, leaving us murmuring about blind luck or about guardian angels. For both reasons, the fault we are trying to capture isn't one of having your child come to great harm, but one of leaving the child exposed to unacceptable risk—regardless of whether what was risked comes to pass. We can use Leroy's behavior to think about what constitutes such behavior.

What he did was to bring his children to a casino, in the wee hours of the morning, and then ignore them for four hours. A casino isn't an inherently dangerous place—unlike, say, the edge of a cliff. However, its clientele between midnight and 4:00 A.M. seems likely to include some unsavory characters, and the danger would lie in exposure to them. There is no reason to think the casinos

Leroy chose were "family friendly," designed to entertain children while their parents gambled, or even to protect children from coming to harm. These were not places where people even *bring* children, and the guards they employed weren't in the practice of looking after children but of dealing with trouble of other kinds. We should add that most 7-year-olds aren't going to sit quietly at their father's knee for four hours. They are going to roam, and if there are places of particular danger, there is a chance they will visit these. All of this serves to describe the way in which Leroy Iverson put his children in harm's way. Finally, we should add that safer alternatives were readily available to him, unlike the case of a parent who must expose his children to risk and can choose only between the devil and the deep blue sea. Leroy could have kept his children much safer, and (I will contend) he could have done so at no unreasonable cost to himself.

To decide whether his behavior was negligent, we can adapt a way of thinking that has long tenure in tort law. Here is a passage from an opinion by Richard Posner, a distinguished judge and a leading figure in jurisprudence.

> …we apply the standard of negligence laid down by Judge Hand…. Under that standard, a defendant is negligent if the burden (cost) of the precautions that he could have taken to avoid the accident (B in Hand's formula) is less than the loss that the accident could reasonably be expected to cause (L), discounted (i.e., multiplied) by the probability that the accident would occur unless the precautions were taken. So:[there is negligence if] $B < PL$.[5]

The right side of $B < PL$ represents behavior as more dangerous the more likely it is to lead to harm, and the more serious the harm to which it can reasonably be expected to lead. In those ways, what Leroy did was certainly not as dangerous to his children as turning them loose in the median of the highway, but more dangerous than a good deal else that a father can do with his children. It was *rather* dangerous, without being outrageously so.

It's also important that he needn't have exposed them to a risk of this order. There were many alternatives, including staying home that night and saving his trips to the casino for times when he could go without his children. Those would have been far safer where the children were concerned. Think of those as "precautions that he could have taken to avoid the accident." Under the formula, before we can tell whether he was negligent not to take those precautions, we must ask about what it would have cost him to take them. The underlying idea is that although it is reasonable to require us to go to some lengths to protect others from coming to harm, there are limits: the cost can be too high.

Since our interests with regard to child neglect differ from those in tort law, we needn't try to calculate these costs entirely in monetary terms. We can employ a different standard for deciding whether forgoing an evening's gambling is a relatively high cost for Leroy to pay, or a relatively low one. We can also think a little differently about how high a cost is *too* high. That's so because we are not constrained by an interest in encouraging commerce to flourish in a community of adults, as tort law is. Our concern instead is to protect children without placing unreasonable demands on their parents. So we are free to say that it is not a great cost to postpone an evening's recreation *because it is only an evening's recreation*, and that it is reasonable to require a parent to pay this cost in order to avoid what is even *rather* dangerous to his children.

That is a moral choice about how careful it is reasonable to require parents to be where their children are concerned. It requires parents to treat their children's important interests more seriously than unimportant interests of their own, even if the parents themselves are inclined to take those unimportant interests very seriously indeed. That requirement seems only fair, and it also seems crucial to the well-being of those who are in a parent's charge. It does demand more of parents where danger to their children is concerned than we ought to require of businesses where danger to their customers is concerned, but this is as it should be. After all, customers ought to be expected to look out for themselves to some extent, rather than having their protection fall entirely to the business. Customers are capable of being alert to at least some dangers and of coping with those dangers if they arise, and it is not unreasonable to expect them to take responsibility for their own safety by doing so. Of course, *children* also ought to be expected to be careful themselves rather than having their protection fall entirely to their parents, insofar as the children are capable of being alert to at least some dangers and of coping with them if they arise. The point is just that children aren't in a league with adults in this regard, and that point makes it reasonable for others to go to greater lengths to protect them from harm. Thus more is required of parents where keeping their children safe is concerned than is required of a business with regard to keeping its customers safe.

What does that amount to, though, where the parents are concerned? The claim is that it is negligent to expose your child to what is even *rather* dangerous to her when you could keep her acceptably safe at what ought to be regarded as a rather low cost to you: in Leroy's case, the cost of postponing an evening's recreation. Of course, Leroy's desire to gamble when he did might have been very strong. That fact wouldn't mean we should regard foregoing the gambling as a *high* cost for him to pay, on the view I am offering. Rather, whether a cost of taking care is high is a matter of what priorities a person ought to have, as opposed to the ones he does have.

That reasoning suggests an objection: what priorities a person ought to have is hardly obvious, and this point might seem to show that we are on the wrong track. After all, we are trying to say when the state ought to intrude on a child's behalf, and it was argued earlier that we should be cautious about authorizing that intercession. This caution won't be achieved if the suggested way of identifying what counts as negligence turns on something highly debatable.

The solution, I think, is to avoid highly debatable contentions about what a person's priorities ought to be, and rely only on the ones that are not debatable. We do exactly that in other contexts, such as when we take some driving to be *reckless* driving, and when we take some behavior with a firearm to be reckless endangerment. Suppose that someone at a party twirls a loaded revolver around his finger with the safety off. That behavior is a paradigm of reckless endangerment, surely. Suppose next that he did this because he badly wanted to impress someone he was with. That certainly wouldn't mean his behavior wasn't reckless after all. It wouldn't even convert what he did to a hard case, one about which we might reasonably debate, even if acting more cautiously would have required overriding a very strong desire, just as Leroy might have had to override a very strong desire to gamble in order to keep his children safe that night. In both cases, what makes the behavior unreasonably careless with the safety of others isn't what the man's priorities actually are, but what they ought to be. In both, it is sufficiently obvious that this person has them wrong. The fact that there are also harder cases doesn't mean we shouldn't think in this way about the easy ones, either with regard to recklessness in general or with regard to recklessness about the welfare of one's children.

A different criticism would be that what I am suggesting asks too little of parents, since it requires only that they avoid behavior that is as reckless as Leroy's. Surely parents should be willing to forego much more than Leroy would have had to forego, in order to keep their children from being at any very serious risk. Actually, I think this is correct as a moral principle, but our question is a different one. It isn't how seriously parents ought to take their children, but what the state should require of them along these lines. Here, as in other contexts, the answer shouldn't be that the state should intervene whenever one person does another wrong. For one thing, the state's ability to tell whether wrong has been done ought to be limited by rights of privacy. We should want the state to pursue only the wrongs that are worth the costs in law enforcement. For another, the state's efforts to make life better for the person it means to protect can actually make matters worse for that person. Those considerations don't mean the state should never intervene, but they do support saying that not every parental failure to take proper care calls for an intervention. So it isn't wrong to have a different standard for what should count legally as neglect or as negligence than we should have for how parents ought to treat their children—in fact, it is right to do so.

The standard I've suggested for the state to intervene takes into account both how dangerous the parent's conduct is and how costly it would be to the parent to act in a way that is acceptably safe. The first of those is a matter of how likely the conduct is to lead to harm and how serious that harm would be. The second relies on a sense in which interests are important or unimportant, and takes an evening's recreation and impressing someone at a party as quite low on that scale. The claim is that the state should treat a parent's conduct on a particular occasion as negligent if it is even *rather* dangerous to the child, and the cost of keeping that child acceptably safe would have been something of that low order. No doubt there are other interests that clearly are similarly unimportant, and other conduct that is similarly dangerous or more so. My suggestion is that these are the terms in which to think when the question is whether the state ought to treat what a parent has done on a particular occasion as negligent with regard to the child.

2.

While to neglect a child is to leave her at unacceptable risk of harm, to *abuse* her is actually to do her the harm. Calling what is done when a child is abused *harm* might already convey that the effects are not trivial, but not all harms are equally serious. So we are left with a familiar question: When should the state intervene on the child's behalf, this time into conduct by which the child suffers at the parent's own hands rather than through the parent's insufficient concern? What should the state treat as *abusing* a child?

As with neglect, there are good reasons not to treat every parental failure in this way. Given that all of us are imperfect, it seemed right earlier to say that all parents sometimes fail to pay as much attention as they should, and that not all such behavior ought to be treated as neglect. The analogue might be harder to accept, but human imperfection also means that all parents actively mistreat their children at times. They overreact, or they make mistakes of other kinds, perhaps realizing later that they didn't act as they should have and perhaps not realizing this: after all, why would we be perfect at parenthood when we aren't perfect at anything else we do? Here too it's only the relatively serious errors that ought to count as abuse and be treated as such by the state—and here too, to say only that is to say very little.

Again as with neglect, we might have any of three purposes in mind when treating what a parent had done as child abuse. One would be to help the child heal rather than leaving her to her own resources. Another would be to protect the child from suffering more of the same, or mistreatment that would be worse still. Obviously, both of these purposes take the child as the object of concern. They invite the thought that what counts as abuse ought to be what calls for these forms of attention to her, so that abuse will be mistreatment that gives reason to think she needs help in healing, and reason to think she is likely to be seriously mistreated again if something isn't done.

The third purpose we might have in treating what happened as abuse is to deal appropriately with the person who mistreated the child, whether through punishment or through therapy. That approach is reasonable—why *wouldn't* we be interested in the person who did something wrong rather than only in the victim? However, it also shifts the focus of concern away from the child. Moreover, it changes what would be relevant about the behavior in our considering whether it should count as abuse. What would matter now would be whether the behavior called for the parent to be punished or to be given therapy. Those are not quite the same as whether what happened indicates that there is more in store for the child if we don't intervene. The behavior might not indicate that there is, and still might merit the parent's being punished or call for us to help him.

In addition, the best way to deal with the parent might conflict with the best way to help the child heal, or with what is best for the child in the long run, or with both. In those cases, I think what is best for the child ought to prevail. We should seek that rather than trying to ensure that justice is done or that the parent gets therapy, given that we can't work toward all three on this occasion. I will give the concerns for the child that same pride of place in trying to say more about what should count as abuse in the first place.

Parenthood carries obligations, of course. At least some of those are positive, so that relatively serious failures in them are neglectful. Others are negative—obligations *not* to do something because it is *your* child to whom you would be doing it, even though others might do the same thing without doing the child wrong. I want to begin in a different place. There are obligations that every adult has to a child, even if he or she is not that child's parent. It is possible for parents to fail in those obligations, treating their child less well than even a stranger should.

That is not always as bad as it might sound. For example, no adult should for frivolous reasons break a promise she made to a child, even if it is only a minor promise. Nor should any adult hold a child up to public ridicule—by making fun of his huge ears, say. It is wrong to do these things, even if one is not the child's parent. It is worse to do them to your own child, but strangers shouldn't act in these ways either. So, if a parent were to do something like this even once, what he did would be a failure to treat his child even as well as a stranger should. Even so, it doesn't seem to be the kind of mistreatment that calls for intervention by the state. Partly this is because even when the parent does it, the wrong done to the child is rather minor (assuming, as we are, that this is a single episode rather than a pattern). Equally important, it seems perfectly possible for a parent who sometimes mistreats her child in minor ways still to do pretty well, over all, as his parent. She could still have considerable concern for the child, despite this regrettable imperfection. To conclude that her child's life with her must be thoroughly miserable or rife with danger would be somewhat overwrought.

By contrast, consider a very different range of actions that it would be wrong for any adult to take toward a child. As Joel Feinberg once observed in a different context, "Willful homicide, forcible rape, aggravated assault, and battery are crimes (under one name or another) everywhere in the civilized world, and no reasonable person could advocate their 'decriminalization.'"[6] Everywhere in "the civilized world," that is, such behavior is not merely taken to be morally wrong and left to individuals to cope with on their own. Rather, the state undertakes to protect people from it, and to punish those who ignore their prohibition—even when both the wrongdoer and the victim are adults. Surely it must also be at least wrong for an adult to do such things to a child.

Well, perhaps not *battery*, some hold. Perhaps it isn't wrong for parents to strike their children in an effort to discipline them. Many people do exactly that. Indeed, it seems likely that there are parents for whom physical discipline is pretty much the same thing as discipline, so that *not* hitting their child means they don't care much about him or about what he is doing at the moment. If so, at some such times they might wrong their child if they didn't commit battery against him, rather than if they did.[7]

These thoughts relate to questions that are deep and important, but also better postponed. Let us begin instead with a different member of Feinberg's quartet, something that no one will be inclined to argue might be acceptable behavior toward his own child. Let us begin with forcible rape.

Unlike a parent who merely broke a promise to his child, or who held his child up to public ridicule on some occasion, a father who raped his daughter would do her a wrong we take so seriously that it is criminal for anyone to inflict it on anyone. It is easy to see why. Even if the rapist had not been her father, the poor child would suffer an unimaginable mixture of pain, injury, fear, and long-term damage. Afterwards, she would have to find a way to "go on with life," despite having precious few of the resources a person would need in order to do that. If it were a stranger who abused her so severely, we would hope her parents would fold her into their loving arms and do whatever they could for her. If it were a parent who raped her, she would be left far more alone, in a hostile territory where the parental embrace is the very place of danger. In short, the harm a father would do in raping his daughter is even greater than the harm a stranger would do her—and we were already prepared to treat the stranger's conduct as a terrible crime. That is suffcient for the conclusion we would expect, that the state should have broad license to protect children from being raped by their fathers.

However, there is also another dimension of the behavior, on which I want to focus. For a father to rape his own daughter is deeply distressing not only in what it does to her but also in what it shows him to be like. There are many powerful, vivid reasons for a man not to subject his daughter to forcible rape, including the signs of what she is suffering as he does it. If these do not deter him, we have very good reason to believe there is something terribly wrong with him, either in how much he cares about his daughter or in his ability to put that concern into action. Try to imagine construing a father's rape of his daughter in the same way that it seemed plausible to construe breaking a minor promise. That is, try to think of the rape as a bad thing for the father to have done but only a sort of *slip*, really, only an imperfection in the conduct of someone who is otherwise pretty much like you and me and who does well by his daughter over-all. That description works well enough for broken promises, because breaking a minor promise betrays (at worst) some minor flaw of character, some degree of selfishness or unconcern that is consistent with treating the child as one should for the most part. It is *ludicrous* as a description of raping your daughter, because doing that to her indicates something of a different order.

To get further would require investigation, since there is more than one possibility. It could be that this father is able to rape his daughter because he does not care what happens to her. It could also be that he actually wants her to suffer, both immediately and in the long term. On either version, her pain is not aversive to him in even the most minimal degree to which the pain of *strangers* ought to be aversive to a person. A third possibility is that the father cares a great deal about his daughter's well-being but is so driven to molest her sexually that he does so anyway.

Whichever of these is the truth, a terrible life lies ahead for the girl. If her father is indifferent to her suffering and to the damage done to her or actually wants to inflict these, he certainly does not care about her in the way he must if he is likely to carry out his various parental duties. Those duties require a parent to take much greater care how his behavior might affect his child than the care we would be required to take about possible effects on strangers. Since the father we are imagining is not sufficiently concerned about the harm and the wrong he does his daughter to treat her with the minimal decency he owes strangers, we must also expect him to fail in the more demanding role of parent. So, her life with him will be painful in many ways, of which his sexual use of her might not even prove to be the most damaging.

An alternative is that the girl's father does care about her well-being, perhaps even to a degree that would normally be sufficient for him to carry out his parental obligations, but he is also in the grip of a pedophilia so intense that he is unable to resist it. It is less clear whether a father of that kind would also fail across the broad range of his parental duties. Even if he did not, her childhood with him would be a time of great damage. For either girl, the only reasonable hope is for someone else to protect her from what her father does to her, and to act as her parent in his stead. That is the only reasonable hope because of the deep, continuing defect that is betrayed in what her father does to her.

I want to emphasize that it is by indicating a defect of this sort that the father's behavior must be taken very seriously where our interest in protecting the girl is concerned. Of course, our first concern should be to comfort her and to help her cope with what has happened, and we should also be concerned to ensure that he suffers whatever penalty he deserves and gets whatever treatment he needs. The point is that insofar as our interest in protecting her is concerned, what matters is what the behavior strongly indicates about him, since that is what should be expected to be in play in his future treatment of her. So far, the argument has run this way: since his behavior does not evince even the most minimal of the concern we are required to show strangers, and the role of parent requires an ability to implement even greater concern for one's child, his behavior provides good reason to believe that he is not equipped to play that role.

The same implication holds for certain levels of neglect. Return, for a moment, to the story of Sherrice Iverson, the seven-year-old whose life ended when a young man raped and strangled her in the stall of a casino ladies' room. It is natural to think that the young man must have had the ladies' room to himself as he did these things to her. Surely anyone who came upon them as it was happening would have put a stop to it. But in fact there was a second young man, a friend of the assailant, who followed them in, saw what was going on—and simply turned around and left. He didn't stop his friend, and he didn't call security guards to stop him. He left and let it happen.[8]

That was a serious moral failure on his part. Even strangers have some obligation to protect children from coming to harm. Accordingly, there is another way for parents to fail to treat their children as well as even a stranger should: namely, by failing to go even as far as a stranger should go to keep their child out of harm's way. When such failures mean the child suffers, they are distressing in what they help to cause, obviously. Even then, though, that is only part of what is distressing about them: they are also distressing in what they strongly indicate about the parent. Even in cases in which a child comes to no actual harm, despite having been neglected to a degree that should shame a stranger, part of what is so appalling about the behavior is what it appears to reveal about the parent.

Namely, what? Again, there seem to be several alternatives, including the following. It could be that the parent pays so little attention to his child's well-being because that is something of little or no interest to him. Or, the parent might actually prefer that the child come to harm and therefore might leave her at risk so that this will happen. Or, the parent might be unaware that his behavior leaves the child at risk: an ignorance so profound, where the danger is this plain, as to be plausible only if he is either mentally incompetent or very young indeed. Whichever of these is the case, his child is in for a very dangerous life.

The reasons to think so follow the earlier pattern. Where the children of other people are concerned, our obligation to keep them from coming to harm requires rather little of us by way of alertness to danger, concern that the child not suffer, and willingness to sacrifice in order to prevent him from doing so. *Something* along these lines is required of us. To revert to our earlier example, when the second young man opened the stall door and saw what was happening to Sherrice Iverson, he could hardly fail to see that the little girl was in terrible trouble, from which she had virtually no hope of escaping without help. It would also have been a very easy rescue, one he might have been able to carry out just by insisting that his friend stop and certainly could have accomplished by speaking to the security guards. That too should have been obvious to him. He behaved dreadfully in being unwilling to do so little. For him to turn away on the ground that Sherrice was not *his* child would be so far from an acceptable excuse as actually to make matters worse.

It is not obvious how far our obligations to protect other people's children extend beyond this clear a case. What *is* obvious, I think, is that they do not extend nearly so far as those of the child's parents do. Seeing to it that the child does not come to harm is much more their responsibility than it is ours. They have a duty to be alert to dangers that are less severe and less certain, to go to greater trouble to fend off those dangers, and to be willing to incur much greater risk to themselves for the child's sake. The rest of us are free to let other matters occupy us to a much greater degree and to fall much further from taking it to be just as bad for something to happen to the child as it would be for this to happen to us. Accordingly, any parent who lacked even the concern required of a *stranger* should be expected also to fail extensively in her parental obligations to look after the child. Since we leave it to the parent to provide that further protection, her child's life will carry considerable risk.

It has that in common with the life of a child whose parents are abusive rather than neglectful and thus are willing to do terrible things to her themselves. The argument that a child who is as neglected as this should be protected by the state is similar: (1) her parent's conduct provides good reason to believe that (for one reason or another) he is not equipped to treat her with the same regard as he would be obliged to treat a stranger, (2) parents are obliged to pay their own children much greater regard than strangers are, and hence, (3) her parent's conduct provides good reason to believe that he will do very badly in the more demanding role of parent.

Our initial question was, from what should the state seek to protect a child, assuming it is able to do so? The answer thus far is, a life with a parent who appears to be seriously defective in concern or in the ability to implement that concern. As to what gives us sufficient reason to believe that is the life of a particular child, the answer thus far is that we are given very good reason to believe this when the parent fails to treat the child as well as even a stranger should, assuming the conduct cannot be dismissed as doing the child only a trivial wrong. A parent who is already doing this to her child gives us good reason to believe she has these defects in concern and, thereby, reason to believe that more of it lies ahead. I want next to address several objections to this line of argument.

3.

One objection is to its accusatory tone: the idea that parents who abuse or neglect their children do so because of some terrible fault that the parents have. It might be urged that we should take a more sympathetic approach, which would acknowledge that someone who abuses her children is less likely to be a bad person and more likely only to have been overwhelmed by the way life is abusing her, lashing out when the situation became too much to bear. She needs help, not blame, and the same holds for someone who can't manage to look after her children as she should despite doing all that her terrible life leaves her the time and energy to do. It's very wrong to regard them as bad people, whose concern for their children is seriously defective.

I don't know enough about the realities of child abuse and child neglect to tell whether it's right to say that the abusers typically are victims themselves of something larger. That would be a theory about why abuse and neglect occur. Empirical studies of this causal question are essential for dealing with questions of what to do with the abusive or neglectful person, whether we should try to reunite the child with the parent, and what we can do to help make life in this family safer. Those questions arise at a different stage: the question addressed here is what sort of behavior calls for the state to intervene on behalf of the child. My answer is that behavior calls for such intervention if it is *as if the parent were* seriously defective in concern for his child. If he has acted that way, then the child needs protection, regardless of whether we ought to blame him for it. It doesn't matter whether he doesn't care about his daughter, just that he might as well not care about her. That will be true if he has acted in a way that strongly suggests he is either seriously defective in his concern for the child or unable to implement his concern for her, perhaps because of his own life situation. Such behavior calls for us to protect the child, regardless of why it occurs—not that abusive or neglectful parents must necessarily be to blame for what they do.

A different objection is to my way of characterizing the behavior in question. I seem to have assumed that what is wrong for a stranger to do where a child is concerned must also be wrong for the child's parent to do, and wrong in some deeply significant way—one that strongly indicates a serious defect of concern, for example. But think again of *striking* a child. Many believe there are situations in which it would be wrong for a stranger to do that but not wrong for the child's own parent to do it. If so, it is a mistake to move from "treated her own child in a way a stranger should not" to "acted in a way the state should take very seriously." The parent might have been acting perfectly acceptably, precisely because she is the child's parent.

Since not everyone agrees that parents have a right to strike their children, however, I will develop this point by means of a different example. Imagine instead John and Sara, who believe very earnestly that no child should play games that involve pretending to do people violence. John and Sara forbid their children to play such games, they confiscate presents that are toy guns or standard video games, and they impose harsh punishments if they find their children pretending that a stick is a gun or a rock is a hand grenade. This reaction strikes some of the neighbors as a little over the top, despite being well intentioned and meant to teach the right lesson. Others believe John and Sara are mistaken in the message they seek to convey about guns and violence. But even they would grant that John and Sara seem to be within their rights as parents when they try to teach their children what they believe on this matter, and also when they try to teach it in the way they do, rather than in a way others might choose.

Imagine next that John and Sara extend their efforts to the other children in the neighborhood. They travel the local places of play with missionary zeal. Like missionaries for a religion, they are well aware that many of those they hope to convert will not be moved by the light of reason alone. So they do not stop at warning the children they encounter about the evils of violence. They also con-fiscate whatever war toys they find these children using, and they punish the ones who resist just as they would punish their own children.

They are going too far, I take it. At exactly what point they go too far is an interesting question, but not one that we need answer here. John and Sara ought not to be doing at least some of what they do to the neighborhood children, yet it is no different from what they (perfectly acceptably) do to their own. Evidently then, what is within their rights as parents is beyond their rights as concerned adults. So, it is wrong to assume that a parent must be misbehaving if she treats her own child in a way it would be wrong for a stranger to treat him—and, as I appeared to argue, possibly misbehaving in a way that raises grave doubts about her broader performance as a parent.

However, I think the challenge this example poses to my argument can be met fairly easily: I have not made the assumption in question. I have not taken the fact that a parent is acting in a way that would be wrong for a stranger to act to be sufficient to place the behavior in a special category where the attentions of the state are concerned. There would be little to recommend such a view, since some of the ways it is wrong for strangers to treat children are rather trivial, and they remain trivial when a parent does them—such as frivolously breaking a minor promise, to use an earlier example. What does call for intervention by the state is behavior that may indicate that the parent (1) does not care about the child in the ways a person must in order to carry out a parent's obligations, or (2) does not know how to implement that degree of concern in even the most fundamental ways, perhaps because of mental defect or extreme youth, or (3) despite caring enough about the child and knowing how to fulfill his or her obligations as a parent, has a condition in which people regularly fail to carry out important obligations, such as addiction to narcotics or sexual interest in chil-dren. Such a parent will fail the child not only on the occasion that betrays the deficiency but also across time, certainly extensively and probably dramatically, and this is why the behavior calls so strongly for protective action by the state. Although some behavior that would be wrong for strangers certainly falls into this category—rape, for example—other such behavior certainly does not, such as breaking a minor promise. John and Sara's campaign of moral education too would be wrong for a stranger to conduct, but when they conduct it with their own children there is no reason to think them seriously defective in their concern for those children.[9]

Why not, though? The answer should clarify what further signs we need for the state to intervene on the child's behalf. Notice first that our reason for saying John and Sara's conduct toward their children is all right for parents despite being wrong for strangers can't be the one we would offer for saying this about breaking minor promises or being occasionally cruel in some petty way. That is, what John and Sara do isn't behavior that does the child only a relatively trivial wrong, and for that reason might be perfectly consistent with deep and able affection for the child. For one thing, it isn't clear that what they do in trying to teach their children to abhor violence wrongs their children even trivially, as opposed to being clearly permissible. For another, if it *were* wrong, it wouldn't be wrong only trivially. What John and Sara do involves taking property that someone else has given to the child and that therefore belongs to the child, not to John and Sara. They also engage in motivation by threat, and they punish their children for disobedience: by depriving the child of a liberty the child had, perhaps, or (ironically but certainly not unimaginably) by giving the child a good paddling. Deprivation of property, motivation by threat, restriction of liberty, and battery are not trivial ways to mistreat a person when they are mistreatment. Yet it is standard to take them to be legitimate when done as John and Sara do them to their own children. We need a different justification for our intuition that it gives us no grounds to believe that John and Sara have what I called serious defects in concern and thus (on the view I am offering) shouldn't be regarded as child abuse.

The answer begins as follows, I think. What John and Sara do is to conduct a project of moral education, and the moral education of one's children is an important obligation of parenthood. Of course, parents are not free to do anything they like under that banner. There are limits both to the lessons they may attempt to teach and to the methods they may use. John and Sara are within both sets of limits, though. They are not attempting to teach their children that it is a good thing to shoplift from the major chains, for example, and their punishments for disobedience do not range into the cruel and unusual. Finally, their methods are not so clearly inferior to some other way of achieving their goal that their inefficiency should give us pause. In sum, it is permissible for John and Sara to act as they do toward their own children because they have an obligation as parents to provide them a moral education, what they do is part of an attempt to carry out that obligation, and both their goal and their methods are within the latitude they have to make choices in this matter.

It is tempting to complete the argument by saying that the reason they are wrong to act in these same ways toward the other children in the neighborhood is that they don't have an obligation to provide those children a moral education. That obligation belongs to the children's own parents, the idea would be. Those parents also have a (limited) right to carry it out in the way of their own choosing, and the objection would be that John and Sara are encroaching on their territory when they extend their program beyond their own family. The matter is more complicated than this, however.

As a start, it isn't true that we have no obligation at all to attend to the moral education of children who are not our own. For one thing, we ought not to lead such children astray, whether intentionally or through failure to take reasonable care in the example we set for a child whom we should know is paying attention to us. That is part of what is wrong with breaking minor promises and indulging in acts of petty cruelty. I think there are also some noncontentious moral lessons—about cruelty and about dishonesty, for example—that we would have an obligation to try to convey to any child we found mistreating an animal, say, or telling a huge and dangerous lie to some trusting soul.

What those various obligations require of us varies. Sometimes we can fulfill them just by openly disapproving of what the child appears to think it would be all right to do. Sometimes we have an obligation to alert his or her parents rather than letting some matter pass. Sometimes we ought to interrupt what the child has underway. The point is that to do *nothing* on such occasions would need a justification. That would not be the case if the moral education of children were none of our business but only that of their parents. It seems, instead, that other adults do have obligations along these lines but these are more limited than the ones the child's parents have, just as other adults have more limited obligations than the parent's to protect the child from danger and to avoid doing him harm.

Also, as with those other areas of obligation, the duty to attend to a child's moral education is a *lesser* obligation for other adults than it is for the child's parents. It holds a lower priority among their duties. That is why a parent who fails in her obligation to look after the moral education of her child will need a better excuse than another adult would need for failing to do what *he* should along these lines, and she will be in for much harsher criticism if she has none. Since it is a lesser obligation for the stranger, he ought not to seek to carry it out at the same cost to his other obligations. That will be too high a cost, since he is a stranger, whereas it would not have been too high a cost if he had been the child's parent. In part, the greater latitude that parents have to threaten and to punish is a way in which their obligation to look after their child's moral education is of higher priority than a stranger's.[10]

It is important that parental latitude has limits of its own, since thise preserves us from the conclusion that parents have *carte blanche* whenever they are engaged in "teaching the child a lesson." No doubt there are parents who take parenthood in exactly this way, but what John and Sara do gives us no reason to think they are like this. As was noted, it is plausible instead to regard what they do as an extended effort to provide their children with what John and Sara are at least not wildly wrong to regard as appropriate moral values. No one who is engaged in a campaign such as theirs can also be thinking of their children as theirs to treat as they wish.

More generally, it is important to note that it isn't simply the fact that John and Sara are trying to carry out a parental obligation that makes it implausible to take what they do as revealing a grave, continuing defect in their concern for their children. A parent's effort to carry out an obligation could be so desultory or so ill-suited to its end that it *should* suggest there is something wrong with him: either that he doesn't care about the child and is only going through the motions, or that he cares but is mentally incompetent or has some debilitating condition. Failures of distinctively parental obligations can belong in our category of special concern, then, along with the forms of abuse and neglect already mentioned. It is only *extreme* failures that belong in this category, though, just as it was extreme abuse and neglect that belonged in it: not only because they strike us as extreme, however, but because of what they give reason to believe about the parent.

A different objection to the view I am offering is that it oversimplifies when it divides adults into the child's parents, on the one hand, and strangers to the child, on the other. Even John and Sara aren't strangers to the neighborhood children, and there are also adults who look after children professionally in one way or another. There are teachers, camp counselors, nannies, pediatricians, and so on. They aren't the children's parents, but they aren't strangers either. Moreover, they seem to have a different set of moral obligations than a stranger would have where protecting the children from harm is concerned.

This is all correct, but it does not undercut the account. My idea was that parents have a greater responsibility for their children than the broad class of other adults: a greater one than strangers have, and also a greater one than the professionals mentioned. I also said that parents shouldn't fail to treat their child as well as even a stranger ought to treat him, and that their failure to do this can be good evidence of the lack of proper concern that should bring the state to the child's aid. Those points are unaffected by an intermediate class of adults who also have special responsibilities to ensure that children fare well.

However, there is another question of interest here. What are these special responsibilities of teachers, pediatricians and so on to ensure that children fare well? What do they have an obligation to do along these lines? It will help to start by explaining why they have a special obligation here at all.

In part, they have it because they are in a position to see things that others won't. If you are teaching a child, working as her nanny, or being his doctor, you can be alerted to signs that the child is in difficulty. The signs would differ in their clarity, of course, and thus in how strongly they called for the professional to come to the child's aid. There are the same concerns here as with the state's interacting on the child's behalf: there must be a sufficient basis for intruding upon the parents' right to raise their children as they see fit and for invading family privacy; care is needed so that the intervention does not do the child more harm than good. The clearer the sign that the child is in trouble and the more serious trouble it seems to be, the more deeply and insistently the professional would be obligated to intervene on the child's behalf.

In that sense, though, the professional's moral obligations to be of help to the child are the same as the stranger has. Each has a duty to act on the child's behalf in the way that is called for by what she sees. The difference is in what the two see and should be expected to see.

In addition, at least some professionals become people the child trusts. The trust allows the professional to see what other adults would not. That can include further signs that the child is in need of help, with the same heightened responsibility to act on the child's behalf that we've just discussed. In addition, this is a case of being trusted by *a child*, and that matters in another way. Even the most inventive and resilient of children are highly vulnerable to harm, both from adults and from other sources of trouble. This is surely a case in which being trusted by someone who can't do much to protect himself gives you an obligation to look after him when he needs looking after. It would be an obligation to be vigilant about this responsibility rather than only to take signs seriously when they came to your notice.

Again, there are the same hard questions about what this concern calls for and what would be an intrusive overzealousness. I can't try to answer them here, but I think the right answers would follow the general outlines that emerged earlier. Those reflect two main ideas thus far. The first is that the state should seek to protect a child from a life with parents who are seriously defective in concern. The second is that we are given very good reason to believe that this is a child's predicament when the parents act in a way that fails to treat the child as well as even a stranger should, so long as this action wrongs the child more than trivially and falls outside the latitude parents have in carrying out their parental obligations. Teachers and pediatricians have a heightened responsibility to attend to such matters because children are in their care; the teacher and pediatrician can see what others will not see, and he or she may have the child's trust.

Since I offer this approach as an alternative to relying more completely on the intuition that what the parent has done is something *very bad*, let me offer two observations on its behalf. First, it accords well with our intuitions in the easy cases, the ones in which it would be stunning to hear someone claim that the conduct *wasn't* very bad. Anyone who, for example, rapes his child, or tortures her, or batters her until her bones break has surely done the child more than trivial wrong, has surely exceeded his latitude as a parent, and has surely provided good reason to believe there is something badly wrong with his concern for her.

Second, the way of thinking that I am recommending has an advantage over relying exclusively on intuitions about how bad the conduct is. When we think only in terms of the parent's having acted very badly, there will be certain logical limits to any effort to be sure we are right in our concern. We can try to confirm that what the parent did was the kind of act we thought it was, and we can reflect on our strong reaction to acts of that kind, thinking about whether our dismay is merited. Both of those things are important to do, but there is a sense in which they do not take us beyond this particular episode.

When instead what is important to us is what the act signifies, we have additional ways to confirm or dismiss our worry about it, quite apart from looking ever more closely at what was done on this occasion. For example, if it were true that a father did not care what happened to his daughter, as his conduct suggests, that attitude should be discernible in other aspects of their life together. The same goes for his being mentally incompetent. Similarly, there will be other ways to test whether he is an addict or a pedophile.

These further explorations will not always be easy to conduct, of course, but they are always possible. To have this range of ways in which to confirm or dismiss our hypothesis is an advantage when we are anxious to be right about something. It is like being able to examine an object from several angles rather than from just one. And, since these are angles anyone can adopt, there is less worry that the conclusion reached is only one person's opinion.

4.

Let us consider, next, one way in which further investigation might show that the parent's behavior did not derive from a serious defect of concern, as we had thought it did. Suppose it turns out that this parent is actually quite concerned about her child's well-being and is amply equipped to implement that concern. Moreover, she is eager to carry out her obligations as a parent, and she is not mistaken about what those obligations are. Rather, her mistake is about the moral limits to what she may do in carrying them out. Unlike John and Sara, she is wrong about what being the child's parent entitles her to do.

As a result, her methods of discipline are somewhat too harsh, or she takes her child's privacy more lightly than she should. Alternatively, what the parent (wrongly) does to the child might be part of a deeply different way of life, according to which the parent's behavior is perfectly appropriate, or even obligatory. As one illustration, consider the Aboriginal father whose daughter commits the offense of being present when an elder dies and who punishes her by putting a spear through her thigh. According to his way of life, only males may be present at such a time, what his daughter did was a very serious matter, and he had an equally serious obligation to carry out what counts for us as an aggravated assault.[11]

Still, when the Aboriginal father put his spear through her thigh, he betrayed no defects in his concern for her well being or in his ability to put that concern into action. His action was different in these ways than it would have been if someone outside this culture had done it to his own daughter: that would simply be a punitive assault, given its very different cultural background. Similarly for refusing to allow a child to have vital medical treatment: for a Jehovah's Witness or a Christian Scientist to do this does not signify the same troubling qualities as it does in a parent who is *not* enacting a different conception of how to serve the child's best interests.

The point of importance about different ways of life is not that someone from another culture must be following one of them when he does something it prescribes that we consider wrong: he may not be. Nor is it that he cannot be mistreating his child if he is following that way of life: a different way of life could prescribe exactly that. It isn't even that what he does cannot be the kind of mistreatment that we should take especially seriously, as if ways of life could differ only insignificantly. Rather, what is important is that when someone who is following a different way of life acts in the way in question, the situation does not provide the same reason to think he is indifferent to the child's well-being or positively hostile or grossly ignorant or in the grip of some disorder.

It might still be true that a life with this parent is one from which the state should seek to protect the child, but if it is, that will not be because of what it is like to live with a parent who is seriously defective in his concern for his child. It will be because of what it is like to live with a parent whose values put the child at this particular risk of mistreatment. The same would hold if the parent's values put the child in peril of rape or sexual molestation, aggravated assault, or homicide, regardless of whether those were the values of a Leroy Iverson or those of someone whose culture prescribed doing so as his parental obligation. If those harms are grave enough to call for the state to intervene when the risk arises from the parent's lack of concern for the child, they should also suffice when the risk is due to the parent's moral values.

That conclusion might be resisted, especially when the parental values that expose the child to these risks are based in an established religion. Imagine, for example, parents who are Jehovah's Witnesses and who will not permit their infant child to have a transfusion without which it appears that she will die. Jehovah's Witnesses believe that to accept the blood of another into one's body is to lose all chance for eternal life, ensuring that whenever one does inevitably die, that will be the end. Someone who lived by this creed would see refusing transfusion to be in his best interest. Parents who lived by the creed might find it terribly difficult to reach this same conclusion about their children, but let us suppose that they did. Then their refusal to permit the transfusion would express their deep concern for her, rather than their failure to have that concern. The trouble with what they do is a different one: what a person may do with her own life, if it has limits at all, has different limits than what one may do with the life of another.

Imagine, for example, that a hero is needed, someone who will risk his own life to save another. Ordinarily, a person is free to undertake to be that hero—but not also free to make someone else do so. If he wants to leap into the bullring to distract the bull from the fallen matador, that is up to him, but he may not throw his small son into the ring for the same purpose. Similarly, if he wants to volunteer for a dangerous medical experiment, normally he may do so and perhaps be admired for it—but to volunteer his children for the same purpose is something else again. His life is his resource to value and to spend, to this extent; his children's lives are not his in this way, but theirs.

The principle that appears to be in play here runs along these lines. There are aspects of life that virtually everyone agrees have a good deal to do with faring well, though there is disagreement over how much they have to do with it. There is staying alive at all, for one thing, being in good health, living without disability, and being free from very bad experiences such as severe pain. The example of choosing to be a hero suggests that a person has the discretion to place considerably less value on these aspects of well-being than she places on other matters: on helping someone in need, for example, or on serving a particular cause, or on preserving what might be a chance to have eternal life. Presumably, this belief extends also to sacrificing a fair degree of physical well-being to her *art*, or to her scholarly or scientific work. We may differ over whether her discretion about these contours of her life is absolute, but surely she is free to accept very reduced circumstances where her physical well-being is concerned in order to serve the cause or help the person she cares about or do her work—or to preserve what she takes to be her chance at eternal life. She is free in this way because it is her life, and she is at liberty to live it as she chooses rather than as someone else would live his.

By the same token, however, she is not free to determine that her child will live by these same lights, since it is not her life about which she would be choosing but his. That is, she is not free to decide that he is to do considerably less well than he could have done with regard to staying alive, keeping in good health, or being free of disability and relatively free of severe pain, in order to serve a cause or help someone else or do work of a certain kind or retain what she considers to be his chance at eternal life. She is certainly free to try to incline him to make those same choices about his life, once he is capable of making them. That is part of her right to try, by means of her centrality to his life, to affect what sort of acceptably-functioning adult he turns out to be. But the choices are his to make, ultimately, because it is his life they will define as certain to be worse off, in certain fundamental ways, than it might have been.

There are two possible explanations. It could be that physical well-being has an inherent priority over other aspects of life, so that to sacrifice it for something else is always a mistake. That might explain why we should let adults make such choices about their own lives—to make mistakes about them, that is—but should not allow them to make the same mistakes with the lives of their children. The other line of argument, which I find more appealing, doesn't take the importance to lie in its being physical well-being that is sacrificed, but in its being a case of accepting relatively certain high costs in the hope of benefits that are nowhere near as certain. One thing that a person may not do with another's life, on my view, is to take certain extreme gambles against the odds when safer bets are available. One may take such gambles with one's own life, in the conviction that what might be gained is so far superior to what is almost certain to be lost that this choice is a rational one. One may do so because one has utter faith that the outcome hoped for will obtain, or that *this* time the costs that seem so certain will not be exacted. What one may not do, on this view, is to take similar gambles with the life of someone else.

Insofar as this line of thought gives physical well-being a priority over other matters, that is so because effects on the physical are generally more predictable than the chances for other kinds of benefits. In our earlier example, the evidence might provide a high degree of certainty that the daughter of Jehovah's Witnesses will die if she is not transfused, while the same cannot be said for the reason to believe that a transfusion will also preserve her chance for eternal life, no matter how compelling a believer finds those reasons. If so, refusing to allow their daughter to be transfused is a gamble her parents may not take with her life, since there are other courses of action without this balance in the odds. They would be free to refuse transfusions for themselves, because it would then be their lives they were defining in accordance with the principles they hold. They would not be free to refuse one for her.

This is a matter of life and death, of course, and it is also possible for another person's values to prescribe courses of action that do not expose the child to

anything of this order. Unfortunately, for some of us, to realize that someone is
(by our lights) immoral is like realizing that what we took to be a stick is actually
a snake. We lose all powers of further discernment, and all concern for anything
but this one fact. That's particularly unfortunate with regard to protecting children from parental abuse or neglect, because a parent's moral failings should
arouse the state's interest in protecting his or her child only if they put the child
at risk of nontrivial harm or wrong. The reason is that we are engaged here in
protecting children, not in the moral improvement of adults. This is also a context in which to be especially careful both that our protective attentions don't do
the child more harm than good and that sufficient regard is paid to parental privacy and autonomy. I think it would be relatively easy to mount an argument to
conclude that a child should have some protection from life with Fagan. I think
it would be impossible to make a similar argument that a child should be protected from life with homosexual parents, for example, or one with parents who
do not disapprove of homosexuality.

Be that as it may, the suggestion so far is that the state should seek to protect
children not only from parents who are seriously defective in concern, but also
from parents whose values put the child at serious risk. When would the state have
reason to fear that a child needed this latter protection? In some instances we
might require a demonstration that this parent's values had already been enacted
in a way that did the child a serious harm or wrong, which the parent regarded as
perfectly appropriate under the circumstances. In others, as in the cases of denying
the child vital medical treatment, we needn't wait until the parent does this at least
once. It would suffice to know that she had decided to do it this time.

5.

To this point, I have been concerned mostly with parents who fail in obligations
that even strangers have to the child. I want now to turn to abuse and neglect
with regard to obligations that strangers do not have but that the parents do.
Later chapters will explore these parental obligations in greater depth, but it is
necessary to say something now about their nature.

The distinctively parental obligations might plausibly be taken to fall into
two broad categories. One set are obligations to look after the child's current
welfare in various ways, so that he or she continues in good health and has a
positive existence. Under this heading, it is up to the parent to try to ensure that
the child is fed, clothed, sheltered, kept healthy, protected from harm, and so on.
(As was suggested earlier, others also have more limited obligations to look after
the child in these ways.) Parents are also obligated to do more than look after the
current well-being of their children, however: they must also attend to what the
child will become. If the child is expected to grow up and become an adult, his
parents have an obligation to raise him to become...well, what, exactly?

Nothing very specific, it seems, since adulthood is not something that comes
in only one acceptable form. There are many ways to function acceptably as an
adult, and so there are many ways for a parent to succeed in raising a child who

does. Nor should we characterize what parents must do in raising their children as if the children fell under no other influences during their youth. Finally, it isn't as if children emerged from childhood as finished products, unchanging in what their parents had provided and set to run mechanically the course their parents had manufactured them to run. Since there are other influences in a child's youth and since children do go on to live their own lives, it can't be a parent's obligation to *ensure* that the child is happy when he or she grows up, for example, or that he or she is morally upright. We would do better to say that a parent's obligation is not exactly to *equip* their children to be happy and to be good but (while they are children) to make a reasonable effort to provide some of what they will need for these goals, including certain resources of character.

Admittedly, a parent cannot be obliged to know precisely what her child will need in order to be happy as an adult, let alone obliged to provide that. To say otherwise overestimates both the predictability of life and our grasp of what makes a person happy. Still, it is reasonable to say, for example, that no one who regards himself as worthless can have much by way of happiness, and that the same is true of those who have developed no ability to look after themselves or no capacity for intimate relationships with other human beings. It is reasonable to require all parents to know such broad, general truths as these. It is also reasonable to require them to know more particular truths about their own children. As one's children grow, a good deal emerges about their personalities, character, intelligence, abilities, and limitations, with corresponding implications about what this person will need in order to be happy. Where those implications are clear, it is reasonable to expect parents to grasp them.

In short, parents ought to know that much about what their children need in order to be happy as adults. It won't quite do to say that they have an obligation to provide it, however, for two reasons. One is just that it might not be possible for the parent to do this. The other is that even if it were possible, providing it would not be the only obligation the parent would have. There is always more to a parent's life than parenthood. How his or her children turn out should be an important part of it, in my opinion, so I would say that raising children requires us to make quite a serious effort to provide some of what they will need in order to have happy lives when they are "on their own"—but not more than that. There are significant sacrifices of other interests that we would be wrong not to make, but we are not obligated to make every sacrifice we could.

Our obligation to raise our children to be good people follows similar lines. Exactly what it is to be good is not so obvious that we could require every parent to know it. On the other hand, it is reasonable to say that no one can be a good person if he or she is utterly without compassion, or regards others solely as potential instruments for use, or is utterly without honesty. It is reasonable to require parents to know broad truths of this kind and, as with similar broad truths about happiness, to make a serious effort to raise their children to have these ingredients of moral goodness.[12]

Two further points will complete this brief, preliminary account of parental obligations. The first is a point of clarification. I distinguished parental obligations into those of looking after the child's current welfare, on the one hand, and those of raising the child to be someone who can be happy and good, on the other. Distinguishing the obligations in that way might suggest, mistakenly, that the looking-after is done in one set of actions and the raising-up in another. What we do (or fail to do) in looking after our children must bear enormously on what they become. For one thing, the family environment is the child's most basic forum in which to learn to see himself as someone of value or to think instead that he is worthless or worse than worthless. It must also be where the capacity for intimate relationships might be either cultivated or virtually extinguished. Accordingly, the obligation to look after our children in certain ways is part of the obligation to raise them as we should. Some of the same actions serve both obligations, and some of the same omissions are failures in both areas.

Second, since we are concerned with failures to carry out obligations toward the child with regard to such matters as self-esteem and self-respect, acquaintance with her own talents and limitations, the sense that others are to be taken seriously and the ability to feel for them, it is important to notice the extent to which these goods do not turn on any single parental act but depend on sustaining a pattern of behavior. No doubt some specific acts or omissions will be more powerful influences than others, and there may be watershed events, but in general it is what parents do over time that will matter the most.

To fail in these obligations, then, will be to fail over time, for the most part, rather than failing to perform some single action. Much the best indication that the failure has happened will be signs that the damage has already been done: behavior that indicates the child lacks compassion or is utterly dishonest, for example, or that he has no regard for himself.[13] Other than that kind of evidence, the only impressive basis for believing a parent is not raising a child as she should would be substantial failure to *look after* him as she should. As was noted, the two sets of duties are interrelated to the point that greatly to neglect to look after a child is also greatly to neglect to raise him or her to have a fair chance to be both happy and good. As was noted at the close of section 3, we are speaking here of failures in parental duty that give their own indication of a serious defect in concern and that should be taken with the same seriousness as other instances of that failure.

6.

I have offered a way to identify parental behavior that indicates the state should seek to protect children, ranging from negligence on a particular occasion through neglect over time to abuse. A different question is what form the state's effort to protect ought to take, since there are many possibilities. Some earlier distinctions will be of help in this regard as well.

Suppose, first, that there is reason to believe the parents have failed to carry out one or more of the distinctively parental obligations. Perhaps their son is not attending school regularly, or their daughter usually seems both ill in some low-grade way and in need of a bath. If it turns out that they are in fact not looking after her as they should, the possible reasons cover a wide span. At the grimmer end of that range, it could be that they are actively hostile to their child or utterly indifferent to her. It could also be that one of the parents is an addict or is in the grip of some other condition that is debilitating to the carrying out of obligations—or that this is true of the child's only parent. It could also be that the parents hold a different set of values, according to which they have no obligation to act as we think they should and as the society in which they live has left it to them to act.

There are further possibilities of a different order: simple ignorance about how to carry out what a single parent recognizes as obligations; a life that does not provide her the resources she needs to carry them out; a life that has overwhelmed her, in ways of which this failure is a sign. A failure may also indicate *nothing* that we should expect to persist and thus lead to further such failures: it is possible just to err, and it is possible to learn from an error on one's own, or to need only to have it called to one's attention. In short, the fact that someone has failed in a distinctively parental obligation is not especially informative about the child's future. It is consistent with many possibilities, which differ greatly in how alarming they are. Accordingly, if it calls for any response from the state, the first stages of that response should be to investigate the possibilities.

The story is a very different one when the parent has failed in an obligation that even a stranger would have to the child, in a way that cannot be dismissed as trivial or as within a parent's latitude to make choices and to make mistakes. Here's why: when we begin with an investigation, we seek to resolve uncertainty about what lies behind the mistreatment and thus about what lies ahead for the child. If a parent has already acted in a way that even a stranger should not, we are already clear enough that we should assume the worst. Our first step should be to remove the child to a place of safety while we do our investigating.

For example, if we knew that a father was already molesting his daughter, we would have an excellent reason to believe that he would do so in the future. The recidivism rate for pedophiles—at least those who have been caught and punished or treated—is exceptionally high. Evidently, using a child for sexual purposes isn't a kind of *slip* a person makes once or twice under some rare combination of circumstances and against the grain of who he is. Rather, it expresses a powerful aspect of who he is and, even if we make our best efforts to change him, who he should be expected to remain.

There are other behavioral signs that are equally good evidence of what I have called serious defects in concern, and these too call for removing the child *before* investigating rather than after. To continue the example, a father who molests one daughter is highly likely to molest another. We should react by removing all his daughters from his custody.

There might be other kinds of evidence that should be taken with this same seriousness even though the parent has done nothing that suggests a serious defect in concern. Among these, I include not only indifference and hostility but also conditions that make the parent unable to put adequate concern for the child into action. There could be a compelling reason to believe someone had such a condition, even though she had not yet mistreated her child: to believe, for example, that she lacked the mental competence to play the role of a parent

with an acceptable degree of success. It is also arguable that addiction to narcotics incapacitates a person for parenthood. If so, the addiction itself would be
sufficient reason to begin by removing the child from the parent's custody.

But what about the idea that parents have a right to raise their children as they
see fit and that the state must give this right its proper due—including, perhaps,
permitting those who have erred to try again? There are contexts in which those
are very important points to raise. A right to do something your way—including
to raise your children in your way—isn't much of a right if it entitles you only to
do the thing perfectly and is lost at your first wobble. But clearly those concerns
are at their least compelling in cases of the present kind, where our immediate
thought is certainly not that what the parent did was to *wobble* in the course of
otherwise acceptable parenthood. Let us pursue the matter further.

On the view for which I argued in earlier chapters, parental rights are rights
to continue with the parenthood that one began either by conceiving the child
or by adopting or informally by joining a single-parent family. That is why
someone would have no parental rights if he had deserted his family, since in this
case he *had* no parenthood underway, because of actions freely taken. Those who
desert their families have no complaint if the state allows someone else to take
up what they have left undone, or arranges for this to happen if the child has no
other parent. And although certainly they might be permitted to return to their
families, they are not entitled to do so. We do need to be careful about what constitutes desertion so as to keep it distinct from forced separations, and also from
voluntary departures that are meant to be temporary but last a very long time.
Those ought not to be treated as *abandoning* one's family in the same significant
way as someone does who leaves willfully and stays away for a significant period
of time, having nothing to do with his children or having only sporadic or casual
contact with them. That is what I would consider desertion that forfeits the right
to serve as parent to the children one deserted.

It is much the same, I want to argue, with parents who are still present physically but who have treated their children in ways that could be regarded as indicating serious defects in concern. Despite remaining a presence of some kind in
the family—often a malign one—they have substantially abandoned parenthood
itself: not necessarily willingly, but as a matter of fact. They may do nothing at
all of what parenthood requires, or they may continue to play some parts of the
role. Even in the best cases, their serious defects of concern mean they omit a
great deal, because such defects undercut repeated self-restraint and the disposition to protect the child from harm. The heart of parenting is left undone, as
opposed to being done badly. Moreover, what is left undone is so pervasive that
others cannot take it up without removing the child from the custody of these
parents, unlike the more limited omissions.

For both reasons, it is best to regard these not as cases in which someone has
been acting as a mother or father in a way he or she might have a right to continue,
but on the model of a family that has been deserted. Because these parents haven't
done enough to count as playing the role at all, they have no right to *continue* to
play it. Nor have they a right to *resume* parenthood, as they would if it were
something they had been doing, but doing imperfectly. As with desertion of the

more conventional kind, it will be important to think in this way only about those who have genuinely abandoned the role of parent: that is, those who willfully ignore its responsibilities for a significant period of time, doing little or nothing of what they should for their children. Briefer periods of distraction are a different matter, however, and ought not to be treated as ceasing to be a parent.

I've claimed that if someone has stopped being a parent to his or her child, concern for parental rights is not a reason to think of the state's intervention as an interruption in something the state should be working to restore. Nor, in a case of this kind, do parental rights give the state the burden of proving that its intervention continues to be necessary. There could be other reasons for taking this position—though I will argue shortly that there are not—but as far as parental rights are concerned, those who have already treated a child in a way that indicates a serious defect in concern should be taken to have no parental rights in play; thus there should be no claim that the state should be working to restore a family in which they will be parents and no claim that the state must justify its continuing intervention. Instead, it is up to such parents themselves to show that they will now play the role that they left unplayed.

The same argument cannot be applied to those who have not yet treated the child as described, since they have not similarly forfeited their parental rights. In some extreme instances, however, it would be arguable that a parent is incapable of playing those aspects of the role that lie ahead. For example, women who were and would clearly remain comatose have been impregnated, as have women who were so severely retarded or so severely deranged that to serve as the child's mother was clearly beyond them. There must also be a degree of youth at which we ought to say the same of a girl who bears a child of her own, or a boy who fathers one. It is arguable that those addicted to narcotics belong in the same category, and also those who have already molested some other child: parenthood is a role they cannot play acceptably well, at least at present.

These cases are different from those in which a parent has already abandoned his or her role, and the rights that role carries, of course. Still, to be unable to play the role has similar implications, because one cannot have a right to do something that is impossible for one to do. So, the wholly incompetent parent is without parental rights, even when the incompetence has yet to cost the child anything. The role of the state is the same: to begin by removing the child to a place of safety while it investigates the contention that the child's parent is as we fear, to work toward the best alternative for the child rather than toward restoring him or her to a repaired parent, and to regard it as the parent's burden to show that things have changed.

It might be argued that parental rights are only one of the reasons why the state always ought to work toward reassembling families and ought to have the burden of showing that their temporary disassembly is still justified. More important, it might be contended, it is in the best interests of the children themselves to be raised by their own parents and therefore we should always work toward reassembling families. Moreover, it might be added, the traditional family is a valuable social institution that our system should seek to preserve, in this venue as in others.

It would be a mistake to cast either of these contentions as absolute rules, however. Some children test both beliefs severely. First, the assumption that children are best off with their own families is based partly on a belief that there is love of a special kind for the child there. But these are children who have never had much of that kind of love and, I will argue shortly, there is good reason to believe they never will have. Partly, too, we believe children are best off with their own families because it is so *wrenching* for a child to lose what is familiar to him or her. Again, though, for these children, paying that cost might well be the best option open. Similarly for the argument that our system should maintain the family as a social institution: whatever the cost might be of not supporting that institution at every opportunity, in these cases that cost is most likely to be worth paying.

In addition, there is good reason to be skeptical that parents this inadequate can be repaired and the child thus restored to a family of the kind the arguments contemplate. What the parent would have to change isn't just a defect in an otherwise acceptable makeup, but something deep and pervasive. The parent might have to begin to care about a child who has counted for little or nothing to her, or, worse, has been considered one more of life's troubles. Some parents might have to emerge from an addiction or a powerful compulsion. Sometimes, it might be necessary to overcome a stunning level of incompetence. Reforms of these dimensions must be among the most difficult of human undertakings.

The arguments in favor of reassembling the families are thus at their weakest when what we fear for the child is the worst. This is a significant factor, since it's when we fear the worst that we should require especially *good* reasons to be willing to risk. Here we have the opposite of what we need, I have been arguing.

Imagine next the kind of case in which what worries us gives no reason to fear that the parent has a serious defect in concern. There has been no failure to treat the child as well as even a stranger should. There has been an apparent failure to carry out one of the distinctively parental obligations, but this is neither so egregious nor so repetitive that it provides its own reason to believe the parent is seriously defective in concern. Here it would not be at all plausible to infer that this child had been essentially without this person's parenthood and was in need of removal to a place of safety. By the same token, it would not be plausible to assume this parent has forfeited his or her rights by abandoning the role. So, the assumption should be that the state's intervention is only temporary and that the parent has a right to have it end when it is no longer necessary and a right also for the state to show that intervention continues to be necessary.

The argument that children are best off when restored to their original families is also on better footing in a case of this kind. The parent we are imagining has erred, but not in a way that undercuts the assumption that she cares deeply about the child and can put that concern into action. If she is concerned about him, she will have a powerful motivation not to repeat the error that brought the family to our attention. So we have a much more encouraging basis for thinking the child's best interest lies with this family than we have when the parent has something far more obdurate to correct and lacks the motivation to correct it.

As a final variation, suppose that although we did have reason initially to fear a serious defect in concern, further investigation showed this not to be the case.

What emerged instead was this: when this child's father did something that alarmed us, he was applying a different set of values than ours to a child about whom he cares deeply. Regardless of whether his moral code differs from ours only somewhat or very substantially, it would be wrong to think of him as having deserted his child by abandoning the role of parent and therefore having no right to continue in that role. It would also be wrong to think of him as having a mental or psychological condition that made him incapable of playing the role acceptably. Rather, he has been engaged in parenthood and has the capacity to continue. He has the right to do so, albeit not in the way that brought him to our notice. Respecting his rights as a parent requires working, in the least intrusive way available, to ensure that he does not continue to implement his dangerous values in the way he has.

What that behavior amounts to would vary quite a lot. We should not undertake to change his values, such as, for example, his opposition to transfusion on religious grounds. If we had reason to believe that someone who opposed transfusion would want his child to receive many other forms of medical attention, it might suffice to make those other services available only if he agreed to permit this one as well, should it prove medically necessary. In other cases, we might prevent the implementation of values dangerous to the child by making it clear that the parent would otherwise suffer criminal penalties, perhaps, or loss of custody of the child, or both.

In addition, when the root of the problem is dangerous values rather than a defect in concern, there is a greater chance that the child is better off staying with the parent rather than in the custody of the state while efforts are made to remove the danger. We are speaking here of parents who care about their child and have provided the child an acceptable life on the whole. To be removed from such a home would be distressing in itself for the child. Moreover, despite our concern, this is a home where there is a lot for the child, unlike the one in which the parent does not care about the child or cannot put that concern into action. From the point of view of the child as well as that of the parents, then, the presumption should be that we leave the child at home while we work to protect him or her.

Both points of view also support directing efforts toward making the intrusion only temporary. Since these are capable parents who have not abandoned their role, they have a right to resume it once we have found a way to cope with the difference in values. There is also better reason to think we can find a way of doing that than there is to think we can repair a parent who hates his child or who is utterly indifferent. Parents who love their children but also have values that are dangerous to the child have their concern for their child to motivate them to change. It is true that they are faced with a choice between something they believe in, perhaps as members of a group whose way of life it is, and looking after the child either at all or without some level of state intrusion, and this might be a difficult choice. Still, it does not seem to be on the order of the change required in someone whose parental failures are due to addiction to crack or to mental incompetence. In short, we should be more optimistic about the proposition that these children will be better off with their original families.

There is one further point. A subculture whose values endorse treating their children in ways that are alarming to the majority will be regarded as strangers among us, viewed with the usual mixture of fascination, disapproval, distaste, and fear. Removing the children from such a culture for their own good is a practice with a long history, and one about which there is good reason to be at least ambivalent. Suppose that to leave the child of Aborigines or Native Americans with his or her family is to leave that child at considerable risk of excessively harsh treatment because of the parents' values. If the only way to eliminate that risk is to remove the child not only from his or her family but from *any* family that practiced those values, placing her instead in a culture where she is viewed as an inferior alien, it is far from clear that doing so will be best for the child. There will be a counterargument that the best life for the child is with his or her parents, even when we are uncertain that we have found a way to ensure that they will not put into action the values that distress us.

7.

Abuse and neglect and what to do about them are matters as complex as they are important, and I have left a great deal undiscussed. On the approach for which I have argued, what calls most urgently for rescue by the state is life with a parent who is seriously defective in concern. The compelling signs that this is the life of a particular child, I have argued, are (1) failures to treat the child as well as even a stranger should, where these cannot be dismissed as trivial or as being within parental latitude, (2) convincing evidence of a mental or psychological condition that would render the parent unable to implement the concern that parenthood requires, or (3) sustained and extensive failures in distinctively parental obligations. In such cases, the state's first step should be to remove the child to a place of safety, while it checks its hypothesis about the parent. If the hypothesis is confirmed, it becomes the parent's burden to establish that he or she should regain custody of the child, and the state's efforts should not necessarily be directed toward reassembling this particular family but should aim toward promptly finding a permanent place in which the child can have a good life.

Other parental failures should be treated very differently, I have claimed, because they do not represent the same forfeiture of parental rights or incapacity to have such rights, and also because the prospects for the child's life with these parents are so much better. At its extreme, this category includes parents whose values do put the child at risk of serious mistreatment. The state should try to protect children from that treatment, of course, but these efforts should be constrained by the rights of the parents and by the distinct possibility that the child will be best off with those parents, both during the effort to correct the problem and even if it cannot be corrected.

I have claimed that evidence that a parent is immoral is of interest only insofar as the parent's values endanger the child, either physically or psychologically, and is far less significant in itself than evidence that the parent is seriously defective in concern. The same is true of failures in a parental obligation that are not so extensive as to give their own reason to postulate that the parent is seriously defective in concern. When the parent does care (though not enough), or is able to put her concern into action (but has some noticeable limitations in this regard), or has values that put the child at some risk of harm (but not at any *great* risk), we have entered the territory of judgment calls. I have said nothing that would help say how those calls are to be made. Which such children the state should help, and in which ways, depends in part on what resources the state has. It also depends on how extensively those resources are drained by cases of the kind I have discussed at length: those, I think, have first call.

Finally, there are good reasons to want the state to be the last resort where families are concerned. The family's first resource should be the parents who are devoted to being good parents, vigilant about errors they might make, and ready to change as needed. Often there are also friends and relatives who take an interest in a family. That should sometimes extend to expressing concern about how the parents are treating their children, despite the intrusiveness of such behavior. As with other moral matters, only a portion of what it is wrong to do as a parent should also be illegal or should prompt the attention of some other official of the state. This is no surprise, since looking after our children and raising them is a deeply personal activity that can be carried out in many acceptable ways and a great deal of which is carried out in private. These are all considerations that argue against giving the state a role in governing what we do.

Although I have offered a view about the set of parental failures that ought to bring the state into play despite those considerations, I've said little about what would count as a parental failure *at all*. This broader morality of parenthood is the subject of the chapters that remain. I begin with what parents owe their children by way of respect for their autonomy.

5

The Autonomy of Children

AMY LYNN HAGEN
Endangered runaway
Race/Gender: White Female
Date of birth: July 17, 1981
Current age: 17 years
Weight: 105 lbs Height: 5' 2"
Hair color/style: Blonde, wavy or straight, long
Eye color: Brown
Date missing: July 27, 1998
Missing from: Riverside, Ohio
Distinguishing marks: One-inch scar on lower back.
Details: Amy ran away from home when she found out charges
would be filed against the man who harbored her when she ran away
previously. She is in the company of James L. Campbell, age 19
(DOB: 12/5/78), and may be with family in Dayton Ohio,
Michigan, or Virginia.
CONTACT: If anyone has information or has seen Amy Lynn
Hagen, please contact the Riverside (Ohio) Police—Officer Morton
at (937) 233–1820, or the Beavercreek (Ohio) Police—Dets. Potts or
McFaddin at (937) 426–1225, or your local FBI or law enforcement
agency immediately.
                    —from http://www.lostchild.net, with photo

If Amy Lynn Hagen wants to go off with James Campbell, why isn't she perfectly free to do so? The short answer is that she is only seventeen years old. If she were twenty-seven it would be an entirely different story, on this view, but at seventeen Amy Hagen's home is where her parents say it is. She is not free to live elsewhere without their agreement, and she is not at liberty to come and go as she pleases.

The posting tells us that Amy ran away "when she found out charges would be filed against the man who harbored her when she ran away previously." It doesn't tell us whether James Campbell is that man, nor how old she was when she ran away the first time, nor what the charges against the man who "harbored her" back then are to be. Perhaps "harbored her" is a euphemism, and perhaps she was young enough at the time for those charges to include statutory rape.

Certainly she would have been young enough for the running away to mean that she missed school. Those are two further matters that are not left up to Amy, at least not in their entirety: what sort of sex life she has, if any, and whether she pursues an education.

There are a number of other respects in which she is simply not as free as an adult would be to live her life by her own lights. Depending on the laws of the particular state, at various ages a child will be too young to hold a job, get married, operate a vehicle on public highways, purchase a firearm or alcohol or tobacco or be present in a place where alcohol is served, authorize her own medical treatment, vote in an election, or serve on a jury. Her city might also have a curfew requiring people of her age to be off the streets by a certain hour, not because the city is so dangerous as to be under martial law but on the theory that children who are out that late must be up to no good, or simply should be home in bed.

If Amy Hagen had gotten pregnant and wanted an abortion, obtaining one might have required that her parents be notified beforehand, or that she consult with them, or that she have their consent, or (in the absence of their consent) that she convince a court "that she has attained sufficient maturity to make a fully informed decision."[1] (Which of these it would be depends on the state and on the point in the legal history of such restrictions.) If some other adult—an aunt, say, or the mother of the boy by whom Amy got pregnant—had driven her to a less restrictive state, doing so might well have constituted "interference with the custody of a minor" and carried a penalty ranging up to seven years in prison.[2] These laws concerning abortions for girls are certainly very different than the ones concerning abortions for women. Where women are concerned, the law treats this matter as a deeply personal one that is within the woman's right of privacy to decide, at least during the first trimester. Where girls are concerned, whether to have an abortion might be just as self-defining a choice as it would be for a woman, just as personal and intimate, just as arguably a choice about her own body, but it certainly isn't left up to the girl in the same way. Instead, she is required by law to allow others to play a designated part in the decision.

At least some of the legal limits on children are imposed partly in order to protect other people from harm we think the children would do them if left to their own devices: if the children were free to own guns or drive cars, for example. A different rationale might be the primary one, though: we want to protect the children from doing *themselves* harm or from ruining their own lives by unwise choices. The state is not our paternalist of choice: that would be the child's parents. Indeed, a parent who gave her child the same liberty that adults ordinarily give each other would be highly likely to lose custody of the child, in the same way as she would if she failed to provide for the child's physical needs. In short, we take paternalism to be at the very heart of parenthood.

And yet, to have a child under your care is not like owning a doll or a toy. This is true not only when the child is seventeen years old but also when he or she is very young. An adult who owned a doll or a toy would be free to move it about in any way that pleased her, with the usual restrictions against harming others with it. Partly that is because dolls and toys have no will of their own that the owner would be ignoring, as children clearly do. A will calls for some respect, even if it is the will of a child. Imagine a parent who insisted that her six-year-old daughter must always step first with her left foot, never her right—something the daughter would be perfectly free to impose on her doll. Clearly, a six-year-old is not entirely her parents' creature but should be free to do some things in her own way.

The conventional view about these matters can be summarized as follows. An adult's freedom to do things in her own way is to be taken very seriously, under the heading of respect for autonomy. A child's autonomy merits some respect, but not to the same degree. We are far readier to say that regardless how the child would act if he were to do things in his own personal way, that isn't the way he will be *allowed* to act. This chapter concerns whether that system is just as it should be.

The question can be sharpened. Consider again the situation in which someone has an unwanted pregnancy, which she might or might not end by having an abortion. For present purposes, let us set aside the important view that abortion is a variety of murder, and thus that every abortion is the proper concern of all. Those who do not hold this view are going to think that whether your next-door neighbor has an abortion is essentially none of your business. This neighbor could *make* it your concern if she were your close friend and asked your advice, but even then the final decision would certainly be hers, and it would also be up to her how much you had to do with what she decided. If you were even to insist on counseling her about it, that would be highly intrusive.

But now suppose it is your fifteen-year-old daughter who has gotten pregnant. You certainly should take an interest in whether *she* has a baby or has an abortion, most would think. She is your *daughter*, after all, and the decision is a major one, likely to have considerable effect on her life. Those facts would be considered quite sufficient to make what she does your proper concern. Indeed, most would say that if you took no interest in so important an event in her life, you would fail the girl in an important way. In short, the common view is that our children should be objects of a paternalistic concern that would be intrusive and inappropriate if it were directed toward another adult.

This point is not limited to major, deeply private matters such as whether to have an abortion. A parent would also be expected to try to control what a child ate and drank, not just so that he did himself no great harm but also so that he developed good general habits and came to appreciate a variety of foods. Similarly, it is thought proper for parents to impose some control on the way their child dresses, on the way she spends her free time, on who her associates are, and a great deal more. To take this same interest in another adult would be extremely presumptuous, clearly, and an adult who permitted it would not be living as independently as most of us would think she should. In short, whereas we don't expect adults to intervene uninvited in each other's behavior unless something fairly substantial is at stake, we expect parents to do so on a much broader range of occasions where their children are concerned.

There is also a difference in how far it is ordinarily thought a person should go when acting paternalistically. In many contexts a parent would be considered justified in going very far indeed: essentially in doing everything she could to prevent her child from putting himself at risk. For example, if a six-year-old who had been a great success in the school play were to announce that he was leaving home to try to make it as a child actor, no one would think his parents could only argue strenuously that this path was a mistake but must eventually allow him to live his life as he chooses. Many would say the same if the child were a fourteen-year-old determined to go to New York and make it as a ballet dancer. Just *don't permit it*, the conventional wisdom would be. Where adults are concerned, however, there is a point at which virtually all of us think we must say, "All right, it's a terrible mistake, but it's your life," and then do no more than be on hand to pick up the pieces. Almost no one would think it right to take the adult's car keys and ready cash, cut off his contact with anyone who might help him do what he has in mind, and so on—the measures his parents might be expected to take if he were a child.

Some arguments for what I have described as the conventional view are reviewed in the first section of this chapter and found wanting. Later sections develop three other lines of thought. One is concerned exclusively with paternalism toward very young children and draws on our general obligation not to put others in great danger. The second concerns the extent to which a child's first character and personality are her own, in a way that is important where respecting autonomy is concerned. The third applies exclusively to paternalism toward adolescents and draws on an obligation that the children have themselves in all of this.

1.

It's obvious that children often make bad decisions, sometimes very bad ones. This is true even of adolescents, who are the oldest group of those we treat as children and the ones it might best be argued should be treated as if they were adults. Actually, treating them that way seems as if it would be a terrible mistake. The typical adolescent is ignorant of many facts but often thinks otherwise, pays insufficient attention to long-term consequences, is unrealistic both about his or her abilities and about his or her vulnerability to harm, has poor emotional control, is too concerned about the opinions of peers, and is perfectly capable of going against good advice or conventional wisdom just in order to be independent. Which of these impairments to rationality happens to be in play varies with the occasion and also with the child, but that is hardly important. What matters is that the typical adolescent would make decisions that would be dangerous to his or her own well-being, or to the well-being of others, or both. That concern is what justifies denying adolescents these decisions, it might be argued.

This line of argument has been challenged on the ground that actually the decisions that typical adolescents would make are no worse than the ones adults would make for them.[3] The basis for one such challenge is a set of experiments employing Lawrence Kohlberg's theory of cognitive development. The experiments are said to reveal that "the attainment of an adult's capacity for moral reasoning [is] at the onset of adolescence, around the fourteenth year."[4] More specifically, the finding is that both adolescents and adults typically reason at

Kohlberg's second and third levels, making their decisions on the basis of "the conventions of individuals immediately around them" and "the conventions of society as a whole."[5]

Replies spring to mind. Even if the quoted remarks are true, there are many reasons to doubt that they mean adolescents will do just as well as adults at avoiding choices dangerous to themselves and/or to others. For one thing, even if both adolescent and adult reason partly by reference to the standards of their peer groups, it is reasonable to hope that the standards of an adult's peers will not be the same as those of an adolescent's. For another, even if it's true that both adolescents and adults refer either to the standards of peers or to the conventions of society as a whole, we might reasonably expect that the typical adult would have a deeper understanding of what those standards and conventions are and of how they apply in a particular case.

For a third, the decisions we reach do not depend solely on our way of reasoning about them, but also on the information about which we reason. So, even if an adult and an adolescent were to reason in the same way, if they applied this reasoning to different bodies of information they might well reach different conclusions. The Kohlberg tests would miss that point, since they do their best to ensure that each subject has the same information by giving each the same story to read and the same alternatives from which to choose. Finally, even if adolescents and adults were to reach the same conclusions in an experimental setting, there are other reasons to believe adolescents will do less well than adults with decisions in the real world: adolescents understand less well the situations in which they find themselves, the alternatives they have, and the consequences of those alternatives. These factors are not covered in the Kohlberg tests.

What is especially interesting in this debate, however, is not who is right about whether some adult would make a better decision than the adolescent would. Rather, what is interesting is the shared assumption that the answer would settle the matter: that whether someone should be permitted to engage in an activity depends simply on whether another person would make better decisions about it than he would. That would hardly be an appealing rule by which to decide what an adult should be free to do. Adults are free to carry out a wide range of activities even if there is indeed someone who would make a wiser decision about it than they would themselves It might be tempting to say that this is because adults are grown up and children are only children. But that statement only emphasizes that it isn't *simply* the child's inferiority to other available decision-makers that is carrying the weight in this argument. If it were, we would be equally ready to control the behavior of adults on the same basis: it wouldn't *also* matter that the person we could replace with a better decider is a *child*. Like children, many adults are inclined to ignore long-term consequences for more immediate gratifications, to place great importance on how they are perceived by others, and to act on imperfect information. But not only are adults left free to act in these ways, we have built whole industries of advertising and credit upon their doing so. In short, what we have here is not a justification for our greater paternalism toward children but another instance of it: namely, our readiness to accept a justification that we would reject if they were adults.

The point is that we don't allow children to choose in ways that we do allow adults to choose. That goes further than the following passage by Samantha Brennan:

> It seems to me that the main reason speaking against rights which protect children's choices is that often children do not choose well or wisely. There are two ways to think of this problem, one of which focuses on the end results of children's choices and another which looks at their process of choosing. The difficulty cannot just lie in the content of their choices since adults too frequently make bad choices. The problem must be with the children's capacity for choosing. Here choosing cannot just mean 'stating a choice,' since children can state choices. There is more to choosing than stating a choice. It is in the process by which the choices are made that children go wrong.[6]

I am claiming, in part, that there is also no "process by which choices are made" that only children use, and that when adults choose in these same ways, it will not be thought right to prevent them from doing so for their own good, as it would if they were children. It isn't the imperfection in the reasoning that is being taken to justify the paternalism, then, or at least it is not only that. It also matters that the imperfect chooser is "just a child." As was noted, what we have found is another way in which adults and children are treated differently, rather than something that explains why they should be.

It might be thought that the explanation is that the children who choose imperfectly are not yet "grown up" and will grow up if we are careful about what we let them do, whereas adults who behave in similar ways have already done so. Brennan is especially illuminating about what growing up could have to do with it:

> How is it that children make bad choices? Let me describe two sorts of ways that children's choosing goes wrong. First, children's choices frequently fail to reflect stable, long-term preferences. The child who loves skating today may hate it tomorrow; the child who will only wear purple today will tomorrow only wear pink; and so on. Second, the ways in which children change represent a gradual change to becoming the sort of being who is able to have stable, long-term preferences and can reflect critically and rationally upon them....Our worries with children are partly concerns about identifying the right unit for moral protection: the person the child is now or the person the child will become....We want to teach our children to be good choosers, and we do that, in part, by letting them try out the business of choosing.[7]

As Brennan urges, it is appealing to say that children's imperfect choices are to be treated differently than those of adults partly in order to help the children become good choosers. But clearly this approach too is another way in which we treat adults differently than we do children. We don't also take adults who are not good choosers in hand in this way, even though adults are also capable of improving the ways in which they make choices. So we will still need to hear why we should do this for children. Otherwise, we will have (once again) a richer description of the differential treatment that needs explaining rather than an explanation for it.

In this case, the reason that children are to be prevented from making certain choices is, at least partly, to protect them from bad consequences their choices might have: here, consequences working against the goal of their growing up to be good choosers. For an adult that reason would suffice only under special circumstances—some would say it suffices if the adult's choice is self-destructive, for example—whereas our paternalism toward children isn't restricted to choices that destroy their chances of becoming a good chooser but includes far milder departures from what we think best.

We could say it isn't just that children will make errors in balancing the interests of their future selves with those of their present ones, but that this is something they cannot do at all, a kind of thinking that is beyond them. It isn't beyond adults, the reasoning would be. So we can leave adults free to do it in their own way but cannot leave children free to do it in *their* own way because they don't *have* one. Doing that thinking for a child is like being the ears for someone who cannot hear rather than for someone we think is just not listening as he should.

However, this reasoning draws the lines between child and adult too sharply. It exaggerates the shortcomings of children, especially as the years pass. They do get better at such choosing, not only when their parents have given them careful instruction and judiciously lengthened their leash but even when their parents have neglected them and let them learn in what we call the hard way.

Robert Noggle develops a related line of thought about paternalism toward children, well worth quoting at length. Here is one of his key ideas.

> A person displays *temporally extended agency* when she has and pursues a set of goals that remain fairly stable over time, or when she provides for both her short- and long-term interests and needs. Temporally extended agents see the goals and projects of their future selves as their own goals and projects; they see their future happiness and pain as their own. They identify with their future selves.[8]

Second:

> The moral community—at least as it exists in contemporary Western liberal democratic societies…assumes a significant degree of temporal extension in the agency of its members. It seeks to provide a setting in which agents can devise and carry out projects over time, and in which they can engage in cooperative enterprises in order to achieve goals that are of mutual benefit…. In addition the moral community typically assumes that individuals are capable of managing their resources over time; economic systems and social institutions provide resources to persons but leave them relatively free to manage them so as to satisfy their present and future interests and pursue their long- and short-term projects. Moral, legal and political practices assume that the mere passage of time neither changes one person into a new person nor dissolves the rights, responsibilities and obligations of the earlier self. In practice as well as in theory, the moral community…assumes that members are temporally extended agents.[9]

This moral community isn't a club for adults only, of course. The family itself is part of that community, I would say, and children also go out into the larger world. So children participate in this community that "assumes temporal extension in its members." They do this even though "Children typically lack the degree of temporal extension that most adults have."[10] Typically, that is, "Their [not merely biological] concerns, goals, and preferences are in flux, and…they have not had enough experience with their own growth to realize how radical— and how inevitable—the coming changes will be."[11] In contrast, "Normally, adult core values and fundamental concerns are relatively stable, changing fairly little in the short run, and changing in a relatively orderly way in the long run."[12]

A solution is at hand: "[T]he parent can provide a kind of 'surrogate prudence' that can provide the temporal extension the child lacks. The parent is not only the agent of the present child, but of the whole temporally extended person: in much the same way as she is the advocate and protector of the child vis-à-vis society, she must also be the advocate and protector of the child's future self vis-à-vis the present child."[13] On Noggle's view, parental control is called for because someone has to be the temporally extended agent for the child that she herself isn't yet able to be, both for the sake of the person she will become and for the sake of the larger moral community.

This view is highly appealing if we think of very young children, who "do not have what we would call commitments, values, or projects at all"[14] and so lack temporally extended agency altogether. If they must participate in a community that requires anything at all along these lines, then someone is going to have to act on their behalf. In the same way, as the biological creatures they are, very young children must take in nourishment that they cannot acquire and consume themselves, so someone must see to this requirement for them. However, the argument is meant also to apply to controlling the behavior of adolescents and post-adolescents such as the seventeen-year-old Amy Hagen. Noggle says that by then "the parental function is less crucial and eventually unneeded. In the transitional period the exercise of parental authority is probably best if it shifts from a directive to a veto role."[15] It's surely right that an adolescent's parents ought not to be as directive as they once were, but why do they remain in authority at all? The answer has to be that even the older child will "typically lack the degree of temporal extension that most adults have," and that this position leaves her still unsuited for solo participation in a moral community that "assumes a significant degree of temporal extension in the agency of its members." We don't have an argument, though, for concluding that what older children have by way of temporal extension isn't enough and that only what is typical of adults will suffice. We also lack an account of why the parental control should be exercised even though we would not veto the choices of an adult we regarded as similarly "immature." Without those arguments, we've come again to justifying parental control on the ground that the person we are controlling is "still just a child" rather than an adult. Why that factor should matter remains unanswered.[16]

2.

To work toward an answer, let us imagine that one afternoon in the park we were to encounter a man and a woman with their daughter. Although the girl appears to be about 15, they are looking after her in exactly the same ways as one would look after a toddler. A good deal of the time they hold her by the hand, and when they do turn her loose they watch her very closely, sometimes calling her back and sometimes moving nearer to her. They hover, and they attend to her assiduously, lest she come to harm.

The natural thought would be that there must be something very wrong with this girl. Normally a fifteen-year-old is very unlike a three-year-old. Normally, children mature, and as they mature we adjust our paternalism toward them more or less automatically. Normally too, maturing children demand these adjustments, not always when their parents are ready to make them, but in any case insisting on greater independence than they once had. The parents in the example have made none of these adjustments, and that is a very good reason to assume that their daughter has not matured in anything like the usual way.

Suppose, though, that actually she is a perfectly normal fifteen-year-old girl, whose parents treat her as if she were three. That is very odd, for the reasons noted. It is also morally dubious. For one thing, it insults her. "You treat me like a *child*," the girl might reasonably complain, if complaints were allowed. If the parents calmly reply that she *is* a child, this would be true, but it would also miss her point: she isn't a very young child, and they are acting as if she were. Children change as the years pass, and to treat one of them in ways appropriate to a much younger child is to act as if this child had not changed. I think there is also another change as the years pass, namely, in the reasons that would justify paternalism toward him or her. In this case the parents are treating their daughter like a child in two ways: first, by believing she still has the qualities of a toddler, and second, by guiding their behavior toward her by a standard that is now out of date. They think of her in the wrong terms, or, better, they no longer think at all about how they ought to act toward her but just proceed as they have for many years.

It will be best to concentrate first on paternalism toward very young children. By "very young children" I mean the ones who would surely perish if they were left to their own devices: newborns, babes-in-arms, toddlers, and those of tender years. These terms are all vague, since there are no sharp boundaries between the times of life they denote. That complication can be put aside for a while, however. We are speaking here of the rough age-group about whom the manifestos of the child liberation movement of the 1970s were at their least compelling. According to those manifestos, children are an oppressed group who should be emancipated from parental control out of respect for their rights as human beings.[17] David Archard characterizes the central idea this way:

> Here there is a direct parallel with contemporaneous feminist writing. Feminists argue that the idea of women as necessarily fitted to occupy certain subordinate roles on account of their female nature is in fact a major element in patriarchal ideology. Weakness, emotion, dependence and illogicality are not the natural properties of women as a sex. Rather they are attributed to the socially constructed category of femininity which endorses the continued oppression of women. Similarly, Holt and Farson seem to claim that "childishness," connoting vulnerability, frailty and helplessness, is not a natural quality of children but rather an ideological construct which helps support the denial of their proper rights....

The adult's concern to assist the helpless child in its development is as patroniz-ingly offensive as the "respect" a man might declare he had for the "weaker sex."[18]

Probably we exaggerate exactly how vulnerable, frail, and helpless small children are, given the occasional story of the lost child who survives a night or two in the wilderness and the more common stories of children coping with abuse and neglect. Even so, however, the assertion that a small child needs no more help to survive than an adult does is simply absurd.

Here is a more technical complication. Although our topic is parental pater-nalism, it might be said that there is a period during which "paternalism" is the wrong term for efforts to protect a child from harm. Paternalism has to do with controlling someone's actions and omissions for that person's own good, or fend-ing off the consequences of those actions or omissions. It's plausible to say that there is a period during which newborn children aren't agents at all but only stimulus-response mechanisms. In these early days a child moves in response to many events both within his body and outside of it, but these are not actions the child performs, any more than the movements in an epileptic seizure are actions the epileptic performs. We would want to protect the child from coming to harm through these movements and failures to move, just as we would want to keep the epileptic's head from striking the pavement. But that protection would not be paternalism on our part, the claim is, because it would not be protection against harming oneself by one's actions or by one's failures to act.

Even if this view is correct, however, it does not matter a great deal. If parents have an obligation to be extensively paternalistic toward their very young chil-dren, they have the same obligation to be extensively protective toward their newborns. Here is an argument concerning both kinds of looking-after.

1. Due to certain facts of biology and the environment, all newborn human beings are helpless, and it is several years before they are able to survive on their own.
2. Accordingly, to bring a child into the world is to create someone who will be in great danger if he or she is not looked after extensively during the first several years of life.
3. We have an obligation not to expose others to great danger.
4. We therefore have an obligation to ensure that any children we bring into the world will be looked after very extensively during the first years of their lives: both "protectively" and paternalistically.

These statements are not quite the same as saying that if we bring a child into the world we must be extensively protective and paternalistic ourselves. They contend instead that we must ensure that *someone* is. There are two reasons to put the point that way. First, as Jeffrey Blustein has pointed out, there are soci-eties in which little if any of the looking-after is done by those who conceived the child: it is simply someone else's job.[19] In a society of that kind, the argument I have offered requires biological parents only to take care that the others are in a position to do their job: for example, to take care that the social resources will not be overtaxed when this particular child is born. Second, in societies in which the biological parents do often raise the child, they may still have the option of delegating some of the raising, and some of the protection and paternalism, to others. So even there, the obligation that biological parents have is properly put as one of ensuring that the child is looked after during this period of great vulnerability.[20]

Now, as the example of the parents in the park reminds us, children ought not to be treated equally paternalistically regardless of their age. If this first argument entailed otherwise, that would be a serious flaw. Fortunately, there are good reasons to think that it does not. The first is just that older children are much better at looking after themselves than very young ones are, so the same extensive paternalism simply isn't needed in order to protect them from coming to great harm. Thus it isn't required by the obligation not to expose others to danger, as it was when the child was very young.

Second: the deeper idea in play is that we ought not to be at fault when others are endangered. It is plausible to say that the parents of a young child *are* at fault if they do not ensure that their child is protected during this time of great vulnerability. They are the ones who brought the child into the world, the world just is an impossibly dangerous place for an infant who is not carefully attended, none of this is mysterious, and the parents were free not to create the child. That makes them responsible for the child's being in great danger if they do not make him safe or ensure that others do.

In contrast, they are not similarly at fault for all that befalls an older child. Of course, it is still true that they brought him into the world and that he would not be in danger if they had not done so, but those facts only make their actions a necessary condition of his troubles. This is not the same as the troubles being their fault, as anyone who is prone to blame himself will often have been told. On such occasions you think that if only you hadn't gone back to be sure you had locked the door we wouldn't have been late leaving and therefore we would have passed through the intersection a few minutes earlier, and so we wouldn't have been at that location when the other driver ran the light and hit our car...all true, but the conclusion is hardly that the damage is your fault. There were the other agents, after all, who acted independently and not in ways you ought to have predicted. The same is true for the parents whose child comes to harm as a teenager. He would never have suffered if they hadn't brought him into the world, but other agents have made their contributions as well, including the boy himself, and these were not actions the parents should have predicted. So his troubles are not the parents' fault in the way those of a young child would have been if the parents had left him unprotected during those early years of human vulnerability. That means the older child's troubles do not in the same way fall under their obligation not to put others in danger.

So far, so good, perhaps, but there is a long way yet to go. Where very young children are concerned, only some of the paternalism we ordinarily expect of a parent has anything to do with *danger*, if we use that term as we should. Sometimes the path the parent sees the child following doesn't lead in front of a truck, but only in front of a tricycle; sometimes what the parent might insist the child learn isn't vital for survival but is only a way in which her life might be richer or happier. And yet it seems that parents ought sometimes to be paternalistic on these kinds of occasions as well. As was noted at the outset, our children seem to be our business in relatively minor matters as well as in major ones. Clearly that can't all rest on the obligation not to put them in *great danger*. So, there is more to be considered where paternalism toward young children is concerned. Moreover, thus far the only point about paternalism toward older children has been a negative one: there is much more to consider with regard to them as well.

3.

Chapter 4, "Abuse, Neglect, and the State," sought to say which of the many possible forms of parental failure should be taken especially seriously. It took the key to be what the behavior showed about the parent: in particular, whether it revealed a continuing, serious defect in concern for the child. The most dreadful of these defects was an abiding inclination to do the child harm. Another was utter indifference to how the child fared, and another was taking little interest in the child's behavior or welfare. Still another was inability to put a proper level of concern into action. It is obvious that these would be serious defects in a parent. It will be useful to say why they are.

First, to be the kind of person described would make one very unlikely to perform acceptably at what parenthood requires. After all, a lot of what parenthood requires has no intrinsic appeal, and some of it is even aversive. So, on the face of it, when parenthood calls, this aspect of it is mostly going to be an intrusion, a distraction from what one *wants* to be doing, unless one has some added reason to do what it says. The added reason might be a sense of moral obligation. Or, it might be a belief that playing the parental role would bring something else one wanted. Those motivations have their shortcomings, however, and can foment their own resentment. It is much better if the child himself is motivating: if the parent has genuine affection and concern for the child, that is, so that what would have been only toilsome or unpleasant or a bother becomes at least tolerable, and sometimes even appealing. Anyone who was seriously defective in concern for the child would lack these important motivations and thus would be poorly equipped for parenthood, the argument would be.

The other answer is that abiding affection for one's child is *itself* a requirement of parenthood. On this view, someone who carried out only the actions we think of as obligatory for a parent would just be "going through the motions." It's also true that he wouldn't go through them perfectly, for the reasons mentioned, but that would only be part of the trouble. He could function adequately as the child's keeper, since all that can be expected of a keeper is that he does the right things, but it is also expected of a *parent* that he care deeply for his child. Someone who does not has already failed the child.

Whichever of these accounts one prefers, they share a contention that genuine affection for your child is necessary if you are to do well as his or her parent. The affection has to hold up when its object is unlovely, and it can't be easily discouraged by rejection: otherwise, it won't last as long as this person is a child, and it is needed the whole while. Nor can parental affection reduce to concern for the child's immediate gratification, of course, since the child continues beyond that moment. As Brennan urged, concern for him is concern for the future version of him as well as for the present one; it is intelligent in that way.

Clearly, no one could have this affection and treat his child in the terrible ways described in "Abuse, Neglect, and the State." Nor could anyone have it without being strongly inclined to protect his child from coming to harm at the hands of others, or from natural causes. But now let us suppose that the child were at risk of harming *herself*, if nothing were done to stop her from acting in the way she has in mind. Surely the same strong inclination to intervene would be part of being a good parent to her, or, if the other formulation is preferred, it would be part of the equipment needed in order to be a good parent. This means that paternalism toward one's child comes with a very good pedigree, especially when compared with paternalism toward random adults.

The point can be put this way. Parents do not need their children's permission to care about them, in the broad, deep, durable, intelligent way described, or to enact that concern in some way. They *must* care about them in that way and they must put that caring into action if they are to be good parents, either because this caring is one of a parent's duties itself or because otherwise they cannot do well at the broad variety of actions parenthood requires, and they do not need their child's permission to be good parents to him. In contrast, we do not need that same kind of concern for random fellow adults if we are to act as we should toward *them*. For one thing, they do not depend on us in the same ways. For another, how we feel about them does not matter to them in the same way. For a third, most of our relationships with them are more temporary. Finally, it is an important aspect of their liberty that they have some control over who enacts a deep and lasting interest in them, and they are thus free to reject at least the expressions of such interest if they do not welcome them. These are all ways in which the lives of other adults have an independence from ours that the lives of our children do not have. This independence is the reason we need not care deeply about most other adults in order to treat them as we should, and it is also the reason we should not put such concern for them into action if this is not welcome. By the same token, the reason we must have and must enact this concern for our children is that their lives are not independent of our own in these ways but are intertwined with ours.

Here is what this has to do with paternalism. One of the original questions about it concerned the sense we have that expressing an uninvited paternalistic interest in a fellow adult is intrusive, while taking that same interest in one's children can be positively obligatory. That distinction seemed true both with regard to major matters such as whether to have an abortion and with regard to the many minor ways in which one might live one way rather than another. There is a basis for this, along the following lines. Our paternalistic interest in our children is an aspect of the broader affection we must have for them if we are to be good parents, whereas paternalistic interest in other adults who have not welcomed that interest is not part of an attitude we must have in order to be good persons where *they* are concerned. Indeed, such interest threatens to intrude on their liberty to define their personal relationships. So, the interest in correcting their behavior for their own good is dubious, whereas it is exactly the interest we *should* take with regard to our children.

Paternalism toward one's children and paternalism toward adults also seemed to differ in how far it was proper to go. Admittedly, some adults do occasionally have Ulysses-contracts with other adults: "Whatever I say at the time, don't let me have 'just one drink' (or: don't let me back down on what I said I'd do; don't let me tell all those stories again; don't let me lose my temper...)." In addition, adults can also be drunk or otherwise incompetent and about to do something truly self-destructive. Such cases aside, however, there seems to be a point at which we should back off and allow this person who we think is mistaken to live her life as she has decided. "It's your life," it seems natural to say on such occasions, perhaps adding one last time that she is making an awful mistake with it. We don't seem to regard the lives of our children as ultimately theirs to live as they choose, in this same way.

Consider here the example of Jessica Dubroff, a seven-year-old girl who died in an attempt to become the youngest person ever to fly an airplane solo across the continental United States. After she got a considerable distance, the plane she was flying crashed and burned during a terrible storm. Her mother said this:

> I'd have her do it again in a second. You have no idea what this meant to Jess....
> I did everything so this child could have freedom and choice, have what America stands for. Liberty comes from being in that space of just living your life.[21]

The contrary intuition is that *whatever* it meant to the girl to try to fly solo across the United States, this was no way to think about a seven-year-old: that her parents ought to have stopped a child this young from doing something so dangerous. Perhaps that view won't turn out to be correct, but if it is correct then it illustrates the other apparent contrast: parents should sometimes go so far as actually to prevent their children from behaving in dangerous ways, whereas with competent adults they should only clarify the risks and argue their case.

Here is an added wrinkle. Imagine that Jessica Dubroff had not been seven years old when she was so determined to fly across the United States, but sixteen. One could still say she should be prevented from doing this because she is "just a child," of course, but at the very least this response is not as automatic as it was for the seven-year-old. Perhaps how decisively children should be restrained for their own good is yet another respect in which it matters how old the child is. (Recall the parents in the park, for example.) It could be that at least some of what would be out of the question for a young child is only something to *reason* about with an older one.

Why should that be true, though? Certainly an older child can *handle* some activities that are beyond a younger one. Perhaps the thought is that a sixteen-year-old might actually be able to complete the flight whereas a seven-year-old has little chance of doing so. The reasoning would thus be that we should let the sixteen-year-old try it, once we make sure she understands the dangers, but we should stop the seven-year-old in her tracks, because the activity remains beyond her abilities even if she does understand its risks. However, this reasoning once again takes the key to be whether things really would go better for this person if we were to control what she did rather than leaving it ultimately to her. (Yes, they would, if she is a seven-year-old who wants to fly around the world, so prohibit this absolutely; maybe they would not, if she is a sixteen-year-old who does, so permit it, in the end.) That isn't our principle with regard to treating adults paternalistically, so invoking it here only raises once again the question of *why* paternalism toward our children should be different rather than answering that question.

As an alternative, we might fasten upon differences in what children can understand at different ages. Surely there is a lot that a sixteen-year-old can grasp that would have been beyond her when she was seven. Perhaps the solo flight is one of those things. Perhaps the conception a seven-year-old would have of such a flight is bound to be rather romantic and unrealistic, that is, while a sixteen-year-old might be able to "know what she's doing," if we are careful to instruct her. Therefore the seven-year-old should be stopped, because otherwise we are allowing her to act dangerously out of ignorance that she cannot avoid having; whereas, that isn't necessarily the case with the sixteen-year-old, which is why it isn't as obvious that she should be stopped.

Unlike the earlier reasoning, this does rely on principles that we also employ with regard to adults. It matters whether an adult is endangering himself knowingly or out of ignorance, just as the argument says it should matter where children are concerned. Notice, though, that the argument concerns ignorance that is supposed to be *inescapable* for the child, presumably because of some truths of human development. One problem is that those truths may not be sufficiently universal to be pictured in that way. To continue the example, it could well be that there are seven-year-olds who *can* understand what is involved in flying across the United States solo, at least to the extent that we would think an adult must understand this in order for us to believe we have to let him go ahead. A seven-year-old who can actually fly a plane isn't so good a bet to be thinking about this activity only romantically and unrealistically.

A second problem is in the assumption that we should prevent people who are acting out of ignorance from endangering themselves, if this is ignorance they cannot correct. Suppose an adult could not get beyond a fairly basic grasp of the risks involved in some activity, understood this limitation perfectly well, and wanted to go ahead anyway. If he did, he would then be acting out of ignorance he could not correct, but it is not obvious that we mustn't let him. Rather, there is something to be said for letting adults decide for themselves whether to act on inadequate information, as far as the risks to them are concerned. The argument denies that privilege to children, since its conclusion is that we must always prevent children from acting out of ignorance they cannot correct—even if the child *does* understand that she has this limitation, that is. Once again, then, the conclusion that children should be treated differently is reached by assuming that they should be, here with regard to ignorance they cannot escape. The next section offers a different way of thinking about the issues raised by these two versions of the Jessica Dubroff case.

4.

What is meant by autonomy in these contexts is making one's own way through the world, putting one's own personality and character into action. To some extent, to be allowed to play your part in what happens is to be allowed to be a person. Whoever we are and however old we are, our claim to be a person of our own should have the same weight, it seems, and so should our claim to act as we choose.[22]

What I will argue is that the actions of children are not always *cases* of "being a person of one's own," "putting one's own personality and character into action," and "making one's own way through the world." The reason is not that children have no personalities or character, of course. They do. However, what they have along these lines is sometimes not their own, in an important sense. Accordingly, when they put those traits into action, it isn't their own way they are making through the world, despite the fact that it is they who act.

I think that underlies the worry about the seven-year-old Jessica Dubroff, who tried to fly across the United States: the idea that she was too much her parents' creature and not enough her own. It seems as if what she did called for certain traits of character and personality. Among other things, it seems to have required a strong sense of adventure, considerable courage and determination, the ability to sustain concentration, and great persistence in the face of obstacles. Not all seven-year-olds have those qualities. For the sake of argument, let us suppose that Jessica Dubroff did have them. My contention is that we should doubt that this set of qualities was a self *of her own*, in a way that is important where respecting autonomy is concerned.

Roughly speaking, to have a trait is just to have a relatively stable tendency to behave in certain ways, including, where traits of character are concerned, a relatively stable tendency to act for certain reasons. Those who like science fiction might now imagine an evil scientist capturing someone and *providing* a tendency of this kind. By means of brain surgery, or pharmaceuticals, or hypnotism, the scientist makes the captured person quite shy, for example, or makes him rather dishonest. However the work is done, the scientist's subject emerges with the trait implanted in his character or personality. My idea is that although this is a trait the subject *has*, it is *not* his trait in a way that calls for us to respect its workings in his behavior, as part of respecting his autonomy. Not at the start, at any rate—not immediately after he wakes up with his newly implanted behavioral tendency and begins to act accordingly.

Even if the science-fiction example gets things off the ground, though, a claim that this was the true story of Jessica Dubroff would belong in one of the supermarket tabloids. We still need to hear how it is supposed to work in real life. It will help if we stay with the science fiction example briefly. Consider, in particular, the intuition that the implanted trait is not the experimental subject's own, in some important sense. This intuition is at its strongest very early in the story, when the man first awakens or first begins to act as his new personality inclines him, and he hasn't yet taken much notice of this new trait. That is when it is most plausible to think he is too much the scientist's creature in this aspect of his personality, and that respect for this man's autonomy ought not to restrain us from intervening in the actions that put these traits into play. Suppose now that some time were to pass during which the man came to realize that he was quite shy, or that he was rather dishonest—that is, the traits the scientist had implanted came to his notice. Suppose further that the man also believed, rightly, that he could change these traits if he wished to. Finally, suppose that he did not make any such changes but continued to live exactly as he had been before recognizing these features of his makeup.

From that point on, I think it would be much less appealing to say there was an important sense in which it wasn't *he* who was in action when his shyness or his dishonesty was in play, but the scientist who had made him that way. If this thought is correct, it suggests one way in which a person might make a trait he found in himself become a trait of his own, in the sense important for autonomy. He could do so by recognizing that he had it and accepting it as part of the person he was.

There would also be other ways, of course. For one thing, it doesn't seem that he must be entirely *right* about the trait he has. Imagine a man who is aware of a quality he regards as great charm, though he is quite mistaken to think that is what it is. So long as he lives as the charming fellow he takes himself to be, that is enough to make this a respect in which he is his own man, it would seem. Once one has some conception or other of a feature, that is, accepting it makes it a trait of one's own in the important sense even if one misunderstands this feature.

It is also possible to undertake a project of becoming a certain kind of person. This endeavor might begin in dissatisfaction with the sort of person one takes oneself to be. The man in our initial example might grow tired of the costs of being shy, resolve to be more assertive, take steps to become so, and succeed. Or, he might be ashamed to realize that he is really rather dishonest, undertake to reform, and become a better person in this regard. According to Aristotle, we develop traits of character by imitating the behavior of those who already have them, coming eventually to have the motivations that define the traits.[23] The man in our example could do that when he came to have a sense of what he was like. His traits would then be his own, this time not by virtue of his accepting them but by his own making.

Clearly, some of our imitation of others isn't part of a project of moral development, but happens more or less unconsciously. This process might still make one like the person one imitated. That would be an unintended self-construction, resulting in features that were also the person's by her own making. Finally, we often modify our personalities in other ways without thinking about it, not by adopting the traits of others but by making unconscious adjustments. Later reminders of what we once were like might bring a cringe or a smile, but they generally wouldn't include a picture of how we strove to be different. There simply wasn't one, even though the changes did happen.

Let us now turn to the ways in which children come to have their first traits of character and personality. Clearly they do not have these implanted by evil scientists, but it is also clear that when they are young they generally do not engage in conscious projects of self-construction. Young children do not set out to become especially honest, or kind-hearted, or bubbly, and then carry this off, in the way a person dissatisfied with herself might. Their early character and personality are simply not their own doing in this self-conscious way.

Instead, if a child has attentive parents, her early traits of character and personality are to a considerable extent *their* doing, insofar as the origin is not genetic. Unlike the child herself, parents often do take what kind of person she is as their conscious project—and they are well-placed to have some success, at least while she is relatively young, since she will care whether they think she is a good girl or a bad one, and they will control other important means of reinforcement as well. Their success will certainly not be perfect, but it would be surprising if they were unable to have a great deal of influence on her early personality and character.

As has been noted, people sometimes construct selves of their own by imitating the behavior of others. Here there are two points of importance where young children with attentive parents are concerned. The first is that the parents themselves are one of the primary models the child has available to imitate; the other is that they have considerable control over the competition. Parents have a lot to say about which other models are available, they have the opportunity to try to correct what they see as bad effects those other models are having, and they have the further opportunity to reinforce what they see as good effects. In short, although children certainly do imitate others, for young children with attentive parents they do so under the parents' substantial domination. That domination is significant, since our question is whether to think of the child as her parents' little girl in some respect or as her own person.

She could affect the answer, I've claimed, by gaining some sense of what she is like—not necessarily an accurate sense—and accepting it. Doing so requires that she have a degree of interest in what she is like, however. That topic does interest many adolescents, though they are usually pictured as anxious about what they think they are like rather than accepting of it. In any event, it would be very surprising to find a very young child who was greatly absorbed in what kind of person she was, as opposed to living more from moment to moment.

This idea invites a different thought about being a person of one's own, however. Consider this point of Aristotle's, about those who are unaware of their vices:

"Well, probably he is the sort of person that doesn't take care." But people get into this condition through their own fault, by the slackness of their lives; i.e., they make themselves unjust or licentious by behaving dishonestly or spending their time in drinking and other forms of dissipation; for in every sphere of conduct people develop qualities corresponding to the activities that they pursue. This is evident from the example of people training for any competition or undertaking: they spend all their time in exercising. So to be unaware that in every department of conduct moral states are the result of corresponding activities is the mark of a thoroughly unperceptive person.[24]

This sounds like another way in which traits might become our own without our recognizing them as qualities that we somehow have come to possess. Indeed, it wouldn't be necessary to have even a mistaken sense of them, like the man who thinks that what he has is great charm. In addition, it seems, people can also make carelessness a trait of their own simply "by the slackness of their lives": just by living that way, that is. It might well be part of the slackness with which they live that they are unconcerned not only about what they are doing but also about what sort of person they are becoming in the course of acting in this way.

Aristotle is speaking here of vices, but it also seems possible to develop virtues through a pattern of good behavior, without any awareness that this change was taking place. Think here of someone who focuses intently on what needs to be done and is utterly uninterested in herself. She too might have made herself the highly admirable person she is by the way in which she lives, with little sense of what she is like. Her admirers might get her to recognize her fine qualities—perhaps with some difficulty—but the woman made these qualities her own well before they were brought to her attention. She did so in the same way as the careless person made himself careless: just by regularly behaving in the ways that are conducive to acquiring and sustaining those qualities.

The interesting question is whether this way of making traits our own is open to young children. If it is, then it does not matter that young children take little interest in their moral character. After all, neither do Aristotle's careless man and our admirable woman, and it seems right to say that the traits they acquire are still fully their own. Like the man and the woman, these children would have acquired the traits simply by living in the way that developed them. They would be unaware of what they had become, just as the careless man and the admirable woman would be, but that is something else. It does not preclude these being selves that we should attribute to them as fully as we would attribute the carelessness to the man and the admirable qualities to the woman. If so, I was wrong to say that we should doubt that a child's early traits of character and personality are his or her own, in the sense important for autonomy.

There was impatience in Aristotle's remarks about those who develop vices by living inattentively, though. The point he was making was that the fact that these people hadn't realized they were developing vices is no excuse for their doing so. The reason it is no excuse is that they should have known better: "to be unaware that in every department of conduct moral states are the result of corresponding activities is the mark of a thoroughly unperceptive person."[25] So the reason that adults are responsible for the character they develop by living in a certain way is that they should have known it would happen, if we follow Aristotle.

That point matters, because it would be wrong to say the same of a child. For one thing, the claim that a person who lives in a certain way will acquire certain traits of character or personality is a causal one. Young children are not generally expected to be aware of causal relationships that are obvious to adults. We expect to have to teach them such things, since they don't have much experience yet with how the world works. The same would be true here, surely, where the connection is between acting in certain ways and becoming a person of a certain kind.

Grasping this particular connection also requires seeing several instances of behavior as cases of the same kind, despite the ways in which they might also differ. That reasoning too is a kind we expect to help a child develop, whereas we are impatient with adults who don't make the connections any more readily than a child. I take these points to show that although adults can make traits their own simply by living in the way that develops the trait, this is not true of children. That won't be enough to make the trait the child's doing. Rather, a trait acquired in this way would be like an illness the child caught by acting in a way that only adults ought to know would put one at high risk. The illness and the trait of character should both be considered something that happens to the child through other agencies, rather than something for which the child is responsible. The child is not to blame for becoming ill, even if an adult would be, and the child is not the author of the trait either, even if an adult would be the author of his carelessness or of her admirable qualities. I have suggested that the child could *make* a trait his own by getting some sense of it and going on as that person. The point is that some next step of this kind is needed.

What all of this suggests is that when a young child with attentive parents puts certain traits into play, it is highly likely that these are not simply the child's own, in any of the ways the traits of an adult are. If the child has had good parents, what he is like will have been substantially influenced by them. We could give him the benefit of the doubt out of concern that we not override what *might* be an exercise of his autonomy, or in order to give him early opportunities to become his own person. That is what we should do when nothing much will be lost if he acts as he wishes. However, it is obvious that parents should also protect their children from coming to harm. The parents of the seven-year-old Jessica Dubroff had very good reasons of that kind to prevent her solo flight, since the flight was an exceptionally dangerous undertaking. Because of her age, they also had little reason to regard undertaking the flight as enacting a self of her own, I have argued, as opposed to one they had created. I would say that the concern to respect her autonomy ought not to have won the day on such an occasion, and also that it was no time to give her space for self-construction. They ought to have prevented her from making the effort, rather than permitting it in order not to disrespect her autonomy, as her mother thought she would be doing if she said "no."

That argument did employ a good deal of vague language, including "*young* child" and "*early* personality and character." It would be a great help if we could be more precise. We should also want to hear more about children who are no longer in this category. What is the age at which a child's traits are her own, so that there is a serious autonomy-objection against controlling her behavior for her own good, and what more can be said about paternalism toward her?

There is no such age, unfortunately, and the vagueness is unavoidable. This fact suggests that there could even be some adults who live apart from their parents but who have not become persons of their own in any respect. Those adults would have no greater claim to have their autonomy respected than a child would, according to this argument. That is an important point, because if there are such adults and they are *not* to be subjected to the same paternalism as children are, then my view is vulnerable to the same objection I raised against several other views. For example, take the view that what justifies our more extensive paternalism toward children is that we need to help them become good choosers.

I objected that many adults are not good choosers either, and we don't regard that fact as justifying our taking them in hand in quite the same way. So, I claimed, we still need to hear why we should do this for *children* who have not yet become good choosers. Otherwise, we will have a richer description of the differential treatment that needs explaining rather than an explanation for it.

The parallel objection to my own view would run as follows. I've claimed that what justifies paternalism toward children is concern that they might not be enacting selves of their own, in which case there would be nothing to be respected as the autonomous behavior of this person. But we ought to have the same concern that an adult is not enacting a self of her own. Therefore this is just another instance of thinking differently about children than about adults, not an explanation of why we *should* think differently about them.

In reply, I want to grant that where there is legitimate concern that a person is not enacting a self of her own, it does not matter how old that person is, but I deny that this fact leaves it unclear why we should be more paternalistic toward children. The reason is that an adult who wasn't yet a person of her own would be an anomaly of a kind that did call for special treatment, unlike an adult who was not yet a "good chooser," for example. It is apparently fairly easy to reach adulthood without becoming a good chooser; reaching adulthood without becoming someone of your own is a different matter. Consider what it would require.

One route would be for this person to be denied the independence through which we ordinarily develop selves of our own during childhood. Even young children escape parental domination to some degree, but much more so as time goes by. All except the oddest of parents gradually leave their children more and more alone to live their own lives, and allow them to take on more and more of what the culture expects of an adult. Recall once again how truly bizarre it seemed for the parents in the park to look after their normal fifteen-year-old daughter just as assiduously as they had when she was three. We simply don't do this. We also shouldn't do it, in part because one of our most important obligations is to prepare our children to live as adults and *without* our close supervision, but more of that later. The point here is that for an adult to lack a self of her own seems to require her childhood to have been controlled and restricted in ways that are difficult even to imagine.

In addition, anyone who lives with others comes to see ways in which she is like them and ways in which she is not. Those others also make observations about what we are like. These are all occasions either to want to change what we see in ourselves or to accept it, which are ways of making it part of a self of one's own. So for an adult not to have a self of that kind requires either that she be incapable of seeing such things or that she be raised in total isolation from others, including those who were raising her. The latter is a character from science fiction. The former, the person who was unable to see what she was like, is someone I am comfortable regarding as needing special care. Neither raises concern that we ought to be more paternalistic toward adults in general than seems appropriate, if we take what matters to be doubts that someone is enacting a self of her own. Those doubts would be unfounded with regard to adults in general, because adults in general have had the opportunities provided by childhood (and by the period during which they have already been adults) to become someone of their own and have been capable of doing so. By the same token, the doubts are increasingly better founded the younger the child is.

As a consequence, the point at which a child's traits are importantly her own is much more complicated than if there were some single age of complete emancipation in all respects. The answers with regard to a sixteen-year-old Jessica Dubroff and a fifteen-year-old Amy Hagen would depend on the independence they had had, and on what they had done with it. Presumably they would have gained some sense of themselves, and perhaps they would have engaged in some self-construction. It isn't possible to know in the abstract what they would have done along those lines, or whether flying across the United States (in the one case) and leaving home (in the other) drew on traits that were their own in these ways, because nothing so specific follows just from a person's age.

What can be said in general is that the younger a child is, the better reason we have to think he has not yet made his traits his own. So, the younger the child is, the better the case that paternalism would not restrict his autonomy. This means that the younger the child, the better the case for acting paternalistically when there is great risk at stake. The older the child, the more concerned we should be that paternalism does restrict her autonomy, since the better the reasons are to think she has made her traits her own. This is a respect in which paternalism toward children is more suspect as they grow older, then, and extremely so after they move away from the parental home to have "lives of their own," as we say. Their lives will typically have been increasingly their own before then, with corresponding changes in the acceptability of paternalism toward them.

If these arguments are sound, they justify the earlier intuition that the scope of parental paternalism should narrow as a child becomes older. For example, it is considered legitimate to control very closely what a younger child eats and drinks, not just so that nothing fatal or truly damaging is ingested but (perhaps) so that he doesn't consume "junk food" or eats only whole grains. To be that solicitous over what another adult ate would be oppressive, and an adolescent might well chafe at it. The question was whether there was any good reason for these differences in when we are prepared to swing into paternalistic action. There is. One part of the answer is that an adult should be presumed to have lived sufficiently independently to have become a person of his own in many respects, including the ones in play in deciding how assiduously to follow a healthy diet, for example. Whether this is also true of an adolescent would be up for argument. It is certainly *not* true of a young child, who will have lived so far with little or no independence. So, to be paternalistic about the diet of the young child would not constrain his autonomy, as it might constrain that of his older sister, and would certainly constrain that of an adult who was treated this way.

A different question of interest was how decisively we should act, when acting paternalistically is appropriate. The thought was that we ought actually to prevent our children from "ruining their lives" in various ways, if we can, by making it impossible for them to do the ruinous thing. That seemed to be the right response to a six-year-old who wanted to run away and become a child actor. Where older children were concerned it seemed less certain, though many would be very confident that no responsible parent would permit a fourteen-year-old to head for New York on her own to become a ballet dancer, for example. Adults, on the other hand, ought not to be *prevented* from doing this sort of thing, the thought was, even if it seems to others to be just as erroneous and destructive. The arguments in this section support those conclusions as well. For, as was noted, we have excellent reason to believe that a self of one's own is in play when the person is an adult, excellent reason to believe it is *not* in play in the young child, and should be uncertain about this matter if the child is an adolescent.

Of course, adolescence is not only a time when children near adulthood, but also a time when some of them are most likely to want to act in certain alarming ways. A seven-year-old who is bent upon flying an airplane across the United States is an extreme rarity, but a seventeen-year-old who wants to leave home with an older man is not. I've said only that it is more likely that the adolescent has a self of her own in play when she wants to do something of this kind. That observation issues a proper caution, where respecting her autonomy is concerned, but it does no more than that. In particular, it is very far from saying what an adolescent's parents ought to do if their adolescent child wants to make what they regard as a terrible mistake of this kind. The closing section takes us further regarding that.

5.

> …there is no doubt that the normal adolescent is capable of recognizing selfhood: a teenager has long since developed the ability to say "'I" with meaning. However, it is not nearly so clear that or when the normal adolescent develops a moral self, so that he or she can say with meaning, "I value this or that," so that a particular decision is *authentic*, an expression of who I am in a moral sense, of what kind of person I am, of what is really important to me.[26]

These words, from Jeffrey Blustein and Jonathan D. Moreno, don't say much more than that about what they mean by a "moral self," but it clearly includes having a sense of what one's values are. Moreover, the implication is that these are values one accepts. If so, what Blustein and Moreno mean by a moral self is one version of what I mean by a self of one's own: the version in which the person has recognized that he is a certain way and has accepted this feature of his makeup. So the points these authors make about what they call the moral self will serve equally well in my own account of respecting autonomy.

Blustein and Moreno are writing about what they call "the adolescent alone," where "alone" means having no parent or other adult with whom the adolescent has "a supportive and trusting relationship."[27] These are children who live on the streets, or have lived in a series of foster homes rather than with an intact family, or have looked after a dying parent and become surrogate parents to younger siblings while still children themselves. Inevitably, adolescents who are alone in these ways come to need medical treatment. Should they be regarded as children, where their right to consent to treatment or to refuse it is concerned? Should they be regarded as adults, with the same right to make an autonomous decision in these matters?

For Blustein and Moreno, the key is how the child's troubled life has affected his development of a "moral self"—or, in my terms, a self "of his own." If no such self were in play, the choice wouldn't be *his* in the sense that demands respect as an expression of his autonomy, any more than it is when the seven-year-old wants to fly a plane across the United States. Here is a point of interest along these lines.

"A child who feels unwanted—whose sense of personal worth is not nurtured and supported by caring adults—is plagued by failure and self-doubt, apathy, and cynicism in later childhood and adult life."[28] Blustein and Moreno connect this feeling with an inability to appreciate the consequences of your actions even if you do grasp those intellectually. What that shortcoming would have to do with lacking a "moral self" is unclear, but the quoted passage also suggests ways in which being unwanted would indeed affect the child's having one.

Suppose first that a child's sense of personal worth *had* been nurtured. This nurturing would happen over time. There would be occasions when the child had just done something that merited praise and had received it. There would be other occasions when things had gone badly for the child and she was in need of reassurance. What a nurturing parent did in both instances would go beyond asserting the rather solemn and abstract proposition that the child is a person of value. It would include conveying some of what is valuable *about* her, and encouraging her to value that too. When she does value it, it changes from something her parents value in her to something she values in herself. So the traits or skills they have praised become part of a self of her own—not by her having acquired them through a conscious project, but through her recognizing them in herself and accepting them as part of the person she is. At some point, her parents' encouragement to do this would also interest her in discovering what else would bring her this same support, and in developing other qualities that would do so. Thus, it would encourage her to become a person of her own in other ways as well.

Now imagine a child who had very little of this nurturing response, one who was never praised and never consoled, or only very occasionally so. It wouldn't be impossible for this child to have a positive opinion of himself even so, and to recognize his good qualities, but he would certainly be at a disadvantage in accomplishing this. That means his later choices might not put a self of his own into play, as they would have if his earlier life had been a more supportive one. So respect for his autonomy wouldn't require honoring those choices, any more than respecting the autonomy of the seven-year-old Jessica Dubroff requires honoring her choice to fly solo across the United States. The best case for thinking that a child's choices might be impaired in this way would be one in which there were both behavioral symptoms of low self-esteem (including "failure and self-doubt, apathy, and cynicism") and a history that made these feelings no surprise.

That way of thinking is another tool for the parent to use in respecting autonomy without misunderstanding what respecting it requires. However, Blustein and Moreno observe that autonomy calls not only for respect but also for efforts to further its development, if such can reasonably be done. So their message is decidedly not that medical facilities needn't go to the same lengths to secure the consent of an "adolescent alone" because it is less likely he *has* a self of the kind about which we should be concerned.[29] Rather, their view is that such facilities must develop processes that encourage these adolescents to "raise their level of capacity, and thus their self-determination."[30] How a medical facility might do this is a fascinating question. The point of interest here is that *parents* should certainly do it. That is, the obligations of parenthood would include both paying proper respect to the extent to which your child is already a person of her own *and* helping her to become one. After all, a central aspect of parenthood is raising one's child to be an adult: what *kind* of adult is a question to be pursued over the next two chapters, but certainly it ought to be one who can act with the autonomy that deserves respect rather than only as the creature of another.

One crucial form of help in becoming a person of this kind has already been noted: it is important to encourage the child's sense of herself as someone of value. Doing so would involve allowing the child to have projects of her own, from which she would learn a good deal about herself. She would accept some of it as part of who she was, especially if encouraged to regard it as good. It's also important that she would sometimes fail in what she undertook. To a certain extent, self-esteem is a matter of knowing that failures don't mean you are worthless.

Still, saying that parents have an obligation both to respect their child's autonomy and to foster it by helping him become a person of his own doesn't exactly settle what they ought to do in the cases of particular interest to us. These are cases in which their adolescent child wants to make what the parents think is a terrible mistake: a fourteen-year-old wants to go to New York to make it as a dancer, or a seventeen-year-old Amy Lynn Hagen wants to leave home with a nineteen-year-old man, or a sixteen-year-old wants to leave school and join the military, or a fifteen-year-old wants to spend his every waking moment writing music and practicing with his rock band. What if the most honest appraisal is that these desires *would* express some aspect of a self of the child's own—but an aspect that the parent thinks is highly unfortunate, at least in this instance? If the child were an adult, respect for autonomy would require allowing her to do what she wanted despite the risks that friends and loved ones saw in it. Does respect for the adolescent's autonomy require the parent to permit it as well?

The answer requires a shift of focus. We have been thinking about the rights of the child and about the obligations of a parent. Nothing has been said about obligations the *child* might have. Those would matter, since if someone has an obligation to do something, we do not violate his autonomy if we require him to do it. He has no proper complaint that we are not allowing him to be himself and make his own way in the world. The same would be true here. The question becomes whether the adolescents we are imagining have obligations that they would fail to keep if they were to make the choices they want to make. I am going to argue that this is true in some cases and false in others.

One premise in the argument is that parents have an obligation to *raise* their children. A careful exploration of what doing so requires will have to wait until the next chapter, but a little can be said at the outset. First, it is an obligation parents owe both to the child and to the larger society in which the child lives and will continue to live as an adult. That means the child is not free to release the parent from it, so long as the claims of the larger society remain in place. Second, raising a child is unlike raising a crop. Corn and beans, for example, are passive, and what they have to do with being raised is entirely a function of biology. In contrast, a child has to *cooperate* with the efforts to raise him to be a functioning adult, to some extent, or those efforts will fail. A *completely* uncooperative child would be unlikely even to survive, since raising him and protecting him from harm aren't entirely independent. Part of raising him would be teaching him what was dangerous, and if he refused to learn any of that from his parents it's hard to see how he would last long. If he did manage to survive, it is barely possible that he might still become an adult who could function in society with others, but that result wouldn't represent a success on his parents' part. It would have happened in spite of his defeating their effort to carry out their obligation to raise him. Here we might also add a point from Jeffrey Blustein's version of this same argument: "Without obedience to parental authority, an obedience based on trust rather than fear, children will not develop the inner discipline essential to complete self-control, and without self-control children will not develop the confidence essential to self-respect."[31] If this is true, the disobedience would certainly sabotage the effort to fulfill the parents' obligation to raise their child to be someone who is reasonably happy with his or her life.

Second, we have an obligation not to prevent others from carrying out their obligations. That obligation applies here: children would have an obligation not to be completely uncooperative. This isn't an obligation to cooperate perfectly and without question with their parents' every directive and plan. Children owe only the cooperation that is needed for their parents not to fail to raise them to be adults who can function acceptably in the larger society and are reasonably happy with their lives, not the cooperation needed to make them turn out exactly as the parents envision. But children do owe that lesser degree of cooperation. To require it of them, therefore, is not an offense against their autonomy.

Not, at least, so long as their parents do still have the obligation to raise them, since that is the source of the child's obligation to cooperate. Once the job was done, it would all change. That is the additional consideration in our cases; in most of these the child wants to part ways with the parent: to live apart while trying to become a dancer, to live with an older man, to join the military. If the child is not yet capable of meeting the society's reasonable expectations of someone who has become an adult, then the parental obligation is still in place, and so is the child's obligation not to act in ways that defeat it by parting ways with the parent to this extent. The matter does not turn on whether this particular decision would enact the child's "moral self," or qualities she has made her own. It turns instead on broader truths about the child's stage of development.

That means that what would have deserved respect as an expression of autonomy if it were chosen by an adult might not deserve this same respect in an adolescent, because the parents haven't yet completed their obligation to help the adolescent become the kind of adult that the larger society has a right for him or her to be. In such cases the parents ought to deny their child the choice that he or she wants to make. There would also be cases in which the larger society had no right to any more finished product than the child already was. Then the parents would already have carried out their obligation, even if not to their liking and even if they wanted more time to do it. The only considerations those parents would have a right to invoke would be whether the child was indeed acting autonomously and whether he or she understood the risks the parents saw in the choice. To put it differently, this child would have the right to be treated just as one would treat an adult and would be allowed to make what the parents regard as a great mistake.

6.

In this chapter I've argued that the autonomy of children deserves respect, even when they are quite small. However, it is also true that to bring a child into the world is to create someone who will be in great danger if he or she is not looked after extensively during the first several years of life. We have an obligation not to expose others to great danger, and so we have an obligation to ensure that any children we bring into the world will be looked after extensively during the first years of their lives, both "protectively" and paternalistically.

In addition, what is meant by autonomy in these contexts is making one's own way through the world, putting one's own personality and character into action. I argued that the actions of children are not always *cases* of "being a person of one's own," "putting one's own personality and character into action," and "making one's own way through the world." The reason is not because children have no personalities or character, but because what they have along these lines is sometimes not their own, in an important sense. Accordingly, when they put those traits into action, it isn't their own way they are making through the world, despite its being they who act. To honor their choices on such occasions out of respect for their autonomy would get this wrong. I think that happened in the case of Jessica Dubroff, the seven-year-old who was permitted to try to fly a plane across the United States.

The final portion of the chapter concerned respecting the autonomy of adolescents. Since the adolescent is no longer seven years old, it can be much harder to tell whether the traits a particular choice put in play are part of a self they have made their own. I drew upon the work of Jeffrey Blustein and Jonathan Moreno for help in doing so. The chapter ends by exploring the idea that there are some choices adolescents shouldn't be free to make, because those would defeat the obligation that their parents have to raise them. That last discussion made use of ideas about that obligation, and it is now time to consider those ideas more thoroughly.

6

Raising a Child

Some children do not go on to become adults, because they die while they are still young. Their early death is sometimes predictable given afflictions with which the child was born. Then being a good parent cannot include the attention to the child's future that we think of as *raising* the child. Instead, the parents are limited to attending to the quality of their child's brief life and in some cases to maximizing whatever autonomy the child is able to have, and that is where their obligations lie.

What those obligations are is a hard question. All parents are called upon to make sacrifices for their children's sake and to redefine their own lives so the child is not simply an intrusion but a source of added value for them. The next thought that comes to mind may be that no parent should take this task to the level of self-abnegation so that the child is all there is to the life that the parent leads. But is this still true when your child's life is to be very short, so that the exclusive focus is just for a time? Is it still objectionable to put everything else aside and do all you can for her before she dies, leaving you to go on as whoever you have become? Keep in mind that except when the child's difficulties are due to errors by medical personnel, they are due to the body that you and your partner gave her. Would her suffering then be that much more yours to reduce, and to compensate for?

There are also children who live for many years but acquire few of the capacities required for life as an adult, again because of the bodies with which they were born. Here too the parents cannot help the child become an adult, though I believe that whatever autonomy is available to the child is just as valuable as it would be if she could eventually become one, and merits the same respect. Once again the central moral questions about the parents' obligations concern what they owe in sacrifice and redefinition of their lives in order to improve the quality of their child's life and to allow her what autonomy she can have. That is both intriguing and important, as are questions about how much this differs from being the parent of a more fortunate child and how much it does not. I believe these issues require a book of their own, however. This chapter will be limited to a different project, concerned with families in which the child *should* be expected to "grow up." Helping her do so is then an important part of being her parent. But what does this call for the parents to do? What are they to accomplish in raising their child, and how are they to accomplish it? A number of factors shape the answers.

Children ordinarily grow up to live in society with others rather than in isolation. The larger society therefore has claims in how they are raised. We will want to say what those claims are. But it isn't only the larger society that can be done a wrong by the way in which a child was raised, of course: that can do the child herself a wrong, as well. So we will also want to say what the parents owe the child in the way they raise her, in addition to what they owe the larger society in this regard. Perhaps they owe the child something more than they owe the society—or, perhaps not.

We should also ask how much control parents ought to exert over the life that their child comes to have as an adult, by the way in which they raise him. Of course, it is impossible for parents to control this absolutely, as if children were wind-up dolls that could be sent on some course from which they would never deviate. Even so, perhaps parents can settle their child's future more completely than they should: a concern Joel Feinberg once expressed by speaking of the child's right to an open future.[1] We will want to see what this cautions against, exactly. In addition, it isn't only when we are adults that we have a right to do some things in our own way but also while we are still children, if arguments in the preceding chapter are correct. How is that fact to be given the proper respect in the way parents raise a child? Finally, there are the parents themselves. It is appealing to say that they should have some latitude in how they raise their children, rather than, say, being required to follow some precise pattern laid down by the state.

In sum, an account of how children are to be raised must give proper weight to the autonomy of the child, to the autonomy of the adult the child will become, to the child's own well-being, and to the claims of the larger society and it should allow parents whatever latitude they ought to have in the way they carry out this important obligation. I begin by considering what the parents should be trying to accomplish as they raise their child.

1.

It is not uncommon for parents to say that all they want is for their children to be happy when they grow up. As I shall use the term, to be happy is to be reasonably content with one's life in general: to regard it as going well, on balance. Parental assertions that this is all they want for their child are usually not to be taken literally. Even those parents who do not actually have their hearts set on anything very specific would be disappointed if the child turned out to be happy with *some* lives she might have. Sometimes the parents think she could be even happier if she were not reasonably content with what she has. Sometimes they had wanted her to "make something of herself" in ways they think she has not done. In either case, if she is happy as she is, they are a little disappointed in her, as well as in how things have gone, which is very far from having only wanted her to be happy.

Those are observations about what parents sometimes want for their children, whatever they might have said (and perhaps believed) that they wanted. Maybe such parents go wrong when they aim for more than what they said would have satisfied them. Maybe, that is, what parents should try to do is nothing more specific than to raise their children to have some happy life or other, with no restrictions on which happy life it is to be.

That goal has the appeal of leaving a great deal up to the child once he is grown, an approach that certainly respects his autonomy as an adult. It also reduces some risks posed by having more specific goals for one's children: the risk of feeling later that the efforts to raise this child were a failure, and the risk that the child himself will regard his life as a way in which he has failed his parents. Those risks are diminished if parents try only to equip their children to be happy in some way or other, since this aim allows a wider range of ways for the child to succeed.

There would have to be at least one restriction, however. Imagine that the life with which a grown child was happy was one in which he often treated others very badly, and took special pleasure in doing so. Suppose that his parents understood that trait in him but said this: "All that matters to us is that our son is happy—what happens to those other people is of no concern to us." The problem is that it *should* be of concern to them. They shouldn't want their son to be happy with a life like that; they should be troubled by the person he has grown up to be, and is happy being.

If they are not, perhaps they too see nothing wrong with their son's way of life. That is, they think he isn't mistreating others but only besting them, or treating them as they deserve, and so they are proud of their son's successes rather than appalled by them. It is much harder to picture the satisfied parents as agreeing that their son's life is morally reprehensible but finding this fact undistressing because, truly, their only concern is that he be happy. For one thing, to find something reprehensible is a way of being greatly bothered by it, and they are supposed to be unbothered by their son's life. For another, to find someone's behavior reprehensible is also to have some serious reservations about *him*, and they are said only to be glad that their son is happy. Still, all of us are capable of inconsistency, and parents can be especially resourceful in this regard where their children are concerned. Perhaps the latter parents are imaginable after all.

Even if they are, though, it is clear that they are less than ideal parents. This point suggests that parents ought to seek not only that their children will be happy as adults, but also that they will be morally good, in ways the son we have imagined is not. Thus one parental goal should be to convey a proper appreciation for the considerations that make it wrong to act in certain ways: for the misery one would cause others, for what it is to break faith with someone who trusts us, and so on. Otherwise, the parents themselves will not have taken these things as seriously as they should have.

As a next point, we might note that it is possible for someone to be happy with a life that has little of what seem to be certain positive features. For example, someone might be happy even though he had no sense of great accomplishment, or had little intellectual stimulation, or had little by way of variety and excitement. There are other goods than happiness, some of them positive, like these. It is reasonable to ask why a parent should not seek to have these other goods included as well in the life she raised her child to have, rather than aiming only for one with which her child would be happy.

This question draws out some important points that are surprisingly easy to overlook. First, the life that a parent raises a child to have is one the *child* will live, rather than the parents themselves, and when the child lives it he might not be the kind of person the parents imagine he will become. Second, what would be a good life for one person would not necessarily be a good life for another. Third, the goal to be sought by the parents is a good life for the child grown to adulthood, not a good life for a different person.

As quick illustrations, consider again the idea that anyone's life is better if it includes considerable intellectual stimulation, or has variety and excitement, even if he is happy with a life that does not include these things. Actually, this seems to be true only for some people. Suppose a man finds variety and excitement deeply unsettling rather than enjoyable, and he is not galvanized by them to improve his life in some other way. Since variety and excitement are not good for him in either of these ways, why say his life would be better if he had them? Why not say *he* would be better off with a more placid and regular life, even though there are also people for whom the excitement and variety would make a positive contribution? Similarly, although great intellectual stimulation can certainly be an important element in the life of someone who is bright and self-confident, imagine instead someone who is dull and who finds the stimulation only frustrating and humiliating. Better for *him* if his life has less of these elements, it seems.

The working idea here is that whether a life is a good one for a person is a matter of how well it suits that person: how well it fits his or her abilities, desires, personality, and qualities of character. This idea has two aspects, the first of which is in play in saying that someone's life suits her abilities. What that means, I take it, is that what her life regularly and importantly calls for her to do are things she is good at doing rather than things she does badly. She then has a good measure of success rather than failure: this is one ingredient of a good life. If so, then since we differ in our abilities and since lives differ in the abilities for which they call, we also differ in which lives would be good for us in this way.

The second respect in which a life might or might not suit a person has to do with his desires. A life that suited you well in this way would be one in which you did well at getting what you wanted and at avoiding what you found aversive, and did well at serving your abiding concerns. Naturally, this success does not reduce to serving your desires of the moment only to find that doing so has cost you more of what you want in the long run, or costs you something more important to you. Those would be ways in which you had failed to serve your desires well. In addition, the desires and aversions that matter include ones that you do not have when you act but that you would have when the consequences of acting in this way occurred. For example, suppose that although you do not particularly relish human company now, you would develop a keen yearning for it if you were to take up a solitary occupation. That would be relevant to whether this occupation would serve your desires well.

That is only a sketch, but it serves to suggest a second way in which your life could go well for you, or could go badly. Since we differ in our *desires* just as we do in our abilities, this too is a way in which we differ in what would be good lives for us. For example, a life that brought lots of public attention might be good in this way for someone who craved it but bad for someone who found the attention intrusive and annoying.

Sometimes qualities of personality and character are like *abilities*, in that they affect what the person will be good at doing and thus whether her life will have a good measure of success. For example, it can require great courage to do what a particular life requires, but not to do what a different life would need. In the same way, one life could require a substantial degree of self-confidence, or a good deal of patience, while other lives would require much less of these traits. For someone who had the *qualities* the life requires—or who would develop them if he lived that life—it would be a good life for him to have in this respect, in the same way as it would be a good life for someone who had the *abilities* it required or who would develop those. That is, such a person would do well in that life, whereas someone who lacked the qualities and would not develop them would do badly in it.

Qualities of character and personality can also function in the same way as desires rather than the way that abilities do. Then they affect what a person will find it satisfying to do. Take, for example, the person who seemed better off with a placid and regular life because for him excitement and variety were only unsettling. They might be unsettling because excitement and change unnerve him sufficiently that he does not function well. In that case, his personality or character would have made him unsuited for that life in the same way as a person's abilities might. However, he could also simply be averse to excitement and change, not because he does badly in such situations but because he very much needs to feel "in control" in order to be comfortable. That is simply what he is like, and so a thrilling life is not in that respect a good one for him to have: not because he won't be successful in it, but because it will regularly be aversive to him.

In sum, there seem to be two different ways in which a life might suit a person: by suiting her abilities (and traits that function as abilities do), or by suiting her desires (and traits that function as desires do). These generally coincide. It is usually satisfying to do what we are good at doing and frustrating to do what we do poorly. Moreover, both doing well in most of what we do and doing badly at it have predictable consequences for how others regard us and treat us, and for how we feel about ourselves. They are connected in that way with other important desires and aversions. So, people generally want to do what they are good at doing, and they look for lives in which they can do it often and regularly. Interestingly, however, these two ways in which a life can suit a person can also come apart.

In particular, it is possible not to want to do the things you are good at doing, and also not to want what doing them would deliver. In cases of this kind, the life that suits the person's abilities seems to offer him little. Since it does not serve him well, the right thing to say seems to be that it is not a good life for him to have, despite his being good at what it calls for. Because being good at what you do is so central to having a good life, one remedy is to find a life in which those abilities are in play in a different way, or perhaps a life that suits other abilities that this person has. It's only when those alternatives fail that he would actually be best off doing things he did poorly, and this person would be an unfortunate one. Still, what matters ultimately is how these various lives do at providing what he wants. A life that serves him well in this way is a good one for him to have, and one that serves him badly is not: being good at what he does is no good *to him* if his desires are not well-served in the bargain.

We began, though, with a different idea: that happiness is the proper goal for parents to have for their children. There is no mention of happiness in this more recent conception of a good life as being one that serves the person's desires well. Of course, we might expect a person to be happy with a life that does well at bringing him what he wants. These do differ, however, and they need not coincide. Indeed, it is possible to be dissatisfied, even with a life that suits one in *both* senses: to be unhappy, that is, even though one is both good at what one does and is doing quite well at satisfying one's desires. It is also possible to be happy with a life that does *not* go well in either of these ways, because one has "come to terms with it," or concentrates one's attention on its bright spots, or has faith that things will improve. Apparently, being happy and having a life that suits you are two different things. It will be worth considering more closely what each has to do with having a good life.

A first thought might be that it is only being happy with our lives that matters ultimately to whether we have good ones, just as it was only serving our desires that mattered ultimately to whether a life *suited* us. The earlier argument contended that it was no good to a person to have a life that suited his abilities unless it also did well at providing what he wanted. The parallel contention would be that doing well at getting what we want is no good to us either if it does not make us happy. But surely this latter argument does not have the same appeal. Rather, to have your desires well served seems to be a good thing in its own right, even if you do not also have the positive attitude about how your life is going in general that amounts to being happy with it. It seems to be a way in which you are well off, even if you are not well off in this other way.

So is being happy, it would seem. An earlier observation suggests that the "good life" that parents should seek for their grown children is one that is good in both ways, rather than one that is going well (but leaves them unhappy) or one with which they manage to be happy (even though it is not going well.) The life that is good in both ways is simply a better one to have, as far as we can see, and there is no apparent reason why it shouldn't be a parent's goal for her child. If so, what parents should try to equip the child to be is a good person whose life does well at delivering what he or she wants and who is happy with it. The next section will fill this idea out somewhat, by considering some cases in which it appears that things have not worked out this well.

2.

Imagine first a man who appears to be flourishing but is not at all happy. Much of what he wants does come his way, but this isn't enough for him, because he believes he should be doing much better than he is. Let us also imagine that this belief is unreasonable, resting on an exaggerated conception of his abilities and his personality, sustained by suspicions that many have kept him down out of envy or concern that he will show them up. What would satisfy him is definitely not in the cards, but he has his heart set on it. Sometimes he believes things are bound to turn his way despite their disappointing state at the moment; sometimes he doubts they ever will. In neither mood is he a happy man.

Those who are impatient with him regard him as someone whose life actually is going very well despite his inability to appreciate this fact. They think he s*hould* be happy, and they have their reasons. The man does have a good measure of material well-being, and creature comforts are important to him. He is also regarded by others as a success, and that perception is important to him too. He has a wife who loves him and children who sweeten his life, and these matter to him as well. And so on. Those who are impatient with him recognize that he is ambitious for much more than he has, so that he has desires that are not satisfied. What they think is that none of us gets everything we want and that this man's life is going very well in this regard, as well as he has any reason to expect. The problem, as they see it, is that he is unable to recognize these facts, and this blindness keeps him from the happiness he should have and risks leading him to cast his good life aside in a destructive search for something better.

Their view is certainly plausible, but actually there is a still better argument for saying that the man is right to think his life is not doing well at serving his desires. Those desires include the second-order desire to be *hugely* successful, a yearning important enough to him to leave him substantially dissatisfied despite how well things are going in these other important ways. Things are going better for someone if he is getting what he wants *more* rather than what he wants *less*—if the hierarchy of his desires is well served, to put it rather grandly. That is why a life that satisfies a good number of one's less intense desires can come out poorly, as it does with this man. His friends are right to think that he ought to have different desires and different priorities than he does, because his are unrealistic, but that is a different point. It is still true that his life does not do well at satisfying the desires he has. His life isn't a good one for him in that important respect—even if we want also to say that this circumstance is largely his own fault.

Several points emerge, I think. One is that the proper referent for how well a life is serving someone's desires must be that person's desires. Even if others regard them as foolish (or as foolish in their intensity), his are the desires that matter when the question is how well his life is serving his desires. Second, what a person wants and how badly she wants it are partly functions of what she thinks she ought to have, given the sort of person she takes herself to be. The man we imagined overestimates himself and is impervious to lessons that he is not the man he thinks he is. This situation goes a long way toward keeping his life from serving him well, and, as the disappointments mount, it is also likely to keep him from ever being happy. There is also an opposite flaw, in which someone underestimates her abilities in a way that undercuts her pursuit of what she cares most about, leading again to a life that neither serves her desires well nor makes her happy.

These examples suggest that if parents are to seek to equip their children to have a good life, part of that equipment will be the ability to have a reasonable sense of themselves and of their possibilities, and another part will be the ability to accept life's lessons about these. Helping the child to understand and appreciate what she is *already* like would be an important start toward these continuing capacities for self-understanding and for realism. Another would be to convey to the child that she isn't all she will ever be, and that understanding what she becomes will be valuable to her when she becomes it, in many of the same ways as her current self-understanding is valuable to her now.

Imagine now a second man, who regularly has much that he wants. Unlike the first man, he has an accurate sense of himself and he does not think that he should be doing much better than he is. He isn't getting everything he wants, of course, but he agrees that on the whole, the desires that are most important to him are being satisfied. That isn't enough for him, though: he is not happy, because there is one area of life that has been a disappointment to him, and this leaves him substantially dissatisfied. Without success in it he cannot be happy, even though he acknowledges that his desires are well served when one takes his life as a whole. Others say that he ought to be happy, because once we give his various objects of desire their proper weight in terms of their relative importance to him, his life actually serves him well.

Here a version of the earlier points applies again. If the question is whether his life is going well for him, it is his standards for "going well" that matter. Others can argue for a change in those standards, but as long as he retains them they are the measure of how good his life is for him. Unlike the first man, this second one is not unreasonable in what he wants in a successful career or a fulfilling marriage or whatever it is that he has found disappointing. His fault, if he has one, is in the standards by which he judges whether his life as a whole is going well: in particular, his requirement that this one aspect of life must itself go well. That is keeping it from doing so and is preventing him from being happy. If so, then a second piece of equipment for a good life would be the capacity to develop attainable standards for when things are going well, on balance.

As a third example, imagine a woman who lives in poverty. She does not manage to get much of what she wants, and she has to endure a great deal of hardship. Fortunately, there are also times when her life is good in various ways, however, and it turns out that for her those times are enough. On their basis alone, she manages to be reasonably happy. This could be a case in which she has ceased to want much, or one in which she wants a good deal but has very low standards for when life is doing well by her desires. Suppose instead, though, that she agrees that most of her desires go unfulfilled, and that even by her own lights her life is not going well, on balance. "But I don't need things to go well in order to be happy," she tells us. "That would be wonderful, but I am able to be happy with much less." Good for her, we might think, if she has little chance of changing things, since she can be happy and happiness is a good thing. In a different situation, such an attitude might immobilize someone who could do better, but that is a different story.

Her example suggests that what a person requires in order to be happy affects whether she can be happy, just as her standards for whether her life is going well on balance can do so. It also suggests that what one should seek to provide one's child in this regard depends on the material circumstances of the life that child will lead, as well as on the child's own abilities and character and the child's conception of those.

As a related example, imagine a different woman who recognizes that her life is going *well* by her own standards but who is still unhappy. What she thinks is that although her life is going well, it could be going better than it is, and that she could change it so that it did. She is correct in both respects. In her case, though, these beliefs keep her not only from resting content with what she has, but also from being even *reasonably* content with it:they keep her from being happy. In her case, to be happy requires more than just that her life go well by her standards for going well, just as the woman in poverty required less. If what this second woman requires is that her life go as well as she can possibly make it go, she is the sort of person we describe as *driven*: someone who is never satisfied and who is rather strikingly absorbed in how things are going *for her*. Those are severe handicaps as far as ever being happy is concerned.

To put it differently, perfectionism is one set of standards we ought to be reluctant to provide a child we hope will have a good life, because perfectionism is an obstacle to being happy and happiness is part of a good life. There would also be an opposite concern with some standards: they might leave a person satisfied with too little, unmotivated to do better when he could easily have done so. At its worst, with this attitude the person would fail to have a good life at all, since he was happy with the life that served his desires badly and thus he had only one of the two elements of a good life. The low standards would have gotten in his way, as they do not get in the way of the woman who cannot rise from poverty. It would be better not to equip him to settle for so little, just as it would be better not to make one's child a perfectionist.

Up to this point I have argued that parents should seek to equip their children to appreciate moral considerations, and to have lives as adults with which they are reasonably content and that serve their desires reasonably well. That goal is quite unspecific, in the same way as "any life she will be happy with" is unspecific. Accordingly, so are the suggestions offered about what it would be to equip a child to have such a life. Those suggestions can only identify what would help a person to have *any* life that would serve his or her desires well and with which he or she would also be reasonably content, or they can identify what would hinder one in having any such life. I suggested that one hindrance of that kind is an unreasonable sense of oneself and one's possibilities, and this is a greater hindrance the more dogged these misconceptions are. One would hope instead to have one's child become someone who liked and sufficiently appreciated the person he actually was that he had no need of persistent illusions.

One would also hope that he would have good judgment both in when to take himself to be doing well at getting what he wanted and in when to be happy. Rather than trying to say what would constitute good judgment in these matters, I offered several ways to have bad judgment about them. Perfectionism is one obstacle to happiness; another is to have standards that incline you to settle for lives that do not serve your desires well even by your own standards, when you could do better. I have also claimed that to find a life that suits your abilities and character is ordinarily to find one that will do well by your desires Doing so is deeply connected with being happy as well. There are several reasons here to believe that knowing where your abilities lie, being able to appreciate them, and knowing how to put them into play are all important equipment for a good life.

There are other points to be made at this same level of generality in regard to qualities that would be helpful in having a good life of any kind. To draw out one more of these, consider the common experience of getting something you want but then finding it disappointing. Sometimes the matter is minor. You order a dessert that sounds wonderful, but when it arrives it isn't good at all. You read something by a favorite author, but it delivers little of what her past work had offered. Those experiences are not greatly troubling, but there can also be disappointment when we have managed to satisfy relatively central and stable desires, sometimes with considerable effort. You wanted this woman to love you, and that puts it far too mildly: your yearning for this defined your life, for a time. In the end, she did come to feel as you had hoped. Now that you have the place in her heart that you wanted so badly…well, you are not *blissful*, as you had expected. In fact, you are dissatisfied, and this dissatisfaction persists.

We can tell a similar story about someone who finally finishes the long and arduous training required to be a physician and then finds that she does not even want to be one, or someone who works very hard at an ambitious project, finally brings it to a successful conclusion, and finds nothing like the deep satisfaction he had expected. The problem is that we have not only desires, but also expectations about what fulfilling them will be like. Some of those expectations are clear to us. They are what we could offer as our reasons, if we were asked why we wanted the thing in question or why we wanted it so badly. But we can also be unaware, or only dimly aware, of some of our expectations. We can even be unable to acknowledge some of them if they are called to our attention, either because we can't see ourselves as someone who wants *that* or because we can't see ourselves as someone who thinks it could be had in *this* way.

What happens when getting what we want leaves us disappointed is that our expectations fall through, to an extent that is important to us. The way in which they have fallen through need not be clear to us, since it needn't be any clearer to us what our expectations were. There is much to avoid here, obviously, if one is to have a life that serves one's desires well and a life with which one is happy.

It would be especially useful not to be the kind of person to whom this sort of thing happened regularly, in some area of life. What is needed more generally is to be clear about what our expectations are and to be reasonable in those expectations. No one is perfectly clear-headed in this way, and so it is also desirable to have some hindsight in such matters: to be able at least to tell what went wrong when a success proved disappointing, so that the same kind of mistake does not become a pattern in one's life. As with the features identified earlier, these abilities would help equip a person not just to have a good life *as a physician* or *in politics*, and so on, but to have a good life of any kind. Therefore they are something else that parents should seek to provide their children, on the view I have offered, along with a reasonable sense of themselves and of their possibilities, good judgment in when to consider that they are doing well, and good judgment in when to be happy with their lives.

On this nascent account, those points matter because we ought to seek to raise our children to be morally good people whose lives do well at serving their desires, and who are happy with those lives. William Irvine would object, in the following way: "While I don't for a moment want to suggest that steward-parents shouldn't be concerned with the happiness of their child, either as a child or as an adult, I have qualms about picking out happiness as a goal of steward-parents."[2] According to Irvine, parents ought not to try to raise their children to have lives with which the children will be happy, because "happiness is, in an important sense, unpursuable as a goal."[3]

His chief argument for that view is epistemic. He thinks we just don't know enough about how to achieve happiness, even for ourselves: "Attaining happiness, then, is not at all like going to the store and obtaining a quart of milk or like going to college and obtaining an education. It isn't as if there is a certain process which, if you go through it carefully, will automatically bring you happiness. Instead, there are lifestyles which, if lived, will tend to produce happiness as a by-product—but there are no guarantees."[4] Similarly, he says that "the best anyone can do is to remove obstacles to happiness…but there is no guarantee that [we] will thereby become happy."[5]

These remarks focus on being happy ourselves, but equipping our children to be happy as adults is even more of a shot in the dark. Whether the adults they become are happy will depend on what sort of person they have turned out to be, at a time that is years away. The same holds for what kind of life will serve their desires: that also depends on what those desires turn out to be. So, Irvine's objection might be offered against both aspects of the life I claimed parents should try to raise their children to have. The objection would be that in neither respect can we know enough to pursue this goal, so we had better choose a different one.

Whether this objection is right depends on what we can know about these things, but it also depends on what we *need* to know about how to achieve a goal if it is to be a sensible one. Irvine's own standards for what we need to know are too high, since he rejects happiness as a goal on the ground that there is no "process which, if you go through it carefully, will automatically bring you happiness…there are no guarantees." No very interesting goal could meet so stern a test, and it is hard to think of anything at all that would meet it as far as our children's future lives are concerned. That is, it is hard to think of any good thing that we would be *guaranteed* to achieve for them so long as we were "careful." It would follow that we should have no goals in raising our children: a more radical conclusion than Irvine intends, and not one we should accept.

Still, we ought not to lose sight of the valid points in his misgiving. It is true that what would be a good life for one's child depends on what she will be like when she is grown. It is going to matter what personality and character she combines with her talents, as well as what she wants to achieve. In her very early years, predictions might be fondly made, but they would also be somewhat fanciful. They might express the parent's hopes, or something the parent meant to bring about, but they could not be predictions the parent should make with much confidence. If we had only very young children in mind, then, we might well share Irvine's intuition that seeking their happiness as adults is too dodgy a business to recommend.

However, since childhood is a period of development, there are changes as the years pass. It isn't as though there is no sign of what sort of person your child is becoming until he or she is actually an adult when all is suddenly apparent. Instead, the child's abilities emerge during childhood, as do personality, character, and some developing interests. We don't reach adulthood as finished products in any of these respects, but neither are the earlier versions of ourselves totally disconnected from the later ones. So parents who are paying attention as their children grow up do acquire a basis for some predictions about what sort of life will suit the child as an adult. I think they get enough to go on that it isn't foolish of them to try to help the child have a life that will suit him. Indeed, I'd say it would be a great disservice to their child if they ignored the signs of what sort of person he was becoming.

A different objection is that although it is right to regard perfectionism as an obstacle to happiness, I have failed to recognize that some dissatisfaction with one's current state is essential to striving for a better one. The underlying idea is that parents ought also to make their children people who strive for better, rather than people who rest content with what they have. I agree, but I think the place I have allowed to raising the child to strive for improvement is actually the proper one.

On the view I've offered, the right parental goal is for the child to be *reasonably* content with her life, not completely satisfied with it. Someone who is reasonably content with what she has still has some motivation to try to do even better. This means the objection is sound only if that wouldn't be sufficient motivation to strive for improvement as much as one should. The issue becomes how much striving there must be for a life to be a good one. It isn't obvious that the answer is "More than there would be if one were reasonably content with what one had."

All I've said is that it is unfortunate if the striving leaves a person greatly dissatisfied with what he has, or if the reason he doesn't strive for better is that he underestimates his possibilities. I haven't also said that there is a particular level of ambition that parents would be wrong not to instill in their children. To me, that goal would be too specific to require parents to achieve. It would be wrong to require this, just as it would be wrong to require parents to ensure that their children had any particular trait of character beyond the ones needed to live in society and to be reasonably happy with their lives. Beyond those elements of character, what sort of person the child becomes should be up to her rather than her parents. That principle holds for how *social* she is (or how private), how *generous*, how concerned about the opinions of others, and so on—including, I am urging, for how much of a *striver* she is. Others shouldn't settle much about what kind of person she is but should allow her to become someone of her own rather than someone of their manufacture. That point is respected, if we take a parent's obligation only to be to equip her to be relatively happy with the person she becomes and the life she comes to have.

This discussion has been cast in terms of what parents should be trying to do in raising their children. Let us look more closely at the concern I've now raised, which is that they ought not to be too greatly in control of how their children turn out, lest the adult the child becomes be too much their creature and too little her own.

3.

An education that renders a child fit for only one way of life forecloses irrevocably his other options. He may become a pious Amish farmer, but it will be difficult to the point of practical impossibility for him to become an engineer, a physician, a research scientist, a lawyer, or a business executive. The chances are good that inherited propensities will be stymied in a large number of cases, and in nearly all cases critical life-decisions will have been made irreversibly for a person well before he reaches the age of full discretion when he should be expected, in a free society, to make them himself.

—Joel Feinberg, "Open Future"

Feinberg's reference to the Amish was prompted by a legal case, *Wisconsin v. Yoder*. The issue in that case was whether the Amish should be permitted their practice of withdrawing their children from school after eighth grade, when the children were typically thirteen or fourteen years old, despite a state law compelling schooling until the age of sixteen.

As Feinberg noted, the Amish are a rather special case:

There is perhaps no purer example of religious faith expressed in a whole way of life, of social organization infused and saturated with religious principle. The aim of Amish education is to prepare the young for a life of industry and piety by transmitting to them the unchanged farming and household methods of their ancestors and a thorough distrust of modern techniques and styles that can only make life more complicated, soften character, and corrupt with "worldliness." Accordingly, the Amish have always tried their best to insulate their communities from external influences, including the influence of state-operated schools.[6]

In *Yoder*, the court found in favor of the Amish, ruling that their First Amendment right to free exercise of their religion did entitle them to limit the formal education of their children to the completion of the eighth grade.

That ruling troubled Feinberg. He found it acceptable, in the end, but only because "The difference between a mere eight years of elementary education and a mere ten years of mostly elementary education seems so trivial in the technologically complex modern world that it is hard to maintain that a child who has only the former is barred from many possible careers while the child who has only the latter is not."[7] He thought it would have been a different matter if the Amish religion had required denying their children any education at all, or required withdrawing them "after two or four years of schooling.... [Then] no amount of harm to the parents' interest in the religious upbringing of their children could overturn the children's rights-in-trust to an open future."[8]

The point of deepest importance to Feinberg is that parents ought not to be permitted to narrow too greatly the possibilities open to their children. What he calls the "critical life-decisions" should be made by the person whose life they decide, he thought, not by someone else. For him, that person is the adult the child becomes: hence the mention of "rights-in-trust." What this means that parents should do while their children are young, he maintains, is to respect what he called "the child's right to an open future." Not that the parents are to leave the child's future *completely* open in their attentions to her, of course, something that is clearly impossible: his closing remarks clarify what he means instead. A parent raising a child is to

> give him opportunities to develop his strongest talents…after having enjoyed
> opportunities to discover by various experiments just what those talents are…steer
> the child toward the type of career that requires the kind of temperament the child
> already has rather than a temperament that is alien to him by his very nature…. At
> the very least…not try to turn him upstream and make him struggle against his
> own deepest currents. Then…the child's future is left open as much as possible for
> his own finished self to determine."[9]

A great deal of this view is congenial to the one I offered in the preceding sections of this chapter. Both Feinberg's view and my own leave the proper parental goal quite unspecific. He puts it in terms of an open future; I had put it in terms of having a *good life*, cashed out only as one that serves well the desires of the person whose life it is and that also makes him or her happy. Similarly, both views take such a life ordinarily to be one that suits the person's abilities and personality. Given this substantial agreement, it is important to consider a central objection to Feinberg's view, to see whether it also applies to the one I have offered.

As David Archard has observed, "Each and every upbringing has an obvious 'opportunity cost,' namely, the absence of some other upbringing."[10] That is certainly true of raising a child in a way that sharply narrows his possibilities, as Feinberg feared that an Amish upbringing did. The trouble is that it is equally true of raising one to have an open future. That too precludes bringing the child up in a different way. For example, it would rule out raising one to be a member of the Amish community, if Feinberg is right that an Amish adult ends up "fit for only one way of life," namely, that of "a pious Amish farmer" or an equally pious Amish woman. Feinberg certainly wanted to allow the Amish their way of life. It appears that he shouldn't have, if he was right both that the Amish upbringing makes the "critical life-decisions" for children before they are grown and that an upbringing ought not to do this.

More generally, to quote Archard again, what Feinberg favors in urging respect for the child's right to an open future is "the classic liberal upbringing— tolerant of diverse life styles, flexible and wide-ranging in outlook, humanistic and tending to secular idealism in ideology."[11] That upbringing certainly has its virtues. However, to raise a child in this way also excludes raising him in a number of the major religions, since these are decidedly not "humanistic and secularly idealist in their ideology," and the moralities they offer are not necessarily tolerant with regard to a number of "diverse life styles." We should be uncomfortable about dismissing these other ways of raising children, even if we do not ourselves have a traditional way of life in which we feel impelled to raise our own.

The question is whether these same criticisms apply to the view I offered, according to which what parents should do is to raise their children to have good lives. I will argue that they do not. As a start, we might observe that life as "a pious Amish farmer" can certainly *be* a good life for someone who is raised to have it. So can life in one of the other established traditions. It sounds as if it would be one of the ways for a parent to *succeed*, then, if this were the life she raised her child to have and if the proper parental goal were for the child to have a good life.

We can also agree with Feinberg's intuition about the hypothetical religion whose believers insisted their children must have no education. That restriction shouldn't be permitted, he thought, even under the banner of a right to practice one's religion. It wouldn't be right on the view I have offered either, if a person with little or no education would be hard pressed to have a good life of *any* kind in the current world. Parents who raised their children in ignorance wouldn't be raising them to have good lives and so would be doing this in the wrong way.

These first points urge that raising children to have a good life does not exclude raising them to have a particular *kind* of good life, including one that would be lived within a particular tradition. If so, raising a child to have a good life is not the same as leaving the child's future as open as possible. This idea returns us to what worried Feinberg the most, though: namely, that a set of parents might have too powerful a role in determining the life their children had as adults. The question is whether that would be true if the parents went beyond providing the realism about one's abilities and in one's expectations (etc.) that are tools for any good life at all, and sought to raise their child to have a good life *as an Amish farmer*, or *as an Orthodox Jew*, or *as a wife and mother*, or *as a professional*, and so on.

The right answer, I think, is "not necessarily." Feinberg does not say how powerful a role in determining what sort of life someone else has would be *too* powerful. Whatever the answer, it does not seem as if every parent whose efforts are to raise his child "in the faith," or to have a particular kind of occupation, or to play a particular gender role, will qualify as having settled this issue more completely than he should. What such parents do need not be decisive, in any very impressive way. Many children so raised go in other directions, not all of them with great difficulty. Indeed, some of the Amish leave their communities and still have happy and productive lives, so even this upbringing is not as narrowing as Feinberg thought it was.

I have put that point in Feinberg's terms, taking the concern to be that we leave important choices open to the future adult rather than deciding these ahead of time. As he put this concern:

> It is the adult he is to become who must exercise the choice, more exactly, the adult he will become if his basic options are kept open and his growth kept "natural" or unforced. In any case, that adult does not exist yet, and perhaps he never will. But

the child is *potentially* that adult, and it is that adult who is the person whose autonomy must be protected now, in advance.[12]

The point thus far is that a parent's efforts to raise a child to have a good life of a particular kind need not foreclose those choices and violate that autonomy.

Now for a different point: Feinberg was concerned about the choices the future adult would make, but not about respecting the current choices of the child. It did not matter to him what the thirteen-year-old's own view was about leaving school after the eighth grade in order to continue the path to the Amish life, only whether taking her out of school would close off choices she would have made when she was an adult. For Feinberg, as for many, raising a child is something parents do to and for the child, with however much cooperation might be forthcoming but in the face of resistance if need be. The choices belong to the parents, and they are choices about how a parental activity is to be conducted.

I want to suggest a different model for raising children who are no longer very young. I agree that very young children are properly under very close control, in order to protect them from coming to harm. Indeed, doing so is a parental obligation, if an argument in the preceding chapter is correct. One effect of that early control is to put the parent's influence at its maximum regarding what sort of person her child is becoming. However, as our children grow up, we are able to leave them more on their own and are less and less a substantial a presence in their lives.

That growing independence allows them to make their own way, to some extent. As they do, they help to shape their character and personalities. In time, they also come to be interested not only in what they are doing at the moment, what they did earlier, and what they might do later, but also in what they are like themselves. Once they take an interest in that, they are soon also in a position to become persons of their own in a variety of ways: by conscious imitation of others, by acceptance of qualities they take themselves to have, by continuing to act in ways they now should know are likely to have certain effects on them, and so on. This self-construction is another set of activities they undertake on their own, and to some extent they do so away from the parental eye that had once rightly watched them so closely. Their work in this development makes them no longer their parents' creatures in these respects, but their own. The choices that express what they have made of themselves then merit respect, as the expression of their autonomy. To put it another way, they become someone whose right to act as they choose has to be taken into account—by the child's parents, among others.[13]

"But he's still just a *child*!" they might want to say. Of course, and his parents still have an important obligation to raise him to become a morally sound adult who has a good life. The difference is that raising him is no longer very much like raising a crop, since he can no longer be thought of as something his parents planted and must protect and nurture if he is to survive. It won't even be enough for them to be careful not to foreclose options that should be open to the adult he will become. He is already a person of his own making, and part of treating such a person with the proper respect is allowing him to act for his own reasons, rather than taking him to be under your direction. This means the older child should *now* play a role in the way he is "brought up": the upbringing should be a joint project in which he takes part.

I don't mean by this that older children should play the same role in the project as their parents. For one thing, it remains the parents' obligation to provide the child the opportunity that Feinberg emphasized, to continue to discover what her possibilities are and to enable her to take advantage of some of them. That will be an important moral claim on the way in which the parents spend their resources and their energies. It is one difference between their role and the child's, and it doesn't change if we think of the older child as properly a participant rather than the passive object of their obligatory efforts to raise him.

It also remains true that parents ordinarily know and understand a great deal about many things that their children do not. Some of this knowledge is about how the world works, some of it is about what qualities the child herself has, some of it is about what a life of a particular kind would probably be like for her, some of it is about whether she would be happy with such a life. Their past record in raising the child can entitle them to some degree of trust in these matters as people who know what they are talking about and who are well intentioned. Clearly, the degree of trust to which a particular set of parents is entitled in a particular matter is going to vary, since not all parents have the same past record and not all new matters resemble past ones. For both reasons, the conclusion of a particular set of parents might not be trustworthy on some occasion, whether on the very broad question of what life the child should seek or on narrower questions about how best to seek it. Still, parents can be reliable sources of information even on these matters.

Clearly, this role falls short of a parental right to insist that even an older child should seek the life the parents think would suit her best, or should seek it in the way they have in mind. Those choices are the child's, and the parent should respect her way of making them. Respecting that means permitting the child to follow a different path of her own choosing, so long as that path has a reasonable chance of leading to a good life of a different kind. Moreover, there is no change in the obligation to support her efforts to have a good life: if her decision is to try to be a dancer, there is the same obligation to help her become one that there was to help her become what her parents hoped she would. It is important to note in passing that to decide to "be a dancer" is to commit oneself to a sustained pattern of activity. That is what the parents have an obligation to support, if she undertakes it, not a momentary change of mind. And, in their role of informed parents who care deeply what becomes of her, they are also obligated to try to make this commitment one she is not unwise to make, by helping her to accomplish it.

The parental role just described does not seem to me to pose the danger that worried Feinberg, which was that parents would *settle* the lives that their children went on to have in ways that should have been left to the adults whom the children became. Here, if anyone settles this it is the children themselves, whose life it already is and who do what settling is done in choices that should already be theirs. If the adult the child becomes is partly someone of her own making, worries that she will be too finished a product during childhood are somewhat undercut: it wouldn't be her parents who had done the job too completely, but she and they together. Clearly, this is also a way to help the child become a person of her own as an adult, able to act with the autonomy that deserves respect rather than only as the creature of others. As was noted in the preceding chapter, helping the child achieve that is an important parental obligation: not only to respect the autonomy the child already has, but also to help in its development.[14]

Let me repeat that there is room here for parents to have a particular version of a good life in mind for their child and to try to get the child to follow that path, including life within a particular religious tradition. The restriction is that the parents can't impose their version of a good life on an older child but must accommodate themselves to his having a good life of a different kind, if that is how things turn out. Of course, it might be difficult for the parents even to concede that there could be a good life outside the tradition, or outside the occupation or gender role they had in mind. If they are mistaken about that, though, parenthood requires them to come to terms with the child's choice and support it in the way decribed.

It is also more than possible that the child will not fall away from the faith in which her parents raised her, or in some other way take a different path than they thought best for her. Archard expresses this principle by saying that if the parents "live their [own] lives in the light of customs and values they esteem [it] is most unlikely that the child will not thereby inherit a respect for its parents' way of life."[15] Parents have the opportunity to be a powerful example of the life they advocate. They also have many years in which to earn their child's respect as people to be listened to, as she decides what to make of herself. That combination will often be enough for things to work out much as the parents hope, and it is all anyone should ask.

We come, finally, to the child who appears to be highly talented to an unusual degree. Even here there are good reasons not to embark on a highly directive effort to develop those talents when the child is still very young. As Irvine observes, with many arresting examples, the lives of children who are nurtured for stardom from a very young age are strikingly similar to those of adults who have hard jobs and whose jobs are virtually all there is to their lives.[16] Even if the very young child *likes* the job her childhood has become, she has lost what might be the only period in her life that could have offered the pleasures of aimlessness and the chance to discover and cultivate other abilities and interests that could have shaped a good life for her. The other concern about this issue is Feinberg's, of course: not that this is a bad life for the child at the time, but that it gives the parents too powerful a role in the life she has as an adult. The worry is that her parents ought not to have foreclosed her other possibilities by focusing her life so exclusively on developing her talent. Rather, they should have raised her in a way that allowed her ultimately to make those choices for herself.

This argument invites certain replies. One is that some choices aren't available when one is an adult but only when one is a child. If this particular life is to be had, it is essential to develop the talents from an early age. Granted, if a parent refrains from doing so, a range of possibilities will still be open to the child, but only at the cost of foreclosing this one, in the field where his great talent lies. It will cost the future adult the rewards of that life, and it will also cost others the rewards of his having it.

This reasoning is correct, but it is also reasoning about which to take great care. The fundamental ideas are that something will be impossible unless the child is given the assiduous early training, and that achieving the goal is worth the costs of that training. These ideas will find ready support among some coaches and teachers, who provide that training and who have more successes of which to be proud the more young children they train. It can also be important for some parents to believe these things. This is so for a variety of reasons, including the enhancement it gives to what is at the end of the path the child undertakes, which must be of great value if it can be achieved only by such assiduous effort...

First, though, what requires all-consuming early training if one is to achieve success isn't always so straightforward. For example, I have a colleague who had a highly successful career in ballet before reinventing himself as a philosopher and who began in dance not as a tiny child but as a fourteen-year-old. Did his "late start" as a dancer still foreclose *some* possibilities for him? Perhaps, but it becomes harder to say what those possibilities were. The thought arises that what the parent is driving for isn't just a rewarding life in a field for which the child has talent, but one in which she is a leading figure. If so, it will be important for the parent to be realistic about how talented the child is, about how dedicated the child is to this same goal, and about the role that luck will play in achieving it.

That is very hard to do. It would be exceptional even to know the child's degree of talent and dedication when she was very young, as opposed to knowing that she had some talents along these lines and was currently excited about developing them. It is also difficult to be realistic about the role that luck plays in being among the very best at something. The conclusion isn't that parents should never treat their very young child as the next sensation in the field, but that it is a hard choice to have right.

It is also important to be sensible about the argument that your child must follow this path lest others lose what they would have had if she had followed it. Generally speaking, we ought not to raise our children for the good of others, or for some abstract good. Nor is it generally true that unless this one person takes up the life in question the loss to others will be incomparable.

Those are reasons to doubt that greatly narrowing the childhood of a very young child in order to develop his talent is a wise choice with regard to the future adult, or a necessary one for the sake of those for whom he will dance, or sing, or paint, or write, or perform athletic feats. The other argument for nurturing abilities at a very early age is that this is what the *child* wants himself. It isn't only his parents who want him to focus so assiduously on becoming a violinist or an Olympic ice skater or a tennis player—this is also what he wants to do with his life. I've been arguing that children have a right to make their own choices and that we should respect that right by making the way they are brought up a joint project that they carry out with their parents. Wouldn't we be doing exactly that if we helped them cultivate the talents they wanted to cultivate?

Actually, this reasoning assumes that the very young child's desire to have the training is properly understood as *his* desire, in the important sense: as expressing a self of his own. I argued earlier that very young children are still very much their parents' creatures. If they are, then beginning exclusive training at a very early age might not be a way of respecting the child's autonomy and allowing him to play a properly participatory role in his own upbringing, any more than we would do this if we allowed him to leave home and make his own way at the age of four because that was what he wanted to do. Neither decision should be taken to demand respect of that kind, when the costs of repecting it are very high.

The choices of an older child certainly can demand that respect, though there can be problems in telling whether they do. As in the preceding chapter's discussion of the fatal attempt by Jessica Dubroff to fly a plane across the United States, the less clear it is that the child is putting a self of her own into play, the less ready we should be to allow her to follow desires that are particularly costly. That caution could certainly be true of some intensive training regimens which, as Irvine emphasizes, make childhood an especially demanding stage of life instead of a playful one, and which greatly narrow the open future for which Feinberg had hoped. We shouldn't allow such things unless they are something this person wants to do, and the younger the child is the harder it will be to be sure it is he, in the important sense, who wants to do it.

There is another wrinkle. An older child can have a powerful desire to do what is important to her parents, and that desire could be at the heart of her wanting to do the assiduous training. This possibility is another risk of being too powerful an influence on a child. The best one could do to cope with it would be to make it plain that no single course of action was essential to her remaining in your affections, and that the rewards for her in what she chooses to do and to be are far more important than the rewards for you. That understanding would express respect for its being *she* who acts and *her* life that is shaped, and it would urge her to make her choices about it in her own terms.

Still, if she wanted to go ahead with the training, it might be very difficult to tell why she was doing so and thus whether providing the training respected her autonomy rather than imposing your choice on her. There would be signs in the pleasure she took in what she was doing (or did not take in it) and in her independence in other matters (or her lack of independence in them). No doubt you would often be uncertain how to add those elements up so as to be sure you were raising your talented child as you should. It is hard to know enough, and it is also hard to separate your own ambitions from the child's.

But in addition, sometimes the choice isn't between acting as you should and acting as you should not, but between two ways of acting as you should. To some extent, the obligations of parenthood are only obligations to proceed in a general way: here, with respect for the child's autonomy and with the proper general goals. They don't amount to obligations to do *exactly this*. They don't define precisely what you must do as a parent. That part of it is left open, as your particular way of being a good parent to your child. There are wrong choices, of course, but once those are avoided, there is more than one way of meeting your obligations as a parent.

4.

I have urged that the way in which a child grows up ought to be something the parent and child bring about together rather than being a parental project of raising this person as one would a crop. I think that approach pays the autonomy of the child the respect it deserves, and does so with proper respect for the autonomy of the adult the child will become. It also serves to help equip the child to have a life with which she will be happy.

One consequence of the recommended partnership between parent and growing child would be a sense on the child's part that what she does is *her* doing, rather than a choice someone else has made for her or the product of external forces. To call this a sense of responsibility for what she does is rather solemn and sounds as if it would come into play only when she does something wrong. What I have in mind is broader than that. Someone who had such a sense would take it for granted that the next moves in what she had underway were up to her, whether these involved dealing with a difficulty, taking proper advantage of an opportunity, or turning in a new direction. She would also have a sense of accomplishment, enriched beyond the sense of accomplishment we can have when we think we have done a good job for someone else.

Those are ingredients in happiness with one's life. For one thing, the assumption that choices are yours to make helps you to avoid allowing others to make them for you. As Mill pointed out, we are generally the best ones to choose how our interests should be served, partly because we are more likely to get this right than anyone else is. Perhaps it is also true that human beings are happier with their lives if they have this sense of *leading* them, other things being equal. Certainly that will be true of someone who is raised to believe that he ought to lead his own life. That sort of person will be happier to the extent that he thinks he is doing so. Fortunately, the sense that you are leading your life isn't all that hard to come by, for anyone who doesn't have an exaggerated sense of what doing so requires. So this is a path to happiness.

Of course, it is a path that could prove to be unhappy: there are none that couldn't. But it is also a way of living that has good prospects for a person who is inclined to follow it. Parents can send their children down that path by enlisting them early in the project of determining what kinds of people they will be and where they will go first in their lives as adults. This means that respecting the child's autonomy by raising her cooperatively is a way of serving the broader goal of raising her to become relatively happy with her life.

I have argued that parents should raise their children to be morally good people whose lives do well at serving their desires and who are reasonably happy with those lives. Some of the equipment for such a life is one-size-fits all: a reasonable sense of one's qualities and possibilities, good judgment in when to consider that one is doing well, good judgment in when to be happy with how well one is doing, a good grasp of one's expectations, and the ability to learn from one's disappointments. Parents should try to enable their children to have these qualities. Whether they succeed will not be entirely up to them, partly because they will not be the only influence on their children and partly because what anyone learns is, in the end, the work of the person who learns it.

Often parents will have much more specific hopes for their children, reflective of their own sense of what would be a good life. This goal is perfectly legitimate, so long as their efforts to bring it about are properly respectful of the extent to which an older child is already a person of his own, who is to live the life and who should therefore define it for himself. As was noted, it is more than possible that the child who has become a person of his own will not deviate sharply from the life his parents had hoped he would take up, especially if he joins in preparing for that life rather than being conscripted for it. The parents' influence on this outcome is something they will have earned by the way in which they carried out the earlier stages of parenthood and will continue to earn by the way they treat their growing child.

Of course, it is also possible that the child will want a very different life than his parents had in mind for him. This fact does not change their obligation to raise him to have a good life, I have argued. It also leaves them free to try to persuade him otherwise, but not to insist or to revoke their support. That is one last point about the proper balance between the respect that must be paid to his autonomy and his parents' interest in raising their child as they wish. The raising should be a joint project conducted by parent and child, I argued, and here the unequal partners in that project would be at odds about its fundamental direction. By requiring the parents to help the child so long as the path he chooses has reasonable prospects of leading to a good life, I've taken the child's autonomy to be more significant than the parents' wishes for him.

Lest this statement be misconstrued, let me emphasize that it doesn't amount to giving the child veto power over everything the parent tries to do. In particular, it doesn't endorse what people have in mind when they speak of children having a right to divorce their parents. That idea emerged in connection with a 1992 case in which a twelve-year-old boy brought legal proceedings to terminate his relationship with his mother—and won the case. The circumstances were as follows. The boy's parents had separated when he and his two brothers were very young. After his mother began raising him on her own "she had a difficult time and repeatedly had to park him with relatives in foster care. By the time he was twelve, he had lived with her only seven months. George R., a visiting attorney, noticed [the boy] when he was living at the Lake Country Boy's Ranch. George and his wife took him in as a foster child and agreed to adopt him if the lawyer they helped him hire succeeded in terminating his legal relationship with his mother."[17] As Laura Purdy writes, "The country was in an uproar. Children, the press suggested, aren't supposed to make those kinds of decisions—and the next thing we know, they'd be dragging their parents through divorce court at the drop of a hat. No longer would parents be able to make children abstain from sex or drugs, do their homework, even take out the garbage."[18]

Indeed, what was feared as a right to divorce your parents might be a version of the adult right to a no-fault divorce. At least in most U.S. states, it's no longer necessary for an adult who wants to dissolve a marriage to prove mistreatment or abandonment or adultery. It is only necessary to want the relationship to end and to cite "irreconcilable differences." Perhaps children might be given the same legal right to divorce their parents simply because they wished to go their own separate way.

Purdy explains why that would be a bad idea.

> If the right to do so is linked with the full liberationist program, there are a variety of good reasons for rejecting it.... That view is based on the false assumption that there are no morally relevant differences between children and adults. Children are not just miniature adults; they need time to mature and to develop the traits that make it possible for adults to live good lives. These morally relevant differences undermine the attempt to show that it is unjust to deny children the same rights as adults; they also suggest that the consequences of equal rights would undermine justifiable parental authority, make schooling optional, and thrust many vulnerable children into the world of work."[19]

As Purdy's reasoning emphasizes, children will be far better off if they *don't* have the same right to divorce their parents that adults in virtually all U.S. states have to dissolve their marriage.

My own arguments against children's divorcing their parents would follow a different course. First, because of the important differences Purdy mentions between children and adults, the larger society is entitled to have adults *raise* children, thereby fitting the children for society with others. That situation is incompatible with allowing the child to decide he has had enough of being raised before this is accomplished, or decide that he wants it carried out by someone more to his liking. Second, since the society is entitled to have someone continue to raise the child, those who have been doing so have a right of their own to continue to be parents to their child. I've argued that they have this right just because they began the project without violating anyone's rights, so long as they are doing no one any significant harm. They are certainly doing their child no harm of that order if his only complaint is that he is sick of being made to do his homework and being required to do chores, or if he chafes under other reasonable parental restrictions, let alone if he just wants to go his own way as in a no-fault divorce between adults.

A more interesting case would be one in which his parents had abused him or neglected him in ways that called for them to lose custody of him. Whether they had done so can be obvious; it can also call for judgment. Chapter 4 offers ideas about how to make such judgments.[20] When the child's parents did indeed treat him in this way, *of course* he would have a right to "divorce his parents"—but this is only to say that the child has the same right as anyone else to bring the abuse or neglect to the notice of the authorities, and the same right that the claim be taken with the seriousness it merits. Children don't also have a more general right to dissolve the joint project of raising them as adults have to dissolve their marriages, for the reasons mentioned.

Finally, it might be objected that my account of what parents should do in raising their child is culturally dependent. I've claimed that parents should be concerned to help their children develop into persons of their own, should grant them increasing independence, should have their participation in the project of raising them, and should be trying to help them become adults who can function without parental direction. That set of contentions might sound awfully American. Aren't there also cultures to which it would be entirely foreign: ones in which children aren't supposed to be increasingly independent as they grow up but must continue under their parent's control, are supposed to be raised as their parents see fit, and are meant to have lives as adults in which they are more a part of their original family?

No doubt there are; what's needed is to be careful about what follows. The existence of other ways of life isn't a reason to reject my account of what parenthood calls for from those of us who live in more familiar cultures. We would need to see that the other way of life is correct not to value the autonomy of individuals as highly as I am valuing it—not to value what I called becoming a person of one's own rather than the creature of another, and having control over the shape of one's life as highly as what the other cultures think is more important. The fact that the other cultures take something else to be more important does not prove that theirs is the right moral view, since if it did, the fact that still other cultures reverse these values would also prove that *theirs* was the right moral view.

Perhaps cultural differences show something more modest: not that my account is wrong about the form parenthood should take in the cultures of most people who would read this, but that it is wrong about the form parenthood should take in the cultures that handle it differently. Actually, that conclusion wouldn't follow either. If we say the fact that they handle it differently means no other approach could be a better one for them, then they must currently have the moral calculus right for their part of the world, or else, although they might get a better idea about it themselves someday, this view cannot be contributed by an outsider. It would also mean that any culture that adopted some aspect of a different way of life would be making a moral error, replacing its own right way of dealing with the matter with the foreigners' wrong one. None of those propositions is very plausible.

What is plausible is that it would be quite foolish to assume the opposite: to think, for example, that if parenthood ought to take the form I've urged for some cultures, then it ought to take that form in all of them. For one thing, how parents and children ought to treat each other is no peripheral matter but is very central to a way of life. Changing it would change a good deal else as well, perhaps in ways that would make it not the right choice after all. For another, any local version of parenthood has developed in a particular empirical setting, where it serves various functions. Think here of the standard arguments that although polygamy is objectionable in some settings, it isn't objectionable when a small population struggling to survive has few men and many women. Then it is a better way to balance what is important. Similarly, the form of parenthood that a different culture developed could be the better way to balance what is important in their empirical setting.

This isn't to revert to one of the positions I've criticized, according to which a culture must have parenthood right and could not do better by adopting some or all of a different approach to it. Perhaps the approach I've urged would be of value for other cultures to consider. That would be enough, if it were also a good account for cultures such as my own to adopt.

Early in this chapter I argued that parents ought to seek not just to equip their children to have lives that will serve their desires well and with which they will be happy, but also to ensure that they become morally good, to some extent. The next several chapters attend more closely to the moral education that should be part of raising a child.

7

Moral Education

The aim of providing a child a moral education isn't only to teach a kind of geography that conveys where various ethical considerations are to be found, but also to get the child to appreciate these considerations. She is meant to find them motivating and to continue to do so. To put it differently, the aim is to provide her with certain qualities of moral character.

Of course, parents are not the only moral influence on their children, or even the only ones who have an obligation to shape the child's moral character, but it would be an odd conception of parenthood that didn't assign them a central role in this process. What, if anything, are they supposed to accomplish? What does accomplishing it require them to do?

The answers must keep the interests of several parties in the proper balance. One is the child himself, both while he is a child and when he becomes an adult. Another is the larger society in which he lives as a child; yet another, the society in which he will live when he is grown. The child's parents also have legitimate interests of their own in what they are to convey, in the course of providing the child a moral education and in what they are to do in order to convey it.

That is enough to eliminate certain simple views. For example, it means that parents are not free to teach their children whatever they themselves believe to be the moral truths. They would be free to do that if the child were theirs to shape in any way they wished. They are not free to do it, however, in part because the child lives among others, who have their own legitimate claims as to how he is to act both while he is a child and when he is an adult. Since parents can have a faulty sense of those claims, they are not free to teach their children whatever they believe. Moreover, in their zeal to make their child the kind of person they believe she should be, parents can fail to give proper weight to the child's own claims in the matter. In particular, the child has a claim to have her current autonomy respected, a claim to the parent's help in becoming a person of her own, and a claim to the parent's help in becoming someone who is able to be reasonably happy with her life as an adult. Those help define the moral education the parent is to provide.[1]

Nor will the parental duty be to instill the local morality regardless of any moral horrors the parents take it to contain. Parents have a legitimate interest of their own in teaching their children what they believe to be right, in the kinds of people their children become, and in what sort of lives they go on to have. As

William Galston points out, the moral education one gives one's children is inseparable from a parent's "expressive liberty":

> Expressive liberty offers us the opportunity to enjoy a fit between inner and outer, conviction and deed...it is a precondition for leading a complete and satisfying life...the ability of parents to raise their children in a manner consistent with their deepest commitments is an essential element of expressive liberty....We cannot detach our aspirations for our children from our understanding of what is good and virtuous.[2]

So parents too have important claims in play when they are providing their child a moral education, no less than the larger society has them. One of our questions is how to keep these in the proper balance. Another is how to balance both the parents' claims and those of the larger society against the child's own claims, which he has as the one who is shaped by the moral education he is given.

In addressing these questions, I will concentrate first on three qualities of character: empathy, a sense of fairness, and a sense of responsibility. I will begin by describing these qualities and the ways in which they develop in children. I will then offer arguments about what parents owe their children along these lines, and what they also owe society where these qualities in their child are concerned. The second section offers two arguments of a different kind. Their conclusions are that parents also owe their children the traits that make a person capable of friendship and the traits that make a person capable of profiting from free and equal discussion with others. A third section argues that parents have no obligation to ensure that their children are good people in any more particular way and, indeed, that a proper respect for the child's autonomy gives the child a primary role in what particular kind of good person he becomes. A fourth section addresses what all of this means parents are to do, exactly, in order to provide their children the moral education they should.

1.

> Perhaps most chilling are statements of young criminals who profess no feelings whatsoever for those whom they hurt. I recall a *New York Times* interview with a thirteen-year-old convicted of viciously mugging a series of older persons, one of whom was a totally blind woman. The boy expressed only regret that he was caught, and went on to say that the blind woman was his victim of choice, since she at least could not provide a legal identification. When asked about the lasting pain that he had caused this unfortunate woman, the boy was surprised at the question and responded, "What do I care? I'm not her."[3]

The author is surely right to find this attitude "chilling." Somehow, it is more chilling in a thirteen-year-old than it would be in a man of thirty. Perhaps this is because we think anyone as coldhearted as this is beyond redemption, and we don't like to think of someone so young as already lost. Or, perhaps we think it should take *time* to become so cold, as if this were the dulling of a capacity we all have at the start and some of us lose.

Be that as it may, scholars of human development mark the first emergence of empathy at a very early age. Martin Hoffman, for example, says that children are "responsive to distress in others" in the *first year* of life.[4] As he notes, that would be "long before they acquire a sense of others as physical entities distinct from the self."[5] But this means their responses couldn't possibly be a matter of realizing that someone else was in distress and being moved by this circumstance, which is what we ordinarily have in mind by *empathy*. The children seem instead just to be bad at telling when it is *they* who are distressed: they hear crying and it upsets them, wherever the crying comes from, but not because it makes them concerned about someone else. This feeling is certainly a way of being responsive to (what happens to be) distress in others, to use Hoffman's phrase, but although he calls it "global empathy," it seems better construed as a precursor to empathy.

In contrast, in the second year of life children can be aware that someone else is in distress, and they sometimes attempt to go to that person's aid. This reaction sounds much more like empathy, although their efforts to help are rather sweetly unsophisticated:

> Hoffman observed a thirteen-month-old who...brought his own mother to comfort the crying child instead of bringing in the child's mother, who was equally available....In other similar cases, toddlers have been observed offering unhappy-looking adults their own beloved blankets or dolls for comfort.[6]

This reaction sounds as if the children do know who is in distress and do want to help this person feel better but lack the experience to know how to accomplish this. They don't know that what makes them feel better might not work for someone else, nor do they know what *would* work for this other person.

One can help a child to learn such things, obviously. To do so would be one way in which to encourage the instinct, endorsing it as a proper reaction by showing how to carry through with it. One can also refine the instinct in various ways, showing when it might be appropriate to have empathy for someone and when it might not, and how the appropriate expressions of this empathy might vary. Alternatively, it is possible to do none of this, or even to actively discourage empathy for others. That is, one could allow the empathy that appears to be natural in children to atrophy, or one could even try to teach a child *not* to be empathetic. I am going to argue that those would be ways to fail as the child's parent. Empathy is one form of moral appreciation that parents have an obligation to ensure that their children develop, to some degree. I believe that at least two other forms of moral appreciation are in this same category. Since the argument is the same for all three, I will postpone giving it until all three are described.

The second of them is a sense of fairness, at the heart of which is a sense that *reasons* are sometimes required if there are to be differences in how we fare. This idea is inseparable from some rudimentary sense of what would be a reason we should fare differently, and of when it would be unfair if there *were* no reason for the difference. Those are deep matters, obviously, and one's grasp of them can be more or less sophisticated. As Michael Pritchard observes:

Most adults would readily acknowledge that fairness is not just one thing. It could be treating equals equally, not discriminating against others, providing equal opportunities, providing people fair compensation for their services, avoiding biased judgment, considering all sides of an issue, taking turns, returning favors, sharing responsibilities and burdens. The list could go on.[7]

For the most part, what Pritchard is listing are occasions on which there ought to be reasons if people are to be treated differently, together with some hints as to what might be such a reason (e.g., what "their services" had been, what previous favors they had done you, whether it was time for them to have a turn with something).

One of the points Pritchard makes is that little children have nowhere near so thorough a grasp of all this as we expect adults to have. On the other hand, many parents will recognize "It's not *fair*!" as a complaint that children make early and often, especially if they have siblings: it's not fair that I have to go to bed and she gets to stay up; it's not fair that I have to carry out the trash; it's not fair that he gets to watch his favorite TV programs and I don't get to watch mine; and so on. Any difference in treatment can bring this complaint from one of the children who is treated differently, or even from both. The complaint always calls for reasons justifying the difference, and it certainly could be the first manifestation of a sense of fairness.

However, as long as the child demands only reasons why she herself isn't faring better, it is also conceivable that she is only using the language of fairness to complain about not getting what she wants. That is, it could be that what bothers her is not the rather abstract fact that someone (who only happens to be her) is being treated less favorably without sufficient reason, but the fact that she is going without something she wants to have. So we might doubt that there is any sense of fairness in play here, as opposed to simple self-interest or self-interest mixed with envy.

Children do also come to complain on behalf of others, however, and they also sometimes limit their own behavior out of what seems to be a sense that they should be fair. Not that this sense is there from the start, as Damon observes: "Fighting over toys begins as soon as children play with other children...in toddler play groups, struggles over toys are the most frequent type of encounter."[8] However,

> ...by the end of infancy, the child begins to hold an *expectation* that sharing will occur in some circumstances. This expectation is most apparent when children take turns while playing with an object. When in control of the object, a child in her second year will often spontaneously offer another child (or a parent) a turn. When not in control of the object, the same child will wait for, and eventually demand, her own turn. The same behavior can be observed with food, particularly if the food is attractive and divisible.[9]

Even here, though, the experimenters do not take the children to be motivated by an abstract belief that there is no good reason why just *one* person should have the good thing and hence it ought to be shared:

> [M]ost turn-taking and "dividing up" between children in the first three years of life is playful, done purely out of enjoyment...it appears that very young children

view sharing as a voluntary and irregular part of social life, unless of course it is demanded by an authority figure who happens to be present. Other acts of sharing may be imitative, strictly in emulation of adults and older siblings. In none of these cases does there appear to be an inner norm or ethic that justifies sharing on its own behalf.[10]

If a sense of fairness is an inner norm of this kind, then, we are still speaking of a precursor to it. Next step: a number of studies "have found four-year-olds already in possession of active, flourishing conceptions of fairness. Most children at this age have firmly internalized the standard of sharing. They know that they have an obligation to share at least some part of their possessions with others on occasion."[11] But their reasons for believing so vary considerably, it turns out. Some of the children in the studies appear to share out of empathy for those who would be left out, some because sharing is more fun than being continually pestered for a turn, and some because they believe that sharing when you have the toy or the food can pay off later when someone else has it.[12] As Damon observes, this is still only a mix of empathy and pragmatism about how best to serve one's own interests, rather than an appreciation of fairness per se. It's not until "the beginning of the school years [that] children begin to express more genuinely objective notions of fairness with some regularity. These further notions include basic categories of justice that have been used throughout human history to distribute goods and to resolve conflicts. Among these ancient categories are the principles of *equality, merit*, and *benevolence*."[13]

Taken together, this is a process of learning that *reasons* are required, where the distribution of good things is concerned, and then of refining and changing one's sense of what counts as a reason. There develops what I am calling a sense of fairness, beginning, as with empathy, with what seem better conceived as precursors to that. Again as with empathy, the opportunity to help a child develop a sense of fairness comes earlier than we might have thought, and without the right encouragement her sense of this might remain very rudimentary.[14]

Consider next a third form of moral appreciation: a sense of responsibility for what one does. This is more than just the realization that you will be judged and evaluated on the basis of your contributions to what happens in the world. That others will judge you is one important fact about the larger world, but to know it is not yet to feel responsible for what you do. Indeed, someone who knew only that others would hold him responsible for what he did might find their behavior rather strange, just as the thirteen-year-old psychopath found it strange for others to have empathy for another person's pain. He would be detached from this aspect of his behavior himself, whereas if he had a sense of responsibility for it, he too would take it as reflecting on him. Shame, guilt, and pride are all ways of doing that, as is embarrassment. Those would be absent in someone who lacked a sense of responsibility for what he did.

Shame, pride, guilt, and embarrassment might sound like reactions to what one had already done, but each has its analogue prior to action. That is, we can regard what we *might* do as shameful, or as something of which to be proud, and so on. Indeed, the fact that we regard actions of a certain sort as shameful can mean they don't even occur to us as alternatives. Finally: part of taking in what you do as shameful, a source of pride, and so on, is taking it to call for certain reactions from others. It isn't just that you realize others will in fact react in these ways: you take it that they should.

Just as with empathy and a sense of fairness, we start developing this sense of responsibility quite early in life. Damon claims that "[T]he child's first guilt experience occurs around the end of the first year."[15] As one might expect, these first experiences often involve confusions: "In Carolyn Zahn-Waxler's studies, toddlers have been observed apologizing to upset mothers and siblings in situations where the toddlers had done nothing wrong."[16] As with empathy and the sense of fairness, no one thinks that one-year-olds have anything like the sophisticated sense of responsibility that we hope to find in an adult, or even in an older child. Again as with empathy and the sense of fairness, for my purposes these need only be early precursors, from which a sense of responsibility might develop and be refined in a variety of ways, given proper encouragement. My contention is that parents have an obligation to ensure that their children do develop all three forms of moral appreciation, beyond the most rudimentary levels.

The argument for that conclusion rests on two premises. The first is that one obligation of parenthood is to equip the child to live in society with others. Perhaps this premise requires little defense, given that it is parenthood as a social institution that is of interest, not parenthood in the biological sense. Of course, the social institution of parenthood does have different forms in different societies, to some extent. However, all forms of parenthood specify particular adults who are to have special responsibilities for particular children, and these responsibilities always include equipping the child to live in society with others. Adults who are not responsible for civilizing the child even to that extent might be the child's keepers, or her cooks, or strangers to her altogether, but to call them her *parents* would be to use the wrong term, it seems to me.

The second premise on which my argument rests is that empathy, a sense of fairness, and a sense of responsibility for one's actions are minimal equipment for living in society with others. There may also be other minimal equipment that I have overlooked; if so, parents have an obligation to ensure that their children develop it as well. Whatever the minimal equipment is, a person who does not have it cannot live in society with others. My own claim is that this means parents must try to ensure that their child is equipped with a certain capacity for empathy, sense of fairness, and sense of personal responsibility.

The defense of this second premise has to rely on a conception of what it is to live in society with others. I take this to involve interacting with these others in ways that take them to be more than simply features of the landscape along with whatever trees, stoplights, and trash baskets one might encounter with equal regularity. Someone for whom other people are only physical objects might live in proximity to them but would not live in society with them. I also take the interactions essential to living in society with others to go beyond making simple use of them, as one might make simple use of a stoplight or a trash basket. Someone for whom other people were only resources for simple use might live as a marauder among them, taking whatever he could, but to live in society with them involves more complicated forms of give and take. Finally, this give and take is with *other persons*, who therefore have some of the same moral claims one has oneself: they have whichever claims we have *as persons*, that is. No one can live in society with them unless he is equipped to think of them in that way, and all societies have rules requiring this attitude.

This section began with a passage describing a thirteen-year-old mugger who took the old and infirm as ideal prey. Obviously, he did not live in society with those people in the way I have been describing. What's more, his genuine puzzlement when asked about the pain he had caused one of them—"What do I care? I'm not her."—suggests that he was not equipped to do so. He seems to have been what we commonly call a psychopath: someone to whom the suffering of others is of no interest in itself, as a motivation not to act in certain ways. He had no sense of what his victims were suffering at his hands. He lacked any ability to appreciate it in a way one must if one is to advance beyond *marauder* and live in any civilized commerce with others.

It might not be within a parent's power to prevent his or her child from being a psychopath. That condition could be in the wiring, so to speak, in a way no one can correct, or at least a way no parent can correct through moral education. If it is something parents can prevent, though, they surely have an obligation to do so. When it is possible to do so, parents have a responsibility to ensure that their children develop some capacity for empathy—and doing so ordinarily is within the parent's power, fortunately. Parents must also nourish this capacity to some stage of development beyond the minimal, or they still will not have equipped their children to live in society with others. Here is Damon, again:

> Even in hardhearted delinquents may flicker a glimmer of empathy from time to time. The problem is that it is only occasionally felt; and, when felt, inappropriately expressed. One psychologist who has studied this problem writes, "Empathy is available in most offenders but is not readily elicited and tends to be either an isolated impulse or a mawkish sentiment. In either case, the empathy is superficial and erratic; when it lingers it is readily suppressed by self-centered motives or aggressive impulses."[17]

The bare ability to feel for some others from time to time isn't enough to enable a person to live among other people. Such feelings need to have potency in the competition against other feelings and desires, or they might as well be absent altogether. They must also attach with some breadth, as opposed to being felt only for one's loved ones or close comrades, for example. The larger populace is entitled to a capacity to live in society with that larger populace, rather than just in society with some subgroup—one's fellow predators, for example. Nothing precise can be said about the strength or breadth the capacity for empathy must have if it is to prevail sufficiently regularly for us to count this as a life *with* one's fellow humans. A parent's obligation in this regard is similarly imprecise then. It remains an obligation, I would maintain, despite the difficulty in telling whether one has done enough to carry it out.

There is a similar obligation to ensure that one's child has a sense of fairness—again, developed somewhere beyond its most rudimentary form. That is so because the members of any continuing collection of persons fare differently from each other, as the child learns very soon. If these people live in society with one another, then there is an order to some of what happens among them, defined by the society's rules. That social order would be missing if there were never any need for a reason why some of them should fare differently than another. Changes would simply occur, according to whoever had the power to bring them about and the wish to do so. In contrast, to live in a society is to live where power is sometimes restrained, and where a different basis for distribution sometimes suffices—one that puts the local social rules into effect.

No one could participate in this life unless she were able to appreciate that power did not always entitle a person to determine the distribution of goods. She would need to appreciate that reasons are sometimes needed instead, if people are to fare differently, and she would need to have some grasp of what might count as a reason. That is what I earlier called a sense of fairness. It must be present, in anyone who is to live in society with others. Like empathy, it must also be sufficiently developed to compete against the countermotivations just to take whatever one wants.

The third element in my list is a sense of responsibility for what one does. As was noted, it is in the nature of societies to have rules—including rules that take individuals to be responsible for some of what they do. No one could participate in the life of this society who regarded what he did as beyond the purview of judgment by others and, indeed, who formed no judgments of it himself. He might be present among these people for a time, until they found him intolerable, but that would be as far as it went. Since he would have no sense of his behavior as rightly falling under rules, he would lack something essential to the rule-governed form of life that constitutes a society.

If a sense of responsibility, a sense of fairness, and the capacity for empathy are indeed essential if one is to participate in social life, it makes sense to say that parents also owe it to the children themselves to ensure that they develop these qualities. On some views our nature is to be social creatures, whose lives are not fully human unless they are lived in society with others. If so, our parents owe us the wherewithal to do that. They also owe us this even if it is not in our nature to be social, because the fact is that almost all of us do live in societies. To deny us what we would need in order to do so would decide for us that we were to be hermits of some kind, and that would be to settle our future too completely. Insofar as parents have an obligation to their children to provide them a moral education, then, they owe the children at least this ability to live in society.

The obligation is also one parents owe to the larger society. As was noted earlier, it is not plausible to say parents owe this larger society an effort to teach their children whatever moral beliefs they hold themselves, however groundless and however destructive of life with others those beliefs might be. It does seem plausible, however, to say that they owe the larger society children who have whatever is minimally required for life in society with others. That is, the parents owe those among whom the child lives someone who can live in society with them, as opposed to someone who has learned only how to prey upon them or who can only be prey for others.

Do parents owe nothing more than that, though? Suppose someone's child grew up to be no more than minimally decent: to have nothing more by way of empathy, the sense of fairness, and the sense of responsibility than was necessary to live in society, with no virtues of any other kind. That ought to be a disappointment to her parents, surely. In addition, the rest of us might well regard it as a way in which they had failed as parents, about as badly as a parent can. It might not be a failure for which the parents were necessarily to blame. There could be reasons why it wasn't their fault that their child turned out no better than this. Still, it seems as though they would *need* an excuse—as though they should have done better in raising their child.

If so, the arguments in this section understate a parent's obligation. It isn't enough just to ensure that one's children are minimally decent human beings, fit for society with others. The next section argues for two further obligations parents have where the moral education of their children is concerned.

2.

William Galston reports that John Stuart Mill's views about education included the following:

> The state has a legitimate interest in enforcing parental responsibility, both to enhance social utility and to create human beings in the "maturity of their faculties" who are "capable of being improved by free and equal discussion."[18]

This appears to say that parents have a responsibility to the larger society to ensure that their children do come to have this capacity to be "improved by free and equal discussion." That is an important capacity, but it isn't obviously a condition of being fit to be in society with others at all, unlike a sense of responsibility for what one does and the ability to see what happens to others as relevant to how one should act. No doubt a person who lacked the capacity and could not profit by engaging in discussion with others would be considerably less than a leading light, and he or she would be detached from the others in a certain way. However, that isn't the same as being incapable of civilized commerce—it seems only to limit the forms that interactions with others could take. So if the larger society is entitled to adults of this different kind, the reason won't be simply that it is entitled to people who can live in society with others.

Perhaps the new contention would be that societies have a right to a kind of participation that requires openness to discussion, or that societies have a right to *originality* in their members' behavior. An argument for those premises would take us deeper into political theory than I can go, however. Recall instead that although parents do owe it to their society to give their children a proper moral education, they also owe this to the children themselves. I think that it is in this aspect that we are to find an obligation to make the child someone who is "capable of being improved by free and equal discussion." That is, parents owe the cultivation of this capacity to the child himself or herself, regardless whether they also owe this to the larger society.

One reason to say so is that parents have an obligation to their children to help them become adults who can be reasonably happy with their lives. An adult who was cut off from all improvement by discussion with others would be terribly alone. In addition, there are simply limits to how well any of us can do with life's problems on our own. We are right to think that the self-sufficient frontiersman had a hard life, and the lives we would have in modern times would be very hard too if no one could show us anything. No doubt there are special personality types who could be happy even so—think here of a survivalist who trusts no one. What follows, though, is that a parent could leave his child ill-equipped to profit from discussion with others only if he also ensured that she had the particular qualities that could make her happy as a loner. That is too much control for a parent to have over what kind of person a child becomes and the kind of life she has, if the arguments in the preceding chapter are correct.

A parent who didn't equip her child to learn from discussion with others would also have failed to help her become someone who can act with the autonomy that calls for respect. That is a kind of growing up, as opposed to remaining just as others have made you in your youth, and an inability to profit from discussion with others would greatly impair your chances of doing so. This inability to learn from others might derive from too great a need of certainties to allow one's current view of anything to be mistaken. Or it might derive from a supreme arrogance that dismisses the possibility that others could have anything to offer. Or such a person might be a kind of drone, who accepted the direction of certain others without question and took "free and equal discussion" to be both overweening and a path to error. This last is the proper attitude toward the Koran, on some views: its meaning is to be revealed by the learned, not worked out by the ordinary believer.[19] Some have the same attitude toward the Bible. But we are imagining someone who is incapable of improvement through free and equal discussion of *any* matter, not just of any matter he took to be theological This sort of person would take herself to need direction in all things, from how to drive a nail to how to raise a crop to how to treat other human beings. None of these personality types is conducive to becoming a person of one's own. Here's why.

One way of becoming someone of your own making is to change who you are. None of the kinds of people we have been picturing would do this. The one who is threatened by any challenge to the way things already are certainly wouldn't change. Nor would the one who was supremely arrogant—why change if you are already perfect? Nor would the one who was a drone in all matters.

A second way to become a person of your own is to recognize that you are a certain way and accept that fact, though you see it as something you could change if you wished. I doubt that the person whose need for certainties is too great to allow him to entertain alternatives would want to think about himself at all. I doubt that the one who needed direction in all things would want to think *for* himself about what he was like, since he would regard this subject too as one in which he needed the help of experts. The one who is too arrogant for conversation with others might seem a better candidate for someone who is self-constructed in this way: someone who has a sense of what he is like, though not necessarily an accurate one, and is content with that picture. Actually this analysis might give the supremely arrogant too much credit, but in any case supreme arrogance is a recipe for unhappiness. So, even if it were a way of being a person of one's own, to equip a child with that quality would be to fail her in another way.

In sum, parents have an obligation *to their children* to raise them to be "capable of being improved by free and equal discussion," regardless whether they also owe this endeavor to the larger society. It comes with their obligation to help their children to become persons of their own who are equipped to be reasonably happy with their lives, and with their obligation to help their children become persons of their own. We ought also to adopt a point of Jeffrey Blustein's:

> If Aristotle is right that the happy man needs friends (*Nicomachean Ethics*, 1169b3–1170b19), then parents ought to give their children the kind of upbringing that is conducive to strong personal attachments later in life. Contrary to what Rousseau appears to believe, friendship is not incompatible with autonomy, and the capacity for friendship should perhaps be included among the objectives of parenting.[20]

It is plausible to say that someone who is incapable of having friends will not have a life with which she is reasonably happy, or at least that someone who could be happy with such a life would have to have been specially constructed for it, to a degree that gives the parent too much control over who she is. If so, the moral education of a child ought also to cultivate the capacity to have friends.

Admittedly, what is required to be someone's friend depends to some extent on the person whose friend you want to be. We are speaking of being capable of friendship with *anyone*, though, and there do seem to be some points to be made about that capacity, deriving from the nature of friendship as such. To be a friend requires the ability to value someone else so that what happens to that person becomes important to you in itself. It also requires loyalty and a capacity both to trust and to be worthy of being trusted. All of these would be traits that parents have an obligation to cultivate in their children under the heading of equipping the child to become someone who is reasonably happy with his or her life.

3.

The next question is whether parents have a further obligation to ensure that their children have some particular set of positive virtues, beyond the ones already mentioned. Consider first a contention that parents owe this commitment to the state or to the larger society.

That could be true only if societies were entitled to virtue in their citizens, and it isn't obvious that they are. If societies are not entitled to that, clearly they cannot have a right to have parents ensure that their children fill the bill. One problem with the view that the larger society *is* entitled to have us be good people is that it gives the society a legitimate basis for arriving, politically, at a conception of what are considered virtues in a person, and for trying to make us people of these kinds. That scenario sounds as if it could threaten our freedom of choice. There is no similar problem if the requirement is only that we have the qualities necessary to live in society with others and that equip us both to be persons of our own and to be reasonably happy with our lives, since it is then left to the individual what more particular form all of this takes.

Alternatively, the contention could be that parents owe it not to the larger society but to the children themselves to provide them with some further set of moral virtues. This would be a preliminary set, as it were, which the child might either discard upon becoming an adult or choose to retain. In response, it has to be granted that the child who has just become an adult will inevitably be someone in particular, with some set of virtues and vices. The trouble is that to regard that result as the parents' doing and (where the virtues are concerned) also their obligation understates the child's own role in his early moral education. The child who has just become an adult isn't his parents' product, if things have gone as they should, but someone he himself has helped to produce. The new adult is partly his doing as well as theirs.

A child has obligations of his own where his moral education is concerned. One is to cooperate—a point noted earlier in chapter 5, "The Autonomy of Children." His parents have responsibilities where his moral education is concerned, and we all have an obligation not to prevent others from carrying out their responsibilities—something true of children as well as adults. So one way in which the child is to participate is by refraining from defeating his parents' effort to make him fit for society with others, capable of learning from free and open discussion, and capable of friendship.

His parents have a further obligation to help him become a person of his own rather than remaining too much their creature. To cooperate with *that* process is to take an active role oneself, obviously. Just as cooperating with someone's effort to help you become a musician requires your trying to become one, cooperating with someone's effort to help you become a person whose moral qualities are his own doing requires your trying to make those qualities your own. Neither need take exactly the form the other person had in mind, but both would have to take some specific form. You couldn't just be a musician—you would have to play the guitar or the piano or the violin or whatever. Equally, you couldn't just be a person of your own without becoming one that had this set of qualities, or that one, or another one.

What this means is that the child must play a considerable role in her own moral education, in order not to defeat her parents' effort to carry out their own obligations in the matter. It has to be a joint undertaking, in which the child is not the passive recipient of shaping by adults but an active party who determines what she learns and what she does not and bears some responsibility for this.

Children make their way through many possible sources of moral lessons, encountering many examples of how to behave, many conceptions of proper behavior imposed in the many small societies through which they travel, and many forms of treatment to which they are subjected themselves. Ordinarily, there is little in all of these influences that endorses behavior that is not even minimally decent. On the other hand, there are genuine constituencies for competing ways of being *better* than minimally decent. To require that any of these sources of moral education succeed in making the child become a person of their preferred kind would certainly be very demanding, even for a source as potentially central to the child's life as her parents. So, an obligation to make the child become the kind of good person you hoped for would be difficult, even unreasonable, to fulfill.

Still, the most central objection isn't that this goal would be hard to accomplish. The more important points are that it misplaces responsibility and undercuts the parent's obligation to help the child become someone of her own. It is up to the child to utilize the sources of moral education in her life. assuming that she is equipped to live in society with others, capable of friendship, andcapable of learning from others. She has a right to determine what more she becomes in addition, and she also has an obligation to do so.

It would not follow that children are responsible for every mistake they make in these choices, of course. It never follows from being an agent that there can be no excuse for acting badly. Nor would it follow that no one must help a child form her moral character beyond the minimum, or even that no one could have an obligation to do so. It never follows from a project being yours that no one must help you, or that no one could have any obligation to help you, and the same is true here. What *does* follow is that children can be responsible for a great deal, both when they are still within the care of their parents and when they no longer are. At both stages of life a child can be responsible for being the kind of person she is, and for the actions that are expressions of her moral character as well as for the actions that are not.

None of these statements can be true, if a child's character is never her doing but always the product of shaping by many forces, principally her parents. Then what she was, and the behavior enacting what she was, would be their responsibility as well. It might be urged that this is true only when she is a *child*, that once she becomes an adult she is responsible for the repair of any errors others have made and for any behavior that manifests those errors. However, one problem with this notion is that it doesn't allow us to hold children morally responsible for anything they do as children, since they are taken to be entirely their parents' creatures at this stage of life. Surely children are sometimes responsible for what they do. In addition, the transformation occurring when the child reaches adulthood is fairly magical, if it is taken to be instantaneous. Until the point of transition children are but children and are the innocent product of others; later they are adults and responsible for who they are, and there is no apparent reason for the change. It is surely better to think of children as gradually becoming agents while they are still children, with some of their agency spent on what sorts of people they are, and being responsible for this and other actions except when they have excuses for having done badly.

4.

The remaining question is exactly what do these obligations require a parent to do. Obviously, they don't specify a particular action to be carried out at a specific time. A moral education is provided over the extended period during which the child is under the parent's care. But what is the parent actually to *do*? The actions required are bound to change during those years, for several reasons.

Most obviously, the children themselves undergo changes during this time, in the natural process of maturation. They begin life unable even to distinguish themselves from others and without any concept of causality. They emerge from this (surely premoral) stage more quickly than we might ordinarily think, but what happens to them before they do has obvious bearing on what will later be their moral education. Nor are they ready immediately for all the abstractions of moral thought as soon as they are ready for any of them, of course. So the lessons one might seek to teach vary with the child's cognitive development, as does the best way to teach those lessons.

Another change over time is in the other sources from which the child might learn ways of behaving. Different people play various roles in her life at different stages of it. They present new examples of how to act and new treatment at the hands of others. There are also changes in the small societies in which the child moves, presenting new sets of moral rules. Helping her make sense of all this variety is part of a parent's role. Since the variety changes, there are also differences in what is required of the parents if they are to do so.

The child's own relationships with other people change as well, bringing new moral issues for him to deal with. What he had to deal with at one time involved taking turns and being careful not to hurt people physically. Those issues still hold, but now there are also questions about what it means to be someone's *friend*, for example. Since the questions change, what a parent would do to provide an education about such questions also changes.

Equally important, the child is developing a morality of her own as she has experiences and makes whatever she does of them. That growth is a work in progress, and there are bound to be substantial differences in it over time. At the very least, it can become inappropriate to act as if she were still at step one, when the moral idea the parent wants to convey would have been news to her. Her development also makes her a different person to deal with, since she continues to bring a different framework to bear on what she encounters. Therefore what would be needed in order to teach her a particular idea might be quite different than it would have been earlier.

Finally, it is important to return to the fact that the purpose of a moral education is to help the child develop moral character of her own. To have your own moral character is, in part, to be disposed to act for reasons related to the kind of action you would be taking, rather than simply because of what is authorized or forbidden by another person. So the aim of a moral education is for the child to become someone who no longer relies completely on another person. We don't want her to be unable to make judgments without her parents' advice, and we don't want her to revise the judgments she makes as readily if her parents disagree: that is all part of her deciding on the merits of the alternatives themselves. Unless those changes occur, she remains their creature, rather than becoming her own. Therefore what parents do in providing for the moral education of their children must change over time, or it will cease to serve its purpose. In addition, the changes should make the parents less central to the process than they once were and should reflect the differences noted in the child's cognitive development, history of past efforts at moral education, and moral character thus far.

So much for differences; now for some similarities. At each stage, only some of what parents must do in order to carry out their obligations to impart moral lessons is overtly instructional. For example, generally speaking when parents permit their children to act in certain ways with regard to others, they don't do so *in order* to teach the child something about how to treat people. Nevertheless, clearly this tacit consent provides an opportunity for the child to learn about how to act. Similarly, if games were always played with one's children in order to teach them something about fair play, empathy, and respect for others, life would be awfully earnest. There would be no *play*. But clearly, play does provide ideas about such things, even when that is not the purpose of the players.

There are other respects in which moral education is inadvertent. Parents provide examples of how to behave in how they treat the child himself, in how they treat other members of the family and how they react to the behavior of others in the family, in how they act toward people outside the family, and in how they treat rules of various kinds. I do not want to suggest that children are always learning moral lessons from these experiences, any more than I wanted to suggest that parents always mean to teach such lessons. I do want to suggest that a child's life with his or her parents is very rich in opportunities to do exactly that, and that the somewhat unpredictable use children make of these opportunities is the heart of their moral education.

It follows that our contributions to the moral education of our children are bound to be more or less ambiguous, and more or less inconsistent. For the child to make something of them is a little like making something of a long and complicated piece of music. In both cases patterns and themes have to be found among a great deal of sound, including themes that begin simply but gain nuance in the context of new elements. Perhaps with both music and a continuing moral example there are always several ways to take what is there. Still, it is also possible for some interpretations to be more strained than others, and it is possible to be careful about what it would be relatively natural to find in what one does. This caution would hold both for composers and for parents, who would be careful partly by checking how the work is going, from time to time, and would be much better at the project the better they understood the ear of those who were listening.

In part, what all of this suggests that parents must do is that they must achieve some degree of consistency in the moral example they set, though it acknowledges that being consistent across very different sets of circumstances is a richer idea than it might sound. Parents play the role of a continuing paradigm for the child, which the child consults both as an example and for clarification of issues in how to act. The clearer this paradigm is, the more naturally it can be taken in one way rather than in another. The ways in which the child consults the parent's paradigm change over time, as do the alternative paradigms available to him. That change is to be hoped for, since it helps in the development of a moral character of the child's own.

"Paradigm" is a term of academic discourse, however, and it has at least one misleading implication. In other contexts the paradigm itself is passive, consulted by others or not, but taking no active part in what they do. Not so with parents as paradigms. Parents have an obligation to monitor what sort of person their child is becoming, providing encouragement, and making efforts to correct what they see as mistakes the child is making. That activity itself is part of the paradigm they provide. It is one example of how important a person's loved ones should be relative to other concerns, and it is also an example of balancing concern for someone's autonomy and privacy against concern for her general well-being. (What the child makes of the example is not within the parent's control, of course, and the implication is not that parents are to scrutinize their every move for its potential moral messages. Doing that would make life as a parent fairly intolerable, and the messages it would convey to the child are far from ideal.)

Presumably one of the ways in which moral education should change over time is in the amount of explicit instruction the parents offer in advance rather than waiting until there are errors to be corrected. As time passes there should be more trust that the child will get things right on his own, on the basis of what he has already learned, and more trust that he *has* gotten them right. That increasing trust would also be part of allowing him to develop his own moral character rather than keeping him under one's direction (with the restriction, again, that children are not free to develop a character that leaves them unfit to live in society with others).

The foregoing, even if correct, cannot be a complete description of what parents are to do, however. They are to be an active paradigm in this way, but an active paradigm of what? Not, presumably, of abuse for anyone weaker than oneself and dishonesty whenever it suits, for instance. Certainly those are examples a parent could set, in the way she treated her children and others. They could even constitute the parent's moral code, conscientiously conveyed to her children as the proper way of life. She would convey her contempt for those who think differently about how we should treat each other, including her own children if they should complain about being bullied or being lied to. On her view, what they were complaining about would be the right way to treat anyone who couldn't prevent it, and if her own children couldn't prevent it then it would be what they had coming to them. On the other hand, she would be visibly impressed when they did the bullying and lying themselves, at least when they didn't try to make her their victim. So she would be an active paradigm of a certain way of life—but certainly she ought not to count as someone who does what she ought to do for the moral education of her children. We need to say something about the content of the paradigm that parents have an obligation to present.

The woman we are imagining seems to be raising marauders rather than people who live in society with others, and it was argued earlier that parents are obligated to ensure that their children are capable of doing that. Perhaps we can go further and hold that this positive behavior is the only active paradigm parents need to present: that is, that their only obligation is to display and encourage the levels of empathy, sense of fairness, and sense of personal responsibility that are needed to enable one to live in society with others. Nothing more along those lines need be a feature of their paradigm, and no virtues of other kinds need to be either.

This view cannot be right, for two reasons. One is that to be an active paradigm of *any* way of life requires that one take a greater interest in the person whom one serves as a paradigm than would express only minimal decency on one's part. To be an active paradigm for someone requires paying attention to how that person is doing in life, and it evinces a considerable sense of personal responsibility for the results of one's own actions. The qualities this behavior displays go beyond the ones needed to live in society with others *at all*. So, the child is necessarily presented with a richer paradigm and thereby encouraged to be more than minimally decent himself, insofar as he is presented with an active paradigm at all.

Moreover, it is part of the concept of parenthood that our children are to be our special concern. They are to be of more concern to us than they are to others, that is. Now, it might be that even those others ought to treat a child with more than minimal decency: that they ought to have more compassion for her than a person actually needs in order to live with others, for example, just because she is a child. If so, this is certainly also true of her parents, whose concern for her is supposed to be still greater. Alternatively, those who are not her parents might owe the child nothing more than minimal decency. It will still follow that her parents owe her more than that, since parents are supposed to have a greater concern for their children than others must have. Either way, the paradigm we present in our treatment of our own children must display more substantial virtues than the ones constituting minimal decency.

It remains true that parents have some latitude in which such virtues they want to exemplify and cultivate in their child. They are free to try to teach their children to be scrupulous about rules *or* fiercely loyal to individuals, to be forgiving and generous-minded toward those who wrong them *or* to be demanding of others but equally demanding of themselves, and so on. There are competing ways in which to be a good person, and parents are free to take any of these for the active paradigm they present to their children. It is also very clear that their children might not become exactly the kind of people their parents presented as paradigms. Neither the parents nor the larger society have a right that the children do so. The parents need to succeed only in ensuring that their children become people who can live in society with others, that they are on their way toward being persons of their own and equipped to continue, that they are capable of friendship, and that they can profit from free discussion with others. If the parents have accomplished that, and have also presented an active paradigm of some more specific form of better moral character, then they have done what they are obligated to do where the moral education of their children is concerned.

A further intuition is that the moral education of one's child is unlike her education in mathematics of her training in athletics or any of a number of other matters, in that her moral education is something a parent cannot delegate to others. Parents have to do this themselves; to have someone else "teach their child right from wrong" is to cede a matter that is too central to being a parent. That intuition fits well enough with the idea that parents do their moral educating by being an active paradigm of how to live. Being one requires being a substantial presence in the child's life; delegating the job to someone else would mean being a parent from a distance. How remote one could be and still be a parent to one's child is certainly not precise, but there does seem to be something to the idea of being a parent "in name only." Such a person has either ignored the responsibilities of parenthood or—in this case—abdicated something central to them. I am claiming that the moral education of one's child is central in that way, unlike a great deal else. Leaving it to others disconnects parent and child so substantially that the relationship becomes one of a different kind.

That contention might be appealing enough for some cases, but it also invites examples of the following kind. Suppose a family emigrates to a large city in a new country. They live in an ethnic neighborhood with others from their homeland but remain aware that the dominant culture in their new country is very different from their own. They also see its influence on other children in the neighborhood, and what they see troubles them greatly. They are worried about the kind of people they fear their children will become. In their optimistic moments, they think they will be able to succeed where other parents in the community have failed, but eventually they become convinced that this is wishful thinking. In their view, where they live is just a very bad place for children to grow up, and if their own children are to become good people, they will have to grow up somewhere else. Ideally, this place would be the old country, but there are reasons why the parents don't want to go back there. Their solution, in the end, is to send the children home to be raised by their grandparents, where the parents believe they are much more likely to turn out as the parents deeply believe they should.[21]

One question is whether this amounts to abdicating the role of parents to their child by delegating the child's moral education to others. I think it certainly could, if the parents truly did leave the moral education of their children to the grandparents. Alternatively, the parents could retain a substantial role in it themselves by visiting often and for extended periods, using computers to maintain a steady "virtual" presence, and using telephones and letters to be present in other ways. In those ways they could continue to serve as an active moral paradigm for their child despite the great decrease in physical contact. But clearly what happened could also fall short of this scenario. If it did, I would say the parents were no longer serving as parents to their children.

In some versions of the story the parents would remain connected with their children in lesser ways that would make this a family of a different kind. In other versions the children would have moved into a family of which the parents were not a part. It's important to say that in neither case does it follow automatically that the parents have done something of which we should disapprove, any more than we should automatically think so when a parent gives a child up for adoption. It isn't as though they have simply neglected their responsibility for the child they brought into the world. Rather, they have come to doubt that they can carry it out in their present circumstances, they have acted at least primarily out of concern for their children, and they have tried to act in the children's interests. That's quite different from leaving a child's moral education to no one while you attend to matters of greater interest to you.

Still, the decision can also be a mistake morally, just as a decision to allow your child to be adopted can be. In both cases, the costs to the child can be considerable, given the points made by Goldstein, Solnit, Goldstein, and Freud about how difficult it is for children to be sent to live with others and thereby separated from those to whom they have developed the special psychological attachment children have to their parents.[22] In this case, the separation wouldn't occur because her "psychological parents" had no right to that position and her grandparents did, unlike the cases in which children were taken from people who shouldn't have become their psychological parents and returned to biological parents who hadn't freely given them up. Instead, the separation would occur because her parents thought it best—so their reasons to think it best would have to be very good reasons indeed. I believe they could be good enough, and also that they could fall short of being good enough, just as the reasons for giving a child up for adoption could make this the right thing to do or the wrong one.

I have concentrated here on what parents have an obligation to provide by way of the moral education of their children, and (a bit) on how they are to provide it. The next chapter completes the discussion of moral education by focusing on bad behavior—up to and including behavior of a kind the state would ordinarily treat as criminal. One question is this: when someone acts badly, should it matter that this person is a child rather than an adult? Another: if age should matter, what difference should it make in how we respond to the bad behavior, and why should it make that difference?

8

Bad Behavior

> . . . the knowledge that an agent is a child rather than an adult often prompts us to modify our "reactive attitudes" toward her. An adult who laughs at your bald spot is to be resented; a child who does the same is to be disciplined—at least insofar as you decide to treat her as a child. In this sense, we do not take child action as seriously as adult action, or, rather, we do not take it seriously in the same way.[1]

These contentions are especially plausible if the children who come to mind are rather young. Suppose the one who laughs at your bald spot is about six years old. When she does, you 'round on her' in the same injured way you would if she were an adult, or else you burn with the same resentment. She is only a *child*, we will tell you. What were you thinking?

Make her a teenager, though, and the matter is less clear. Perhaps you should still treat her laughter as that of a mere child, but perhaps you should respond as if she were an adult. Make her behavior less childish, and a new thought occurs: perhaps the right reaction to what adolescents do depends partly on what they've done, so that we should sometimes react as if they were "only children" and sometimes as if they were adults.

Putting adolescents aside, what is it about the *young* child who does wrong that changes things? What more can be said about the changes it makes? If (as Schapiro suggests) we are to take the bad behavior of children just as seriously as we do that of adults but *in a different way*, what is that different way? As for adolescents, are they like young children and their behavior therefore call for a different reaction, either whenever they do wrong or when their wrongs are "childish" in some way? If not, are there other reasons to react differently when an adolescent does wrong than when an adult does, or is it only *young* children whose bad behavior should draw a response of a different kind?

The answers will apply to something at the heart of parenthood, since every parent has to deal with bad behavior from time to time. There will also be implications for the way in which the criminal justice system should respond when a juvenile appears to have broken the law. At least in the United States, the trend is toward "getting tough" on juvenile offenders. In recent years almost every U. S. state has made it easier to try juveniles as adults, and studies show that juveniles who are tried as adults and convicted are sentenced just as severely as an adult would have been.[2] Apparently, the thought is either that a great many juvenile offenders are no longer children in the way that matters, or that even if they are, this fact should be overlooked. Whether either thought is correct is hugely important.

I will explore two lines of thought about the bad behavior of children, then argue for a third.

1.

Someone has laughed at your bald spot, and you are upset. Your friends tell you to calm down, because the person who laughed was only a little girl. It does seem as if that fact should make a great difference in your response—but why? The answer might emerge more readily if we looked closely at the difference her youth is supposed to make. Here is Schapiro on that point: "An adult who laughs at your bald spot is to be resented; a child who does the same is to be disciplined—at least insofar as you decide to treat her as a child."[3]

That opinion sounds right, but while it could certainly be appropriate to resent an adult who laughs at your bald spot, a different reaction could be appropriate instead. You could just dismiss him as a little foolish, not worthy of resentment, because he is not to be taken that seriously. Or, if you saw his laughter as an attempt to curry favor with others at your expense, you might hold him in contempt rather than thinking him a fool; or you might pity him for being inclined to act in this way. Then again, what you felt when he laughed might be disappointment, because you had had reason to expect better of him.

These reactions differ. Pity and disappointment are not dismissive or scornful in the way that resentment and contempt are. They are not "hard feelings" toward this person, but something with a different tone. And, of course, pitying someone is not the same as being disappointed in her, nor is resenting her the same as holding her in contempt. On the other hand, all of these reactions have this is common: they characterize both what the person did in laughing and the person who laughed. They take the laughter to have shown something of what she is like.

For example, to take what someone did as an effort to embarrass you can be part of regarding him as a cruel person. It can also be part of taking him to have it in for you personally, or to have an abiding hostility toward anyone who is like you in some way (male? black? liberal? highly educated?). The rest depends on your attitude toward those with whom you now categorize him. Perhaps you are afraid of them: the cruel, that is, or those who have it in for you personally or for anyone they take to be "your kind." Perhaps instead you think that people like this are to be told off, or that they are to be quietly resented, or that they aren't worth troubling with. These are different ways in which you are now inclined to *go on*, where this person is concerned. The differences are in how you are now inclined to behave toward him, to take what he does, and to react to things that happen to him through other agencies.

The same would be true if you had taken his laughter only to have been thoughtless immaturity. Depending on what you are like yourself, you might regard those who are thoughtlessly immature as fools, or as objects of pity or of contempt, so that you now take up those attitudes toward this man. Of course, these are all what we might call *definite* reactions. We can also react more tentatively or with mixed feelings, uncertain what to make of the laughter or of the person who laughed. But to be made tentative about someone or to have mixed feelings about him also defines a pattern of behavior, the specifics of which (again) depend on the person who has been thrown off balance. Finally, it could be that this man's laughter at your bald spot doesn't change the way in which you have always thought of him, but only confirm it. That reaction too affects how you go on from here, by reinforcing the attitude you already had.

The general point is that to resent someone as cruel or hostile sets up one sort of future between you, to dismiss her as a fool sets up quite another, to regard her as contemptibly weak in betraying you changes things yet again, and so on. The reaction to what she did casts her for one sort of future rather than another. It does so in virtue of what you take her to have shown herself to be like in acting as she did, your broader attitude toward persons of that kind, and the sort of life you wish to have (one in which you "don't let people kick you around" or one that is free of confrontations, or one in which you are a positive influence on others, or . . .).

This means there is considerable individuality in the way we take the bad behavior of others. We should be free to put our personalities and character into play in this way, casting others as we choose where our future with them is concerned. They are at liberty to try to correct any mistakes we make in this reaction, if they wish to. They are also at liberty to reject at least some roles for which we have cast them, as an expression of their own individuality.

There are limits, however. Although we should be free to form our own reactive attitudes toward others, this freedom does not include the liberty to deprive them of anything to which they are actually entitled. You are free to regard me as treacherous if that is how you take behaving in the way you think I did, and so to have little to do with me if that is how you treat the treacherous, even if you have me wrong. You are not free to fire me from my job just on this basis, because I am entitled to retain my job unless you have *good* reasons to let me go, and we've said nothing yet that ensures that you have them.

Consider next another possible limitation: namely, that the object of one of these reactive attitudes must be an adult. The idea would be that only adults are to be resented for what they have done and cast as enemies, or regarded as contemptible and cast accordingly, or viewed as pitiable specimens of the human race and treated that way, and so on. Suppose further that the reason offered is the very point I have been urging, namely, that these reactive attitudes involve an assessment of what this other person is like and will continue to be like, and an associated sense of how one wants to go on where he or she is concerned.

That would have some plausibility, where very young children are concerned. Although a very young child might be putting a certain unpleasant personality into play when she behaves badly, there is an important sense in which this personality is not yet her own, if earlier arguments are correct. Whatever she has along these lines at this point is not yet her doing, or even something of which she is particularly aware. It has been contributed by other sources, and she is yet to recognize it and either accept it or change it. So, if there is someone to resent when *she* laughs at your bald spot, it isn't her: it's her parents, and even they are not to be resented for her every imperfection.

This same reasoning wouldn't apply to older children, who would have become interested in what sort of person they were, and acquired a sense of themselves, and perhaps also made conscious efforts to be someone of one kind rather than of another. Thus, if a child at this later stage of life were to laugh at your bald spot, the personality and character on display could be his own in a way the younger child's is not. Even for the older child, however, this character may be only a *persona* he is trying out. Schapiro regards trying out personalities as the way in which children "work... through the predicament of childhood":

> By engaging in play, children more or less deliberately "try on" selves to be and worlds to be in. This is because the only way a child can "have" a self is by trying one on. It is only by adopting one or another *persona* that children are able to act the part of full agents, to feel what it must be like to speak in their own voices and inhabit their own worlds.[4]

When he or she is engaged in this role, "the action of a child has a provisional status, the status of a rehearsal or an experiment."[5] The experiment is with being a person of a particular kind—as the child conceives it, a kind who would laugh at something like your bald spot. The trouble with the reactions described earlier is that they take the characteristics exhibited to be relatively stable and thus to be a basis for casting this person as someone to have as an enemy, or to regard watchfully, or to avoid at all costs, and so on. That reaction will be a mistake, the claim is, if the child is only trying out the personality.[6]

However, this claim is plausible only for some children doing some wrongs, not for all children regardless of the wrong they are doing. At least by the time of adolescence, some children aren't only trying the personality out, only *playing* at being bad in a particular way: they already are. Their behavior provides just as good a basis for thinking that they are as it would if they were adults, and they are old enough for the bad character to be their doing. If so, we would need a different argument against using their behavior as a basis for casting them for future roles in the way one would with an adult.

The central premise of one such argument is that becoming a good person is not easy, and we should all be permitted both a period of time in which to accomplish it and considerable help in doing so. During this period we have the opportunity to learn a great deal about what it is like for others if we act in various ways, to come to appreciate this information, and to develop powers of concentration and self-restraint with which we certainly did not begin. No one can be this way immediately, any more than we can be artists immediately, with all of the knowledge, appreciation, and control that are part of being an artist. Similarly, we should have time for moral development.

We should also have help with it, the argument would urge, as opposed to being turned loose to become whatever we will. In particular, we should have parents who love us, who take their role in our lives seriously, and who play that role at least reasonably well. A child who does wrong has not had the time to become a good person, since he is still a child. A great many such children have not had the help either, and often it is worse than that. Far too many have been not just ignored but abused, in ways that make becoming a good person that much harder.

The children who are already bad human beings in some way have constructed themselves too quickly, without assistance, and often under adverse conditions. For them to make a bad job of it is no surprise but a confirmation of the premise that this development takes time and requires assistance. Reacting to them in the same way as we would to an adult negates the idea that there should be time to get this right, and often it also holds the child to account for the failures of others to provide him the help he should have had or for their abuse of him. The conclusion is that we ought not to have the reactive attitudes toward any child who does wrong, not because no child can rise above such hardships and be a good person despite them, but because it is unreasonable to require a child to do so. What it requires is too hard to expect a person to do on his or her own, especially when this person is only a child, and it is something that takes time to get right.

Where children are concerned, there is the further worry that to treat them as if they were bad people who are worthy of our contempt and resentment will confirm the child's own sense of himself as exactly that. That attitude is undesirable for many reasons. It is bad for us if he is not a moral person, it is bad for him, and it perpetuates a life he was entitled to have begin very differently.

These are important points, I think, but it is also important to be careful about what they establish. First, even though children certainly should have help in becoming morally sound people and time in which to do so, we cannot be precise about how much time and what kind of help they are entitled to have. So, we can't confidently conclude (for example) that the grace period should extend to all wrongdoers who are younger than eighteen. Second, it is implausible to think that every aspect of moral development requires the same amount of time and the same degree of help. Some expectations might be unreasonable but others not: perhaps the child in question *has* had enough time and enough help not to be a vicious thug with no regard for human life. If so, it also matters what his misdeed was, not just that he is a child. Third, what the argument counsels is that we ought not to treat a child as the bad person he has already become, because if we do we will sustain the unfairness in his early life. But we can't know whether doing this is the worst alternative we have until we know how we are supposed to treat him instead, and what that will be like both for him and for those who are at risk from the person he has become.

What these doubts suggest is that these arguments, like their predecessors, fall short of showing that no child who does wrong should ever be treated as an adult, regardless of the child's age, the wrong he has done, and what it will be like if we treat him as a child instead. Rather, the arguments identify considerations against treating particular children as adults, which are stronger in some cases than in others. They are not always strong enough, in my opinion. I think there are lost children, whom it is better on balance to treat as adults despite the unfairness to them in doing so. However, the case for that conclusion must wait until we are clearer about what it would be to treat them as children: so far we have only Schapiro's passing remark that they are to be disciplined, and there is much more to say.

The case for saying there are lost children must also wait until we see whether there are other compelling reasons for saying that there are none and that every child is to be treated in a way reserved for children rather than a way appropriate for adults. A leading defense of that position is that children are not responsible for what they do in the way that adults are. The next section explores that point of view and argues against it.

2.

We might begin by noting that to say children are not responsible in the same way as adults is not entirely separate from saying they shouldn't be resented when they do wrong. Resenting someone is a way of blaming him for what has happened and thus taking him to be responsible for it. That's why it is inappropriate to resent him, if it turns out that he wasn't responsible for what happened. Perhaps someone else was; then it is she whom you might be entitled to resent. Or perhaps no one was to blame for what happened to you, unfortunate though it was. Then there is no one to resent. You are entitled only to be distressed over your bad fortune, not to hold anyone responsible for it.

This means that if children are not morally responsible for their actions, then it is wrong to resent them when they behave badly. They are entitled to a different reaction, because when it comes to responsibility for wrongdoing, they are only *children*—persons who are not responsible for what they do, that is. It is wrong to resent them, just as it is wrong to resent an adult who is not to blame when things go badly for you. Both are entitled to a different reaction.

That is a coherent argument, but should we say that children are never responsible when they do wrong? Consider again the little girl who laughed at your bald spot. Those who hold the view I've sketched might say this: "Perhaps she had no idea that she was doing anything wrong. Or perhaps she did know that she was misbehaving, but even then she wouldn't be to blame for yielding to the impulse to laugh. She had never seen anything like your careful comb-over with the shiny pink skin peeking through, it struck her as amusing, and she laughed. To respond as if she were an adult is to act as if she knew better, or should have known better, or should have resisted the humor in the situation. None of those propositions is true, because they ask too much of someone who is—after all—only a child."

This reasoning might be fair enough, but it can't be stretched to cover every instance of bad behavior by a child. Children do not remain as innocent as babes until they are no longer young, or as blameless for yielding to their urges. Rather, as they mature, they become responsible for increasingly more of what they do. If they didn't, it would always be just as wrong to punish a child as it is to punish a baby for dropping her rattle, and clearly it is not. That poses a problem, if the conclusion we want to support is that all children who do wrong should be treated differently than adults regardless how old the child is.

So, suppose we abandon the view that children are never responsible for their bad behavior and say instead that they are always less than *fully* responsible for it. Our new idea will be that part of being a child is that you always have one or more of the excuses that reduce a person's blameworthiness for what she has done. A child is someone who either does not fully appreciate the wrong she is doing, given her youth, or acts under pressure from her friends, or is at the mercy of emotions she has not yet learned to control as she should, or something else. So we should never act as if a child were fully to blame but should reserve that response for adults.

This approach echoes the fond presumption of parents who are told that their child has misbehaved and are confident that there must be more to the story. Sometimes there is, and sometimes it is right to think there must be—but neither of these is always true. This point can be overlooked if we idealize full responsibility in a certain way. A child's understanding of what he has done is imperfect. So, if full responsibility requires a perfect understanding of what one has done, it follows that children are never fully responsible and that we are always wrong to act as if they were. But the same would also be true for adults, since they too fall short of perfect understanding. Therefore we would not have the desired distinction between children who do wrong and adults who do, but a way in which they were alike.

It also seems wrong to require perfect understanding for full responsibility: something much thinner should usually suffice. But then there is no reason to think that children cannot have it where a great many forms of misbehavior are concerned. So a contention that they are never fully responsible because they never sufficiently understand what they are doing would turn out to be false.

Similar points can be made about other excuses children might have: about vulnerability to peer pressure and to emotions, for example. Suppose we were to grant the hopeful thought that no child knowingly does wrong except when under pressure from others or under emotional stress. It would not follow that they lacked full responsibility for the wrongs they do, unless full responsibility required complete freedom from these. But *complete* freedom from pressure and emotional stress is hardly typical of adult wrongdoers either. So we would again have failed to find the sweeping difference we had sought between children who do wrong and adults who do.

Moreover, we ought to reject the idea that it is only those who are completely free of peer pressure and emotional stress who are fully responsible for any wrong they do. Instead, whether they are fully responsible should depend on how powerful the peer pressure or emotional stress was, what was done in yielding to them, and what alternatives were available, so that someone who is under *some* pressure or *some* emotional stress might still be fully responsible for some wrongs. But then it might well be that children often do attain the requisite degree of freedom, despite not being perfectly free.

Finally, suppose it were true that children were always less than fully responsible when they did wrong. This fact would not establish that we should respond differently to them than we would to an adult unless adult wrongdoers *were* fully responsible for their wrongdoing and it was that responsibility that called for the different response. Both suppositions are dubious. As to the first, it's clear that many adults are not fully responsible for the wrongs they do, any more than children are. To assume that all adult wrongdoers are simply bad people who are doing as they like is clearly too harsh. So, if we take the key to be full responsibility as opposed to partial, once again we will not have found a sweeping difference between adult wrongdoers and youthful ones. As to the second supposition, suppose the response properly reserved for adults is resentment, as Schapiro suggested. Why should we think that only those who are *fully* responsible are to be resented? To see the problem, imagine someone who yielded to pressure that was impressive enough to diminish his responsibility but that still should have been resisted. It might be appropriate to resent him for yielding: for being too weak to do the right thing. If so, it turns out that we should resent children for something different than we should resent adults for: for caving in under mitigating circumstances, rather than for having done the misdeed. That wasn't the conclusion we were seeking.

As a third version of the responsibility view, consider the idea that children who do wrong are at least *less* responsible for what they have done than adults who do the same wrong, and that is why they should be treated differently than the adult. Justice Stevens took this view to be clearly the truth of the matter, in the majority opinion in *Thompson v. Oklahoma*:

> Thus, the Court has already endorsed the proposition that less culpability should attach to a crime committed by a juvenile than to a comparable crime committed by an adult. The basis for this conclusion is too obvious to require extended explanation. Inexperience, less education, and less intelligence make the teenager less able to evaluate the consequences of his or her conduct while at the same time he or she is much more apt to be motivated by mere emotion or peer pressure than is an adult.[7]

Despite the phrasing, surely Justice Stevens doesn't think that every teenager who commits a crime is inferior in these ways to every adult who commits the same crime. He can't mean that the adult must have significantly more experience and education and be more intelligent than the teenager, because this is obviously false. Since it is false, it too fails to explain why we should always respond differently when a child does wrong than we should when an adult does the same wrong. Moreover, suppose it were true that a particular adult wrongdoer was more experienced, better educated, and brighter than an adolescent who had done the same wrong. It wouldn't follow that the adolescent was less responsible for doing it, because the differences cited could be irrelevant. It could be that both what was wrong with acting in a certain way and what one might do instead were so glaringly obvious that even the adolescent should have been fully capable of seeing them. But then we still haven't found a way to support saying that we should *always* respond differently when it is a child who did the wrong: that will also depend on what the wrong was.

One response to the difficulties I have raised for views on responsibility is to weaken them. Suppose we give up the claim that differences in a child's responsibility for wrongdoing mean that *every* child who does wrong is to be treated differently than any adult who does the same wrong. Suppose we say instead that every child is entitled to a presumption that she is "just a child," with regard to her responsibility for what she has done. This stance will allow the possibility that there are children for whom the presumption should be abandoned, perhaps partly because of what they have done and partly because of their age. It would take the burden of argument to fall upon those who contend that in a particular case the presumption should be abandoned and the child treated as if she were an adult.

Many juvenile justice systems take this form. They treat youthful offenders as juveniles unless there are special reasons to bind them over for trial as adults. It is still a way in which to respond differently when the wrongdoer is a child, because adults do not begin with this same presumption. For them, the presumption is that they are to be treated as if they were adults, whatever that turns out to involve. It is only for children that the default is to be treated as children, whatever *that* turns out to involve.

In the next section, I will defend a view of this kind. Doing so will require addressing the following questions. First, when a wrongdoer is to be treated as a child, how is this treatment to differ from the way an adult would have been treated? Second, what is it about being a child that calls for this distinction? Third, how strong should the presumption be that anyone below a certain age is to be treated as a child? What would call for that presumption to be abandoned, in a particular case? Fourth, what weight is to be given to the age of the child, and to what wrong she did?

3.

A factor central to the view I want to offer is the time it takes for a child to develop a personality and character traits that are his own, in an important sense. Some of what very young children appear to have by way of personality is genetic. That is why everyone who raises more than one child speaks of how different the children were "almost from the start": where else could the differences have come from? Naturally some ways in which the children go on to act are reinforced, and others are discouraged. The ways in which these responses shape the child are hardly automatic, but they do induce dispositions to act in some ways rather than in others. It is years before the child takes much interest in how she is being shaped, as opposed to being engaged in life at a much less abstract level.

The point can be put this way. A young child is not the way she is because she has cultivated these characteristics, or because she has recognized that she has them, was content, and chose not to try to change, or because she has chosen to live in a way that she should have known would make her this kind of person. Those would be ways of making her traits her own in an important sense, but they are years away. This is just a little girl, and she will not have made her traits her own in any of these ways.

I think it follows that we should respond differently when the traits she puts into play are unfortunate. Essentially, our primary aim at such times should be to help her become better in this respect. If we are to punish her, we should do so only in order to help her improve her nascent moral character, not simply because she *deserves* to be punished. That is the difference between responding to a wrongdoer as if she were a child and responding to her as if she were an adult, on the view I am offering. It isn't that we should treat her as she deserves and since she is a child she deserves to be treated less harshly, as the responsibility-views would have it. Instead, to respond as if she were a child is to take her bad behavior primarily as an occasion to contribute to her moral education, rather than an occasion for ensuring that she is punished as she deserves. The other views still take it that our response when children do wrong should be punitive. I am claiming that it shouldn't be.

One view about the proper response when adults do wrong is retributivism, according to which our primary goal *should* be to ensure that they are punished as they deserve. Adding that view to the one I am offering would be nicely symmetrical, and if retributivism is correct, then it is what should be added. I am inclined toward something milder where adults who do wrong are concerned, but this is not the place to argue for it. So, I'll say only that when adults do wrong, they give us a reason to respond retributively in a way that ought to bear considerably on how we treat them, and that retribution should not have this same bearing on how we respond when a child does wrong. The presumption regarding the child should be that this is someone to educate, not someone to punish in order that justice is done.

I take the basis for this to lie in the phenomenon of making one's character one's own. I need to explain why it should make the difference I say it does. As a start, consider the objection that it is only rather *young* children who would typically differ from adults in this regard. Granted, the process of making your traits your own takes time, it is abstract, and a young child is occupied by a great deal else. Granted, concern about what kind of person you are comes only grad-ually—but it does come well before adulthood. Why say that adolescents are to be treated as having no selves of their own when they do wrong? They have had time to take an interest in what they are like, and indeed some adolescents are preoccupied with this idea. In addition, the ones whose nascent character is bad in striking ways will probably have been encouraged to recognize this problem and do something about it. So the plausible assumption about adolescents appears to be that they are *not* "just children" in the way young children are. To grant them the presumption that I've said all children should have seems just to be a mistake.

I think granting them the presumption is better pictured as charity, which there is good reason to provide. As an analogy, consider the excuse of ignorance. "I didn't know" sometimes excuses a person altogether, but it does so only when the ignorance itself is excusable. To put it differently, the fact that you didn't know will mean you are not to be blamed only if we are not inclined to say that you *should* have known. This means that whether to grant someone this excuse is a matter of how charitable we should be with regard to what he should have known. We can be very demanding in that regard, or we can be less so. It can also be clear that we are unreasonable in what we think he should have known or that we are expecting too little of him. The point is that being too demanding and being too lenient are not the only possibilities. There are also many cases in which it wouldn't be unreasonable to deny him the excuse on the ground that he should have known better, just a little *hard*, and it wouldn't be unreasonable to allow him the excuse, just a little *soft*. What are needed at those times are reasons to be more charitable or to be less so.

Just as the question with regard to whether you should have known better is whether you had sufficient opportunity to find out, the question with regard to making the traits you put into play our own is whether you have had sufficient opportunity to do so correctly. The very young child is an easy case: it's clear that he hasn't had sufficient opportunity to do so, for the reasons given earlier. The older the child, the more the question becomes how charitable we ought to be in this regard: how much time and opportunity we should allow before we conclude that the child should be treated as if his opportunity had been sufficient and he had simply failed to make proper use of it.

My answer is not that we should be so charitable that every adolescent is regarded in this way, any more than we should be so generous about what people ought to know that we never say someone "should have known better" and punish her for what she has done. What I am arguing for is a lesser degree of charity. This approach would presume that not even an adolescent has had sufficient opportunity to become someone of his own and behave correctly, but it would allow that there are times when this presumption should be abandoned. That is charity, in that we could have taken a harder view without being unreasonable in the way we would be if we took even young children to have had sufficient opportunity to learn. My task is to show that it is a way in which we ought to be charitable.

In other contexts, one argument for being charitable is that doing so helps those to whom we are charitable, and we can afford it. Some would add a further requirement that the beneficiary's need for charity must be no fault of her own. I take it that all three points apply here. Generally speaking, it is of benefit to adolescent wrongdoers to try to educate them rather than to treat them as adults who are to be punished. Generally speaking, this is also charity we can afford to grant. And, generally speaking, the child has not made such poor use of such substantial opportunities to become a good person of his own that we should regard his failure as his own fault. The arguments that the presumption should be abandoned in a particular case would be arguments that we ought not to extend the same charity on this occasion. They might be arguments that it is of no benefit to the person to whom we would extend it, who would be no worse off—and perhaps be better off—if we didn't try to educate him. They might also be arguments that this time we can't afford the charity, because of what granting it to this child for this act would cost. Or, if we think charity should go only to those who need it through no fault of their own, the arguments would be that this child had exceptional opportunities to become a good person of his own and failed to take advantage of them. The next section will offer a potential illustration, but it is important first to address an argument that this whole project is misguided.

That argument concerns my central contention: that if someone's traits are not yet his own, when he does a wrong that puts those traits in play, that wrongdoing calls not for a retributive response but for an effort to educate him. Consider an adult who acts out of character. It might be urged that she too is not enacting traits she has "made her own," since she isn't enacting any traits she has. Instead, her behavior is uncharacteristic and thus out of keeping with the way she is. But surely that wouldn't mean we shouldn't punish her for what she did and should treat it only as an opportunity to educate her. At most, it might mean that we shouldn't punish her as severely as we should if the act had been in character. The claim would be that the same holds when a *child* does a wrong that does not reflect a trait she has made her own. That is, this too should mean at most that the child is to be punished less severely, not that we should seek only to teach her.

The point to make in reply is that the children are actually quite different from adults who act out of character. The adult *has* character, which she has had sufficient opportunity to make her own. Her behavior reflects that character, despite also being "uncharacteristic." Victor Tadros puts the point this way, in defending a view about criminal responsibility: "The inclination to be cruel, and hence the cruel action that followed, may be out of character, but that he performed it still reflects on his character."[8] Where his example of uncharacteristic cruelty is concerned, what the behavior reflects is vulnerability to inclinations to be cruel on occasions such as this, despite not being a cruel person. Where cruelty is concerned, that is a lesser flaw than many he could have had, and therefore it calls for a less punitive response. It does so because the character it reflects is less objectionable, not because it does not reflect character for which he is responsible.

Compare the case in which it is a child who has been cruel. Here the supposition is that she has not had sufficient opportunity to make her character her own with regard to cruelty. But then that will be as true of lesser faults as well as more serious ones. She wouldn't be responsible for being a cruel person, but this fact doesn't mean that when she is cruel, her behavior reflects a lesser flaw for which she *is* responsible and is therefore to be punished in a suitably lesser way. Rather, it would mean she wasn't reflecting any character for which she was responsible. The way we should react to her behavior doesn't follow from the way we should react when adults act uncharacteristically, because the two are not the same.

Still, why say the response should be to try to educate the girl, rather than to punish her? Actually, this contention is simply part of a broader view we will not want to discard, namely that children are not responsible for their own moral education in the way that adults are. The primary responsibility falls to the child's parents, whose failures here are terrible faults as a parent. Other adults have lesser obligations where the child's moral education is concerned, and central authorities should intervene if it goes badly enough in certain ways—which it has done, in her case. To think we should help with her moral education is in line with all of that; to think we should mainly seek to punish he as she deserves is not.

Notice too that if it is education that children are to receive, we have another reason why children are not to be resented. Resenting someone is ill-suited to educating him, and it does not ordinarily have that intention. That is why resentment can be kept to oneself, or the reasons for it kept to oneself, even as it burns within. Discipline, on the other hand, is ordinarily imposed in order to teach or to train, in exactly the way that resentment ordinarily is not. Thus discipline is suited to children, if we have an obligation to educate them, and is ill-suited to adults, since *their* moral education is not up to us in this way but to them.

The broader point is that no one stands in the relationship to another adult that parents stand to their young children. No one has the primary responsibility for what sort of person another adult is like, or is coming to be. That falls to the adult himself or herself. Therefore no one has a parent's responsibility to respond to an adult's bad behavior in this same way, pondering it for the messages it carries about the person who behaved in this way and using these as an occasion for change or correction in the moral education she is providing him. Indeed, I doubt that we owe other adults any help at all in becoming better people, as a general rule. I don't mean by this that we should never speak to someone for the sake of others whom he mistreats—but that is an obligation we have to them, not to him. I also agree that there are personal relationships that include being honest about what bothers us. Aside from those relationships, though, we do not owe it to others to convey what we take to be their moral failings or what we think is wrong with their behavior. We are free to keep such observations to ourselves.

To put it differently, we do not owe adults an educative response to their misbehavior, let alone the kind that parents owe their children. It is certainly possible to say that this point remains true when an adult is found to have done something so seriously wrong that it is against the criminal law. That is, we could say that the state's response should simply be punitive. Alternatively, we could sometimes be generous to those who have failed in this responsibility, taking this as an occasion to educate rather than to punish after all. The more the adult's life had been like that of a child and the less serious the crime he had committed, the better the case for doing so. The reason is that those factors are what bear on being charitable to the child, and (as everyone realizes) they do not change automatically when a certain chronological age is reached. There is no reason not to extend the same charity to an adult whose life has been like that of a child in these ways. There is reason only for this reaction not to be the norm, as, I've argued, there *is* reason for it to be the norm with regard to children who do wrong.

The final section of this chapter will offer two clarifications. The first is meant to show what it would be to take a child's wrongdoing as an occasion to educate him rather than to punish him. The second concerns when we should abandon the presumption that this is what we ought to do, even though the wrongdoer is only a child.

4.

One aim of moral education when a child has acted badly is to ensure that she understands what was wrong with acting as she did. Another is to get her to take what was wrong with it as a reason not to act as she did, and to give that reason the weight it should have. We also want her to know that she should take responsibility for what she does. Finally, we want her to understand what it will be like if she does not become someone who has all of this understanding. This last is information about how the world works, as she chooses what kind of person to be and so what kind of life to have.

In some cases, what the child does can provide some of these lessons itself. That result is most easily imaginable for thoughtless or careless behavior by a good person, who has now seen quite vividly what her behavior can cost others. Even this child should have to make restitution as best she can, as a way of confirming that we are responsible for the consequences of what we do. Sometimes that amounts to doing what she can to reimburse financially. Other times, it amounts to trying to make up for a loss that can't be covered in that way, as many of the deepest losses cannot be. This situation too provides a lesson in what she actually did to this other person, and in what there is to take seriously where others are concerned. Here, and also when she can't pay the financial cost of what she has done, she is in the position of being unable to right the wrong she did. The fact that this can happen, what it is like when it does happen, and how much it delivers a person of conscience into the hands of the one she did wrong are all valuable lessons.

In short, there is a good deal to be learned from being required to take responsibility for what one has done, even if one is not punished for it. For the child we are imagining, nothing is needed to make her take the costs to matter in the way they do, since she wasn't indifferent to those but only oblivious. The criminologists John Braithwaite and Stephen Mugford take that to be the norm where youthful misbehavior is concerned, at least when it is misbehavior of a kind that gets the child arrested:

> Much delinquency is casual and thoughtless.... The offenders...thought all they had done was to take 50 dollars from the house of a faceless person [but] find that person is a vulnerable elderly woman who did without something significant because of the loss of the money. They learn that as a result of the break-in she now feels insecure in her own home, as does her next door neighbour. Both have invested in new security locks and are afraid to go out in the street alone because they have come to view the neighbourhood as a dangerous place.[9]

If it is true that these offenders would never have done such a thing if they had known it would have these costs, then all that is needed is to enlighten them and to require that they do what they can to bear those costs themselves. But not all offenders are like that, of course. Some are simply indifferent to what happens to others. A vivid depiction of the costs and a requirement to compensate the victims might change this attitude—but it also might not. Other wrongdoers are quite aware of the harms they are doing but do not take these as sufficient reason not to act as they do. Still others actually set out to do the harms. Here again the vivid depiction might change this person's ways, bringing him to appreciate why he should not act in such a way—but certainly it could also fail.

What Braithwaite and Mugford recommend for wrongdoers of these latter kinds is that we make them aware that their behavior also has other costs that they do care about:

Many of the worst offenders have developed a capacity to cut themselves off from the shame for exploiting other human beings. They deploy a variety of barriers against feeling responsibility. But what does not affect the offender directly may affect those who…support her. The shaft of shame fired by the victim in the direction of the offender might go right over the offender's head, yet it might pierce like a spear through the heart of the offender's mother, sitting behind him. It is very common for offenders' mothers to start to sob when victims describe their suffering or loss…the anguish of the offender's mother…may succeed in bringing home to the offender the need to confront rather than deny an act of irresponsibility.[10]

Clearly, this tactic would work only if the child cared about causing his mother pain. It could emerge instead that he does not find her distress motivating, or even that he seeks to provoke it, and perhaps that he is cynical about its true source. ("My parents don't care about me, they are just embarrassed and ashamed to be my parents. Why should it bother me if they are upset?") These are deeper problems than parents can handle without professional help, partly because the child does not take them to have authority over him and may even resist their efforts on principle. His initial misbehavior serves as an occasion to attend to the deeper problems, rather than calling only for an adjustment in the continuing moral education his parents are providing him.

There is also this: the point of the moral education is to help the child become a person of good moral character, appropriately sensitive to the considerations that matter. The goal is for him to be someone who does the right things *for the right reasons*, that is, not because doing them pays off personally or because failing to do them distresses his mother. Those other considerations are only supposed to provide added motivation, at best. So, the idea in showing him how deeply his behavior pained his mother wouldn't be to teach him not to do such things *for that reason*. The idea would be to use something that matters to him— her distress—to capture his attention, thereby enabling us to teach him about something else that should matter to him but currently does not. The fact that he cares about the mother he knows he has distressed leaves the door open for a proper moral education.

It does so because it means the child is not entirely disconnected from others but is of great concern to at least one other person who matters to him. In that respect, attending to the interests of someone else has a place in his experience. He has seen the distress in her, she has required concern from him in this regard, and he accepts this requirement, since it bothers him that she is so upset. Good. This is what a very wide range of moral considerations urge: that what happens to others should matter to us. He is open to that possibility.

All of this confirms a sense we might have that if a parent's response when a child behaves badly is to have the effects we hope for, it has to be the latest episode in something much larger between them. What is needed is a relationship in which the child knows that he is held dear—and that he continues to be so. To see that his bad behavior dismays or angers his parents can show him exactly that. To see instead that it leaves them indifferent would provide a very different message. To see that he is resented for what he did or is held in contempt for having done it can convey unfortunate messages as well, because resentment and contempt are dismissive in a way that anger and dismay are not. They mean he is an outsider now, and will be for a while. They can also mean that he has been cast out permanently, and they can mean that he already had been. These latter messages certainly need not be true: we can resent or have contempt for someone we used to hold dear, and we can get over these feelings. Still, they are potential messages that can require countering, where a particular child is concerned, if parental efforts at moral education are to have good prospects.

The moral could be that one important part of providing your child a proper moral education is to be (visibly) angry or dismayed when she behaves badly rather than indifferent, or resentful, or contemptuous. But clearly how one feels on these occasions is not simply a choice made at the time. It has a great deal to do with the broader attitude one already has toward this person. That is a second way in which effective parental moral education occurs within a context of durable mutual affection, built and sustained at other times.

It remains painfully true that some children also behave in ways we have made criminal, which quite properly brings them to the attention of the state. The state is charged with carrying out the punishments that the law threatens. The classic claims on behalf of those punishments are that they deter such behavior in the future and that they treat the wrongdoer as he or she deserves to be treated. Where the punishment includes confinement, it also protects the broader society from repetition during the period of confinement, and where the punishment is execution the protection afforded to others is permanent.

Imprisoning or executing a child, however, is very much at odds with the idea that we owe children who do wrong an *educative* response. Obviously, ending the child's life offers little as a way of educating him. It could be argued that the prospect of being executed might make the child see the light and be a better person for however long he has left, but that isn't much of a hope. As for imprisonment, it should not be expected to help a child become a better person, but to help make him a worse one. Moreover, both execution and imprisonment are ways in which we cast the offender out. Where imprisonment is concerned we do say that he can earn his way back, but despite this idea and the phrase "paying his debt to society," someone who goes to prison for a few years is not at all like someone who has simply purchased something and then left the store to go on with life as before. Instead there is a stain, on the basis of which others cast this person for some roles and exclude him from others, just as with the reactive attitudes. Earlier, reasons were offered not to characterize children in this durable and dominating way, and institutionalizing them does exactly that. It gives up on treating the child as a child, and there is much to be said against this policy. The default should be that we don't do it. However, I want to argue that it is sometimes the right course to follow even so.

As an illustration, consider Heath Wilkins, who robbed a convenience store and murdered the clerk, a woman named Nancy Allen:

> Wilkins' plan was to rob the store and murder "whoever was behind the counter" because "a dead person can't talk." While Wilkins' accomplice, Patrick Stevens, held Allen, Wilkins stabbed her, causing her to fall to the floor. When Stevens had trouble operating the cash register, Allen spoke up to assist him, leading Wilkins

to stab her three more times in her chest. Two of these wounds penetrated the victim's heart. When Allen began to beg for her life, Wilkins stabbed her four more times in the neck, opening the carotid artery. After helping themselves to liquor, cigarettes, rolling papers, and about $450 in cash and checks, Wilkins and Stevens left the clerk to die on the floor.[11]

When he did these terrible things, Heath Wilkins was sixteen years old. The argument against reacting as if he were as bad a person as they make him appear is that either he *isn't*, but is only trying on one possible identity, or that he *is*, but it will be unfair to react accordingly because he has become this way so young and on his own. After he was convicted, evidence gathered for a punishment hearing revealed that Wilkins

> ...had been in and out of juvenile facilities since the age of eight for various acts of burglary, theft, and arson, had attempted to kill his mother by putting cyanide into Tylenol capsules, and had killed several animals in his neighborhood. Although psychiatric testimony indicated that Wilkins had "personality disorders," the witnesses agreed that Wilkins was aware of his actions and could distinguish right and wrong.[12]

Assuming that the "personality disorders" were not ways in which Wilkins should be considered to be mentally ill, it is hard to maintain that he is not yet a bad person but is only a child experimenting with a possible identity.

The same data strongly suggest that it is not his fault that he is the person he is. Heath Wilkins hasn't had the help a child should have in becoming a good person, if we are right to be skeptical about the "moral education" provided in the juvenile facilities Wilkins had visited repeatedly for eight of his sixteen years on earth. It would be unfair to treat him as if he had had the childhood he should have had. Those are reasons to treat him instead as if he were a child, by attending only to his moral education. That course of action has grave flaws of its own, however.

For one thing, Heath Wilkins is certainly a candidate to be regarded as a lost child, in the sense of not being open to moral education at this point in his life. If so, then even though our response when the wrongdoer is "only a child" ought to be educative, to do so in his case would be futile. For another, even if he is still a child, what Heath Wilkins has become is something very dangerous to others. They should be protected from him even though it is not his fault that he is dangerous, just as they should be protected from a person who is mentally ill in a way that makes him highly dangerous even though the illness is not that person's fault. Moreover, those in danger from him are not an identifiable subset from whom we could simply keep him away. What will be needed is an extensive limitation on the kind of contact Heath Wilkins can have with anyone. His liberty will have to be limited, if we are to protect others from him, probably by confining him.

A second argument for reacting as if he were a bad person is retributive. Heath Wilkins is responsible for what he did. Even if his youth diminishes that responsibility, he still robbed a store with the full intention of murdering the clerk so as to escape detection, and then carried out a murder that took a fair amount of time and a series of violent acts to accomplish, performed over the victim's pleadings for her life. That behavior calls for a severe punishment, if there is anything to retributivism, even though Heath Wilkins became someone who would behave in this terrible way because he did not have the help he should have had in becoming a different kind of person.

Suppose it is urged that we should still take this action only as an occasion to contribute to the moral education of Heath Wilkins. The contention would be that avoiding the unfairness is more important than the right others have to be protected from him and more important than his being treated as he deserves, even when the contribution to his moral education seems bound to fail. We should still try again, and, presumably again, for as long as Heath Wilkins is less than eighteen years of age. That is a possible view, but it is hard to see why it must be correct.

I suggest instead that we consider his life to date only as a reason to have mercy in the punishment we impose. Heath Wilkins should be confined for some period of time, but not punished as severely as someone we expect to take full responsibility for the sort of person he has become. The reason for being merciful in this case is that Wilkins, unlike an adult offender, has not had sufficient opportunity to overcome the ways in which others failed him so badly. The reasons *only* to be merciful in our punishment appear above.

A similar argument can be made concerning juveniles whose offenses are far less serious than the one Wilkins committed, but for whom offending has become a way of life. According to a number of studies, over half of juvenile offenses are carried out by a relatively small core of repeaters.[13] Here too the offenders are only children, and I expect that the early lives of most are far short of what they should have been. This means that to treat them as if they were adults will sustain a way in which life has been unfair to them, and that point has to be taken seriously. However, there is also reason to believe that efforts to educate will simply fail, and to believe also that potential victims are entitled to protection from them and that their punishment is deserved. All of that has to be taken seriously too, and to act as if these offenders too were *only* children does not do this.

As with Heath Wilkins, presumably it is possible to be merciful in the ways in which we protect ourselves from the children I've just described. As with Wilkins, the mercy would be granted because the offender was only a child, who had not had sufficient opportunity to become an acceptable person or the help he should have had in becoming one, and who had not had the same opportunity to overcome this background that an adult would have had. That approach would be a way of allowing it to matter that these are children, without (I think) allowing it to matter more than it should.

Whether that is the right conclusion about juvenile offenders is certainly open to debate. That particular debate is not about what constitutes good parenthood where bad behavior is concerned, which is our principal subject. I have argued that good parenthood on such occasions presumes that the bad behavior is an occasion to contribute to the child's moral education, in whatever way is appropriate to the child and to the wrong she has done. I have also suggested that when parents and children love one another, the child is easier for the parent to teach on such occasions than he is if they do not. That issue invites us to consider the topic of the next chapter: do parents have a moral obligation to love their children, or is love outside the domain of obligation?

9

Loving One Another

Home is the place where, when you have to go there, they have to take you in.

> —Robert Frost, "The Death of the Hired Man"

Prisons are like a home of that kind: if you have to go there, they have to take you in. So are emergency rooms at U.S. hospitals, if you arrive with a medical emergency. If you have to go there, they have to take you in, and they have to see you through the emergency before they may send you elsewhere.[1] But clearly emergency rooms and prisons are not at all what we want *home* to be like. Neither of them is an unfailing refuge from anything that we can't face alone and a place where people know us and love us.

The hired man in Frost's poem doesn't have a home to go to, in that sense. He is dying, and he can go only to a family in whose fields he had labored for a time, and hope they will be kind to him. That's what gives the poem its poignancy. They do take him in, and that is far better for him than if he had had nothing like this available—but it is also far less than we hope would be available to us. We want to be able to go to people who love us, and not just as our lives are coming to an end.

Do our parents have an obligation to be such people for us, so that they would do us wrong if they did not love us? I will argue that parents do have an obligation to love their children while they are raising them, but that they have no obligaton to love their child after he or she is grown—at least, none that follows just from his being their son, or from her being their daughter. I will begin with the very different idea that love can never be a matter of obligation and so cannot be something parents owe their children at any stage of life.

1.

According to Harry Frankfurt, "Love is irreducibly a matter of personal circumstance. There are no necessary truths or *a priori* principles from which it can be established what we are to love."[2] It would follow that we have no obligation to love our country, and none to love any particular man or woman, whether this is someone to whom we are married, or one of our parents—or our child. A few pages later, though, Frankfurt begins another sentence this way: "Even if parents

are somehow morally obligated to love their children."[3] The phrase suggests that
he thinks there might be at least *one* "necessary truth or *a priori* principle" about
the people we are to love, namely that we are to love our children.

Ambivalence about such an obligation would be understandable. Love within
a family is like romantic love in that it involves feelings that are certainly not
under our voluntary control at a moment's notice and that might also be beyond
our power to develop over time. Where romantic love is concerned, those same
facts are commonly taken to mean there can be no obligation to "fall in love"
with someone: either it will happen or it won't. So it seems that the same should
hold for loving our children or our parents: no one can be obligated to love a son
or a daughter, either it will happen or it won't.

That same thought about familial love might derive support from this. To
love someone either romantically or in the familial way is to take what happens
to this person greatly to heart. Whether we open ourselves to someone in this
way surely depends on what we are like ourselves. When we do love someone,
there are deep and abiding truths about us in play, and they are also in play when
we might have loved someone but do not. Those wellsprings might be too little
under our control for loving someone to be a matter of choice. It could be that
the most that should be expected of us is that we try to love certain people. We
could not be blamed for failing to manage it, on this view, if we had made every
effort we should to love this person.

Love could be like that. However, it could also be that loving someone *isn't*
too much a matter of luck to be expected of someone, at least under some circumstances. Imagine a woman who has been done a minor wrong by someone
she loves. The man who did her wrong is very sorry for what he did, and that
wrong runs counter to his many demonstrations of love for her in the past. He
begs to be forgiven and to have her love again—but she will have nothing more
to do with him. It certainly isn't unthinkable to criticize her for this attitude, for
taking herself so seriously that every offense is unforgivable, and for her hardness
of heart. Those criticisms hold her failure to love him against her. They regard
her as wrong not to go back to loving this man, and if she is genuinely unable to
manage to do so, they take her to be at fault for this inability.

Which way we ought to think about love depends on what control a person
must have over an outcome, ultimately, if it is to be a matter of obligation, and
on whether we have that control where love is concerned. Whatever we do, when
we act there are always matters beyond our control, including some that have
helped to make us the kind of people we are. The question is always whether
what we do is still sufficiently up to us, or up to us in the right ways, to be
something that we are responsible for handling in the right way. The trouble is
that there is no general test for when something is still up to us in the right ways
and when it is not. Nor is the answer clear in the case of loving someone, or the
more particular cases of loving our children or our parents. It could be up to us
in the right ways whether we did those things, or it could be that they are always
too much a matter of luck to be regarded in this way.

The right conclusion to draw is that neither alternative can be dismissed. We
shouldn't be certain that anyone who does not love her children or her parents is

a bad person instead of someone who is afflicted in a way that makes her life poorer than it could have been. But we ought also to be open to the possibility that love is sometimes a matter of obligation and should consider whether that is the case with love between parents and children. This chapter follows that second path.[4]

2.

Here is a sentiment with which many would agree, offered by Neil MacCormick:

> Let me start from what seems to me a simple and barely contestable assertion: at least from birth, every child has a right to be nurtured, cared for, and, if possible, loved, until such time as he or she is capable of caring for himself or herself....I should regard it as a case of moral blindness if anyone failed to recognize that every child has that right.[5]

In preceding chapters I argued that parents do indeed have an obligation to see to it that their children are "nurtured [and] cared for," and to provide their children with a moral education by serving as an active paradigm of how to live. The question now is whether parents also have an obligation to *love* their children at this stage of life if they can, as MacCormick thinks they obviously do have.[6]

We have already seen at least one reason to agree with him. Chapter 5, "The Autonomy of Children," drew upon the following observation by Jeffrey Blustein and Jonathan D. Moreno: "A child who feels unwanted—whose sense of personal worth is not nurtured and supported by caring adults—is plagued by failure and self-doubt, apathy, and cynicism in later childhood and adult life."[7] Their argument is that the nurturing and support that are part of loving a child are crucial to the child's coming to understand the ways in which she is *worth* loving. I urged that a sense of who you are is crucial to making those traits your own so that when you put them into play you are acting with an autonomy that calls for respect. Parents have a central obligation to help their children grow up in this way of great moral importance, as opposed to maturing only physically and intellectually: a child who did not do so would remain too much the creature of others. If loving the child were inseparable from carrying out this obligation, there would certainly be an obligation to love her.

However, it might seem that there would be other ways of carrying it out, and thus that this hypothetical language is the strongest we can use—that is, that there isn't really an obligation to love our children, but there would be one if love were essential in a way it is not. But what would those alternatives be?

To be affectively indifferent to your child wouldn't help her understand herself, since it would simply withhold the reinforcement parents can provide and the messages about what matters and what does not. But imagine a parent who wasn't indifferent and also had no love at all for his child, but regarded her as a burden and an affliction. As part of this attitude, he belittles the child at every turn, harping mercilessly upon her faults. Often he exaggerates these and sometimes he blames her for what isn't her fault at all, just as loving parents sometimes exaggerate their praise and sometimes give credit where none is due. The venomous parent's message is that the child is worthless and this is why, just as the loving parent's message is that the child is wonderful and *this* is why. If one of those messages is a way to help the child come to understand at least some aspects of who she is and either accept these truths about herself or work to change them, don't we have to say that the other one is a second way of doing the same thing?

Not really. First, accepting your current characteristics isn't a way of making them your own unless you believe that you can change them. Without that belief, accepting what you are like is only resignation to remain as others have made you. Second, believing you can change is also essential to *trying* to change, and thus to becoming a person of your own by trying to reform, or at least that belief is essential to succeeding. The parent we are imagining doesn't include a message that his child can improve, but only a steady barrage of criticism. If Blustein and Moreno are right, the likely outcome isn't a child who strives to improve but one who is "plagued by failure and self-doubt, apathy, and cynicism," so it is highly unlikely that this approach is a way of helping.

Moreover, children who are belittled in this way are hardly on their way to becoming happy adults, even if their self-image were correct because their parents' abuse had made it so. Parents who were responsible for doing that would have failed in a different obligation of great importance. Even if they had helped the child to become a person of her own, they would have done so in a way that failed to help her become an adult who was reasonably happy with her life. Instead, they would have greatly hindered her in that endeavor.

Finally, suppose that their child managed somehow to make use of their steady criticism to become a better person than she might have been, and to have a life with which she was indeed reasonably happy. There must be some children who are that resilient, at least if others help them. However, even if in that case we have to think of the parents as having done things that helped their child, the help is so inadvertent that it shouldn't count as carrying out the obligation. In addition, there would surely have been a kinder way to do so. Parenthood is concerned not exclusively with the child's future life as an adult, but also with the life she has as a child. Love adds immeasurably to the quality of the child's life, in ways that the campaign of telling the child how she is worthless obviously does not. For a time, parents are in a unique position: they have the power to make this other person as happy as it is possible for her to be. That is an opportunity one shouldn't miss. Finally, quite apart from whether one occasionally provides sheer bliss, there is a broader obligation to make your children happy rather than unhappy. The parent who has only venom for his child fails abysmally in that.

In sum, there are several parental obligations in play here, Therefore even if unrelenting venom were somehow to help the child become a person of his or her own, it would fail in other responsibilities a parent has. In contrast, loving your child and showing this love in the nurturing responses that Blustein and Moreno have in mind is a way in which parents carry out this set of responsibilities.

It serves to make the child happy at the time, it helps him become a person of his own, and it helps him become an adult who is equipped to be reasonably happy with his life. That makes the love an obligation parents have while their children are in their charge.

I want next to develop one of these ideas more fully, namely the idea that love is essential to raising a child in the way one should. I will make use of ideas developed by Loren Lomasky in *Persons, Rights, and the Moral Community*,[8] though perhaps not in a way of which he would approve, and certainly not in a way for which he bears any responsibility.

3.

Some of our actions are simply responses to a need of the moment. Lomasky's example is the scratching of an itch, which can occupy us quite completely while we are doing it but has little connection with what we do at other times. Scratching an itch is also rather simple, in that we ordinarily do it all at once, rather than in steps. There are special cases in which it is done in steps, as when the itch must be scratched surreptitiously; but mostly we just scratch, and that's that.

Even eating breakfast is more complicated, since it is done in steps as a matter of course. Still, actions at these two levels do not bring us to what we might regard as the themes in a person's life, or at least it would be a sad life indeed in which they did. No one wants his obituary to observe that he was assiduous about scratching when he itched or that he always ate breakfast. We hope instead to have been engaged in many more significant activities and to have pursued them in ways that speak well of us. Take Sam Kleiner, for example, who is remembered in the following death notice from the *New York Times*:

> Sam...was our invaluable partner, confidant, and most importantly great friend...an astute, fair-minded businessman, profoundly respected by all....His warmth, gentleness, wisdom, and pure sweetness will never be forgotten.[9]

Those phrases convey some of what Lomasky would call Mr. Kleiner's *projects*, by which he means this:

> Some ends are not once-and-for-all acknowledged and then realized through the successful completion of one particular action. Rather, they persist throughout large stretches of an individual's life and continue to elicit actions that establish a pattern coherent in virtue of the ends subserved. Those which reach indefinitely into the future, play a central role within the ongoing endeavors of the individual, and provide a significant degree of structural stability to an individual's life I call *projects*.[10]

Being a partner in the firm could be a project in that sense. So could being a good friend, or being an astute businessman who was also fair-minded and respected. The projects that a person has help to mark him as the distinctive individual he is. So does the way in which he pursues those projects, balancing them against each other and against other goods. For Sam Kleiner, presumably his projects and his way of balancing them would have been places in which to find his "warmth, gentleness, wisdom, and pure sweetness" in play. As Lomasky says, "When we wish to understand or describe a person, to explicate what fundamentally characterizes him as being just the particular purposive being that he is, we will focus on his projects rather than on his more transitory ends.... Projects explain more than an action; they help to explain a life."[11]

I think there is considerable moral value in being responsible yourself for what explains your life in this way. It was a good thing for Sam Kleiner to be able to determine which projects he pursued as well as the way they were to be balanced against each other, as opposed to having those matters determined for him by someone else or by factors beyond his control. This autonomy helped to make his life the mark that he left in the time that he had. It isn't quite that if these things hadn't been up to him then his obituary couldn't record his life as *to his credit*, in the way such remembrances do (or, as they do much more rarely, as to his discredit).[12] After all, if we have free will, then there is always *something* we did, even if it is only the particular way in which we carried out what life assigned to us and scratched our momentary itches. The idea is just that it is better if the larger themes are also up to us.

I am claiming that this independence has moral value in itself. What we do also shapes us in return, over time. Indeed, it is plausible to think that the extended enterprises to which we devote ourselves usually have more to do with what kinds of people we become than any conscious efforts we make to cultivate traits of character or of personality. That is so because our extended enterprises reward some features and penalize others, so that pursuing them inclines us to be more open to others (or more remote), to be more patient (or to expect success to come quickly), to be hard workers (or to be more relaxed in this regard), to be very honest (or not entirely so), and so on. If we have the liberty of choosing those enterprises, then we also have a measure of control over what sort of person we come to be over time. On the other hand, if we do not choose them, who we become is ceded that much more fully to whatever imposes the patterns of activity that are in our lives: we become their creature, rather than our own. My claim is that individuals should be taken to have moral claims in this regard as well.

Let us consider what follows about an obligation to love our children when the children are young and under our care. Lomasky's own chief claims about children are these:

1. "...children do not pursue projects...."[13]
2. However, children "are numerically identical to the project pursuer that will emerge"[14] when they reach that stage of development, or that would emerge if this were not prevented from happening. Each child is a particular person who would pursue projects as an adult.
3. This gives each child a right not to be *spoiled* as a pursuer of projects before he or she even reaches this stage.[15]
4. That is a welfare-right the child has to be provided the "food, shelter, emotional and intellectual stimulation"[16] that he or she needs in order to become this future pursuer of projects.

Despite saying that "children do not pursue projects," for the majority of the time Lomasky does not say that *no* child pursues projects, but only that babies, infants, and very young children do not. It seems clear that older children do sometimes begin personal projects that they continue as adults. To use Lomasky's examples of projects, an older child might begin "...serving God...following the shifting fortunes of the New York Yankees come what may...developing a beautiful body...facing testing situations courageously, overcoming shyness, becoming an accomplished disco dancer, [or] staying sober,"[17] and might stay with this activity to whatever extent an adult must if they are to count among the adult's projects. In addition, there are also children who devote themselves at a fairly early age to becoming professional athletes or professional musicians, or to excelling as students, and who don't abandon this later in the month for something quite different. Instead, they stay with it in its original conception, or else they develop it into something related, just as an adult would do. These undertakings contribute to the child's sense of identity and give his or her life a degree of coherence, in the same way as an adult's pursuit of projects would.

In short, it seems right to say that older children (at least) are pursuers of projects, and also that they sometimes engage in some activities that, although they might not "reach indefinitely into the future" and so wouldn't meet Lomasky's definition of a project, certainly do "play a central role within the ongoing endeavors of the individual, and provide a significant degree of structural stability to an individual's life."[18] This means that the children who have these projects and quasiprojects have two kinds of rights on Lomasky's way of looking at things, not just one, as his argument suggests. On the one hand, they have the same kind of right that he takes adults to have as pursuers of projects, against encroachment upon whatever they have underway. On the other, presumably they also have the rights he says children have by virtue of being identical to the project-pursuers they will later become, when some of their projects will be different ones.

This duality might appear to generate a problem. The first of these rights would militate against a parent's controlling what her adolescent child did, for his own good, since that control would encroach upon his right as a pursuer of the projects he had underway. The second might require the parent to do exactly that, in order to protect the child's future self from impairment. Thus it appears that any parent whose older child has taken up a project that puts his future as a pursuer of projects at risk must do him a great wrong whichever course she chooses. It will be worth taking a moment to explain why this is not the case.

The solution lies in a difference between older children and adults who are pursuing projects. The child's parents have an obligation to *raise* the child, and, of course, no one has an obligation to raise someone who is already an adult. In part, parents have this obligation because a child who is not raised by anyone has a very hard life, both as a child and (if he or she survives) also as an adult. Creating a child gives one the responsibility to see to it that the child does not have a life of that kind, just as it is always our responsibility to see to it that our actions cause no one any great harm when there is no justification for doing so. That responsibility requires biological parents either to raise the child themselves or to arrange for someone else to do it. It also requires adoptive parents to keep the commitment they make in adopting the child or, in some cases, to arrange for yet another person to do so.

As was noted earlier, part of what is required in raising the child is to help her become a good person whose life does well at delivering what she wants and who is reasonably happy with it.[19] Although we have this obligation where our children are concerned, we do not have it where other adults are concerned, unless we are pastors with a flock, psychologists with a client, or the like. It is decidedly not our responsibility to help other adults to become better people or to help equip them to be happy. That is their own responsibility as part of being adults. We are free to offer them our help if it is welcome, but not to assume the control that we are obligated to take when we are raising a child.

This responsibility gives a parent's intrusions upon her child's nascent projects a route to legitimacy that they could not have if he were the man who lived next door. What the mother does to rein in her child is legitimate so long as it is a reasonable way for her to carry out her obligation to raise him. If her actions were meant instead to help her next-door neighbor be a better person or have a happier life, they wouldn't have this same justification, since she has no obligation to raise *him*. Worse, for her to act as if she did have this obligation would be to treat her neighbor as less than an adult.

Thus, these two kinds of intrusions upon a person's present projects are very different. Parents aren't in the dilemma that was imagined earlier, forced to choose between encroaching upon their child's right to pursue his projects and violating the rights he has as a future pursuer of projects. They have the third alternative of acting in ways that constitute reasonable efforts to raise their child. Still, children do have rights as future pursuers of projects—including, I will argue, a right to their parents' love while they are children.

4.

Generally speaking, a child's rights call for more from her parents than they do from others. Presumably, adults who are not the child's parents must refrain from impairing her progress toward pursuing projects of her own. There might also be ways in which they must help her to do so. Only the parents are required to *raise* her, though—indeed, no one else is even free to do that without the parent's consent, since the obligation to raise a child is also a right to be the one who does so. Raising the child is a particularly active role to play in her becoming a pursuer of projects, as opposed to the more limited one of not interfering, and it must be played for many years and across many aspects of life. Whatever help others give the child in growing up to become a pursuer of projects will be more occasional, and more limited.

Even so, it will be useful to start with what the child would be entitled to from everyone, *including* her parents, by virtue of her being a future pursuer of projects. Here is Lomasky, again: "Children will eventually come to have projects of their own for which they will require noninterference, but they do not have them yet. The wherewithal to achieve that state can be claimed for them as a matter of right."[20] At a minimum, this means the child is entitled not to be killed before she gets that far, and also not to be damaged so severely that she never develops beyond the stage at which she is able only to scratch some of life's momentary itches and perform simple actions. Perhaps it is also possible to do something that would allow her to become a pursuer of projects but would severely impair her ability to succeed at any that she undertook. Although that child's life would have what Lomasky sometimes describes as "the coherence that characterizes a fully human life,"[21] it would also be filled with failure. The person who lived it would come to regard herself as a failure as well, given how intimately we connect our sense of ourselves with how well we are doing at what we undertake. A right not to be derailed as a future pursuer of projects ought to include protection against that eventuality as well.

Consider next another point Lomasky offers by means of a rather alarming example: "To chop off the left arm of a baby will be accounted a violation of its rights. Mutilation now impedes successful project-pursuit later."[22] Of course, the first worry about a parent who chops off his baby's left arm is not that he has impeded future projects., Nevertheless, as Lomasky says, the mutilation does "impede successful project-pursuit later," though not in the same way that killing the baby, or freezing her development would. Those make it impossible for her to pursue projects at all. Removing someone's left arm doesn't do that, nor does it mean she must be less successful at the ones she undertakes. However, it does rule out any project that requires a left arm, and it does increase the difficulty of a great deal that is easier to do when a person has two arms. Moreover, the projects that are excluded or impeded in this way include many that would be perfectly acceptable for a person to pursue. Doing that to someone needs justifying, at the very least.

Admittedly, there would be special cases. It could be necessary to amputate a baby's arm in order to save his life, and not only so that he would survive a few weeks longer before he died of his injures or his disease. Therapeutic amputation ought not to count as violating his rights, even though it would leave him at the disadvantages mentioned when he came to pursue projects. However, a therapeutic amputation isn't a *mutilation*. There are also said to be parents who do mutilate their baby in this way, in order to improve his chances at the only "career" they see in his future: that of a professional beggar. This action would raise questions about the degree of control that a parent should exert over a child's possibilities, even when the parent does this for the child's own good— questions I have addressed in an earlier chapter.[23] For now, let us address only the kind of case Lomasky meant to offer, in which those who remove the baby's arm do not do this for his sake. If (as it seems) what they do violates his rights as a future pursuer of projects, what follows about those rights?

We could take it to mean that these are rights not to have some acceptable projects ruled out entirely, and not to have some other projects made more difficult. This assessment is too restrictive, however. Suppose that a child's parents cultivate some of his talents and interests rather than others, as interested parents normally do. Their doing so would make it harder, and perhaps even impossible, for the child to follow a path that called for his other interests and talents to be cultivated. Thus it would count as a violation of his rights, on this first idea. Better not to cultivate any of them then? But that would put the child at a disadvantage across the board, so that solution too would violate his rights. Clearly, this first idea is too greatly at odds with saying that parents must be of help to their children as they raise them. Let us try for another.

There are at least two respects in which the impairment inflicted by removing the baby's arm is especially egregious. One is that it is gratuitous. It isn't the inevitable result of doing something else in order to help him have a good life, as when some talents go undiscovered because we are helping the child to develop others. Instead, removing a limb just makes life harder and more limited. Second, it does so to a substantial degree. The degree would vary: for example, it is far worse to lack an arm if the only sort of work available to you is manual labor. That aside, we use our limbs in daily life, and so to be without one requires regularly making accommodations that others need not make. That intrusion into how one spends one's time is limiting in itself; the more obvious point along these lines is that a good deal of activities would have become either more difficult or even impossible. The point to be gleaned is that a child has a right not to be substantially handicapped before he ever becomes a pursuer of projects, in addition to having a right not to be prevented from reaching that stage at all and not to be rendered unlikely to succeed at anything he undertakes.

Those would be rights that children have against everyone, including their parents. A child's more extensive rights where his parents are concerned include a right to have help in becoming a good person who is reasonably happy with his life. I think that goal gives parents an obligation to love the children they are raising. Here are the reasons why it does.

Keep in mind that those who raise a child are especially central figures in her life. Suppose that they do attend to the child's physical needs and do see to it that she has an education, but have no love for her. This lack won't end the child's life, of course. Nor will it freeze her psychological development at the stage of living from moment to moment, or mean that she must be greatly impaired in every project she will undertake. Still, to be unloved by those who raised her would handicap the child substantially in an important part of life: namely, in what we might call "intimate relationships."

The damage done would vary. The way the child's unloving parents treated her might have taught her that although there are people who ought to be loved, she isn't one of them. Or she might have gotten a message that love is a foolish affectation, since it isn't something her parents have for her, so she would regard the inclination to love others as a flaw to be overcome. Then again, she might believe that her parents do love her and might take their example as her paradigm for loving—in which case she will take loving someone as having nothing to do with being greatly affected by what happens to this person, and still less with being willing to make sacrifices for his sake. No doubt there are other possibilities.

There will be countermessages for the child, of course, and it is possible that someone else will provide the love that her parents do not. That means a particular set of unloving parents might not burden their child in any of these ways, despite their own failure to love her. But a parent's responsibility isn't only to refrain from *harming* his or her child as a future pursuer of acceptable projects, but also to help her in this. That help includes raising her in a way that helps to equip her to be at least reasonably happy with her life. Intimate relationships are at least as important to an adult's happiness as having a left arm, so part of the help that parents owe their child is preparation for those relationships. They owe their child a decent paradigm of what it is to love someone, and a sense that she or he is worth loving herself or himself. Parents who do not love the children they are raising do not provide them this help, even if someone else steps in and saves the child from the handicaps this deficit threatens to impose.

It would also be wrong to think it is only the capacity for fulfilling intimate relationships that is put at risk if you are unloved by those who raise you. A parent who loves a child is a help and a comfort in a great deal that happens in the child's life, and some of what the parent does helps or comforts only because the child knows it is done with love. The child who doesn't have this is much more completely *alone* in dealing with what he is to do and with what happens to him. To be unloved imposes a variety of handicaps, then, and it would certainly fall short of nurture in how to live.[24]

Earlier I argued that parents have an obligation to love the children who are under their care in part because that love has so much to do with the children's being happy as children and in part because it is crucial to helping them become persons of their own. Here the argument has been that parents have this obligation because it is they who are raising the child, because their task in raising her is to help equip her for a life with which she will be reasonably happy, and because if they do not love their child during their long years together they will be so far from helping her in that way as to greatly burden her if someone else does not come to her rescue.

5.

With any luck at all, when children are young and growing up their parents do love them, and the children love the parents in return. It is also true that those who love their children while they are raising them normally continue to love them after the children are grown. Certainly what they feel for the child can't end promptly upon the child's reaching adulthood, or it won't have been love at all. Rather, parent and child continue to love one another and want to continue to be a family of some kind even though the child's life is now to be more independent of the parents. Although that is the way life very often goes and the way the parties want it to go, I want to argue next that it is not an obligation of parenthood to love one's grown sons and daughters no matter what happens after they are adults. That is one of the ways in which this later stage of life differs from the time when the children were young and under their parents' care.

Notice first that the same arguments said to show that there is an obligation to love our children while they are young don't work equally well with regard to loving them once they are grown. This is easy to see in the case of the argument that derived the obligation to love our children while they are young from the obligation to raise them to become reasonably happy with their lives. Clearly, we do not have the latter obligation, once they are adults. A parent who acted as if he did have it would violate his grown child's autonomy. That parent would take this grown person as still to be in his charge rather than an adult who now has the primary responsibility for what sort of person she is and for how her life goes. So if we have an obligation to love our grown children, it certainly isn't because we are still responsible for them in the same ways.

An earlier point was that although older children are project-pursuers-in-the-waiting, as Lomasky takes them to be, they also have projects and quasiprojects underway already. Adults too are both project-pursuers and project-pursuers-in-the-waiting. One of the main reasons that our projects do not remain unchanged for our whole adult lives is that *we* change, both in what matters to us or in our manner of pursuing it. This factor suggests that adults, like children, have rights with regard to these future selves as well as rights against encroachment upon their current projects.

Even that fact wouldn't help to establish a parental obligation to love adult sons and daughters, however. In part this is because it is the adult sons and daughters who should author their future selves, and not their parents. That task has become theirs to do in part because, as adults, they have a fair chance of having the resources with which to do it reasonably well, as children do not. Even if it is also part of the human condition that life is very hard for *adults* whom no one loves, it is not too much to ask an adult to find someone other than his parents to do so. It *is* too much to ask a child to find an alternative to his parents if they do not love him, for a host of reasons. So an adult's need for love does not entitle him to be loved by someone who put him in a position in which he is helpless to avoid the harms in being unloved, as a child's need for love entitles him to have this benefit from his parents.

Finally, I also asserted that a parent's obligations don't all look to the child's future but also include some obligation to ensure that the child is happy while he is still a child. The idea was that a parent's love is essential to that happiness, so it is our obligation to love our children at this stage of their life. It isn't as though part of becoming an adult is no longer caring whether your parents love you. Certainly their love can still be important to a person's happiness. However, there is an argument that this situation does not equally lead to a conclusion that parents must love their grown children.

A first point is that the parent of an adult is not central to his life in the way the parent of a child is, even if the adult loves the parent and would be distressed if the parent were not to love him in return. I mean this as a causal claim. The parents of a young child have a rare power to affect the child's quality of the life. When he is young, he is in their hands, and therefore they have an obligation to make his life a happy one. The only analogy that comes to mind is one in which someone very ill is under your care. Then too the quality of the other person's life is very much up to you, and I think you have this same obligation to make it positive: to do some things just because they will make her happy, because she is in your hands. We do not have that same responsibility when the other person's happiness isn't so greatly up to us but has multiple sources.

As our children grow up, we become less central to their happiness, and they become more responsible for it themselves. We no longer have the same obligation to ensure that they are happy, because that obligation derived from the special ability we had then to control what life was like for them. So, for older children and for adults, an obligation to take special care that they are happy would need a different source. For older children, it has several such sources, in the responsibilities we still have to raise them. They are still in our charge in those ways, and loving them is part of carrying out those responsibilities, so it is still our obligation to love them. Since they are not in our charge once they are adults, we don't have a similar obligation to love them.

I am claiming here that parents are not responsible for the happiness of their grown children. For example, if a particular father did not love his grown son and this lack of love impaired the grown son's happiness, it would not follow that the father had failed in an obligation. Let me emphasize that this is a claim about parenthood *as such*, about what follows just from the fact that A is the parent of B. It doesn't mean that no parent has an obligation to help her grown child be happy. Many do, but it derives from their more particular relationship. It is due to the way in which they are parent and child to one another, rather than to their standing in this relationship at all. So, there will be parents who have no obligation to help their grown children be happy, because of what has passed between them. The obligation to love a child who is young and under your care, however, does derive just from his being your child. All parents have that obligation to a child they are raising; not all have it to one they have already raised.[25]

So far, I've contended only that certain arguments for a parental obligation to love a grown son or daughter won't do. I've given no reasons to think there cannot be any such argument. I think those reasons emerge if we recognize that love plays the same role in an adult's life as do the projects that we have a right to choose for ourselves and to pursue without encroachment. Projects and love are both forms of commitment, the former to an end ("striving to bring about the dictatorship of the proletariat, serving God...writing the Great American Novel...")[26] and the latter to the person one loves. Both kinds of commitment "reach indefinitely into the future, play a central role within the endeavors of the individual, and provide a significant degree of structural stability to an individual's life"[27]: what you felt for someone wouldn't be love if it didn't fit this description. Both "explain more than an action; they help to explain a life"[28]: that you were a devoted husband to this particular woman for forty years does that, as does having raised children who loved you, and so on. Just as we should be at liberty to choose what projects shape both our lives and ourselves, we should also be free to choose which people shape these by being the ones we love.

We do not live alone, as my emphasis on projects might suggest, but with others. What is involved in loving a particular person is worked out between the two of you: what you expect of each other, that is, what is acceptable without question, what would require explaining, what would put the relationship at risk, and what would put an end to it. Of course I don't mean that there is a written contract, or even that these matters are defined once and for all, but only that they come to be the particular way in which the two of you love each other. This is done mutually, though one party can certainly be more in control of the shape the relationship takes than the other. Since you remain in the relationship by choice, all of this remains your own doing in an important way. It is just as important for all of it to be up to you as it is for you to be free to choose which projects you pursue and when you abandon one project and take up another. Both are ways in which we define the particular life we live and thereby also create the people we become through the way we live.

It isn't going to follow that we can't treat anyone wrongly where love is concerned, any more than we can't do anyone wrong in the course of pursuing our projects. There are also projects we ought not to undertake because we are bound to act wrongly in the course of carrying them out: "being able to kill in cold blood without a glimmer of remorse" could be one, to use one of Lomasky's examples.[29] If there are people we ought not to love, it will be for reasons of that same kind: that is, it will be because loving that person will require acting in ways we should not.

There are also projects we have an obligation to pursue, but only because we have acted in ways that require doing so. For example, fathering a child puts one under an obligation to raise that child, although that obligation can be shifted to others if they will freely undertake it. There are no particular projects we have an obligation to pursue *as such*, in virtue only of the projects they are. The choices are ours, including even the choice of what sort of good person we wish to become.

The choices of whom to love are the same. That's the sense in which Frankfurt is right to say, "There are no necessary truths or *a priori* principles from which it can be established what we are to love."[30] Whom we love is up to us, assuming we have done nothing to freely accept an obligation to love someone or something in particular. We get to choose whom to love, as part of choosing what life we have.

It follows that there is no parental obligation to love our children after they have grown. If there were, it would mean that adults are not free after all to decide whom to love. It would also mean they do not have a choice whether to act in the ways that will retain someone's love, since parents would be obligated to continue to love their grown children no matter how those children treated them. Both states of affairs would leave us at too little liberty to choose what sort of life we are to have.

I did argue earlier that all parents have an obligation to love their children at an earlier stage, while they are raising them. It might seem that this obligation too must conflict with our being free to choose the lives we are to have, but it does not. That obligation is incurred by our own actions: by having created the child, or by having adopted her. To do either of these is to choose a life that includes an obligation to love her, for reasons offered in earlier sections. This circumstance illustrates one legitimate limit to our liberty to choose what sort of life to have: we aren't free to choose one that includes accepting obligations that we don't keep.

It also suggests the way in which parents can come to have an obligation to love their grown children. What they have done in the past can commit them to this love, just as creating the child committed them to loving him while he was young. In the next chapter I will argue that what commits us to loving our grown children is exactly that: loving them while they are young. It commits us to continuing, for reasons to be explained.

10

Having Grown Children

Raising children to have good lives when they are adults is a long-term project, and it is also rather abstract. Fortunately, it blends nicely with the day-to-day. Carrying it out requires lending the child more particular aid in everything from how to tie her shoes to how to treat his sister to how to deal with disappointments. Good parents help their young children in many such ways, and in doing so they are also preparing them for life as adults.

That is what parenthood is like when the children are "still children," at any rate, but childhood does come to an end. In the normal course of events children become adults, both biologically and in the expectations that their society has of them. What becomes of parenthood then?

One possibility is that it too comes to an end. Certainly some parental responsibilities do. Part of being an adult is being free to decline the help that others might provide. So although parents certainly can still be of help to their adult sons and daughters, they can no longer impose their help in the way they once could have done (and, under some circumstances, would have had an obligation to do). Nor is an adult entitled to expect her parents' help in all of the ways she once was entitled to expect it: when we are grown up, there is a good deal we ought to manage on our own, at least if we are able to do so. More generally, we are free to work out with other adults whether the two of us are to play a role in each other's lives and, if so, what that role is to be.

It could be that parents are no different from anyone else in these respects once their children have become adults. That is, they might have no special obligations to their grown sons and daughters, nor might they be at liberty to treat them any differently than anyone else would, nor might they be owed any special obligations themselves by the children they had raised. In short, it could be that nothing at all follows from the fact that this person is their daughter or their son, where so much once did; the end of one person's childhood could also be the end of another person's parenthood.

That certainly wouldn't be what most parents and grown children would want, and it would also be remarkable. Ordinarily, an intimate relationship of many years' standing leaves moral remainders. We are imagining that a history as parent and child is different, leaving the parties as strangers to each other. It is hard to see why that should be true. It is much more plausible that what parent and child were to each other in the earlier years has great bearing on how they should act when the child is grown, just as past behavior bears on this in other contexts. The question of interest is what differences it makes in this case. What is the moral relationship between a parent and a child once the child has become an adult? This chapter and the next two offer an account of that issue.

I begin by arguing that parents do still have what we might call special liberties where their grown children are concerned, and I explain both why that is true and what these liberties are. I also argue that parents have obligations to their grown children and offer a view of what those obligations are. Since I maintain that their moral relationship after the child is grown is greatly affected by the life they had when the child was under the parent's care, it will be important not to ignore the ways those earlier lives can differ. Some people are good parents to their children at that time, and some are not. I discuss the differences that conduct makes once the child has become an adult.

Finally, the parents of grown children face a particular risk of acting as if their grown son or daughter were still a child. I close by discussing what constitutes going wrong in this way.

1.

Imagine a father who takes great interest in what his growing child does and in what happens in her life. It is important to him to be a good father. However, the regard that he has is like that of someone who trains horses for a living and whose concern for them is a deep interest in his own record as a trainer. The father and the trainer both pay careful attention to their charges, but it is really attention to how they are doing themselves. This father does not exult *for his daughter*, or feel hurt or disappointed *for her*, but only for himself. This attitude is certainly better than indifference, but it also misses one of life's great opportunities to have someone whose fortunes matter to you in the same way as your own, and sometimes more intensely.

I argued that parents ought to love their young children; those who do are not like this father at all. They are extremely empathetic where their children are concerned. It hurts them when their child has a bad experience, and they are delighted when he has an especially good one. If he faces a dilemma, this engages them as if the choice were their own. They can be proud of what their children do in the same way they would have been if they had done it themselves, and they can also be made deeply ashamed by what their children do.

This connection couldn't possibly end automatically when the child reached adulthood, or it would not be the identification with the other person that I've described. It is a variety of love, and love does not end on a schedule but only upon some sundering event or through some gradual process. So the norm is for parents who love their children—as good parents do—to continue to love them when they reach adulthood. Since we do not love most people, that is one way in which our children are different to us than most other people are, if we were good parents to them. We love them at least at the start of their adult years and often for the rest of our lives.

So what? The fact that one person loves another might appear to have little moral force. In our case, perhaps it entitles the parents to be treated with some kindness by the objects of their affection. It's plausible to say that we owe those who love us some consideration of that kind, since we have such power to wound them—but that's not much. It's also true that those who love us take a great interest in us and want to play a part in our life—but surely this factor alone doesn't entitle them to play that part.

Suppose next, though, that you were aware that someone loved you, you accepted this fact, and you conveyed your acceptance to him. Then you would have agreed to something, and this would make a great difference. There are special circumstances under which you would have agreed only that this other person might yearn for you, keeping you in his heart but doing no more than that. Perhaps you are adults who are married to others, and although you will allow this person to pine for you that is all you will allow. Or you are of the same gender, and although the other person is "out," you are not ready to be. Those situations are a little cruel in the constraints they impose. What is of interest is that they do impose constraints: ordinarily, to agree that someone is to love you is to permit him some ways in which to put his love into action. It is also to agree that he may know much more about you than you allow just anyone to know. The specifics are worked out between you. They needn't be unchanging, and there can be points of disagreement, but they do serve to define a different role that this person is to have in your life.

Here is what that has to do with children. The ones who are raised by loving parents accept their parents' love, ordinarily, and convey that acceptance to them. They do not regard their parents as one would a *stalker*, or even as some unthreatening suitor who annoys them and who they wish would leave them alone. Children do say hurtful things along these lines to their parents, of course, and they can heartily dislike some of the ways in which their parents put their love for them into action. That isn't at all the same as actually wanting their parents not to love them, though. The norm for children who have good parents is to accept their love while chafing at some of the forms it takes, and to convey this acceptance to the parents through their own behavior, if not also verbally. That response gives permission for the love to continue, and encourages it.

This permission is not automatically revoked upon one's reaching adulthood, any more than the love itself ends automatically at that point. What ordinarily do change are the ways in which the love is put into action—as they should. For example, adult children are right to resist if their parents continue to monitor their behavior as closely as they did when the children were young and under their care, or continue to be as vigilant about who their companions are. Again, though, for the grown son or daughter to reject these manifestations is not a way of rejecting being loved at all. Ordinarily, the love is still accepted and encouraged, and the agreement that it is to continue remains in place. The question of interest is what a grown child grants in this way.

The specifics will depend on the individuals, but they will be variations on the themes noted earlier. By agreeing that her parents are to love her, a grown child agrees that they are not to be kept at the same distance as people in general where information about her life is concerned. She also agrees that her parents may act in ways that express their love for her. The parties work out the particulars: what the parents may know and what is to remain private, how the parents may express their love and how they may not. Those boundaries give their relationship as adults its distinctive contours, are subject to change over time, and can certainly be objects of disagreement, just as they might always have been. Still, in accepting her parents' love, the grown child agrees that they may act in a range of ways that are not open to others, because (1) one needs permission to act in those ways and (2) others do not have that permission. This arrangement is a first respect in which parenthood continues when childhood ends, in the case of those who have been good parents to their children.

2.

Of course, to be at liberty to act in certain ways is not the same as having an obligation. I believe the parents we are considering do also have obligations to their grown children. In particular, they have an obligation to be of help to them, beyond the obligation they have to be of help to just anyone. To see how this obligation arises, let us first imagine two adults who are not parent and grown child. One of them regularly provides the other with a ride to work. The driver never promises that she will come every day, but she knows that the passenger has come to expect her—or at least, she should know this. I think her practice of faithfully appearing entitles him to expect her, so that if she simply fails to appear one morning she will have done him a wrong.

The underlying principle is that we ought to keep our commitments. The other claim here is that there is a commitment in regularly acting in a way that has some importance to others, if you know or should know that you are nurturing the expectation that you will continue. This is true only if your regular behavior is not wrong for independent reasons, it is worth noting. So, for example, a faithful record of perjuring yourself or of murdering those who anger you doesn't put you under a moral obligation to do these things again, even if you know that others have come to expect that you will. However, when it is *not* wrong to act in a way you have knowingly encouraged others to expect and it is important to them that you do so, you have a moral obligation to come through as expected. Here is what that has to do with parents and grown children.

As has been noted, good parents love their children while the children are young and this feeling ordinarily continues after they are grown. It is part of loving someone to be disposed to be of help to him, to a much greater extent than one is disposed to help just anyone. Of course, there will be differences in how this disposition is put into action, because there are differences in the help that a particular child needs, the help he will permit his parents to give, the help they are in a position to give, and the help they are inclined to give. Still, those differences provide variety within a norm, which is that parents regularly do in fact help their children in time of need, more substantially and at greater cost to themselves than they help just anyone. This practice nurtures the expectation that their help will continue. Parents know that it does, or should know this, and ordinarily their help also meets the extra condition mentioned, in that providing it is not morally wrong for independent reasons. So, the parents acquire a moral obligation to behave in this way in the future, by virtue of their behavior in the past, just as the driver acquires an obligation to continue to provide her passenger with rides to work.

As was noted, we do not love everyone as we do our children, so parents do not act in this way toward just anyone. As a result they don't in this way come to have the obligation in question to everyone. This is a second way in which parenthood is a different moral relationship than we have to others even after our children have become adults, at least in the case of those who have been good parents when their children were young and under their care. What more can be said about the content of this obligation?

In the initial example, regularly providing rides to work led to an obligation to continue to provide them. We can also be of help to someone generally, rather than helpful only in one particular way: think here of friends, of whom this is surely true. When we are, this behavior too encourages the other person to count on us for "more of the same." Here the expectation we have nurtured is for him or her to count on us in general, and certainly for needs of a similar urgency that could be served with no more effort than we have expended in the past. There will be room for disagreement over exactly what should be expected, and thus over when our friend would be entitled to be disappointed in us. That's life, but life also includes clear cases. A past pattern of general helpfulness obligates a person at least to continue to be generally helpful, just as faithfully providing one specific kind of help obligates one to continue to do that.

It can also be clear from our behavior that the reason we do not currently help a particular person in a certain way is that we are unable to do so, or that she does not need help of this kind at present. It can also be clear that we would be of help in this way if things were to change: that we would help her financially if we had resources we do not have or if she had needs she does not have, for example. This is another respect in which it isn't only a pattern of providing a particular kind of help that serves to encourage the other person to rely on us for it and commits us to providing it under the right circumstances, as it was with the woman who provided rides to work.

There are several implications of interest. Typically, those who have been good parents are *generally* helpful to their grown children, rather than helpful only in a single way. Many also make it clear that they would be helpful in ways they have not yet had occasion to be, if the need were to arise. Doing that entitles their grown children to rely on them in general and makes it the parents' obligation to generally come through. On the other hand, some who were good parents when their children were young are not generally helpful after the children are grown, and some are never helpful in particular ways even though the need for help of that kind has arisen. For example, they might not be helpful financially, or they might not help by looking after the grandchildren. *These* parents have certainly not encouraged their children to rely on them in these ways. That encouragement would have been the source of an obligation to act accordingly, on the account I am offering, so these parents come out as having no such obligation. Their children are certainly free to ask them for financial help, or to ask them to look after the grandchildren, and so on, but doing so will be asking for favors rather than for something their parents have an obligation to provide.

That situation would change if the parents regularly helped *when asked*. If they did, their children would be entitled to expect that variety of helpfulness to continue, assuming the parents did not make it clear that they were not to be counted on for this. But let us imagine instead that the parents are never specifically asked for help of a particular kind, or that they decline to help when they are, and that they have not nurtured any expectation of general helpfulness. As a result, the parents have no obligation to provide help of this kind, on the view I am offering. Does this take a parent's obligations too lightly?

Bear in mind first that these people had been good parents when their children were young, and they continued to love them after they were grown. We are not yet considering parents who played the role very poorly when the children were young, or who are not helpful to their grown children in any way. The current question concerns those who simply will not help their children in some ways, though they do love them and would help them in others.

Their behavior does fail to meet some standards for what a parent should be, and it will earn the disapproval of those who hold those standards dear. However, the standards in question call for something more specific than loving one's children and being helpful to them. I recommend that we construe standards that call for these expectations as personal ideals, rather than as marks that all parents must meet if they are not to do their grown children wrong. This recommendation needs clarifying.

To many, what they do as parents is hugely important to their sense of themselves, in the same way as performance in a career can be crucial to someone's sense of whether he or she is a good person. Such people may hold themselves to high standards in the matter in question. Living up to those standards is what matters to them, and it matters deeply. Not all their failures to accomplish this end should even be occasions for self-reproach, in my opinion, but that is a separate issue. What is of interest here is judging *others* by the high standards to which one holds oneself: taking *them* not to have succeeded in their careers, or not to have been the parents they should have been, because they have not met one's own standard for doing so. That practice will be mistaken, if one's standard is unreasonably high or reflects only personal preferences.

It will also be an easy mistake to make in those aspects of life where there is much room for argument about what should count as falling short, once we are beyond the obvious, and much room for individuality. What constitutes having the career you should have had is one example. So is what constitutes being the parent you should be, I believe. The view I have offered has the virtue of respecting the various standards. It leaves room for differences in the ways in which people are good parents to their grown children, including some differences in the amount and kinds of help they wish to give. Not all of our differences in these respects are moral failures on someone's part, I am suggesting.

For a related point, consider next a parent who has been helpful to his child in some way and now wishes to stop. In the earlier example of someone who regularly provided another person a ride to work, it was objectionable for her simply to fail to appear one morning. But all she need do to avoid that complaint is to give fair warning that she won't be coming. If she tells her usual passenger this in time for him to have a reasonable opportunity to make other arrangements, she has played fair with the expectation she has nurtured. In the same way, if parental obligations follow this same model, it isn't even necessary to continue to help one's grown child in the ways one has in the past. It is necessary only to give him fair warning that one will no longer do this.

Are parental obligations so easily eliminated? I think that they are, but the act of eliminating them is subject to moral evaluation in its own right. Think first of someone who breaks off an expectation for no good reason, heedless of the difficulty that this cessation causes the other person. That behavior is inconsiderate, sometimes especially so, and we ought not to be inconsiderate. It is an especially poor way to treat a friend, because we should be particularly averse to causing trouble for our friends, and doing so for no good reason strains both the friendship and the contention that we *are* friends. It isn't that we cannot treat our friends inconsiderately, and it isn't that doing so is bound to end the friendship. We can act inconsiderately by canceling an obligation without due regard for its effects on our friend or in some other way, and the friendship might survive. The point is just that it is very clearly something we should not do.

The same holds for parents and grown children. The problem isn't that parents cannot end their obligation to provide the child the kind of help they have always provided. It's only that for them to do so for inadequate reasons casts doubt on the sort of relationship they have had before now, it is inconsiderate, and that is no way for them to treat their child, just as it is no way to treat a friend. In short, what is objectionable isn't the idea that parents can cancel obligations to be helpful to their grown children, but rather their doing so for inadequate reasons. That behavior would cast doubt on whether they loved their children, since we have a good deal more concern for those we love than such behavior suggests that they have for their children.

In contrast, imagine a parent who does have good reasons for telling her child that she will no longer help in the way she has helped him in the past. For example, she might tell him that she won't get him out of a certain kind of trouble again, because her record of doing so seems to have encouraged him to be reckless in this regard. Or she might tell him that she will not provide the financial backing for yet another business venture, given his history of losing interest in these once they are underway. Those warnings relieve her of the obligation to help him in these ways, on the view I am offering. I think this view is preferable to alternatives under which parents must always continue to help in any ways they have helped in the past or they do those children wrong. It allows the parents to treat their grown children as adults in a certain way, by not always protecting them from the consequences of their own behavior, as one might a child. It also allows love to include withholding something the other person wants, on the ground that he would be ill-served by having it. Love for an adult should permit that, so long as it is only occasional rather than a regular practice where this person is concerned.

3.

I have focused so far on what it is to continue to be good parents to our children after they have become adults. Consider next those who never were good parents when their children were under their care. They did nothing beyond what was needed for the society to allow them to remain in the role of parents; perhaps they were also sometimes abusive as well. I argued that the parental obligation to be of help to one's grown children derived from nurturing the expectation that the help would continue. If so, these parents seem to be off the hook entirely. They have no such obligation to help their grown sons and daughters, precisely because they were bad parents to them all along.

Actually, I think it is true that they do not have the same obligation to be of help that better parents have, but they do have another. They have done their children a great wrong by being bad parents when the children were under their care, and they have an obligation to make up for that wrong. That isn't an easy obligation to discharge, just as it isn't easy to do this on other occasions when one person has badly damaged another person's life. Think here of civil wrongs in which one party has made it impossible for another to pursue what would have been her livelihood, or has caused the death of her child, or has removed some other great source of joy and meaning from her life. There is no way to "make the victim whole" in such cases, and there is also no way for thoroughly bad parents to compensate their children for the harm they have done them. However, in both kinds of cases there are gestures of acknowledgement that can be made, and, inadequate though these gestures are, there is an obligation to make them. In part, this is an obligation to be of help to this person, if she will accept the help. That obligation isn't the same one that good parents have to help their grown children, but it shouldn't be.

Consider next an example offered in a different context by Terrance McConnell:

> Suppose that Mark has good parents. They have tended to his material needs, provided him with emotional support, encouraged him in his various endeavors, and paid for his college education. Upon graduation from college, however, Mark secures a high-paying job and then severs all ties with his parents. He tells them that he no longer wants their help, nor will he do anything for them. Because of their lack of higher education and because of the menial nature of their jobs, Mark regards his parents as inferior.[1]

This isn't a single hurtful declaration that Mark makes one day and then apologizes for. It is meant to be a permanent break. Suppose Mark follows through. He goes about his new life with the people he regards as more his kind, and he has no more to do with his parents, rejecting their efforts even to contact him. Suppose further that a time comes when things go very badly for Mark, and he is in need of both emotional support and financial assistance. I have argued that there is a parental obligation to be of help to one's grown children, both for those who were good parents when the children were young and for those who were not. Do Mark's parents still have this obligation, despite his having discarded them so ungratefully?

I would say that they do not, even if they have continued to love their son and to make it plain that they would be more than willing to help him in any way they could. It's true that this assurance would have encouraged him to believe he could count on them, just as their behavior before he dismissed them from his life would have encouraged him to expect this. However, the encouragement after he discards them does not have the same significance it had in the earlier days.

One argument for this position takes it to be positively wrong for Mark's parents to help him. The premise of such an argument could be that helping him would be a failure of self-respect on their part, or that he deserves to suffer for his mistreatment of them and that what will happen to him without their help is no worse than he deserves, or that it is wrong to encourage anyone to believe he can act as Mark did without repercussions. If it is indeed wrong for them to help him, then his parents have no obligation to do so, despite the encouragement they have given him to expect they would, any more than we incur a moral obligation to perjure ourselves or to murder someone by leading others to believe that we will do these things. That's a different situation from the days before Mark disowned them, when there was nothing at all wrong with their being of help to him and when encouraging him to believe they would do so did commit them to doing so.

Not everyone will agree that it would be wrong for Mark's parents to help him after he rejects them, however. Perhaps their son is like a swimmer or a mountain climber who has gotten into terrible trouble by flaunting all the rules. It isn't positively wrong to rescue such people, at least if it can be done without high cost to others. On some views, helping them is an act of generosity rather than an obligation. On other views, though, there is an obligation to rescue foolish swimmers and mountain climbers if we can, even though it is their own fault that they need rescuing, at least if the rescue is a relatively easy one. It might be thought that Mark's parents have a similar obligation to come to his aid, despite his mistreatment of them: to rescue him even though he doesn't deserve it, at least if doing so won't be terribly costly to them or to others.

If they do have this obligation, though, the reason is not that they are his parents and he is their son. Rather, they would have the obligation because he is someone who greatly needs help that they are in a position to provide, just as the reason the potential rescuer has an obligation to save the foolish swimmers or mountain climbers is that these people badly need rescuing and he can rescue them. If Mark's parents have an obligation of that same kind, it isn't an obligation of parenthood. It is only another instance of this general obligation to help others who are in need. Mark has no greater claim to their help than anyone would who found himself in similar straits—the fact that he is their son is not relevant.

Shouldn't that relationship still count for *something*, though? Well, if he was their son biologically, then he is still their son in that sense, despite his having disowned them. He is also still their son in the sense that he is still someone they raised. Those ways to speak of someone as "our son" rest on facts about the past, and nothing Mark does after becoming an adult can change them. But he also did everything he could to sever the *continuing* relationship once he was grown: to stop having any special moral relationship to them as their son. If a person can succeed in that, then it isn't true that Mark is their son where special obligations are concerned, when he comes to need their help, and that they have obligations to him as his parents at that point. This is true even if they have encouraged him to rely on their help after he dismissed them and even if that encouragement did obligate them to come through for him. It still wouldn't be an obligation they had *as his parents*, that is, if Mark had put an end to that aspect of their lives.

The same is true if we believe, as I do, that Mark cannot entirely escape being his parents' son by declaring that he wants no more to do with them, because he cannot eliminate his own obligations to them in that way. It need only be true that he can relieve them of their obligations to him. I would say Mark is a good example of someone who has done exactly that. If his parents do help him, their help will be a gift, for which they are either to be admired or criticized depending on the soundness of the arguments against their helping him.

I have argued that there is a parental obligation to be of particular help to one's grown children, though it has a different basis for those who were good parents than for those who were bad ones. I have also argued that a grown child can release his parents from this obligation—yet another difference from the time when he was young and under their care, since he could not do that then. I have also claimed that parents can cancel their obligations to their grown children by making it clear that they are not to be counted on in the ways in question, noting that it can certainly be wrong for them to do this as well as right for them to do it. The next chapter returns to the idea that grown children cannot similarly cancel their obligations to their parents simply by declaring in a timely fashion that their parents are not to count on them. But first, the next section explores a special problem for those who want to be good parents to their grown children.

4.

The worry is that an effort to help one's grown son or daughter might treat this person as if he or she were still a child. Perhaps it would be perceived as such, and resented. Perhaps the child would tolerate it as a fault in someone she loved. Perhaps neither parent nor childwould see it for what it is, though it still seems to be the wrong way to act. The fact is that your adult son or daughter is not your child in the sense of still being under your care, and you are acting as if things hadn't changed in that way.

The risk of parents' making this error can be reduced while the children are still young, by permitting them to lead their own lives to an increasing degree. Then the child's becoming an adult calls only for more of the same, rather than for a radical change. Still, even those who raise their children as I've just described can certainly find it difficult not to be as central figures in the child's life as they once were, especially if they have greatly enjoyed that role and played it well.

What now, given that they still care deeply about their children? How are the expressions of their concern to change so that they treat their children as adults?

Two observations will help to sort this issue out. First, because the children are adults, the final choices about what they do are now theirs, including the choice of whether to have their parents' help. The grown children are the ones who should make these choices, rather than ceding them to their parents, because to have your parents continue to guide your life is to avoid adulthood and remain their child, in a significant respect. Second, when the children were still under their care, the parents bore considerable responsibility for the child's moral character, and, accordingly, were entitled to try to correct it as they saw fit. Neither of these things is true any longer. The responsibility for what grown children are like as people is their own, and there are new limits to the extent to which their parents are free to try to change them.

Failing to treat one's child as an adult is a matter of acting consistently as if one or more of these points were not true. By saying the fault is in behaving in this way *consistently*, I mean that we do not necessarily treat someone as a child every time that we do something for her, rather than (at most) helping her to do it herself. Doing something for someone on occasion can simply be a favor, and there is a difference between doing a favor and treating this person as if he were a child.

It can also be a favor to do something for someone not just on some occasion, but regularly. For example, the fact that you bring your neighbor's paper up from the street every morning doesn't make this a case of treating him as if he were a child, even though you are doing this for him rather than helping him to do it and even though you are doing it "all the time." It might seem that the reason this is true is that there is no implication that your neighbor is incompetent to do the thing in question, or at least far less competent than you. Certainly that implication is sometimes the complaint when a parent is said to have treated her grown child as if he were "still a child."

However, even if there were an implication that the other person were less than competent, that wouldn't actually be enough to make helping her a case of treating her like a child. To see why not, suppose that someone who is adept with machines regularly solves my problems with them rather than helping me to do the solving. He just takes over the task, that is, as a parent might take over the task facing a child. His help implies (rightly, as it happens) that he is more competent than I, if not that I am incompetent, but it does not treat me as if I were a child. Something further is needed: something suggesting that the trouble is that I am a child, or childlike, and so the other person must take over. Here are some thoughts about what that situation comes to.

It is one part of our conception of a child that children are not just less competent in a particular matter, as another adult might be, but less competent broadly speaking. With admitted exceptions, children are not just less adept with machines, for example, but generally less adept at anything complicated that an adult might be called upon to do. To treat someone as if *that* fact were true in her case would be to treat her as if she were a child. It would be done by taking over not just some particular area of life, but very generally, when there was something of any difficulty or any importance to be done. If so, then part of treating one's child as an adult is just avoiding that pattern. It doesn't require that you never take over the task but just confine yourself to helping him do it. Unfortunately, what it does require is less easily identified, and hence more subject to error and to disagreement over when the boundaries have been crossed.

There might also be matters that no normal adult would be incompetent to deal with. Regularly to do a wide range of those things for someone would be insulting, implying that this person was like a child in these respects. That behavior too could count as failing to treat her as an adult. This issue shades into the different idea that these are not things for this particular person to do, despite their being what the culture expects of adults. Your doing these things would keep her as your child in these respects: something she might resent or might readily accept, not wanting to be an adult in those ways just yet, if at all. If so, another part of treating one's child as an adult is declining to do regularly for her what the culture expects of adults.

Third, insofar as a child is less competent at something than an adult, that is often due to differences between a child's level of experience and that of an adult. Those differences do not vanish instantly when the child becomes an adult, but they do fade away in time. At some point, it is no longer true that the parent has had more experience in some matter or that the child has had insufficient experience, but only that the experiences each has had have been different ones. That difference changes the kind of help the parent can offer. To assume instead that one's grown child's experience is inadequate is a third way in which to treat him as if he were still a child—as if he had had only very little of life rather than merely a different life than yours. That error can be made in taking over a decision, but it can also be made in the way in which advice is offered.

Finally, it is easy to forget that not all differences over what is to be done are disagreements between one person who is correct and another who is incorrect. Often there is simply more than one way to do the thing in question, each with its own virtues and its own drawbacks. The choice between them can be personal, in several ways. Preferring one of the options can reflect features of personality: it can be gregarious rather than retiring, for example. It can also reflect competing features of perfectly acceptable character: it can be courageous while the alternative would be more protective of one's family's interests. Or, it can require one set of talents rather than another. In cases of these kinds, there is not much difference between insisting that the other person do the thing in the way you think it should be done and insisting that he be like you. When our children are under our care, we have some liberty to try to make them become like us, as part of urging them to become the kind of people we would like them to be. When they are adults, it is up to them who they are, and we are no longer entitled to press our favored conception of it in the same ways. To do so is to treat them as if they were still our children; to treat them as adults requires allowing them to be as they are, when that is just a different way in which to be a good person. Doing so can include allowing them to act in their way, even though it isn't *our* way.

This chapter has discussed how grown parents should act toward their grown children, given that their grown children are still their sons and daughters. The next chapter takes up the other half of the story: how grown sons and daughters ought to act toward those who are, after all, still their parents.

11

Filial Obligations

Do grown children have special obligations where their parents are concerned? The belief that they do is deeply held. As Simon Keller observes, "It is common for people to make large sacrifices in order to provide for their parents, and to do so, in part, because they feel that it is their duty...think of a rich son who cannot be bothered to do anything to help his parents—his lonely and impoverished but perfectly loving parents, who did all they could to give him the best possible opportunities in life—and try not to disapprove."[1] If we do have these obligations, though, why do we have them, and what do they require of us? Do we have them as long as our parents are alive? Can we fulfill these obligations once and for all, so that a time comes when we have no further filial duties? Can our parents act in ways that release us from them? I shall try to say.

1.

One view is that we do indeed have filial duties and that these are debts of gratitude that we owe to our parents for all they did when we were young and under their care. According to Keller, this is "by far the most popular account of filial duty in the recent philosophical literature."[2] It has also been heavily criticized, on the ground that although we can owe debts of gratitude to some people, we cannot owe them to our parents for what they did when we were only children. According to one argument, this is so because we didn't ask our parents to do those things for us, and we were not even in a position to refuse to allow them to.[3] According to another, we owe our parents no gratitude because they had an obligation to do what they did for us during that time, and we ought not to be grateful to someone just for carrying out her obligations.[4]

The conclusion to these arguments remains startling. Think again about the "rich son who cannot be bothered to do anything for his parents—his lonely and impoverished but perfectly loving parents, who did all they could to give him the best possible opportunities in life." Surely the terms that come to mind for him include *ingrate*, or possibly *ungrateful wretch*, whereas the arguments entail that it is deeply unfair to think of him in that way, because he is not at all the paradigm of ingratitude that he seems. I believe this view is mistaken: children do owe their parents their gratitude. However, I want mainly to pursue this excellent insight of Keller's: "while it may well be true that parents merit gratitude and children have a duty to engage in acts of gratitude, filial duties in general cannot be understood as duties of gratitude."[5] That is, filial duties are something else, over and above whatever debts of gratitude we owe our parents.

That proposition might remind us that gratitude is not ordinarily all that parents want from their grown children. Ordinarily, parents don't hope only to be fondly remembered and honored for what they did in days gone by, but to have some more current role in their children's lives. If it's true that there are filial duties over and above the debts of gratitude, they would be right to want more.

The first question, however, is why gratitude theories err in taking filial duties to be duties of gratitude if not because gratitude is altogether out of place where our parents are concerned. Keller's arguments on this score take gratitude theories this way: "The gratitude theory says that to fulfill your filial duties is to perform appropriate acts of gratitude in response to the good things your parents have done for you.... What are duties of gratitude? As Fred R. Berger has argued, they are best construed as duties to demonstrate or communicate feelings of gratitude, which is to say they are duties to show that you feel appropriately grateful (or perhaps to act as you would if you did feel appropriately grateful) for a given benefit."[6]

Keller's first argument against such a view is as follows: "Filial duties are direct duties to help, respect, please or benefit parents, not duties to do these things in order, or in so far as they are required, to demonstrate gratitude. Suppose that you go out of your way to be sure that you are with your mother while she goes through a difficult medical procedure. What (conceivably) makes your act obligatory is the fact that she needs or wants you there, that things will be better for her in certain respects if you are around—not the fact (if it is a fact) that your presence will be understood by her to show that you are grateful for the sacrifices that she has made for you in the past."[7]

He is certainly right that what lies at the heart of your duty to be with your mother at this difficult time is the good it would do her, not the fact (if it is a fact) that she would take it to show that you were properly grateful. However, this might mean only that the gratitude theory should be formulated differently. Suppose the theory held that what we owe our parents isn't proof of our gratitude but the gratitude itself, understood as a particular kind of good will that we should have toward them in connection with what they had done for us. This good will wouldn't be a disposition to *show* our parents that we were properly grateful. It would be a disposition to help them to fare well, which we had because of what we took them to have done for us.

Of course, one way to help your particular set of parents fare well could be to show them that you were appropriately grateful. Whether that was important to them would depend on them, as would how much reassurance they needed on this score. Obviously, though, there is also more to what would help a parent than this reassurance. Being there for your mother when she has a difficult medical procedure is also highly likely to help her precisely because "things will be better for her in certain respects if you are around." If so, on this version of the gratitude theory the reason you would have an obligation to do this wouldn't be that it would show her you were grateful, and that such demonstration is what we owe someone to whom we owe our gratitude. Rather, the reason would be that this is what you would do if you cared about her as you should: if you were as grateful as you should be, given what she did for you. It is what you would do if you had that degree of good will toward her, because her faring well in this way would be sufficient motivation for you to do it despite what doing it would cost you.

This notion does not make the good it would do your mother the entire explanation for why you should be there. The reasoning doesn't come down to this: she's your mother, and it would be good for her if you did this, so you have an obligation to do it. Rather, on this version of the gratitude theory, whether you have an obligation to be there depends on how valuable it would be for her if you were, on how costly it would be to you to be there, and on whether what she had done for you called for you to pay such costs in order to provide her benefits of that value to her. Perhaps this reasoning is objectionable, but the objection can't be the one Keller offers. That is, it can't be that this theory takes the matter of importance to be that "your presence will be understood by your mother as showing that you are grateful for the sacrifices that she has made for you in the past." On the version of a gratitude theory that I've suggested, her understanding that you are grateful is not the heart of this matter but is only one of the ways to help her fare well.

There could also be a secondary obligation, not just to be grateful but to convey this gratitude *when that is needed*. That would accommodate a related point Keller makes:

> Some people are uncomfortable with or uninterested in displays of gratitude.... Parents can be just like this....If you have such parents, then your duty to demonstrate your gratitude to them is less demanding than, or at any rate calls for very different actions from, the duty that you would have otherwise. But you do not thereby have less demanding or very different filial duties generally. If you choose to play golf instead of visiting your mother after her operation, then it is no excuse to say "She is not one for constant displays of gratitude."[8]

Keller's golfer poses a problem for the first version of a gratitude theory, the one that says filial duties are duties to *demonstrate* your gratitude. On that theory, the golfer would have no filial duty to see how things had gone for his mother, and it certainly seems as if he does. However, the example poses no problem if the theory is instead that the man should be grateful enough to care a good deal about how things go for his mother, and it takes demonstrations only to be a secondary obligation that we have in the event that a demonstration is called for. That secondary obligation wouldn't obtain, in this case, but the primary one certainly could, leaving him with the obligation we think he has.

How so? As was noted, there is much more to how things go for his mother than whether she values displays of gratitude. The other ways in which it would be good for her if her son were there could make it very much in her interest if he were to come, and thus something he would do if he had the gratitude to her that he should. In addition, part of caring about someone is to have that person on your mind when you know that she is in difficulty. So, it could also be that if his mother mattered to her son as much as she should, he would be unable to go on with business as usual—or, in this case, with golf as usual. For both reasons, the obligation to be properly grateful could call for the son to visit his mother instead of playing golf even though she "is not one for constant displays of gratitude," on the view I've offered.

I think that response disables Keller's first objection to gratitude theories, but he has others. "Secondly, the extent of duties of gratitude depends upon how much discomfort, exertion and sacrifice is involved in the provision of the relevant benefit, and [this] makes such duties different in a further respect from filial duties."[9] Other things being equal, we ought to be more grateful when someone has given up a lot in order to help us than when it was very easy for her to do. Accordingly, if your parents have to make great sacrifices in order to give you a good upbringing, you ought to be especially grateful to them. But now suppose that they had been persons of a different kind, who "find that they are just made to be parents; they love being parents and can think of nothing else that they would want to do with the time and energy involved; they find it an exhilarating breeze. It might make sense for children of sacrificing parents to feel an extra kind of gratitude for their upbringing. But the children of effortless parents do not have lesser filial duties, speaking generally, than those of sacrificing parents. Your duty to look after your father in his old age is not mitigated by his having found parenting so much fun."[10] It's the same filial duty regardless of his sacrifices, and that means it *isn't* a duty to be as grateful to him as his sacrifices call for you to be.

These are points about being grateful for someone's *actions*, however. It will be worth exploring the reply that a child can also have something else for which he should be grateful: namely, the place he had in the affections of his parents. As with the good will expressed in beneficent acts, the continuing good will that another person has toward us comes in degrees. Unlike the acts, however, the measure of a person's continuing good will toward you isn't the sacrifices she makes for you, because that depends on what sacrifices the circumstances call for her to make. If it were what determined how greatly you mattered to her, there would be no difference between the following two people who had never given up anything much for your sake: one who would have done so if the occasion arose, and one who wouldn't have dreamed of it. The second of these is indifferent to you, but the first is not. The first is only someone who hasn't had the opportunity to demonstrate in this way how important it is to her that you fare well.

There are also ways in which good will toward someone affects both what is a sacrifice for us and what we experience as a sacrifice. Think again of the son who will have to miss his golf game if he is to be present when his mother emerges from surgery. Suppose that the appeal golf has for him lies in how greatly he enjoys the experience of playing: it's just a highly pleasurable activity, for him. The round he would play when he knew his mother was emerging from surgery would lose a lot of that appeal if he cared a great deal about her. Perhaps it would lose all of its appeal—the amount depends on how much he cares about her. In either case, that morning's round wouldn't be the pleasure that golf usually is for him, precisely because he cares too much about what happens to her.

If so, missing this particular round wouldn't be a sacrifice (or wouldn't be much of one) since it wouldn't be something of great value to him that he would have to give up in order to be with her. If the only sign of the place she has in his affections is the degree of sacrifice in his actions, missing his golf game would count for little or nothing. But clearly there is a different way in which there is considerable good will toward his mother in his skipping the round in order to be with her.

Suppose next that what he values in golf is something quite different than the pleasures of playing, namely the advantages he gains in business from playing with this particular set of partners. Suppose too that those partners would hold it against him if he were to cancel, even for this reason. In that case he clearly *would* be sacrificing something of value to him if he were to skip the game and tend to his mother. Here the interesting point is that although it could feel to him as if he were making a sacrifice when he went to the hospital, it could also feel as if this were no sacrifice at all even though, as was noted, it does cost him something of importance to him. Because how she fares is so much more important to him than the business opportunities, it could be that once he knows his mother needs him in this particular way this is the only thing on his mind, and it gives rise to fewer regrets in the aftermath. The extent to which this was true would indicate how central a place she held in his interests.

These points suggest that how important you are to someone is not a matter of how much this person has sacrificed for your sake. Instead, the measures are (1) the sacrifices he would make for your sake if he were called upon to make them and (2) the power you have to alter the appeal of various courses of action. It is plausible to think that the child of the effortless parents would score high by these measures. On the one hand, he would be someone for whom they would sacrifice a great deal if such a sacrifice were needed—though in their case it is not. On the other, he would be someone whose prospects greatly affected what they wanted to do and enjoyed doing, and who had considerable power to change what would otherwise seem like a sacrifice into something they did as a matter of course. Having him matter to them in these ways would be part of what made parenthood such a delight to them. If so, the child of the effortless parents would have that to be grateful for, as well. She wouldn't owe her parents her gratitude only for what they (effortlessly) did for her, but also for the place she had in their affections. If this reasoning is sound, it is not very plausible to say, as Keller does, that such children have less to be grateful for than those whose parents found parenthood a struggle. It is no longer clear that gratitude theories entail that the children of effortless parents have less to be grateful for, and thus that our filial duties are weaker or less demanding the easier our parents found it to raise us.

There is still a serious problem here, though. Suppose we ask *why* a grown child should be grateful to his parents for the place he had in their affections. Having that place was a great benefit to him, of course, and not only because of what they did for him. It is also a great benefit just to know that you are loved and that you matter to someone in this way. But when we were thinking about being grateful for someone's actions, your benefiting from those actions did not entail that you owed her your gratitude. It was also necessary for there to be good will toward you in those actions. Since we are still speaking of gratitude, the same should be true of being grateful for your place in someone's affections. That is, the fact that you benefited from having that place could be a happy accident, not something for which you should credit this person by being grateful to her. Rather, you should be grateful for your place in someone's affections only insofar as having this place showed good will toward you.

This line of thought grants that if it was *work* to keep you as central to someone's affections as you are, and if that work was motivated at least in part by her wishing you well, then you ought to be grateful that she cares about you as she does. No doubt some of us are in exactly that position. It might even be argued that we all are, on the ground that every child sometimes strains the love his parents have for him—but this will still be a matter of degree. Suppose you were an especially difficult child, either because you were willful or for reasons outside your control: you had a degree of autism, or physical difficulties that made you hard to care for and rather unlovable in personality. For your parents to continue to care about you in the way they did took a good deal of effort on their part, and let us suppose that they did this work at least partly for your sake. That would mean you owed them considerable gratitude for the place you had in their affections, because you had it through their considerable good will toward you.

The problem is that this way of thinking generates a second version of Keller's argument. Parents who were blessed with an easier child than you were would have had little or no difficulty continuing to give her a central place in their affections. That would mean they deserved less gratitude than yours deserve for continuing to love you, difficult child that you were. This factor would reduce their child's duties toward them once she was grown, if these were duties to be as grateful as one ought to be. But that's counterintuitive thinking, as Keller would surely urge. A person's duty to look after her father in his old age is not mitigated by his having found her easy to love, any more than it is mitigated by his having found parenthood so much fun. Once again, filial duties don't reduce to obligations to be as grateful as we should be—not even if we agree that gratitude can be owed for the place we have in the affections of our parents.

I take this conclusion to mean that gratitude theories are in trouble. Recall, though, that gratitude is rarely the only thing that parents want from their grown children, if it is something they want at all. That applies not only to gratitude for sacrifices made in order to provide material goods, send the child to a good school, and so on but also to gratitude for having loved her when she was still a child. But what is it that parents want of their grown children, beyond gratitude for what they once did and for how deeply they cared for them? I would say it includes a further place of their own in the affections of their grown sons and daughters. I will argue that this is also what grown children *owe* their parents, if certain further conditions are met. On this view filial duties are not duties to be appropriately grateful, although children have those as well. They are duties to give your parents a place in your affections that goes beyond being grateful to them, because of the place you had in theirs.

Since giving them that place is not a matter of being grateful to them, it does not require that their affection for you was the product of work they did for your sake. Nor does the degree of affection you should have for them turn on how difficult you were to love, unlike the degree of gratitude you should have for their continuing to do so. It turns instead on how much they loved you: on how central a place you had in their affections. If the earlier arguments are correct, the measure is not in the sacrifices they actually made for your sake. Instead, one measure is the sacrifices they would have made if these had been called for. Another is the extent to which your fortunes dominated their interests, changing what would have been a sacrifice into none at all and affecting the extent to which they experienced it as a sacrifice when they did have to give up something that was of value to them.

Not all parents and all children are alike in how central a place the child has in the parent's affections. It follows that we differ in the duties we have to our parents once we are grown, because we differ in the place we would give them in our affections if we responded as we should to the place we once had in theirs. This point is consistent with saying there isn't *much* difference ordinarily. When the difference is considerable, the idea would be that although a person's duty to look after her father in his old age is not mitigated by his having found it easy to love her, she *does* have a lesser duty in this regard if he cared little for her when she was a child than if he had loved her dearly. That view does not seem to me to be objectionable. If it isn't, then this account of filial duties isn't undercut in the way the gratitude theory seemed to be undercut by the fact that even though parenthood is harder for some than for others, this doesn't mean that the grown children of parents who found it easy have fewer or weaker duties to look after them if such is needed.

The next section offers arguments for construing filial obligations in the way I am suggesting: namely, as duties to give our parents a place in our affections that roughly corresponds to the place we had in their affections when we were children.

2.

It might seem that no such view can possibly be right, because it would posit an obligation to *feel* in certain ways and to have certain *dispositions* to act. One objection to positing that would contend that our feelings and dispositions aren't sufficiently under our control for us to have obligations where they are concerned. Another would contend that others are affected only by what we actually *do* and have no claim that we should also *regard* them in one way of another or be *inclined* to act in certain ways. Thus there couldn't be, for example, an obligation not to become angry when you were spoken to in certain ways. There could only be an obligation to exercise self-restraint on such occasions: not to "lose your temper" and put your anger into action. (Not to put your anger into action at all, if we want to say you would be "wrong to be angry," and not to act it out in certain ways, if we want to say it is all right to be angry but not to "fly into a rage.") Similarly, the argument runs, although there could be an obligation to act in certain ways toward your parents, there couldn't be one to give them a particular place in your affections, because (1) how you feel about them and are inclined to act toward them isn't sufficiently under your control and (2) how you feel and are inclined to act has no effect on them except through the behavior that expresses it, and that means they have no claims except where such expressions are concerned.

Consider first the idea that we cannot control how we feel about someone or are inclined to act toward him. This is most appealing when we are thinking about what are called occurrent emotions: immediate reactions, such as the *flush* of anger when the words are said. Actually, however, even those can be worked on over time, so that what once angered you no longer has the power to do so. A flush of anger may be beyond immediate control, but such flushes need not be beyond control of any kind.

Moreover, emotions also come as dispositions rather than only as feelings of the moment. Thus you can continue to be angry at someone well after his offense, rather than forgiving him. It is certainly not obvious that we cannot control our lingering dispositions, including whether we forgive someone or remain angry. If it *were* obvious, the contention that we should always forgive those who do us wrong would urge something that would clearly be impossible rather than just very difficult. Then the powerful appeal so many find in the principle that we should forgive all who wrong us would be a great mystery. Nor could it be appealing to say that we should sometimes forgive people, since that would say we should *sometimes* do what is beyond human control. Clearly, both views about forgiveness regard changes of heart as within human capability. Of course, both must deal with special cases in which a particular person is unable to forgive someone, but that notion is very different from holding that whether we forgive just isn't up to us and so cannot be an obligation. Similarly, although it will be well worth discussing the grown child who isn't able to give his parents a particular place in his affections, acknowledging that there are such people is very different from saying that no one can control this feeling and so it cannot be a matter of obligation.

The second objection was that others are affected only by how we act toward them, not by how we feel about them or how we are inclined to act toward them, and therefore we are free to feel however we like and to have whatever inclinations we turn out to have. That contention divorces feelings from actions in a way that should seem incorrect, if the example of forgiveness is still fresh in our minds. At least in continuing relationships, when someone wants to be forgiven, what he seeks is not just for the other person to act as if she had had a change of heart. He wants her to *have* that change of heart, which will work its own changes in how she acts toward him. There is also an important sense in which what she does won't be the same actions if they don't proceed from a change of heart, or from an effort to make one. In that case, if it is wrong for her not to forgive him, then the change of feelings is included in what she owes him. That point gets lost if we claim that our only obligations are to act in certain ways, not to feel in certain ways.

I hope that explication is enough to allay the initial reaction I identified, which was that to say grown children owe their parents a place in their affections is to make a fundamental mistake about what one person can owe another.

Perhaps the view I've offered will nonetheless seem very wrong in a different way. It seems to say that if someone loves you, you are obligated to love that person in return. But isn't that up to you? Suppose you were stalked by someone who actually did love you. If you chose not to return his love, surely you did him no wrong.

That's true, but now suppose you have welcomed and encouraged someone's considerable affection for you. In that case I think you do owe some degree of affection in return, partly because to have a central place that you welcome in the affections of another person is so great a good. It is sometimes said that to have a *friend* is to have another self: a second person who takes what happens to you to heart and acts accordingly. Now there are two of you, so to speak, and that fact is of great value if this friend is one you welcome. For a child to have a parent who cares for her in the way that loving parents care for their children is of even greater value than that of having a friend. First, it is no less central a place in the parent's affections than the one that even the closest of friends give each other. Second, it is part of the very concept of childhood that children *need* "another self" in ways that adults ordinarily do not. If a child were the only one who took his interests to heart, he would be at a terrible disadvantage, not only in his current life but also in the one he would have as an adult if he managed to grow up. Those are respects in which it is of enormous value to a child to have a parent who cares about him in the way parents ordinarily do care about their children. Moreover, aside from some special cases, children do welcome having a place in the affection of the parents who are raising them. If so, my argument is that they incur an obligation to give their parents a place of roughly the same order in their own affections, if they are able to do so.

That proposal is not as radical as it might seem. Actually, it follows the same lines as the familiar idea that we ought to be appropriately grateful to those who do us good turns. To be appropriately grateful to them is to have a particular kind of good will toward them, roughly corresponding to the good will that was expressed toward you in what they did. This gives them *that* place in your affections. It isn't at all the one your parents would have in your affections if you cared about them in roughly the same way as they cared about you when you were a child. For one thing, your gratitude to your benefactor has its source in a particular deed she did and is perfectly consistent with having no broader affection for her at all. For another, ordinarily your gratitude wouldn't dominate your other interests to the extent that your good will toward your parents would. (For example, it wouldn't ordinarily be as distressing to know that someone to whom you owed a debt of gratitude was in difficulty as it would be to learn that your father was.)

Finally, good will toward someone to whom you were grateful would follow a different course, over time, than the affection you would have for your parents. This difference is overstated, if we think both that the good will we owe those to whom we should be grateful is *spent* once we do a suitably good deed in return, and that the affection we owe our parents is open-ended.[11] The truth is that we should continue to be grateful for what someone has done for us even after we have reciprocated, rather than having no further good will toward her because now we have "repaid" our debt of gratitude. So gratitude is permanent too. The difference is that there is nothing wrong with its fading over time, so that whereas once your gratitude was strong enough to motivate the good deed you did in return, now you might be properly grateful as long as what she did is an occasional positive memory of her. Proper affection for your parents wouldn't fade in that same way if they had cared for you in the way parents ordinarily do.

Those are three ways in which the place in your affections occupied by someone to whom you are grateful differs from the one I am claiming that parents should typically have in the affections of their grown children. To say that others sometimes deserve our gratitude for what they have done for us is to say that they deserve *that* place in our affections because of the good will they exhibited toward us. My claim is that others can also deserve a very different place in our affections by virtue of the very different good will that *they* exhibited toward us. It's the proper reciprocation for parental love that we accepted and encouraged, just as gratitude is the proper reciprocation for the regard shown us by someone to whom we ought to be grateful.

Since a place in our affections would be reciprocation for something that happened when we were "only children," this view invites some of the same objections that have been offered against gratitude theories. If there are features of childhood that imply that we do not owe our parents gratitude for what they did, perhaps those features also imply that we do not owe our parents a central place in their affections. I don't think this is true, and I will close this section by addressing it.

One such objection was that children do not ask for what their parents give them and do not have any reasonable alternative to accepting it. They don't ask to be fed, sheltered, clothed, and so on, and they have no remotely comparable way of obtaining those goods. So, the argument was, they owe no gratitude for these gifts, as they would if they had accepted them of their own free will. The parallel contention would be that the same goes for the place they have in the affections of their parents. To have that place is a great good for them, but it isn't one that they choose to accept over some reasonable alternative. Rather, they are forced to accept a place in their parent's affections and therefore owe no affection in return.

This argument has weaknesses. Consider the idea of being forced to accept a place in someone's affections. Imagine that you did have such a place and wanted that person not to regard you in this way. It may be that you couldn't make him stop, but there are various steps you could take. You could make it clear that nothing like this was welcome and that it would not be reciprocated, and you could reinforce these messages as needed. If you did, that response would constitute refusing to accept the place you have in this person's affections.

You needn't be an adult, in this story. A child could do these same things, not only where unwanted friends and boyfriends or girlfriends are concerned but also with regard to unwanted parental affection. The child has the alternative of refusing to accept a place in their affections. So in order for the objection to work, it must be an alternative that would be unreasonable to take, because the life the child would have if he rejected his parents' affections would be so inferior to the one he would otherwise have. That could be true, though I think there is a reason to doubt it: parental affection is ordinarily very durable, quite resistant to efforts to reject it. That means a child who refused to accept the affection would not go without it, unlike a child who refused to accept food and shelter from his parents and so had to seek these elsewhere. This circumstance weakens somewhat the argument that the child has no reasonable alternative to acceptance. It isn't as clear that refusal is so much worse than acceptance that no reasonable person would choose it.

That aside, the broader picture the argument has of childhood is that it is like being under the control of a benevolent captor. Someone who had been kidnapped wouldn't owe his kidnapper any affection if this person took a great liking to him and acted accordingly. If childhood is like being held by a kidnapper, the same holds for owing your parents any affection. You might be fortunate that they cared for you while you were in their captivity, but you would owe them no affection in return.

However, there are no good arguments that parents are like kidnappers. The wrong that a kidnapper does is to take control of what his victim may do. That undercuts any claim to affection in return for what the kidnapper does while he has that control. To extend this situation to parents would require that they too are wrong to control what their children do—not just that some parents exert control that they should not, but that all parental control is illegitimate. Assuming we don't agree with that claim, children are not captives who should resist any natural inclination to return their captor's affection even though they find that they welcome it. The affection their parents gave them is not corrupted by the way they came to be in a position to give it. Thus the parents are not wrong to expect that they have earned their own place in their children's affections, and it is a place their children should give them.[12]

A different objection to gratitude theories is that parents have an obligation to do what they do for their children, and that if someone is only fulfilling an obligation, she does not deserve our gratitude. I think this contention confuses carrying out an obligation with doing something entirely because it is an obligation. Consider the latter: if someone acted entirely out of a sense of duty, it would follow that she wasn't motivated by good will toward the person who would benefit from her action. That person would owe her no gratitude, then, since benefiting him was at best a welcome side effect and at worst an unwelcome one. In contrast, if all we can say is that she had an obligation to do what she did, we don't know *why* she did it, only that she would have been wrong not to. Her entire motivation could have been the good it would do the other person, so the fact that it was her duty does not rule out his owing her his gratitude for doing it. Surely all we can say of parents as such is that they have an obligation to do (much of) what they do for their children, not that they do these things only because they have a duty to do them. So there is no good reason here to say that children cannot owe their parents gratitude.

The parallel objection to saying that children owe their parents a place in their affections fares even worse. The claim at its heart would be that if the other person had an obligation to care about us as he did, then we would owe him no affection in return. Why not? The answer can't be that then there would be no affection for us in his affection for us, as there might be no good will for us in his doing something that was to our benefit. The affection is perfectly genuine even if he would have been wrong not to have it, and it also remains a good he could have withheld. So, if it is welcome to us, it is a good we should reciprocate.

It might still seem that children cannot acquire the filial obligation I've claimed they have, in the way that I've claimed they do acquire it. First, when children are very young, surely their acceptance and encouragement of their parents' love is instinctive, rather than a considered choice. Second, when they are older but still under their parents' care, their lives would be much worse if they rejected their parents' love, so they are heavily constrained to accept it. Finally, if accepting their parents' love did commit them to giving those parents a similar place in the child's own affections many years later, this obligation would have to be assumed unwittingly. It is doubtful that a child could be expected to understand that this was what she was getting into.

These misgivings rest on views about when our actions can incur an obligation. One of those views is that we can't incur one by acting in a way that is instinctive, as a very young child does in loving her parents. But suppose that someone angers you and you fail to restrain the instinct to retaliate. Striking back was instinctive, but you still incur an obligation to bear responsibility for it. You still have some explaining and some justifying to do, and you might have a penalty to pay or some damages to cover because of what you instinctively did. The same would be true if you had followed an instinct to flee what you believed was endangering you, and doing so had meant rushing heedlessly out of a place festooned with delicate glassware. In short, we can incur obligations by acting in ways that are instinctive.

It's more plausible to say this is true only when we can be expected to restrain the instinct, and that this *can't* be expected of very young children. That would mean that very young children don't incur the obligation I've proposed. It wouldn't mean that even older children can't incur it, because we become capable of restraining our instincts while we are still children. That's why it isn't unreasonable to expect an older child to resist the promptings of an instinctive fear or an instinct to retaliate. So we would need a different reason to say that even older children cannot acquire the obligation to love their parents by accepting and nurturing their parents' love for them.

One reason offered was that the older child is so much better off if she accepts her parent's love that she "has no choice" but to accept it: any other course of action would be unreasonable. That can be true, but I don't think it undercuts the view I am offering. I think we can incur an obligation by acting in a certain way, even if it would have been unreasonable for us not to do so.

I hasten to say that this theory doesn't hold when the constraints on our choices are imposed by someone who is acting for purposes of his own. For example, suppose you are ordered at gunpoint to unlock your neighbor's door. You follow your instinct of self-preservation, and you unlock the door. Your doing so enables the men who held you at gunpoint to enter the premises and make off with your neighbor's goods. Clearly, your behavior does not obligate you to make good for your neighbor's losses. However, the reason is that you were coerced—not that you were following an instinct, and not that you had no better alternatives. Compare a case in which there were no armed thieves, but your own circumstances were so dire that you "had no choice" but to unlock your neighbor's door and take her goods yourself. You "had to do it," or do something very like it; you had no reasonable alternative. There would then be good reasons to say you shouldn't be punished for your actions. That's not the same as saying you are perfectly free to do what you did, though. Instead, if you are ever able to repay your neighbor for what you took in your time of need, you ought to do so. Taking the goods obligates you to do that, if you can, even though you "had no choice" but to take them.

I think the same is true of the older child, who "has no choice" but to accept and encourage her parents' love in the sense that this is by far her best alternative. She is not coerced by another to accept her parents' love. Accepting it is easily the wisest course of action for her to take, but doing what is wisest can incur an obligation to do something in return. In her case, I've claimed, it incurs an obligation to reciprocate. I could be wrong about that, of course, but the objection was that accepting her parents' love can't incur *any* obligation. I hope to have shown that it can, and I think it's plausible to say the obligation is one to reciprocate.

That theory is denied by a final strand of objection, according to which no child can be expected to understand that accepting and encouraging her parents' love obligates her to give them a similar place in her own affections when she is grown. So, even if it could incur an obligation, it couldn't incur that one. To me, this notion is correct about a very young child, but not about an older child whose parents have loved her and conveyed this love to her. Certainly the idea that accepting love obligates you to love in return is not so mysterious that we should expect it to be beyond an adolescent's ability to grasp. Indeed, the ability to grasp it is very close to a requirement for a life with which one can be reasonably happy, and part of raising a child is helping her to become able to have a life of that kind. So I would say that it is a parent's obligation to enable his or her child to see that love is to be reciprocated. Of course, it would be up to the child to apply that lesson to the case of her parents: to see that they did love her and that accepting and encouraging their love did obligate her to give them a similar place in her own affections. That is reasonable to expect of an older child, and this means the obligation is not accepted unwittingly after all. At most, it is an obligation that isn't fully understood when it is incurred, but that can be said of many obligations.[13]

3.

One question with which we began was this: if we have filial duties, what is their basis? My answer has been that these arise from our having accepted a place in our parents' affections and encouraged them to continue to love us, when we were young and under their care. A second question was what these duties require of us. My answer has been that they require us to give our parents a roughly similar place in our own affections. There are good reasons not to say instead that we owe our parents exactly the same place in our affections as we had in theirs.

One such reason is just that there is nothing very exact about the place that one person has in the affections of another. The idea of exactly matching what is inexact has a certain charm, but not as an obligation. Second, what calls for reciprocation from the grown child is the place she had in her parents' affections while still a child. That is a period of years rather than a moment in time, and during those years the child undergoes great changes, as do the other matters about which the parents care. (For example, the demands imposed by a parents' career are likely to differ at different stages of life, and so is how vital the parent thinks it is to succeed in that career.) So we should expect there to be some variation in the place the child holds among these concerns, and this means that to speak of the place he or she held "during childhood" is to generalize. Since it is a generalization, matching it only roughly is a more plausible requirement than matching it precisely.

Finally, it is conceivable that a parent could give a child too central a place in his affections, engaging in something close to self-abnegation. Similarly, parents of a different kind can live their own dreams through their child in so oppressive a way that she has too little to say about who she is and what she does and is under intense pressure to succeed. Then their affection for her can be tied too closely to her success in accomplishing their plan, with the broader suggestion that affection has to be earned by the child's acting as they direct. These are moral errors on the part of the parents. Their child can't have an obligation to make the same errors toward them once she is grown, and she would have such an obligation if children owed their parents exactly the same place in their own affections. It is better to say only that she ought to care a great deal about them.

When we ask what our filial duties require of us, though, what we want to know in the end is what they require us to *do*, and what might be beyond the call of duty where our parents are concerned. On the view I've offered, the answer is that they require us to do what we would do if our parents had the place they ought to have in our affections, given the one that we had had in theirs. That answer remains rather abstract, obviously. What it amounts to where particular actions are concerned is still to be said.

Suppose we begin with some of Keller's central examples of filial duties: looking after your father in his old age, being with your mother while she goes through a difficult medical procedure, and visiting her after her operation. A first point, only slightly less abstract, is that unless you were exceptionally unfortunate as a child, you would owe your father and mother quite a lot in these matters. All children except those who are exceptionally unfortunate are greatly cherished by their parents, so that a place even roughly similar in the grown child's own affections would be quite a central one. How their parents fared would matter a great deal to them, in the ways mentioned earlier. First, they would be motivated to make considerable sacrifices for their parents' sake if those were called for. Second, when their parents were in distress or at risk, that fact would have considerable effect on the quality of their own experiences. Third, there would also be considerable effect on what they experienced as sacrifices.

For those reasons, grown children who felt as they should about their parents would do quite a lot when their parents were in need in the way the mother emerging from surgery and the father in his old age might be. There could be costs that the grown sons or daughters regretfully chose not to pay, but these would have to be substantial.

Of course, there is more to having considerable affection for someone than a strong motivation to come through when you are badly needed. You should also want just to be in that person's company from time to time and to do small things that you knew she would enjoy. Those would be filial obligations too, on the account I am offering. They could certainly be part of "looking after" your father in his old age. It isn't solely a matter of paying bills and seeing to it that he doesn't come to great harm; it is also a matter of making his life a happier one during this period, if you can. Your presence at times of no particular need could be of considerable help in caring for him, especially if he understood you to be there because you wanted to be. Fathers would vary in this desire, of course. The idea isn't that all grown children have an obligation to be in their aged father's company at all times because that is always a pleasure to the man no matter what he is like and what his broader life is like. Rather, knowing what was required of you along these lines would require understanding what he was like and allowing him to be who he was.

Moreover, on this view your father needn't be in his old age for efforts in large matters and small to be your filial duties, since it isn't only in time of need that you would be strongly motivated to do these things if he had the place in your affections that we are imagining him to have. The obligations would hold at earlier stages of your adult life as well. However, it is when our parents are elderly that we might most need to recall that it is an adult for whom we have this affection, not a child. That fact isn't meant to be lost in the principle that we are to care about them now roughly as they did about us when we were children.

There are mistakes along these lines that no one would make: no one would think the principle meant that the expressions of that affection would be exactly the same. An easier error to make would be in the relationship between what you thought would be a pleasure for this person and what would in fact be in his best interest. Suppose that when you were a child, your father's affection for you sometimes inclined him to allow you to have or to do what was probably not in your best interest. I'm not inclined to say that this choice would always have been wrong on his part, but it certainly shouldn't have been the routine one. It should only have been the occasional treat. The error would be to think that the same holds now that you are an adult and are giving your father roughly the same place in your affections as you had in his. He is now fully entitled to make mistakes that he should have kept you from making, at least if he is able to make them without your help: to do what is not good for his health, for example. Your affection for him does not entitle you to prevent his eating what isn't good for him, or smoking, or getting less sleep than he should, even though he once had an obligation to prevent you from doing these things. That isn't a way in which you are to care less about him than he cared about you, but a way in which it matters that he is an adult about whom you care this much and you were a child about whom he did.

Finally, there is a sense in which affection is always imperfect. Someone can have a certain place in your affections even though you have not acted as if she did. Knowing this is not a motivation to fall short, for someone who feels as he should about this person, but a matter for regret. Still, it offers a consolation to someone who worries after his parents are gone that he didn't act toward them as he should have. The consolation is that the failures were inevitable imperfections in the expression of affection. To find no consolation in that is to require more of yourself than you were morally required to give. We are free to do that, and to regret failing to meet our standards even though those are remarkably high. However, it might be of value to understand that our regrets represent a failure to be perfect, rather than a failure in our moral duty to someone whose forgiveness we can no longer seek.

4.

A third question with which we began was whether filial duties are permanent. An alternative was that they might be fulfilled once and for all, as keeping a promise fulfills the duty we undertake when we make it. Keller rightly thinks that filial duties are not like promises in this way.[14] Nor would they be if (as I've urged) they were duties to give our parents a certain central place in our affections. This is because there are no actions that allow us to say, "There, now I've given them a central place in my affections, and I need have no more to do with them," as we could say, "There, now I've kept the promise I made, and that's all there is to *that*." Nor is this a duty to give our parents this place in our affections for a time period corresponding to our childhood, for example, on the ground that that is how long our parents had the affection we ought to reciprocate.

The more intriguing alternative is that our filial duties can be eliminated by something our parents have done, rather than by our having fulfilled them. Keller thinks so: "If your parents choose not to carry out their duties toward you, make unreasonable demands, or are otherwise to blame for the deterioration of the relationship—if they disown you without good reason, for example—then your duties to provide the special goods to them is [sic] mitigated or dissolved, even if you are still able to provide these."[15] It seems right to extract the case in which your parents disown you and think of their doing so as a way of formally renouncing the claims they have on you. I would say that parents can do this. The child who helped her parents despite their disowning her "without good reason" would be forgiving them for a wrong they did her, rather than carrying out a filial obligation.

A different question is whether parents can sever their grown children's obligations just by the way they treat them, even though they don't formally disown the children. Keller would say that they can: "This is an instance of a broader principle applying to relationships within which each party has duties to the other. It can be compared with a student's duty to obey a teacher. Should teachers fail to care about and make an adequate effort to advance their students' education, the latter do not have the same duty of obedience they would otherwise have—even when they are still capable of obeying, and even when their obedience would still be of benefit to the teachers."[16] I've been arguing that the duty grown children have is to give their parents a central place in their affections. If we follow Keller, we will say that the parents also have obligations in this relationship and that if they fail to play their part this failure can release their children from the obligation to continue to care about them to that extent, or perhaps at all.

In the ordinary case, that would be true if the parents had ceased to care greatly about their children, because ordinarily they will have had an obligation to do so. This is so because parents ordinarily have welcomed the great good of their grown children's affection for them and so owe it in return, just as the children owe the parents *their* affection in return for the way the parents cared about them when the children were young. So, for the parents to cease to care as they should about their grown sons or daughters will be to cease to play their part in the relationship, and that withdrawal will release the grown children from the obligation to play theirs. This will be true even though the parents' current indifference (or worse) doesn't erase the past, in which they felt very differently and so acted very differently, and even though that past is the source of their children's obligation to love them. The happier past becomes a source only of debts of gratitude. Those might be considerable, but when they are all that remains, the moral relationship between parent and grown child is quite a different one.

The next question is, what conduct should be taken to mean that a parent no longer cares appropriately about her grown child, thus ending the child's own filial duties? Notice that it would be the conduct of someone about whom the child ought to care a good deal himself. One aspect of caring about her would be a certain generosity of spirit in interpreting what she did, assuming the better understanding of it rather than the worse when it could be taken either way. That is also an aspect of having thought of this person as someone who cared a good deal about you, and the child should be assuming that as well. For both reasons, an inference that your parent didn't care greatly about you (and you therefore needn't care greatly about her) is one that would require a great deal of evidence. Moreover, we are speaking here of the parent's continuing disposition toward the child, rather than how she might feel on some particular occasion. The proper conclusion is that although parents can sever their grown children's obligations by acting in ways that show the parents no longer care about the children as they should, this severance would happen only if the parental behavior were extreme. Short of that, the child has only someone it is difficult to regard as he should, not someone he needn't greatly care about any longer.

There is also a difference between a parent who could care about her grown children as she should but does not, and someone who is not able to care because, for example, she is in a late stage of Alzheimer's disease and is no longer able even to be sure who her children are. Since the parent with Alzheimer's can't care about her grown children in the way their concern for her would otherwise call for her to do, she has no obligation to do it. So her failures in this regard aren't moral ones of a kind that releases her children from their obligation to care greatly about her. Their filial duties haven't been eliminated but made more difficult, in part because it has become harder to see what proper affection calls for them to do. The parent has changed in ways that make proper behavior uncertain—but the obligation to care and to act accordingly remains in place.[17]

Finally, suppose it isn't the parent who cannot care about her grown child as she should, but the child who cannot care about the parent as he should. Doing so is beyond his emotional capacities, in the way that it might become impossible for someone to continue to love his spouse of many years even though she continued to love him. That response might speak badly of him, and it would be deeply regrettable, but couldn't it be the recalcitrant fact of the matter? And if it were, should we draw the same conclusion that since he *can't* care about this person as he should, he can have no obligation to do so? Then, it seems, a grown child who just couldn't find it in his heart to care about his parents as he should would have no filial duties, on the account I've offered.

I think he would still have an obligation to act as if his parents had the proper place in his affections, just as someone who cannot manage to feel the gratitude he should feel toward his benefactor would still have an obligation to act as if he did. It is less appealing to say the same of the spouse: that is, to say that if one spouse cannot care about the other as he should, then his obligation is to act as if he did. The spouse is entitled to honesty, instead, and an opportunity to decide whether to continue in the relationship. Why wouldn't the same be true of parents whose grown children are unable to care about them as they should?

Part of the answer is that an effort to act as if you cared as you should about your spouse would be a very poor substitute for the real thing. Another part is that this isn't true of acting as if you cared as you should about your parents. You would still come to their aid when they were in great need, you would still sometimes provide what it was simply a pleasure for them to have, and you would still appear for family occasions and be convivial. Those actions would be less than ideal, but they would also be a good deal of what parents need from their grown children. It is plausible to say they are entitled to this much, when they can't have all from you that they should. It is further from what a spouse should have from a spouse, which in these circumstances would make much more of their life together a counterfeit.

5.

I have argued that grown children do have filial duties, that these are duties to give our parents a place in our affections that is roughly equivalent to the one we had in their affections when we were young and under their care, and that if we are unable to do this our obligation is to act as if we did feel this affection. I've also explored the idea that parents can act in ways that sever these obligations. Parents can do that, in my opinion, but the obligations are also highly durable and open-ended, and though they are not the same for every child, they are ordinarily considerable.

There is a further dimension of parenthood to explore. It is one thing to ask something of one's children and another to allow them to do it. The final chapter considers whether there are limits to what we should permit our children to do for us. Put differently, the question is whether we can be too costly to our children, even though the costs are ones that the children want to pay.

12

The Graceful Exit

Let us suppose that you are in great need of help, the kind that is not easy to provide. Someone comes to your rescue, at considerable personal cost. You ought to be very grateful to her, it seems. But is it also possible that you should never have allowed her to do what she did? Are there sacrifices that we should not permit others to make for our sake, even if they want to make them? Here might be an example, offered by John Hardwig.

> Consider Captain Oates, a member of Admiral Scott's expedition to the South Pole. Oates became too ill to continue. If the rest of the team stayed with him, they would all perish. After this had become clear, Oates left his tent one night, walked out into a raging blizzard, and was never seen again. That may have been a heroic thing to do, but we might be able to agree that it was also no more than his duty. It would have been wrong for him to urge—or even to allow—the rest to stay and care for him.[1]

Hardwig's larger point concerns those who grow old in modern industrialized societies. He expects to be among their number, and he is greatly distressed by the thought of what that eventuality might cost his wife and children. As he rightly observes, for people in the position he anticipates "The costs—and these are not merely monetary—of prolonging our lives when we are no longer able to care for ourselves are often staggering."[2] When those costs fall largely to our loved ones, Hardwig thinks that we too might be "too ill to continue" and "wrong to urge—or even [to] allow" them to do what it would take for us to go on living. He thinks our proper course instead would be to follow the example of Captain Oates. We ought to bow out gracefully, either by declining the costly care for which our loved ones would pay so dearly or by taking our own lives; which of these it will be depends on the details.[3] Finally, it isn't only when we are already dying that this is what we should do, in his view. Rather, "there may be a fairly common responsibility to end one's life in the absence of any terminal illness at all."[4]

Presumably there are also times when the cost of helping us would not be too high, and we would be perfectly free to fall into the arms of those who wanted to look after us, or even wrong not to do so. That possibility makes it important to be able to tell when we would have the duty that Hardwig has in mind, and when we would not. He declines to say anything very definitive about this matter, though: "I cannot say when someone has a duty to die. . . . I can

[only] suggest a few features of one's illness, history, and circumstances that make it more likely....I present them here without much elaboration or explanation."[5] Moreover, since he is concerned exclusively with a duty to *die*, Hardwig does not address situations in which we wouldn't die if the sacrifice were not made, though we would have to do without whatever the sacrifice would have provided. Perhaps there are also sacrifices of this second kind that we shouldn't permit—or perhaps there are not. What we need is a general theory that is applicable to both situations. What I will offer is meant to be one, though the discussion will focus on cases in which we can assume the parent will die if the grown child does not make the sacrifices in question.

1.

It might be thought that any such theory is misguided, because it can *never* be wrong to allow someone to make a sacrifice for your sake, at least if this person is a competent adult who is acting of his own free will. After all, your would-be benefactor has decided that the sacrifice is worth making, and he is the one who would make it. For you to overrule him out of concern for him would be to insist that he live by your assessment of the matter rather than by his own. That behavior sounds paternalistic. The idea would be that we shouldn't impose our will in these matters, any more than we should impose it on someone who is choosing an occupation, or a mate, or a religion. Rather, we should show proper respect for his right to make his own decisions about what to do with his resources, by accepting the help he has chosen to give us.

This argument is persuasive only if it is always wrong to act paternalistically, however. The more common view is that we sometimes *should* intervene in another person's behavior for his or her own good, especially when this person is not thinking clearly and will come to great harm if we do not intervene. That description fits the people in Hardwig's examples. The costs that the grown children propose to pay in order to save their parents are said to be "staggering," and their decision to pay them is surely emotionally charged. Similarly, the explorers on the expedition with Captain Oates would have perished in the cold if he had not prevented them from acting as they chose, and they were certainly under great stress when they made their choice. So, both examples might be just the kind in which we *should* be paternalistic. This fact makes the complaint about refusing to allow the sacrifice inconclusive, at best.

A different point will take us further. It's true that to refuse to allow someone to sacrifice for your sake out of concern for him is paternalistic, but it isn't *simply* paternalistic. It is like simple paternalism in that your concern is for him and for what he would suffer if he were to act as he prefers, and it seeks to overrule his estimation of the costs to him. It is also unlike simple paternalism in that the suffering would be endured *for your sake*. You would have that part in what happened to him if you allowed him to go ahead; you don't have it when you intrude paternalistically into his choice of occupation, or mate, or religion, or in order to try to prevent him from taking up hard drugs. In these latter cases it isn't the pain he would suffer *for you* that moves you to stop him;. the fact that his choice in this case is for you ought to give you some standing in whether he suffers it.

Moreover, the powerful desire your son or daughter has to come to your aid will ordinarily be partly your doing. That's so because parents ordinarily encourage their children to love them, showing over many years that they both welcome and expect this love and that they love the child as well. Obviously, children who love their parents are much more vulnerable to events in their parents' lives than they would have been otherwise. Part of the love is a strong disposition to help, when things threaten to go badly for their parents, and the more they love their parents the stronger this disposition is. This factor is another difference from simple paternalism, in which it isn't your doing that this person wants to act in a way you think will do him harm. Here it would partly be a consequence of your own past actions that your child wants to act in this way. Not that you would be the sole cause of this, of course, as if you had instilled some programming that the child must now follow. Still, you would have had a great deal to do with his wanting to help you in this highly costly way.

These considerations give parents an important standing in whether their grown children are to make great sacrifices for their sake. Of course, the children themselves also have important standing in the matter, since it is they who would either make the sacrifice or stand aside and allow their loved one to suffer. The question is how the parent and child are to respect the standing that each has in the matter. That can't be settled by observing that we ought not to be paternalistic toward our grown children, or that they ought to be free to live as they choose.

A different thought is that it might be *selfish* for the parent to permit her grown child to make an enormous sacrifice for her sake, and wrong for that reason. I think that is one of John Hardwig's own chief concerns. It is easy to see why it would be, since there is ordinarily a great deal to be said against being selfish.

A selfish person takes more than her fair share of something. It might be that she has never thought much about this behavior, having always taken it for granted that she is entitled to have what she wants. Or it might be that she knows she is taking more than her share but she also knows there is nothing others can do to stop her. Selfishness of these first kinds is arrogant and insulting. It can be pathetic, instead. Picture a selfish person who is *weak* rather than full of herself, and who yields to temptations that she knows she should resist.

Generally, it is also bad behavior to allow others to be selfish in their dealings with you. Allowing them to do so can be a failure of self-respect on your part: a mistaken agreement that this person is entitled to the lion's share, or a lack of the courage to protest. Admittedly, to let a selfish act pass can also be the best choice available. Perhaps protesting the boss's selfishness is likely to cost you your job, and others rely on you for support. Or perhaps one of the guests is taking much more than his share of the hors d'oeuvres, true enough, but there is also some obligation not to disrupt polite gatherings, and to make a point of it later would take it too seriously. Better just to let it pass. Still, even on those occasions the selfishness itself remains objectionable. The other person is still acting unfairly in taking more than her share, and it is still arrogant and insulting for her to act as she does, or else it is weak of her to do so.

In short, if it *would* be selfish to allow a loved one to make a particular sacrifice for your sake, it seems to follow that you shouldn't allow her to do this. I am going to argue against that view, however. I think that acts of selfishness need not be objectionable at all, if they occur within the kinds of relationships that we have in mind when we speak of loved ones making sacrifices for one another. I will have to say why this is true, and what follows about permitting sacrifices or refusing to permit them. A fuller version of the selfishness criticism is in order first, however.

2.

Here is John Hardwig's own central example of a person who should not have permitted certain sacrifices to be made for her sake.

> An 87-year-old woman was dying of congestive heart failure. Her APACHE score predicted that she had less than a 50 percent chance to live for another six months. She was lucid, assertive, and terrified of death. She very much wanted to live and kept opting for rehospitalization and the most aggressive life-prolonging treatment possible. That treatment successfully prolonged her life (though with increasing debility) for nearly two years. Her 55-year-old daughter was her only remaining family and her caregiver, and the main source of her financial support. The daughter duly cared for her mother. But before her mother died, her illness had cost the daughter all of her savings, her home, her job, her career.[6]

Hardwig thinks it is obvious that the mother in this example should not have allowed her daughter to make those sacrifices. He offers the following thought-experiment to explain why we should agree.

> Ask yourself which is the greater burden.
> a. To lose a 50 percent chance of six more months of life at age 87?
> b. To lose all your life savings, your home, and your career at age 55?
> Which burden would you prefer to bear?...
> I think most of us would quickly agree that (b) is a greater burden. That is the evil we would more hope to avoid in our lives."[7]

Hardwig's reasoning in this passage might be taken to invoke the following principle: if you would not sacrifice *your* X in order to have Y, it is selfish to allow someone else to sacrifice *his* X so that you may have Y. The mother in the example is like most of us, presumably, and that means she wouldn't have given up her own life savings, home, and career at age 55 in order to have this chance for six more months of life at age 87. According to the principle, then, it is *selfish* of her to allow her 55-year-old daughter to make the sacrifice for her. That is, it is selfish to let her daughter sacrifice *her* life savings and so on in order to provide what the mother wouldn't think worth the price if she were spending her own resources.

This reasoning has an unfortunate implication, however. It means that we are always selfish when we allow someone else to consider it more important for us to have something than we do ourselves. Suppose this person loves you and is therefore quite willing to make sacrifices for your sake that he would not make for himself, and that you would not make for yourself. For him, the difference is that what he does is done *for you*, as the daughter's sacrifices are made for her mother rather than for herself. Sacrifices made for another person's sake represent a value placed on that person, and on her having good things or avoiding bad ones; that value might very well be higher than she would place on herself. The principle says that if she allows someone to make such a sacrifice, she is selfish. That is too hard on love.

As an alternative, it might seem that when we consider which burden is heavier and which is lighter, we should go by the values the parties themselves place on what is to be gained and what is to be lost. The mother is "terrified of death." She "very much wanted to live," and she "kept opting for rehospitalization and the most aggressive life-prolonging treatment possible," in spite of the pain, discomfort, and intrusive stays in the hospital that this course of action must have involved. It was worth all of that, to her: her daughter's sacrifices provided something of very great value indeed, to her way of thinking.

The daughter thought so too. Perhaps what she valued so highly was also her mother's having the chance at continued life, or perhaps it was relieving her mother's terror, or the combination of those, or something else altogether. Whatever it was, the daughter thought it worth the cost she had to pay in order to provide it. In short, if we go by these women's values, it *wasn't* a bad exchange for the daughter to make the sacrifices, but a perfectly appropriate one. Should we conclude that it wasn't selfish of the mother to permit them?

Well, no. The women's values might themselves reflect a self-centered mother and a subservient daughter. It could be that the two women favor the daughter's making the sacrifices for the mother because they agree that the mother is everything and the daughter is nothing. They might have been this way for a very long time. We wouldn't see the selfishness and subservience in this latest episode if we went by their assessments of what is most important, because the assessments are imbued with those very attitudes.

Let us consider instead a very different relationship that they might have—the kind we would hope to have with our own loved ones. This time the mother and daughter are of deep concern to each other. That is a change. In the first version of the example the mother does not care about the daughter, and the daughter might not actually *care* about the mother either, as opposed to only being thoroughly dominated by her. In our new version, each of them cares very deeply about the other. Each would go very far to provide what was important to the person she cared about, because she wanted that person's life to go well. Each would readily sacrifice a great deal in pursuit of that end.

Here is a wrinkle. To *cost* someone you cared about something that was important to him would fall far short of helping him to have such things. So each of the women we are imagining would want to avoid "being a burden" to the other, as this is sometimes put. That means the mother we are imagining would be inclined to refuse to allow her daughter to give up anything important for her sake, as the daughter must if the mother is to put off the death of which she is so terrified. Notice, though, that to refuse her daughter's help would also cost the daughter something of great importance to her, namely, the opportunity to be of great help to her mother. Both choices have the same drawback: each costs a loved one something that is important to her.

The daughter has the same problem. If she allows her mother to refuse her help, this choice will cost her mother something upon which her mother places great importance: the chance to continue living. But if the daughter imposes her help, that too will cost the mother something of importance to her. It will mean she will be a burden to her daughter: something that is important to her to avoid, because she cares deeply about her daughter. In sum, if those who care deeply about someone ought never to cost that person anything of great importance to her, then these women shouldn't allow each other to follow either course of action.

I don't believe that deep mutual concern has to be impotent at such times. Here we might return to Hardwig for a different idea about being costly to those we love. Suppose that A needs help if he is to have something important to him, and that providing the help would be costly to B. Suppose first that this cost to B is relatively low, compared to what it would cost A to do without what the help would provide. Then A should have no reluctance about allowing B to help him, it seems. But now suppose that it would cost considerably *more* for B to provide this than it would cost A to do without it. Then we might say that A shouldn't allow B to do this, if they love each other, or that for A to allow it casts doubt on the claim that he does love her.

I want to argue that actually neither of these latter claims is true. It isn't part of loving someone that you will allow her to help you only in ways that are cost-efficient, and it isn't wrong of you not to follow that principle where those you love are concerned. Rather, it is both possible and unobjectionable for the love that two people have for one another to include the willingness to draw more deeply on each other than that.

This needn't be a matter of each regarding anything that is his as the other person's to spend as she wishes, just as if it were her own. More commonly, there will be limits. There is also trust, both that these limits will be respected and that your own importance to the other person will affect the uses she is inclined to make of you. My thought is that cost-efficiency need not be one of those limits. Instead, each can want the other to make very broad use of him or her in matters of importance, and each can gratefully do so.

We are not perfect, of course, and those who care for each other in this way can certainly do each other wrong. For example, A might tax B dearly for something that is actually of no particular importance to A, or for something A could easily have gotten in some other way, or simply for something he could have paid for himself.[8] Or he might draw heavily on B in what he should have realized would be a wasted effort, unredeemed by benefits to either party. Those choices would be failures to be as careful about B as A should be. They certainly can't be the routine, if A cares deeply about B, and they ought to cause A regret, but they could happen on occasion nevertheless.

I would say that *except* when either A or B errs in such ways in the uses they make of each other, any selfishness in their behavior is unobjectionable. Indeed, the devotion to each other that their action represents is something of great value, both in itself and in the way it expands the possibilities for each of them. It is admirable for them to be so selfless in matters of importance to the other person and to entrust themselves to each other in this way. And though they must certainly take care not to abuse that selflessness and t trust, they are not always wrong to make use of it. If they *were* always wrong to do so, their selflessness wouldn't be admirable after all, since it would only invite the other person to mistreat them.

The objection will be that the people I am describing sometimes act selfishly and accordingly sometimes allow themselves to be treated selfishly. They do so when one of them spends the resources made available out of devotion to him in a way that costs the other person more dearly than it would cost the beneficiary to do without what the sacrifice would provides. Doing that is selfish, the objection would be, a mistreatment of the person who trusted you, and to allow it is objectionable in its own right. The mother and daughter in Hardwig's example are an illustration.

My idea is that they illustrate something quite different, if they are mutually devoted to each other. Then if there is selfishness in permitting the sacrifice, it need not be *objectionable* selfishness, and the submission to it need not be morally dubious. Let us begin with the daughter. She allows the mother to whom she is devoted—and who is also devoted to her—to make use of her in this way. There is no subservience in that behavior, no agreement that she is simply less important than her mother. There certainly can be subservience when we are selfish with regard to someone to whom we are *not* devoted and that person puts up with our action. Here, though, their arrangement is that the daughter may make similar use of her mother in matters of similar importance to her when their positions are reversed. Neither is accepting second-class citizenship. Nor is the daughter letting her mother treat her in a way that she knows is wrong but lacks the courage to protest. There is no cowardice in what the daughter does; there is only devotion.

The critic might urge that the daughter *ought* to protest, because the selfishness itself is a mistreatment of her even though she fails to see it that way. To the critic she is like the mother and daughter who have simply long agreed that the mother is everything and the daughter is nothing, their selfishness and subservience present in the way they value courses of action. But these two aren't like that at all, of course. They both value themselves, and they both value each other.

Nor should we say the daughter goes wrong in a more occasional way, whenever she submits to what is actually selfishness on her mother's part. That view would require regarding the selfishness as mistreatment, and it is not: it does not have the qualities that make it objectionable for one person to treat another selfishly. There is certainly no arrogance in it, no assumption on the mother's part that she is simply of greater importance than her daughter. There certainly can be arrogance of that kind when we are selfish toward someone for whom we have no regard. But in this case the spirit in which the mother accepts her daughter's sacrifice includes a willingness to allow her daughter to make similar use of her if their positions were reversed. There is no assumption of moral priority in that.

Nor is the mother's behavior quite like that of someone who is too weak to resist the temptation to act in a way that he knows is wrong, and whose selfishness is therefore tinged with self-recrimination or protected by self-deception. Certainly the mother might wish very much that she were not so costly to her daughter, but that is not the same thing. She might also be afraid that she is doing something wrong, but that fear won't suffice either. To say she is being *weak* means she is giving in to a temptation to do something that is wrong, for some independent reason, or against her principles, or in violation of a resolution she has made. The weakness can't be the whole story itself but needs this added element. I think it is absent in this case.

For the same reason, it won't do to claim that mother and daughter are mutual enablers, each helping the other to act wrongly. That contention would require that they each go astray in some way, when it is their turn. To put it differently, there is nothing wrong with enabling someone to act in an unobjectionable way. And the independent fault we would need to find in what each enables the other to do can't be what is usually wrong with selfishness. To repeat, there is no arrogance in what they do, no assumption that one is better than the other person, or that even though one is not better, there is little the other person can do to stop one. And to say there is weakness in it begs the question.

One suspects the claim will have to be that it is just always wrong for one person to be *imprudent* with the resources of another, to spend them in ways that are not cost-efficient even if that person urges that he do so. This claim is most plausible at great extremes, when A ruins B in order to have something absolutely trivial: for example, in order to have a soothing massage from the ridiculously expensive Marco the Master Masseur. That seems wrong for A to do even if B is all for it, and even if A would make similarly ridiculous sacrifices for B.

My first reaction is to doubt that we can affect in this way someone we care about deeply. To do so would ruin someone to whom we are devoted. If anyone were able to do that *lightly*, it would mean that he wasn't devoted to this person after all. Moreover, ruining someone to whom we are devoted is too serious a matter to occur as a moment of uncharacteristic behavior. It would have to enact some continuing features of our character and personality, as opposed to being totally uncharacteristic of what we are like from day to day. What could those features be? It could be that A is able to do this because he is very self-centered— but in that case he wouldn't also want B to make costly use of him when B feels the need, and that disposition was part of their being devoted *to each other*. It could be that A is uncomfortable with his life and always looking for magic solutions to his problems, of which a massage from Marco is only the latest. But then A would be broadly or consistently selfish in his dealings with B, as he implemented his steady search for magic solutions to his problems. That behavior is difficult to square with his being devoted to her, and also with his being available for B to use selfishly in matters of importance to her. This reasoning suggests that the extreme cases of selfishness occur only *outside* relationships of mutual devotion. If so, they aren't a problem for the view I am offering, which is that mutual devotion can redeem what would otherwise be objectionable as an act of selfishness.

3.

A different concern remains. Although it's hard to imagine that the prospect of going without a massage could overwhelm your love for those to whom you are devoted, it's not hard to imagine that a fear of *dying* could do this. The prospect of dying could have you acting in ways of which you would be ashamed if you could regard them with a cooler eye. You could become a coward when something of which you are very afraid threatens to occur. It could also be that when you will die unless something is done and your loved ones would go to any extreme to save your life, you will let them do so, rather than having what it takes to stop them—even though you do love them, and even though you should stop them.[9]

But when *should* you stop them, and when are you free instead to fall into their loving arms? We are likely to want a precise rule for this situation, a clear test for which costs are too high to let others pay for our sake and which are not. We are also likely to recognize that there isn't going to be such a rule and to say only that although those who love us may certainly make great sacrifices to save us, we mustn't let these be *too* great. We mustn't let them bear *crushing* burdens for our sake, John Hardwig says in a different argument, not even if their doing so would save us from bearing an even greater burden ourselves.[10]

This argument doesn't tell us which burdens are the crushing ones, of course. That decision is left to our intuitions, and we are not a great deal wiser about what we should permit and what we should not. So we are left free to color the conclusion in our own favor except in very clear cases, just as we were when the question was whether the costs to our loved ones too greatly outweighed what their sacrifices might do for us. There isn't a great deal of protection against our favoring ourselves, if these are the terms in which we are to think, and the worry was that we *would* do it.

I think the worry is overblown, actually, and that it is adequately addressed if those in the situations we are imagining take a different kind of care not to do their loved ones wrong. It isn't helpful to have them agonize over how much it is worth to save their life if the sacrifices were made, or over whether the costs to their loved ones have entered a realm of the inherently unacceptable. Very often there is no decisive answer to those questions, and that is precisely when the agonizing would be done. Agonizing over them also distracts us from thinking in a different way, which I want to recommend.

Some aspects of this alternative emerged earlier: that we ought not to tax our loved ones dearly for something that is actually of no particular importance to us, or for something we could easily have gotten in some other way, or simply something we could have paid for ourselves, or in what we should realize would be a wasted effort, unredeemed by benefits to either party. Certainly our love for those who would pay these costs would strongly disincline us to do any of these things. It could still be necessary to take *care* not to do them, however, if it appeared that our lives would otherwise come to an end. For many of us the prospect of dying has a dreadful power, and a special effort would be needed if we were not simply to grasp whatever hand we saw extended toward us to save us from it. It would be very hard for us to think instead about what that help really offered, what it would cost, and whether there were better alternatives. But if we were able to do so, it might emerge that remaining alive in this particular way wasn't of great value to us after all, despite our powerful first impulses. Or we might come to realize that what we valued so highly in the effort to save us wasn't the chance it gave us to remain alive, but the place it showed us to have in the hearts of others. We could then see that they had already given us this great good, in their willingness to go to these extremes for us—certainly a way in which we could have it without taxing them so dearly after all. That would mean we shouldn't accept such help, any more than we should exhaust their financial resources to pay our medical costs instead of spending our own.

It would be a moral error to allow our loved ones to make those kinds of sacrifices for our sake—though an error that we might be forgiven under these circumstances. After all, a great deal stands in the way of realizing that you do not value staying alive as highly as your loved ones and your culture both assume you must, or, in a different case, in the way of your deciding that what life offers you now isn't worth a great deal to you. So, being careful about your loved ones in these ways could be greatly to your credit.

That said, notice that this approach does not involve identifying a price that is too high to allow your loved ones to pay in order to keep you alive, or too high to let them pay no matter what it purchases. You do need to be able to see that the price would be a high one, but which prices are high is much less problematic than which prices are *too* high. You also need to be able to see that it is a price that is unnecessary for them to pay, for either of two reasons: because nothing of great value to you would be gained by their doing so, or because you can have what you would gain without this cost to them. We owe our loved ones that kind of concern for their well-being, and we can provide it without encountering the conceptual difficulties we do if we think in terms of costs that are either too high for what they purchase or inherently too high.

The same holds for another form of care that we must take about accepting sacrifices. Allowing someone to pay dearly so that you can have something of great importance to you puts you deeply in that person's debt. You may not *want* to be in that debt, even to someone you love. It is also possible that you *shouldn't* be, that you should do without what you want rather than incurring the debt. You would owe her a level of gratitude that knows few parallels. This level of help would call for much by way of willingness to reciprocate—including, perhaps, carrying out obligations this person can no longer fulfill herself because of what she gave up in helping you (looking after her children, for example). It would also call for you to greatly appreciate this person, in your heart as well as in your actions. Those are obligations you would incur if you were to let her try to save you. If you were unwilling to carry them out, unwilling to be in her debt in this way, it would be wrong for you to accept what puts you in that debt. It would also be wrong for you to do so if you knew that it just wasn't in your nature to be this grateful to her. In that case you would lack the resources to be this indebted to her, which is also a reason not to allow yourself to be.

Of course, debts of gratitude do demand something very different from us than monetary debts, but they are genuine debts just the same. It is wrong to incur them unless we are both willing and able to do what they call for us to do, just as it is wrong to incur monetary debts unless we are able to repay them and willing to do so. If the likelihood is that you will die before you can repay the debt in full, the debt must be one that you will honor as completely as you can and would honor in full if you could. Again, that is just as true when the debt is one of gratitude as it is when what you will owe is money. To act otherwise is to *use* the person who helps you, treating her as no more than a means to your end.

We ought not to do that even in our hour of need, and perhaps especially not to those who love us. Whether we would be using them is also an entirely different matter than how great a sacrifice they must make to to help us. So, we can be careful not to treat our loved ones in this way without sorting out how much it would actually be worth to save the life that is in store for us, or deciding whether the costs of doing so are too high a price to pay for *anything*. That is an advantage, since those matters are desperately unclear.

What prompted this closing discussion, though, was concern that we might be so afraid of dying that our devotion to our loved ones wouldn't keep us from acting in shameful ways, just as a soldier might prove to be a coward under fire. I've offered nothing to rule that out that possibility, it might be objected. I would say that nothing *can* rule it out. The best a person can do is to try to break the hold that fear might have on her, by refusing to focus exclusively on what she is afraid of and how to escape it. The thinking I've recommended does that. It shifts to what is fearful about what frightens you, to whether there are alternative ways of escaping it, and to what we might call the aftermath of escaping it in a particular way. Whether we are able to think in those ways when what we fear threatens us will depend on our deeper character. If we are able to do so, those thoughts should help prevent that fear from dominating our actions.

However, the broader original concern was that we might cost our loved ones too dearly when they come to our aid. What is to prevent our doing exactly that, if we take only the care I've urged? One factor is our love for them. Loving them means that we would be greatly averse to their losing what is important to them, as they would if they were to make sacrifices for our sake. We would certainly not want to permit this unless it were for something exceedingly important to us. Loving them also means we would not want to be wrong about how important it *should* be to us: we would not want to err at their great cost. Those aspects of loves protect against our making great errors of this kind, as A does when he ruins B so as to have a massage from Marco.

Second, if we loved this person, we would permit the sacrifice only if we thought ourselves able to carry out the obligations we incurred by doing so. For example, imagine an elderly father whose grown daughter wants to greatly impair her health and shorten her life in order to prolong his, and who has children of her own. If she did this for him, he would owe it to her to make up for what it would cost her children. It does not seem to me that he *could* make up for that cost, because of the great extent to which it is their mother herself that her children would lose. If I am right about that, it isn't a sacrifice he should permit her to make, on the approach I have recommended; no doubt there are others.

Third, it would never be sufficient that we alone believe the sacrifice the other person would make for our sake is worth the cost to him. He must think so too. Since we have a relationship of mutual devotion, he is not some poor servile soul or someone who is simply self-destructive, but rightly expects that we would also make great sacrifices for him. So his opinion isn't to be discarded.

I think that is all the care we can reasonably take not to be too costly. Once we have taken it, we should trust ourselves and our loved ones not to be gravely wrong about what it is worth to be of help to one another. That will be our way of being *us* with what is ours, rather than two people who each have their own.

Finally, it has to be acknowledged that those who are confronted with the situations we have been imagining might never have faced choices of this order before. Take again the mother and daughter in Hardwig's example. It is plausible to picture the daughter as never having been called upon to make a sacrifice this demanding for her mother's sake, and the mother as never having had anything this important to her for which her daughter is her only hope. Even if they *are* devoted to each other, this is new territory. Their relationship will change, and I have claimed that the mother shouldn't allow the sacrifice that changes it unless she is both willing and able to live accordingly.

But what will it *be* to live accordingly? If I owe you money, ordinarily it is quite clear what I am to do: how much I am to repay you and when I am to do this. If I owe you my gratitude, as the mother will the daughter, my debt is in the imprecise currency of good will, and there is latitude both in how I am to repay you and when I am to repay you. There would be more personal changes between the mother and daughter as well, and what those would be would also be more or less unclear. So the choice to permit the sacrifice that changes things between them, and to live accordingly, would be something of a moral adventure.

Such adventures aren't to be undertaken lightly, certainly, but only in good faith. I have urged that they aren't ruled out by an imbalance between what the mother would lose if the sacrifice were not made and what her loving and beloved daughter would give up if it *were* made. That factor alone doesn't make permitting the sacrifice an exploitation or something of which to be ashamed. Sometimes instead, to allow a loved one to make a great sacrifice for your sake is the perfectly permissible acceptance of that person's deep devotion to you.

Conclusion

The relationship between parents and children ordinarily lasts far longer than friendships, or marriages, or jobs with the same employer. Often it begins when the parents create the child, and many adoptions also occur when the child is very young. In both cases, they remain parent and child to one another until one of them dies many years later, unless one of them has what we call an "early death." In short, we are usually our children's parents (and our parents' children) for a very long time indeed.

We should expect there to be patterns in the way the two people treated each other over such a long time, rather than expecting them periodically to begin wholly anew. There are also patterns in the way parents and children *should* treat each other, as each grows older. In a way, that is a remarkable phenomenon. After all, at various times one of them is an adult who is parent to a baby, then to a small child, then to an adolescent, then to a grown son or daughter. The other is a child who is under the parent's care, then the parents' adult child while the parent grows old and the adult child undergoes changes of his or her own. But despite this great variety in what kinds of people they are at any given time, there are commonalities in the ways they should act toward each other. I will close by noting some of these that have arisen in the preceding pages. All are ways in which the ethics of parenthood is shaped by the right to have one's autonomy respected and by the role of love in the relationship.

On the view I offered, the right to have one's autonomy respected first comes into play in a different way. I argued that it is what gives those who create a child a powerful claim to "keep" that child and to serve as his or her parents. Few would now support that claim on the ground that our children are our property, but it is equally unappealing to say that those who create a child are no different than anyone else where that child is concerned. My claim was that biological parents do have a special standing, not as a property right but as an instance of our general right to continue whatever we have begun.

The argument for this view takes creating a child to be the first act of parenthood where that child is concerned. Those who carry it out are then said to be in the same position as someone who plays the first note in a piece of music. Both have a right to do what comes next, rather than being no different than anyone else who might continue what they had begun (or might choose to bring it to an end). This is true of musicians even when what they are playing is not particularly constrained by a score. Similarly, creating a child gives one standing to continue as the child's parent, even though parents have considerable latitude and room for improvisation.

Imagine that we had no such claim to continue what we had begun, and thus that others needed no particular justification for interrupting what we were doing. That would mean we would not control our actions insofar as we did anything beyond what we could do all at once, before there was time for others to interrupt. So we would not be at liberty to be agents in any but the most fleeting ways, and our right to do things in our own way would come to very little—possibly to nothing, since it's hard to see why we would be entitled to do what could be done in one step but just nothing more complicated. In short, if our autonomy is to have any value, it has to carry a strong claim to continue what we have begun.

Creating a child is one way to begin parenthood, and thus to have this strong claim to continue to be a parent to the child. Another is to adopt a child whose parents have died or have chosen to give up their special standing in the child's life. Another is to join informally a "single-parent" family, with the single parent's consent, and to begin to join in raising and looking after the children. Those are different ways to begin parenthood, but each carries exactly the same parental rights, on the view I've offered.

One caveat is that we do not have this claim to continue what we are doing if we began by violating someone's rights. Thus robbers and thieves are not entitled to carry on with their "ill-gotten gains," precisely because the gains were ill-gotten. An analogy for parenthood would be a rapist who impregnated his victim. That would give him no claim to continue as a father to the child, despite his having carried out what I've called the first act of parenthood, whereas, his victim would have every right to be a mother to the child, if she wished to. They differ in this way because the rapist began parenthood by violating someone's rights, and his victim did not. That's why he has no right to continue, and she does.

That conclusion will be welcome to all, but sometimes matters are less obvious. There are cultures in which women have little choice but to agree to have a child, if that is the man's wish. Should this system too leave the man with no right to be a father to the child, as it would if he had raped her? Not necessarily, I argued. My contention was that although those circumstances are ripe for coercion and exploitation, it wouldn't be a necessary truth that whenever a child is created under them the man has either coerced or exploited his partner. The ones who don't would have the same strong claim to be fathers to their biological children as they would have had if the conditions had been less oppressive to women, on the view I offered.

I made an argument of this same kind with regard to those who employ surrogate gestational mothers or donated eggs when they create a child. That is, I contended that although those practices are ripe for coercion and exploitation, not every surrogate mother is coerced or exploited, and neither is every woman who donates an egg. Therefore employing a woman for these purposes can simply be a different way to begin parenthood, carrying the same right to continue as those who create children the "old-fashioned" way have.

A different point of interest is that if we cannot do a thing at all, then we cannot have a right to do it. That should be true even if we have managed what could have been the first step in what we would be unable to carry out. We would have no right to continue beyond whatever stage was within our capacity, because doing so would be a right to do what we could not do.

What's interesting here is that the first step in parenthood, the one in which two people create a child, is so easy that even a child can do it; what's hard is going on from there.[1] Suppose a young girl who became pregnant were incapable of going on to do what parents must do for their children, or that a young boy who impregnated someone were incapable of this. That would mean neither of them would have a special claim to keep the child. It would still be her baby in the biological sense (or his baby), but this fact wouldn't matter in the way it ordinarily does. Instead, the proper course would be for others to think in terms of what was best for the child, even if that meant taking the child away from a mother or father who wanted to keep her. Very sad, but they are just too young to have a child, the reasoning would be.

The reasoning is perfectly sound with regard to girls and boys of very tender years. However, it is unsound with regard to the wider class to whom it is often applied: it doesn't hold true of unwed teenagers who manage to make babies, because teenagers are not literally incapable of being parents to their children, especially if they are given help. So a more interesting question about teenagers is whether they have a right to that help, either from their families or from the state. If they do, their claim to keep their babies would be as strong as an adult's and would carry obligations for those who were to provide the help. I discussed this line of thought, and argued that it does not hold true for all teenaged mothers and fathers but does hold for some.

A different strand of reasoning about teenagers abandons the idea that parenthood is wholly beyond them, in the way it would be beyond someone who was comatose or someone who was unable to distinguish reality from illusion. Those people couldn't be parents at all, but clearly teenagers aren't like that. Rather, the thought would be, the trouble with teenagers is that although they could be parents to their children, they would be terrible ones: so terrible that we shouldn't regard them as having a right to try.

The principle in this reasoning is also sound. As an analogy, suppose that you had begun to drive a truck that you could barely control down a crowded street. The fact that you had started what you "couldn't do" would give you no strong claim to continue. But the reason isn't that your destructive path wouldn't be a way of driving the truck down the street; it's that your way of doing this would put others at unacceptable risk. We aren't called upon to let you do that out of respect for your autonomy, any more than we would have any such reason to allow you to continue to drive a truck that you had stolen. We have a right to continue only what is innocent with regard to others, not what begins in violation of their rights and not what would violate their rights if it were to continue.

If that's correct, it isn't only those who are literally incapable of carrying on as parents who have no special claim to keep the babies they have created. The same is true of those who cannot perform acceptably as parents. The harder question is when we are entitled to say this of someone and take that person's child away.

I argued that the criterion for doing so should be very conservative. It should capture only those whose conduct as parents would quickly amount to levels of abuse or neglect that would call for the state to take the child into protective custody: the ones we know would fail very soon if they were allowed to take next steps. It's not at all clear what would entitle us to believe this of someone. What *is* clear is that we wouldn't be entitled to believe it just on the grounds that she (or he) was a teenager. There is quite a range of competency in that class of possible parents. In sum, neither argument that teenagers have no right to be parents to the children they create is a good one, if parental rights are rights to continue what you have begun. It isn't true that they can't serve as parents to a child at all, and our routine assumption shouldn't be that they cannot do this acceptably well.

I offered a similar argument against the view that children should be taken from homosexuals for the child's sake. A crucial assumption of that view is that homosexuals either cannot be parents at all or that they should be regarded as incapable of being acceptable ones. That assumption is the basis for saying that they do not have the standing that a heterosexual parent would, and hence we are not only free to place a child they have created or adopted where we think best but morally bound to do so. But the reasons to think so are easily refuted. So on the account I've given, homosexuals who begin parenthood without violating anyone's rights have the same strong claim to continue as heterosexuals who do. Interventions must be based on their behavior as parents, and sexual orientation is not a sufficient basis for concluding that it will be unacceptable and acting preemptively on behalf of the child.

Our terms for the conduct that does forfeit parental rights are "abuse" and "neglect." But what should count as those? Every parent makes mistakes, and if we were entitled to continue only what we could do *perfectly*, then this right would amount to nothing much. Abuse and neglect have to be errors of a different order, not only for that reason but also because they call for intervention by the state. If we were to set the bar too low, the system meant to protect children would be overwhelmed. Moreover, a state's efforts to make things better for a child often have costs of their own for that child, sometimes terrible ones. We wouldn't want to wield so clumsy a tool whenever the parents were falling somewhat short, but only when their own errors were serious ones. Finally, we should be free to raise our children in private. That right certainly doesn't mean we should be free to treat them as we wish, but it also introduces limitations. It means that what entitles the state to intervene must also entitle it to intrude, to the extent that it must intrude first in order to detect the wrongdoing and then in order to deal with it. That's another reason to say that only relatively serious parental misconduct should count as abuse or neglect.

We want to be able to say much more than just that abuse and neglect have to be serious misconduct, though. The analysis I offered distinguished three rough categories: abuse, neglect over a period of time, and negligence on a single occasion. My account of negligence on a single occasion was modeled on some thinking in tort law. My accounts of abuse and long-term neglect emphasized a way of understanding what the behavior shows about the parent. That is what signifies what lies ahead for the child, I contended, and when our aim is to protect the child, our sense of what lies ahead is what should guide us in deciding what to do. What the conduct shows about the parent helps determine whether intervention is called for and, if so, what form the intervention should take, including whether it should be geared toward returning the child to this family.

Those discussions are about ways in which parents are not at liberty to continue to treat their children. A question of a different kind arises when there is a time during which someone wants to resume parenthood after a period of absence. If (as I contend) parental rights are rights to continue what we have underway, the question is when an interruption costs us those rights and when it does not.

It seems clear that not all interruptions are alike in this regard. At one extreme are interruptions that occur because someone simply abandons his or her family and later wants to return. Surely that person has no strong claim to do so. At the opposite extreme are cases in which a baby has been kidnapped from a hospital nursery. Here too the baby's parents do not act as parents to her for a time, but surely they would have as strong a right to the child's return as we can imagine. There are also more difficult cases, however, where our intuitions are not so straightforward. The harder cases confront us with a second issue as well. Suppose we decide against allowing someone who had been apart from his or her child to have the child back. Should the law grant this person some lesser role in the child's life? Or should that determination be up to whoever does get to be the child's parents, as part of their right to decide who interacts with their child and in what ways? These too are questions about what the right to continue what we have started amounts to, here in connection with how interruptions affect that right.

My way of answering them acknowledged several potential claims in play in these cases, sought to evaluate those, and then gave them their proper weight relative to each other. That approach differs from far simpler views, according to which, for example, biological parents ought always to prevail, or, for another example, we should always resolve cases of disputed parenthood by attending solely to the best interests of the child. I gave arguments against those simpler views and in favor of the more complex one that I offered. I then applied the view I offered to the cases of Baby Jessica and Baby Richard, to what is sometimes called "prenatal abandonment," to cases of separation by war or natural disaster, to cases in which babies are switched at birth, and to cases in which a child is conceived through a casual sexual encounter and the child's mother chooses to deal with it on her own.

This process served to say still more about what parental rights amount to if they are rights to continue what we have begun, but I hadn't yet said anything much about what parenthood calls for parents to do. In turning to that issue, I chose to focus on cases in which their child should be expected to grow up to be an adult. That isn't true of every child, and the ethics of being a parent to a child who should *not* be expected to become an adult is a rich topic in its own right. The questions it poses are no less interesting or important, but I did not pursue them here.

When the expectation is that a child *will* become an adult, one obligation of parenthood is to raise that child. Doing so includes an obligation to provide a moral education. These and other obligations are part of what parenthood is. There are related rights, to be the ones who do these things for the child. Moreover, there is some latitude in the way the obligations are to be carried out. Some of what the obligations require can be accomplished in more than one form, and all of them can be accomplished in more than one way. Part of being the child's parent is being at liberty in these respects to carry out your obligations in the way of your choosing. This flexibility allows parenthood to be personal and allows parents some ways in which to shape the kind of person their child becomes. That choice is part of what makes parenthood an exercise of autonomy that is so rich in potential rewards, and how well it goes has a great deal to do with how good a life someone who has children has had.

One set of limits on parental latitude lies in what the larger society is entitled to expect. The child already lives among others and will almost certainly do so as an adult. Therefore others are entitled to have the child's parents ensure that he or she develops the character traits required of one who lives as a member of the larger society (rather than, say, a predator within it). I offered a view about what those traits are and what parents are thus free to do in shaping their child's moral character.

There is also a different factor limiting what parents may do in raising their child: the fact that it is a *child* they are raising. Even young children have some right to do things in their own way, I argued, and that right is to be respected. Moreover, as Joel Feinberg famously marked in speaking of a right to an open future, the adult whom the child becomes will also have a right to autonomy, and parents can foreclose it too greatly by what they do while the child is still a child.[2] These points enrich the idea that parenthood must include respect for autonomy, since they mean it's no longer only the *parent's* autonomy that has moral weight. Moreover, although children do have a right to autonomy, parents also have obligations to protect them from harm and to raise them to become adults of an acceptable kind. The issue is how to balance the several claims to have one's autonomy respected and the parental obligations.

In addressing that issue, I made a distinction between simply having traits of character or personality, on the one hand, and making those traits one's own, on the other. Even very young children have personalities, as all parents can attest, and the personalities appear so early that the initial source must be genetic. Various traits are then nurtured, molding the kind of person the child becomes. For a good while the children themselves have no particular sense of what they are like as people, and no great interest in it. They are still the creatures of other people and outside sources: they have traits, but in an important sense the traits are not yet their own. At this point the value of allowing children to do things "in their own way" lies in helping them develop a way that is *truly* their own, in the sense I have in mind, rather than only something with which they've been imprinted.

That situation changes, with time. Children become interested in what kind of person they are, and they act in ways that take ownership of these traits. One of these ways is to get a sense of who they are in some respect, find it satisfying, and accept it even though they think they could change. Another is to make a conscious effort to be a different kind of person, either by imitating others or in some other way. Whatever results from this effort is then the child's doing. Yet another way to become someone of your own is to continue to act in ways that you know will affect the kind of person you are, when you could act differently. Children can engage in any of these behaviors, as part of "growing up." As they do, they come to be a person whose autonomy merits respect, because their way of doing a thing becomes *their* way of doing it, in the sense that matters.

It's obvious that children don't become persons of their own all at once and in every particular. It happens over time, it is uneven, and it varies with the child. The only generalization available is that the younger the child is, the weaker the basis for thinking that he must be allowed to do things in his own way out of respect for his autonomy. This is so because the younger he is, the weaker the basis for thinking he has an autonomy to respect. That explains why extensive paternalism toward children is less objectionable the younger they are, since there is less basis for thinking we are overriding a self of their own and their right to autonomy. It also explains why it is a moral mistake to let a very young child do something highly dangerous because you think you must respect her autonomy, as Jessica Dubroff's mother and father did when they allowed their seven-year-old daughter to try to fly solo across the United States.

I argued that children should play an increasing role in the way they are raised, so that this is increasingly a joint activity rather than something their parents do to them or for them. This isn't to say parent and child should be equal partners in the project, even when the child is an adolescent, or that children are free to "divorce" their parents and carry out the project alone or change to parents of their choosing. None of those are true, any more than it is true that parents have a right to decide in its entirety what kind of person their child becomes or what kind of life he or she will have as an adult. I offered a different account of what raising a child amounts to, if parent and child carry it out properly as a joint project. I also argued that this way of raising a child allays Joel Feinberg's concern that parents must not settle their child's adult life too completely while the child is still young. It respects the autonomy of the adult the child becomes as well as that of the person she already is, to put the point differently.

In another context, I made a different use of the ideas that it takes time to develop a self of one's own, and that only then should our actions be regarded as *ours* in an important way. There is a strong intuition that when a child does wrong, we should react very differently than we should if the wrongdoer had been an adult. That intuition underlies the construction of separate juvenile justice systems. It is also in play in our everyday reactions when people behave badly. In addition, it is another respect in which we aren't entirely sure whether adolescents should be treated as children or as adults.

On the view I urged, children who do wrong (including adolescents) are entitled to a presumption to which adults are not. The presumption is that the self the wrongdoer put into play is not one for which he is responsible, and that he is still entitled to our help with his moral education. Sometimes the child is entitled to this presumption because we ought to regard the self he put into play as the artifact of others rather than one he has made his own. Then it's reasonable to assume that this is someone we should still be helping in that project, rather than someone we should regard as responsible for what he has made of it.

In a different kind of case, the child has been forced to become a person of his own far sooner than he should have been, without the help that children should have from their parents and often with hindrances in the form of abuse and neglect. This child too is entitled to a response meant to educate rather than to give "just deserts," because otherwise we perpetuate the ways in which life has been unfair to him. If adults with terrible backgrounds are not equally entitled to this response, the reason is that the adults have had sufficient opportunities to overcome their pasts, whereas children have not.

This presumption is rebuttable, on the view I offered, both with regard to treating adults who do wrong as adults and with regard to treating children who do wrongs as children. The chapter closed by discussing what is to be done with regard to children for whom the presumption ought not to win the day. The contention was that although our primary concern at those times should be to punish them rather than to contribute to their moral education, we should temper their punishment with mercy.

Those discussions continue to work out what is called for by respect for autonomy and what is not. But of course respect for the child's autonomy is hardly all that parents owe their children. I argued that while children are young and under their care, their parents also have an obligation to love them and to convey this love to the children. Of course, doing that is also part of what makes parenthood sweet, both in its own right and because children love their parents in return.

This all occurs at the time when the child is still a child, however, and although childhood comes to an end, parenthood does not: it only changes. The last three chapters of the book sought to say what special rights and responsibilities parents have when their children are grown, and what rights and responsibilities their grown children have with regard to them. I think love and respect for autonomy play powerful roles at this stage of life as well.

The chapter titled "Having Grown Children" is partly about respecting the autonomy of one's grown child, which calls for something different than it did when she was under one's care. This chapter also argued that parenthood does not include an obligation to continue to love your grown children come what may. It explained why many parents do have this obligation even though it isn't an obligation of parenthood as such, and it also offered a view about what can sever it. A separate chapter developed Simon Keller's important idea that the filial obligations that grown children have are not debts of gratitude to their parents.[3] (Almost all grown children do owe their parents debts of gratitude, I contended: the idea is that those are not their filial obligations, which are duties of a different kind.) In my version of this view, filial obligations are duties to give our parents a place in our affections that is roughly equivalent to the one they gave us when we were young and under their care. I said what that amounted to, and also what can sever these filial obligations—and what cannot.

The final chapter concerns the intuition that there are sacrifices we shouldn't allow our grown children to make for our sake, even if the children want to make them. I addressed this topic in connection with John Hardwig's contention that when our continuing to live would be too burdensome to our children, we have an obligation to die.[4] I argued that Hardwig's way of thinking about this subject undervalues the place that love can have in a relationship between a parent and a child, and the extent to which those who love each other can act selfishly without this action being morally objectionable. My claim was that simple cost-benefit reasoning misconstrues what parents and their grown children can have together. That is a way in which love and respect for autonomy ought to shape the last days of parenthood, as they should also have shaped the days that came before.

Notes

Notes to the Introduction

1. Tamar Schapiro, "What Is a Child?" *Ethics* 109 (July 1999): 717.
2. Simon Keller, "Four Theories of Filial Duty," *Philosophical Quarterly* 56 (April 2006): 254–274.

Notes to Chapter 1

1. Greg Smith, "Baby Jessica Takes to New Life, New Name," *L.A. Times* (August 7, 1994): A 10.
2. Lucinda Franks, "The War for Baby Clausen," *The New Yorker* (March 22, 1993): 72.
3. *In the Interest of B. G. C., a Child*, 496 N.W. 2d 239 (Iowa 1992), 245. Indeed, he had refused even to meet the other daughter he fathered. (Franks, "The War for Baby Clausen," 65)
4. *In the Interest of B. G. C., a Child*, 496 N.W. 2d, at 246.
5. *In the Interest of B. G. C., a Child*, 496 N.W. 2d, at 241.
6. *In re Petition of Kirchner*, 649 NE 2d 324 (1995), at 328.
7. *In the Interest of B. G. C., a Child*, 496 N.W. 2d, at 241, quoting *In re Burney*, 259 N.W. 2d 322, at 324 (Iowa 1977).
8. *In the Interest of B. G. C., a Child*, 496 N.W. 2d, at 241.
9. Marilyn Firth, "The Stolen Generation," *The Age* (June 15, 1996): A 24.
10. Firth, "Stolen Generation," A 24.
11. Sian Watkins, "Single Mothers Were Told Their Babies Had Died," *The Age* (June 12, 1996): A 4; Andrew Darby, "Opposition May Force Inquiry," *The Age* (June 15, 1996): A 24; Firth, "Stolen Generation," A 24.
12. Firth, "Stolen Generation," A 24.
13. Firth, "Stolen Generation," A 24.
14. Martin Guggenheim, *What's Wrong with Children's Rights?* (Cambridge, MA: Harvard University Press, 2005), 24–25. Laurence Houlgate, "What Is Legal Intervention in the Family? Family Law and Family Privacy," *Law and Philosophy* 17, 1998, attributes the following position to Andrea Dworkin, Catherine MacKinnon, Martha Minow, and Frances E. Olsen, among others: "... there is no such thing as the family as a separate and distinct entity into which the state sometimes intervenes.... Since the state constantly defines and redefines the family, there can be no such thing as non-intervention. The legal system *must* intervene in the family" (Houlgate, 143). Houlgate offers important criticisms of this view. Even if it were correct, a state "intervention" in which biological parents were allowed to raise their children would leave them to act as they have a right to act, rather than preventing this and empowering others who have no right to be parents

to the child. If we must choose between state intervention that respects rights and state intervention that does not, we will certainly need a powerful justification for choosing the latter. For positive presentations of the view, Houlgate refers the reader to Andrea Dworkin, *Intercourse* (New York: Free Press, 1987), 97, 122, 155–159; Catherine MacKinnon, *Feminism Unfolded: Discourses on Life and Law* (Cambridge, MA: Harvard University Press, 1987), 100; Martha Minow, "Forming Underneath Everything That Grows: Toward a History of Family Law," *Wisconsin Law Review* 4, 1985; Frances E. Olsen, "The Family and the Market," "The Politics of Family Law," *Law and Inequality* 2 (1984); "The Myth of State Intervention in the Family," *University of Michigan Journal of Law Reform* 18 (1985).

15. For both reasons, this isn't a project over which the parent has a great deal of control. Often there are no clear indications of how to do it, and what the parent does is also constrained both by love for the child and by moral restrictions that range from the obvious to the subtle. A project of this kind couldn't possibly appeal equally to everyone any more than an occupation that was like this would engage everyone. This might sometimes be the reason why a particular parent is rather remote from his or her child and only has a parent's powerful influence in that distant way, for as long as he or she has it at all.

16. William Galston, *Liberal Pluralism* (Cambridge: Cambridge University Press, 2002), 102. The particular piece cited by Eamonn Callan is *Creating Citizens: Political Education and Liberal Democracy* (Oxford: Clarendon Press, 1997).

17. Ferdinand Schoeman, "Rights of Children, Rights of Parents, and the Moral Basis of the Family," in *Morals, Marriage and Parenthood*, ed. Laurence D. Houlgate (Belmont, CA: Wadsworth, 1999), 224. Schoeman's description idealizes the relationship, since certainly some parents are more withdrawn from their children than this and do not make their family lives as central to defining who they are. All we need say, though, is that parenthood offers the opportunity for the richer and deeper relationship. That will be enough to explain why a right to continue the parenthood one had underway would be something of great importance.

In *Children: Rights and Childhood* (London: Routledge, 1993), 124, David Archard identifies several respects in which the relationship between parents and children is not intimate in the same sense as one between lovers and friends. There is still intimacy of another sort, however, and that suffices for the argument here.

18. Joseph Goldstein, Albert J. Solnit, Sonja Goldstein, and Anna Freud, *The Best Interests of the Child* (New York: The Free Press, 1996), 11.

19. Goldstein et al., *Best Interests of the Child*, 11.

20. Goldstein et al., *Best Interests of the Child*, 59, emphasis added.

21. Goldstein et al., *Best Interests of the Child*, 50.

22. Goldstein et al., *Best Interests of the Child*, 6.

23. Goldstein et al., *Best Interests of the Child*, 53.

24. Goldstein et al., *Best Interests of the Child*, 56.

25. Goldstein et al., *Best Interests of the Child*, 19.

26. Goldstein et al., *Best Interests of the Child*, 12, 19, 20.

27. Interestingly, Goldstein *et al.* don't deny that the biological parents in such cases have rights. Instead, their view is that this is a special situation in which those rights are less important than protecting the child from harm: "Justice Heiple failed to recognize that at the time the case came before his court the *Does* were in fact Richard's parents. Consequently the burden should have been on *Otakar* to disqualify the Does as parents, not the other way around...To make this observation is not to deny that wrongs may have been inflicted on Otakar by Daniella, by the Does, and by the entire Illinois justice system....But [the court] made the wrong choice when it decided to remedy the harm to

Otakar by doing harm to Richard—what amounted to violence against him." (Goldstein et al., *Best Interests of the Child*, 60.)

28. Guggenheim, *What's Wrong with Children's Rights?* 88.

29. Guggenheim, *What's Wrong with Children's Rights?* 89.

30. Guggenheim, *What's Wrong with Children's Rights?* 90.

31. "Adam and Eve, and after them all parents were, by the law of nature, under an obligation to preserve, nourish and educate the children they had begotten, not as their own workmanship but the workmanship of their own Maker, the Almighty, to whom they were to be accountable for them." (Treatise II, sec. 56.) See also section 66, and Treatise I, sec. 54. I owe the latter reference to Jeffrey Blustein, *Parents and Children* (New York: Oxford University Press, 1982).

32. Treatise II, sec. 27.

33. Treatise II, sec. 40.

34. It might be objected that this line of reasoningt is at odds with the Millian account I have been giving. On a Millian account, a person should be free to decide what form her project took, as long as she violated no one's rights, and this would include similar liberty in the way in which she served as a parent to her child. Yet here I allow cultures to determine what the role of a parent involves, which seems to restrict that liberty.

Actually, though, there is no conflict. Cultures get to define what counts as *parenthood*, including some of the rights that must be respected by those who are acting as parents. This means it isn't up to the individual to determine whether it is parenthood he has underway, any more than it is up to me to determine whether writing this sentence is part of my own peculiar way of drinking tea: that would belong in *Alice in Wonderland*. Nothing in the Millian perspective requires it: the kind of activity in which I am engaged isn't up to me to determine, only the way in which I carry it out.

Notes to Chapter 2

1. Martin Guggenheim, *What's Wrong With Children's Rights?* (Cambridge, MA: Harvard University Press, 2005), 63–69, 97–101.

2. For a superb exploration of what ought to count as rape, see Sarah Conly, "Seduction, Rape, and Coercion," *Ethics* 115 (Oct. 2004), 96–121.

3. Uma Narayan, "Family Ties: Rethinking Parental Claims in the Light of Surrogacy and Custody," in *Having and Raising Children*, ed. Uma Narayan and Julia J. Bartkowiak (University Park: Pennsylvania State University Press, 1999), 68.

4. For instances of this argument, see Billie Wright Dzeich and Linda Weiner, eds., *The Lecherous Professor: Sexual Harassment on Campus* (Boston: Beacon Press, 1984); Dzeich and Weiner, *The Lecherous Professor: Sexual Harassment on Campus*, 2nd ed. (Champaign-Urbana: University of Illinois Press, 1991); Billie Wright Dzeich and Michael W. Hawkins, eds., *Sexual Harassment in Higher Education: Reflections and New Perspectives* (New York: Garland Publishing, 1998); P. Rutter, *Sex in the Forbidden Zone* (New York: Fawcett Crest, 1989); Louise F. Fitzgerald and Lauren M. Weitzman, "Men Who Harass: Speculation and Data," in *Ivory Power: Sexual Harassment on Campus*, ed. Michele A. Paludi,(Albany, NY: SUNY Press, 1990); Louise F. Fitzgerald, "Sexual Harassment: The Definition and Measurement of a Construct," in *Sexual Harassment on College Campuses: Abusing the Ivory Power*, ed. Michele A. Paludi, (Albany, NY: SUNY Press, 1996); and Leslie Irvine, "A 'Consensual' Relationship," in *Sexual Harassment on Campus*, ed. Bernice R. Sandler and Robert J. Shoop (Needham Heights, MA: Allyn and Bacon, 1997). Let me emphasize that this is a minority position in the literature on sexual harassment—not because that is an argument against it, but so as not to misrepresent.

It is also obvious that the parties need not be a male professor and a female student. It will be convenient to write only of that case, since (in my view) the gender and sexual preference of those involved don't change the issues or their proper resolution.

5. For an argument that the disparity in power between the genders means a woman's consent to sex with a man is never free, see Carole Pateman, "Women and Consent," in her books *The Sexual Contract* (Cambridge: Polity Press, 1988), and *The Disorder of Women: Democracy, Feminism and Political Theory* (Cambridge: Cambridge University Press, 1989).

I think it would also follow that no confession to the police can be made freely, since the police are far more powerful than the person they have under arrest. This suggests that the Fifth Amendment right not to be compelled to testify against oneself ought to make every confession made to police inadmissible in U.S. courts.

6. Sometimes the risk that a powerful position will be abused is great, the abuse is highly objectionable when it does occur, the temptations to abuse might be considerable, and it can be difficult even for the participants to tell whether what happened *is* an abuse. There is a very strong argument to try to change such structures: for example, to require that prisoners who are to be questioned must be allowed to have counsel present rather than being left completely in the power of the questioners. Where the structure remains in place, the conditions provide an excellent reason for the powerful not to risk what could be abuse of their power—for example, for professors never to have sex with any student.

Disparities of power deserve caution of those kinds. What I have opposed is the different view that disparities of power mean the rights of the relatively powerless *must* be violated if the two interact within this sphere of power, and the relatively powerful person must therefore fail to acquire whatever rights he or she would have acquired in the absence of their power differential.

7. For an argument that the power differential between faculty and students means any sexual relationship between them exploits the student, see Sue Rosenberg Zalk, "Men in the Academy: A Psychological Profile of Harassment," in *Ivory Power: Sexual Harassment on Campus*, ed. Michele A. Paludi (Albany: SUNY Press, 1990).

8. There is also a great deal that could be said about what would be wrong with a professor's getting one of his students to have sex. For a particularly compelling account of this, see Leslie Irvine, "A 'Consensual' Relationship," *Sexual Harassment on Campus*, ed. Bernice R. Sandler and Robert J. Shoop (Needham Heights, MA: Allyn and Bacon, 1997).

9. It could happen instead that it was necessary to have a child for economic reasons, as I imagine would be true if a family had to work the land under harsh conditions and wasn't in a position to hire help. This wouldn't be a case of the man exploiting a position of power over the woman, even if he had such a position, because it wouldn't be the man who got her to have a child because she had to or believed she had to. It would be their circumstances that had done this. That situation does not have the same implications as when an individual does it, for reasons parallel to the ones offered for thinking that "coercion" by hard circumstances doesn't have the same implications as coercion by individuals.

10. Centers for Disease Control and Prevention. *2003 Assisted Reproductive Technology Report*. Section 1, overview.

11. Centers for Disease Control and Prevention. *2003 Assisted Reproductive Technology Report*. Section 1, overview.

12. The CDC does not keep data on gestational surrogacy. The American Society for Reproductive Medicine does. According to its Registry, in 2000 in the United States there were 1,200 "cycles using a host uterus, with a delivery rate per transfer of 35.8%." This figures to only 429 births. ("Assisted Reproductive Technology in the United States: 2000

results generated from the American Society for Reproductive Medicine/Society for Assisted Reproductive Technology Registry," Society for Assisted Reproductive Technology Registry and the American Society for Reproductive Medicine, *Fertility and Sterility*, vol. 81, no. 5, May 2004). The states prohibiting the enforcement of surrogacy contracts are: Arizona, Ariz. Rev. Stat. Ann. 25–218 (1995); Indiana, Ind. Code 31–8–2–2 (1996); Louisiana, La. Rev. Stat. Ann. 2713 (West 1995); Nebraska, Neb. Rev. Stat. 225–21.200 (1994); New York, N.Y. Dom. Rel. Law 122 (McKinney 1996); North Dakota, N.D. Cent. Code 14–18–05 (1995); Utah. Utah Code Ann. 76–7–204 (1995); Washington, Wash. Rev. Code Ann. 26.26.240 (West 1996). The District of Columbia also does so, in D.C. Code Ann. 16–402 (1995). I owe this last reference to John A. Robertson, "Assisted Reproductive Technology and the Family," 47 *Hastings Law Journal* 911, April 1996, fn. 46.

13. Narayan, "Family Ties," 69–70.

14. Since the job is 24/7, it would involve 40 hours per week at $5.15, plus 58 hours per week at $7.63.

15. Laura M. Purdy, "Surrogate Mothering: Exploitation or Empowerment?" *Bioethics* 3 (Jan. 1989), 18–34.

16. Narayan, "Family Ties," 70.

17. Laura Purdy makes this same point about an analogous argument that surrogacy ought to be made criminal because "women are less free not to sell such rights against their will if they have succumbed to the low social evaluation of women's worth. That is, they may value themselves primarily in terms of their sexuality and reproductive capacity. Temporary prohibition of such selling might be a reasonable part of a larger strategy aimed at eliminating the underlying denigration of women. As this approach is one more instance of restricting women because of men's attitudes, however, we should have only reluctant recourse to it." Laura M. Purdy, "A Response to Dodds and Jones," *Bioethics* 3 (Jan. 1989): 43.

18. Narayan, "Family Ties," 66–67, emphasis hers. For instances of this argument, she directs the reader to Martha A. Field, "The Case Against Enforcement of Surrogacy Contracts," *Politics and the Life Sciences* 8 (1990): 199–204; Mary Gibson, "Contract Motherhood: Social Practice in Social Context," *Women and Criminal Justice* 1–2 (1991), also published in *Criminalization of a Woman's Body*, ed. Clarice Fineman (New York: Haworth Press, 1992), 55–99; Susan Muller Okin, "A Critique of Pregnancy Contracts," *Politics and the Life Sciences* 8 (1990): 205–210; and Mary Lyndon Shanley, "'Surrogate Mothering' and Women's Freedom: A Critique of Contracts for Human Reproduction," *Signs: Journal of Women in Culture and Society* 18 (Spring 1993): 1–22.

19. Purdy, "Surrogate Mothering," 32.

20. Purdy, "A Response to Dodds and Jones," 41.

21. Purdy, "Surrogate Mothering," 34.

22. Elizabeth S. Anderson, "Is Women's Labor a Commodity?" *Philosophy and Public Affairs* 71 (1990), 80.

23. Anderson, "Women's Labor," 81.

24. Anderson, "Women's Labor," 72.

25. Anderson, "Women's Labor," 77.

26. Anderson, "Women's Labor," 83.

27. Anderson, "Women's Labor," 82.

28. Here is Diana Tietjens Meyers, for example:

"One issue concerns the birth mother's investment in the baby she bears. In light of the emotional attachment a woman may come to feel for a baby as a result of the experience of pregnancy and giving birth, the protections afforded to women contemplating giving babies up for adoption should be extended to birth mothers. It seems cruel not to grant the birth mother a decision period after the birth during which she would have the prerogative of keeping the baby.... From the standpoint of women, the key to a morally tenable practice of contract motherhood seems to be giving priority to the possibility that the contract mother will bond with the baby she has carried. In other words, unless women's nurturant responses are recognized as valuable and accommodated, contract motherhood is patently immoral.

From *Kindred Matters: Rethinking the Philosophy of the Family*, ed. Diana Tietjens Meyers, Kenneth Kipnis, and Cornelius F. Murphy, Jr. [Ithaca, NY: Cornell University Press, 1993], 97. See also Sharon Rush, "Breaking with Tradition: Surrogacy and Gay Fathers," also in *Kindred Matters* 128: "Because so many uncertainties surround a woman's decision to be a surrogate contract mother, she simply cannot know how she will feel about her decision until it becomes more than a mere abstraction. If the parties fail to provide for the possibility that the surrogate contract mother might want to keep the child, then she, as bearer of the child, should have presumptive custody. These protections of the mother from patriarchal attitudes that elevate the father's importance in procreation could even be provided by statute."

29. Anderson, "Women's Labor," 79.

30. Hugh LaFollette, "Licensing Parents," *Philosophy and Public Affairs* 9 (1980): 183–197.

31. LaFollette, "Licensing Parents," 190.

32. Joyce A. Martin, Brady E. Hamilton, Paul D. Sutton, Stephanie J. Ventura, Fay Menacker, and Martha L. Munson, "Births: Final Data for 2003," *National Vital Statistics Reports*, v. 54, n. 2 (Sept. 2005), 8.

33. William Galston, *Liberal Purposes* (Cambridge: Cambridge University Press, 1991), p. 284. For criticisms of his arguments that life is better for children in two-parent families, see Iris Marion Young, "Mothers, Citizenship, and Independence: A Critique of Family Values," in *Having and Raising Children*, ed. Uma Narayan and Julia K. Bartkowiak (University Park: Pennsylvania State University Press, 1999), 15–38. For a careful earlier discussion of the benefits two-parent families can offer children, see Jeffrey Blustein, *Parents and Children: The Ethics of the Family* (New York: Oxford University Press, 1982), 240–252.

34. "Of course, a general preference for the intact two-parent family...does not mean that all single-parent families are somehow 'dysfunctional.' That proposition would be not only false but also insulting to the millions of single parents who are struggling successfully against the odds to provide good homes for their children." (Galston, "Liberal Purposes," 284–285.)

35. Maynard, R. A., ed., *Kids Having Kids: A Robin Hood Foundation Special Report* on the Costs of Adolescent Childbearing. New York: Robin Hood Foundation, 1996. [Online] Rev. June 2004. Available at http://www.healthyteennetwork.org. [July 13, 2009].

36. Maynard, *Kids Having Kids*.

37. Maynard, *Kids Having Kids*.

38. Joyce A. Martin, Brady E. Hamilton, Paul D. Sutton, Stephanie J. Ventura, Fay Menacker, Martha L. Munson, "Births: Final Data for 2003," *National Vital Statistics Reports*, v. 54, n. 2, (Sept. 8, 2005), 4–5.

39. Partly that is so because it isn't their daughter to whom they have the duty to do these things. Instead, they owe this to those who have claims against their daughter that she cannot satisfy: in this case to the girl's baby and to the larger society.

40. Maynard, *Kids Having Kids*.

41. M. Courtney and I. Diliavin, "Struggling in the Adult World," *Washington Post*, July 21, 1998.

42. The first figure is from Lynn D. Wardle, "A Critical Analysis of Interstate Recognition of Lesbigay Adoptions," *Ave Maria Law Review* 3 (2005): 566. The second is from Andrea Stone, "Drives to Ban Gay Adoption Heat Up in 16 States," *USA-Today*, Feb. 21, 2006, at 1A.

43. Sharon Rush, "Breaking with Tradition: Surrogacy and Gay Fathers," in *Kindred Matters: Rethinking the Philosophy of the Family*, ed. Diana Tietjens Meyers, Kenneth Kipnis, and Cornelius F. Murphy, Jr. (Ithaca, NY: Cornell University Press, 1993), p. 112. The studies Rush cites concerning what is needed for capable parenting are from *See How They Grow: Concepts in Child Development and Parenting*, 2nd ed., ed. Thomas Draper, Marilyn Coleman Ganeng, and Virginia Goodell (Encino, CA: Bennett and McKnight, 1987); *Non-Traditional Families: Parenting and Child Development*, ed. Michael E. Lamb (Hillsdale, NJ: Erlbaum Associates, 1982); and Ralph Larosse, *Becoming a Parent* (Beverly Hills, CA: Sage Publications, 1986).

44. Rush, "Breaking with Tradition," 118.

45. Gregory M. Herek, "Gender Gaps in Public Opinion about Lesbians and Gay Men," *Public Opinion Quarterly* 66 (2002): 63.

46. Herek, "Gender Gaps," Table 2.51.

47. Herek, "Gender Gaps, Table 2.51.

48. Carole Jenny, Thomas A. Roesler, and Kimberly L. Poyer, "Are Children at Risk for Sexual Abuse by Homosexuals?" *Pediatrics* 94 (July 1994): 44. See also Kurt Freund, Robert Watson, and Douglas Rienzo, "Heterosexuality, Homosexuality and Erotic Age Preference," *Journal of Sex Research* 26 (1989): 107; "Erotic impact was measured by phallometric test…This measures penile volume changes during the presentation of potentially erotic stimuli. Homosexual males who preferred physically mature partners responded no more to male children than heterosexual males who preferred physically mature partners responded to female children."

49. Charlotte J. Patterson, *Lesbian and Gay Parenting* [Online] Rev. July 13, 2009. Available: *APA Online* (http://www.apa.org/pi/parent.html.) [July 2007].

50. Patterson, *Lesbian and Gay Parenting*.

51. Patterson, *Lesbian and Gay Parenting*.

52. Rush adds this further argument:

But let's assume that a parent can teach sexual orientation…given the social reprobation that at present attaches to being homosexual in the United States, and given the love and affection that most parents feel toward their children, I find it unbelievable that any parents—heterosexual or homosexual—would teach their children to be homosexual. Responsible and loving parents who were given a choice, in my opinion, simply would not choose to subject their child to the pain and isolation that inevitably attach to being a member of a socially disdained group.

From Rush, "Breaking with Tradition," 119.

53. The classic source of the premise that societies have at least a right to use the criminal law to preserve their way of life just because it is their way of life is Lord Patrick Devlin, *The Enforcement of Morals* (Oxford: Oxford University Press, 1965).

54. The figure is from the Statistical Abstract of the United States 2000, compiled by the U.S. Bureau of Statistics, section titled "Vital Statistics," p. 65, table number 78.

Notes to Chapter 3

1. This chapter applies equally well to women whose parenthood has been interrupted, but I will write mostly in terms of absent fathers. That approach simplifies the

prose, and it is also truer to the facts, at least in my culture: it is far more often the father who goes missing than the mother. For similar reasons, I will usually write as if it were a biological father, though in several of the kinds of case to be discussed it could be an adoptive father instead.

2. Suppose a man were to donate sperm that produced a child via artificial insemination. Unless there were an explicit agreement that he would play some later role in the child's life, the assumption would be that he would play none. Entering that arrangement would be a way of waiving the rights he would have had.

3. Martin Guggenheim, *What's Wrong with Children's Rights* (Cambridge, MA: Harvard University Press, 2005), 152.

4. Joseph Goldstein, Albert J. Solnit, Sonja Goldstein, and Anna Freud, *The Best Interests of the Child* (New York: The Free Press, 1996), 59, emphasis added.

5. *In re Kirchner*, 649 NE 2d. 324, at 326.

6. *In re Kirchner*, at 342. According to Justice Miller's dissenting opinion, the record from the trial court is insufficient to determine this.

7. In saying this, I take Schmidt's poor track record as a parent not to be so poor that it undercuts his claim to be a father to this child. It would certainly do so if he had abused or neglected a child in his care to an extent that justified taking that child from him. I think we should regard declining to return a parent's child in the same way as taking the child from the parent, so I would favor requiring that the poor track record be as bad as that needed before we would take the best interests of the child to call for us not to return her. Since Schmidt doesn't approach that level, I regard the best-interests considerations as relatively weak in this case (though, of course, they aren't so weak as to have no weight at all).

8. *Department of Health and Rehabilitative Services v. Privette*, 617 So.2d 305 (Fla. 1993), 309.

9. These are taken from *Twigg v. Mays*. [Online] Available: http://law.jrank.org/pages/13234/Twigg-v-Mays.html, [July 29, 2008].

10. Six months later, with the permission of Robert Mays, Kimberly moved to a YMCA Youth Shelter for runaway and troubled youths. She later left that shelter, not to return to her home with Robert Mays but to live with the Twiggs.

11. During the legal battles, a book was published suggesting that the switch had been intentional (*The Baby Swap Conspiracy*, by Loretta Nobel): *Twigg v. Mays*.

12. Petr Bokuva, "Switched at Birth: The Story Continues," *The Czech Daily Word*, October 10, 2007.

13. *Id. at 746*. In a footnote to his dissenting opinion in *C.V. v. J.M.J and T.F.J. (In re Baby Boy G.)*, AL Court of Civil Appeals, Judge Crawley identifies Florida's sister states in this venture as California, Minnesota, New York, Nevada, and Wisconsin. He adds this note: "In addition, the following...states have adopted the Uniform Adoption Act: Arkansas, Louisiana, Montana, North Dakota, Ohio, and Oklahoma. Section 3–504 of the Act (9 U.L.A. 52) allows for a finding of pre-birth abandonment based on the father's conduct during the mother's pregnancy."

14. *In re Adoption of Baby E.A.W.*, 658 So.2d 961, at 965.

15. *In re Baby E.A.W.*, at 966.

16. *R.S. v. State of Utah*, 940 P.2d 527 (Utah App. 1997), 528–29. I thank the Honorable Judge Scott M. Johansen of the 7th District Juvenile Court, Utah, for providing me this case.

17. *R.S. v. Utah*, at 532.

18. *R.S. v. Utah*, at 532.

19. *C.V. v. J.M.J. and T.F.J. (In re Baby Boy G.)*, 810 So. 2d 629, at 693, 696–697. The parties gave greatly opposed versions of the facts in trial court. This version is selected for purposes of illustration.

20. *Ex parte C.V.*, 810 So. 2d 700 (Ala 2001), at 710–711.

Notes to Chapter 4

1. David Archard, *Children: Rights and Childhood* (London: Routledge, 2004), 149.

2. Archard, *Children*, 154–155, and also Chapter 9.

3. I argue exactly that in Chapter 9, "Loving One Another."

4. "Out of Focus, a Child Is Lost," by Patricia Smith, which appeared (among other places) in *The Tuscaloosa News*, June 4, 1997.

5. *Brotherhood Shipping Company, LTD. v. St. Paul Fire & Marine Insurance Company and City of Milwaukee*, 985 F.2d 323, 331.

6. Joel Feinberg, *Harm to Others* (New York: Oxford University Press, 1984), 10.

7. For arguments that corporal punishment is not always wrong, see David Benatar, "Corporal Punishment," *Social Theory and Practice* 24 (summer 1995): 237–260. For empirical studies indicating that spanking does not increase aggressiveness in children, see Robert E. Larzerlere, "A Review of the Outcomes of Parental Use of Nonabusive or Customary Physical Punishment," *Pediatrics* 98 (Oct. 1996): 824–828.

8. See in particular "Pal Detailed Strohmeyer's Play with Girl," by Bill Gang, *Las Vegas Sun*, August 15, 1997. The young man, David Cash, later appeared on *60 Minutes* to defend his behavior. According to an account of the interview, Cash said that he saw Strohmeyer restrain the girl, "muffling her screams," and heard him threaten her life, but said he chose not to intervene because he thought Sherrice would survive. He also said that since Strohmeyer was his friend, "I didn't want to be the one who turned him in." ("Cash Tells 60 Minutes He Couldn't Have Done Much Differently," by Glenn Puit, *Las Vega Review-Journal*, September 25, 1998.)

9. For ease of exposition, from here on I will use "defective in concern" to refer not only to parents who do not care as they should but also to those who are unable to implement that concern.

10. In addition, strangers have an alternative to the morally dubious techniques: they can hand the matter over to the child's parents.

11. This example comes from the experience of an audience member who contributed to a discussion of "Parental Latitude," a paper I presented to the conference Children, Rights and the Law, Melbourne, 1996.

12. This obligation is explored more fully in Chapter 7, "Moral Education."

13. The only reliable sign prior to this that comes to mind is truancy. If school is essential to developing abilities needed to function as an adult and it is the parent's obligation to ensure that the child attends, a parent who doesn't accomplish this is failing to raise the child as he or she should.

Notes to Chapter 5

1. Teresa Snodgrass, "Minor's Right to Privacy: Bypass Procedures to Notification Statutes," *Journal of Juvenile Law* 10 (1989): 243. Missouri's law requiring the written consent of a parent before any unmarried woman under the age of 18 could obtain an abortion was overturned in *Planned Parenthood v. Danforth*, 428 U.S. 52 (1976). The state of Massachusetts required either that both the girl's parents consent or that a judge of the Superior Court do so. This ruling was overturned in *Bellotti v. Baird*, 428 U.S. 132 (1976). Massachusetts subsequently softened the first alternative to require only that the girl consult with her parents, even if this consultation did not result in their written consent, but this requirement too was overturned. Utah required neither consent of the girl's parents nor consultation with them but only that the parents be notified, an arrangement challenged in *H. L. v. Matheson*, 450 U.S. 398 (1981).

2. One such instance is reported in "Woman Convicted for Taking Girl to Abortion Clinic," an Associated Press item appearing (among other places) in *The Tuscaloosa News* of October 30, 1996.

3. Robert Batey, "The Rights of Adolescents," *William and Mary Law Review* 23 (Spring 1982): 363–384. Adolescents are "categorized as those minors fourteen or older" (364).

4. Batey, "Adolescents," 367.

5. Batey, "Adolescents," 365.

6. Samantha Brennan, "Children's Choices or Children's Interests: Which Do Their Rights Protect?" in *The Moral and Political Status of Children*, ed. David Archard and Colin M. Macleod (New York: Oxford University Press, 2002), 59.

7. Brennan, "Children's Choices," 60.

8. Robert Noggle, "Special Agents: Children's Autonomy and Parental Authority," in *The Moral and Political Status of Children*, ed. David Archard and Colin M. Macleod (New York: Oxford University Press, 2002), 101–102.

9. Noggle, "Special Agents," 104.

10. Noggle, "Special Agents," 102.

11. Noggle, "Special Agents," 103.

12. Noggle, "Special Agents," 102.

13. Noggle, "Special Agents," 103.

14. Noggle, "Special Agents," 102.

15. Noggle, "Special Agents," 105.

16. It is also important both that that we have an appropriate way of holding children responsible when they do wrong and that parents do not greatly foreclose the options open to the adult the child becomes. Each is a problem for the view we have been discussing, according to which parents are to guard the child's adult self against the errors of his present self and are (in essence) to be a temporally extended self for the child. Each is also a problem for any view, however. I take up the first of them in chapter 8, "Bad Behavior" and the second in chapter 6, "Raising a Child."

17. Leading texts of the child liberation movement included Richard Farson, *Birthrights* (London: Collier Macmillan, 1974); John Holt, *Escape from Childhood: The Needs and Rights of Children* (Harmondsworth, UK: Penguin, 1975); and Shulamith Firestone, chapter entitled "Down with Childhood," in *The Dialectic of Sex, The Case for Feminist Revolution* (London: Jonathan Cape, 1971).

18. David Archard, *Children: Rights and Childhood* (London: Routledge, 1993), 49. For an excellent careful discussion of the liberationists' position, see his chapter "Liberation or Caretaking?"

19. Jeffrey Blustein, *Parents and Children* (New York: Oxford University Press, 1982), esp. 142–147.

20. Prospective parents ought to refrain from having a child if the chances are great that the child would not be looked after in the ways that would keep his or her life from being a misery. Those who live in a time of war might be in this position. So might those who live in a place of great poverty. Even in good times and hospitable places, it is arguable that prospective parents ought not to have a child if their genetics make it highly probable that the child would suffer from one of the truly grievous birth defects: the kind taken to mean that life is "not worth living." Suppose, for example, that it is highly likely that any child of theirs will suffer from Lesch-Nyhan Syndrome. Children afflicted with this syndrome

...appear normal at birth, then at approximately six months begin a process of neurological and physiological deterioration first evidenced by athetosis (ceaseless, involuntary writhing movements). Along with severe mental deficiency, the most striking neurological feature of this condition is compulsive self-mutilation that requires placing the elbows in splints, wrapping the hands in gauze, and sometimes extracting the teeth. Even then, children with this condition often bang their heads against inanimate objects or take out their aggression on other persons.... there is *no curative or corrective treatment.*... Little can be done for these children other than marginal life prolongation, palliative care, and institutionalization in a custodial ward...[the] progressive neurological deterioration...is simply impossible to prevent or minimize.

From Robert Weir, *Selective Nontreatment of Handicapped Newborns* (New York: Oxford University Press, 1984), 237. The italics emphasizing that there is no curative or corrective treatment are Weir's but I have reversed the order of the passages so that the descriptive one comes first. The idea is that if this were the life very probably in store for your child, you would have an obligation not to bring the child into existence, as an instance of our general obligation not to expose other human beings to risks as severe as those facing your child.

21. Quoted in "Fly Till I Die," Richard Stengel, *Time* (April 22, 1996), 38.
22. This is a version of what has been called the *choice* theory of this particular right, rather than the *interest* theory:

On the interest model, agency rights are vital because of their indirect contribution to well-being, rather than because choice is given an intrinsic value of its own. The contribution of agency rights to welfare depends on the assumptions that adults can choose with some level of competence, and that for them having a choice is a powerful mechanism for inducing identification with the activity chosen.

From Harry Brighouse, "What Rights (if any) Do Children Have?" *The Moral and Political Status of Children*, ed. David Archard and Colin M. Macleod (New York: Oxford University Press, 2002), 39.
23. See in particular Book II, Chapter 1 of Aristotle's *Nicomachean Ethics*, trans. J. A. K Thompson (New York: Penguin Books, 1965).
24. Aristotle, *Nicomachean Ethics*, Book III, 123–124.
25. Aristotle, *Nicomachean Ethics*, Book III, 124.
26. Jeffrey Blustein and Jonathan D. Moreno, "Valid Consent to Treatment and the Unsupervised Adolescent," *The Adolescent Alone*, ed. Jeffrey Blustein, Carol Levine, and Nancy Neveloff Dubler (Cambridge: Cambridge University Press, 1999), 101.
27. Blustein and Moreno, "Valid Consent," frontispiece.
28. Blustein and Moreno, "Valid Consent," 106.
29. See in particular Blustein and Moreno, "Valid Consent," pp. 104 and 109.
30. Blustein and Moreno, "Valid Consent," 109.
31. Jeffrey Blustein, *Parents and Children: The Ethics of the Family* (New York: Oxford University Press, 1982), 170. He also adds that insofar as parental obligations are owed to the children themselves rather than to the larger society, the child's right to them is inalienable. That would mean the child could not waive this right, releasing his parents from their obligation to raise him (see 171). I am not sure how a right that could not be waived squares with allowing children to petition the state for release from parents who are badly failing them. I think they have the right to do that, and it sounds as if doing so would waive their right to be raised by these particular parents.

Perhaps it would be better to regard the obligation as one that the parents owe to the larger society rather than to the child. That view would explain why the child can't waive it, since we can't waive an obligation someone owes to someone else. It would also become reasonable for the child to be allowed to contend that the parents were not keeping this obligation, to his or her detriment, and to seek relief.

Notes to Chapter 6

1. Joel Feinberg, "The Child's Right to an Open Future," in *Whose Child?* ed. William Aiken and Hugh LaFollette (Totawa, NJ: Littlefield, Adams, 1980), 124–153.

2. William B. Irvine, *Doing Right By Children* (St. Paul, MN: Paragon House, 2001), 256.

3. Irvine, *"Doing Right,"* 258.

4. Irvine, *"Doing Right,"* 258.

5. Irvine, *"Doing Right,"* 259.

6. Feinberg, "Open Future," 131.

7. Feinberg, "Open Future," 136.

8. Feinberg, "Open Future," 137.

9. Feinberg, "Open Future," 150–151.

10. David Archard, *Children: Rights and Adulthood* (London: Routledge, 1993), 56.

11. Archard, *Children*, 56.

12. Feinberg, "Open Future," 127.

13. A fuller discussion of becoming a person of one's own appears in Chapter 5, "The Autonomy of Children."

14. "It is a commonplace of autonomy-based ethics that one not only should respect an individual's autonomy but, where reasonable, should also promote it." From Jeffrey Blustein and Jonathan D. Moreno, "Valid Consent to Treatment and the Unsupervised Adolescent," in *The Adolescent Alone*, ed. Jeffrey Blustein, Carol Levine, and Nancy Neveloff Dubler (Cambridge: Cambridge University Press, 1999), 104. What doubts one might have about an obligation to help others to become autonomous agents would spring from doubts that others are in your *charge* to any great extent, as opposed to being people you are to take as they come. That thought is not relevant when the person is your child, obviously, at least during the time when one of your central obligations is to raise her to become an adult.

15. Archard, *Children*, 57.

16. Irvine's very good discussion of "child stars" occupies chapters 2 and 3 of *Doing Right by Children*.

17. Laura M. Purdy, "Should Children Be Able to Divorce Their Parents?" in *Having and Raising Children*, ed. Uma Narayan and Julia J. Bartkowiak (University Park, PA: Pennsylvania State University Press, 1999), 155.

18. Purdy, "Divorce," 153.

19. Purdy, "Divorce," 156.

20. Here is Purdy, again:

> What, for instance, are we to do about gay children of actively homophobic parents? Many such children now run away from home or are thrown out, but what about those who feel trapped in a situation where they are made to feel like the scum of the earth? Or what about children who feel the weight of their parents' sexist stereotypes especially strongly? What if a parent undermines a girl's attempt to be strong and independent? Or repeatedly punishes a boy for crying or for allegedly sissy interests? More generally, what about the many fundamental conflicts that may arise in matters of religion or politics? (156–157)

My claim in Chapter 4 was that the question turns on whether the parental conduct displays an inability to have the proper concern for one's child, or an inability to put that concern into action. What that situation dictates in these examples depends on more detail than we have, but it is certainly imaginable that those details would show that the parents had indeed become unable to care enough about how their child fared or unable to put their concern for him into action.

Notes to Chapter 7

1. Arguments that children do have these claims are to be found in chapter 5, "The Autonomy of Children," and in chapter 6, "Raising a Child."

2. William Galston, *Liberal Pluralism* (Cambridge: Cambridge University Press, 2002), 101–102.

3. William Damon, *The Moral Child* (New York: The Free Press, 1988), 18.

4. Martin L. Hoffman, "Empathy, Social Cognition, and Moral Education," in *Approaches to Moral Development: New Research and Emerging Themes*, ed. Andrew Garrod (New York: Teachers College Press of Columbia University, 1993), 159.

5. Hoffman, "Empathy," 159.

6. Damon, *Moral Child*, 16.

7. Michael S. Pritchard, *Reasonable Children* (Lawrence: University Press of Kansas, 1996), 26.

8. Damon, *Moral Child*, 33.

9. Damon, *Moral Child*, 34.

10. Damon, *Moral Child*, 34.

11. Damon, *Moral Child*, 36.

12. Damon, *Moral Child*, 37–39.

13. Damon, *Moral Child*, 39.

14. It might seem that empathy and the sense of fairness also differ in that to be distressed by someone else's being in distress "comes naturally," whereas this is not true of a sense that something is unfair unless there is a reason for it. That is, the thought that a *reason* is needed isn't something that will occur to you on its own, one might think, where the troubled reaction to someone crying out not only *will* occur on its own but had better, or you are some kind of monster.

Even if this is true, however, anyone who lives with others is often urged to see that reasons are required. A sense that they are required and some appreciation of what those reasons are might thus become "second nature" to us, even if they are not an aspect of our first nature. Or, it could be that empathy isn't natural either but occurs only when encouraged in a child: presumably no one would want to do the experiments that seem required to find out. The answers do not matter to my argument that parents have an obligation to see to it that their children develop both of these traits.

15. Damon, *Moral Child*, 24–25.

16. Damon, *Moral Child*, 24.

17. Damon, *Moral Child*, 18. The quotation he offers is from J. Gibbs, "Social Processes in Delinquency: The Need to Facilitate Empathy as Well as Sociomoral Reasoning," in *Moral Development through Social Interaction*, ed. W. Kurtines and J. Gewirtz, (New York: Wiley, 1987).

18. Galston, *Liberal Pluralism*, 98. The phrases in quotes are to be found on pp. 13 and 14 of *On Liberty*, ed. Currin V. Shields (Indianapolis: Bobbs-Merrill, 1956).

19. Rory Stewart asserts this view in *The Places In Between* (Orlando, FL: Harcourt, 2006), 236: "The Koran's dense network of metaphor, poetry, and allusion is traditionally interpreted with reference to the Hadiths [sayings] of the Prophet and long traditions of legal and theological exegesis. As a result, public pronouncements on the meaning of the Koran are ordinarily reserved for the most learned and senior of mullahs."

20. Jeffrey Blustein, *Parents and Children: The Ethics of the Family* (New York: Oxford University Press, 1992), 192.

21. I am grateful to an anonymous reviewer for Oxford University Press for providing a version of this example.

22. Joseph Goldstein, Albert J. Solnit, Sonja Goldstein, and Anna Freud, *The Best Interests of the Child* (New York: The Free Press, 1996).

Notes to Chapter 8

1. Tamar Schapiro, "What Is a Child?" *Ethics* 109 (July 1999): 717.

2. Thomas Grisso, "Society's Retributive Response to Juvenile Violence: A Developmental Perspective," *Law and Human Behavior* 20 (1996): 231.

3. Schapiro, "What Is a Child?" 717.

4. Schapiro, "What Is a Child?" 732.

5. Schapiro, "What Is a Child?" 733.

6. It will also be a mistake to react as one would if this were an *adult* who was still trying out selves. An adult of that kind would have had time to become a person of her own but has become one who is still trying out selves, rather than one who is more settled. The child hasn't become that way yet, so she doesn't merit the same reaction. This is why adults who are unstable in this way can be a worry or an irritation in ways that children who are like this are not.

7. *Thompson v. Oklahoma*, 108 *S.Ct.* at 2690.

8. Victor Tadros, *Criminal Responsibility* (Oxford: Oxford University Press, 2005), 9.

9. John Braithwaite and Stephen Mugford, "Conditions of Successful Reintegration Ceremonies," *British Journal of Criminology* (Spring 1994): 144. As a source of the premise that "Much delinquency is casual and thoughtless," the authors cite I. O'Connor and P. Sweetapple, *Children in Justice* (Sydney, Australia: Longman-Cheshire, 1988), 117–118.

10. Braithwaite and Mugford, "Reintegration Ceremonies," 144.

11. *Stanford v. Kentucky* 492 U.S. 361, at 366. *Wilkins v. Missouri* was consolidated with this case, on the ground that both raised the same issue: whether capital punishment would violate the Eighth Amendment prohibition against cruel and unusual punishment if it were imposed upon someone who had been sixteen or seventeen years of age at the time of the crime. The Court ruled that it would not.

12. *Stanford v. Kentucky* 492 U.S. 361, at 367.

13. M. E. Wolfgang, R.M. Figlio, and T. Sellin, *Delinquency in a Birth Cohort* (Chicago: University of Chicago, 1972); results replicated in Paul E. Tracy et al., "Delinquency in Two Birth Cohorts," Executive Summary, U.S. Department of Justice, Office of Juvenile Justice and Delinquency Prevention 15 (Sept. 1985).

Notes to Chapter 9

1. The Emergency Medical Treatment and Active Labor Act requires this, in 42 U.S.C. sec. 1395dd. I am grateful to Professor William Brewbaker of the University of Alabama School of Law for providing this citation.

2. Frankfurt, "Autonomy, Necessity, and Love," in *Necessity, Volition, and Love* (Cambridge: Cambridge University Press, 1999), 130.

3. Frankfurt, "Autonomy," p. 140.

4. There is also this further thought. Suppose the capacity to love a particular person is outside a person's control in the same way as a capacity to solve extremely difficult

problems in physics might be: something that can be cultivated, but only within limits. Imagine someone who has reached her own limits where her child is concerned and just cannot manage to love him. Rather than saying that she has no obligation to do so (since she cannot), the right response might be that she was wrong to get herself in a position in which she could not carry out her obligations, as we might say of someone who just couldn't do the complex problems in physics that her job required. What she should now do is not an easy question, since it depends on what the alternatives are, but it seems to be a way in which she might have an obligation to love her children even if she is personally incapable of carrying out that obligation.

5. Neil MacCormick, "Children's Rights: A Test-Case for Theories of Right," in *Legal Right and Social Responsiblity* (Oxford: Clarendon Press, 1982), 154–155.

6. He is hardly alone in this belief. For example, here is Elizabeth S. Anderson on the subject: "The most fundamental calling of parents to their children is to love them. Children are to be loved and cherished by their parents." ("Is Women's Labor a Commodity?" *Philosophy and Public Affairs* 71 (1990): 75.)

7. Jeffrey Blustein and Jonathan Moreno, "Valid Consent to Treatment and the Unsupervised Adolescent" in *The Adolescent Alone*, ed. Jeffrey Blustein, Carol Levine, and Nancy Neveloff Dubler (Cambridge: Cambridge University Press, 1999), 106.

8. Loren A. Lomasky, *Persons, Rights, and the Moral Community* (New York: Oxford University Press, 1987).

9. The phrases are taken from a death notice for Samuel K. Kleiner, which appeared in the *New York Times*, Wednesday, November 19, 2003.

10. Lomasky, "Persons," 26.

11. Lomasky, "Persons," 26.

12. For example: "SIMON ARTHUR NOEL RAVEN (1948) died on 12 May 2001 at the age of 73 after suffering a stroke. *The Guardian* said that his long life and peaceful death provided 'proof that the devil looks after his own. He ought, by rights, to have died of shame at 30, or of drink at 50.'" (*King's College Cambridge Annual Report, 2003*, published by the Council of King's College, p. 89.)

13. Lomasky, "Persons," 163.

14. Lomasky, "Persons," 162.

15. Lomasky, "Persons," 154–165.

16. Lomasky, "Persons," 164.

17. Lomasky, "Persons," 26.

18. Lomasky, "Persons," 26.

19. The argument for this responsibility is set out more completely in Chapter 5, "The Autonomy of Children," especially sections 2 and 5. The argument that raising them is partly a matter of helping them become equipped to be reasonably happy is in Chapter 6, "Raising Children." What raising them also requires by way of making them morally good is explored in chapter 7, "Moral Education," and chapter 8, "Bad Behavior."

20. Lomasky, "Persons," 165.

21. Lomasky, "Persons," 35–36.

22. Lomasky, "Persons," 162.

23. I have pursued those questions in Chapter 6, "Raising Children."

24. This returns us yet again to the point expressed by Blustein and Moreno (in "Valid Consent") in this way: "A child who feels unwanted—whose sense of personal worth is not nurtured and supported by caring adults—is plagued by failure and self-doubt, apathy and cynicism in later childhood and adult life." That isn't a way in which the parent who doesn't love her child fails only the adult the child will become. It fails the person he

already is, and, as is argued in chapter 5 and also by Blustein and Moreno, it also fails to help him become a person of his own.

25. This position does commit us to approving of parents' reacting very differently when their grown son or daughter does them wrong than they would if this had happened when the child was young and under their care. They would have been wrong to stop loving the young child for what he did to them but wouldn't necessarily be wrong to stop loving their grown son, on this view. Reasons to think so can be drawn from Chapter 8, "Bad Behavior." One change is in how seriously they should take any insult in what was done to them—not very, when the insult is by a child, but it's different when he is an adult. Other changes are in the extent to which he is who he is going to be, the extent to which he is responsible for who he is so far, and their obligation to help him become someone better. All of those elements argue for a different reaction when our young children mistreat us than when our grown ones do: a change is part of treating them as adults rather than continuing to treat them as children.

26. Lomasky, "Persons," 26.

27. Lomasky, "Persons," 26.

28. Lomasky, "Persons," 26.

29. Lomasky, "Persons," 26.

30. Frankfurt, "Autonomy," 130.

Note to Chapter 10

1. Terrance McConnell, *Gratitude* (Philadelphia: Temple University Press, 1993), 216.

Notes to Chapter 11

1. Simon Keller, "Four Theories of Filial Duty," *Philosophical Quarterly* 56 (April 2006): 254.

2. Keller, "Filial Duty," 257. He cites the following as advocates of the view that our filial obligations are debts of gratitude: F. R. Berger, "Gratitude," *Ethics* 85 (1975): 298–309, at 298–301; Jeffrey Blustein, *Parents and Children* (New York: Oxford University Press, 1982), part II, ch. 3; P. J. Ivanhoe, "Filial Piety as a Virtue," in *Working Virtue: Virtue Ethics and Contemporary Moral Problems*, ed. R. Walker and P. J. Ivanhoe (New York: Oxford University Press, 2006); Nancy Jecker, "Are Filial Duties Unfounded?" *American Philosophical Quarterly*, 26 (1989); C. H. Sommers, "Filial Morality," *Journal of Philosophy*, 83 (1986); Mark Wicclair, "Caring for Frail Elderly Parents: Past Parental Sacrifices and the Obligations of Adult Children," *Social Theory and Practice* 16 (1990).

3. This is Jane English's central argument in "What Do Grown Children Owe Their Parents?" in *Having Children*, ed. Onora O'Neill and William Ruddick (Oxford: Oxford University Press, 1979), and it appears again in David Archard, "Filial Morality," *Pacific Philosophical Quarterly* 77 (1996). There is a great deal for which children do ask, of course. More important, gratitude can also be due for what is not requested if it would clearly be welcome. For example, suppose someone were rendered unconscious in a traffic accident and measures were taken to save his life. He should be grateful to those who saved his life, surely, despite not having asked them to do so, because the reasonable supposition is that he would want this done.

We should also be grateful for what we didn't request even if *hadn't* been clear we would be glad it had been done, if we later are pleased to accept it. That is one way in which relationships deepen, by one party's doing more than the other person expects, and the two of them finding this arrangement to their liking. It would be an extraordinary child who never welcomed what he didn't ask for and shouldn't have been assumed to find it welcome, as opposed to disliking only some of what his parents did for him. So, it would be an extraordinary child who owed his parents no gratitude.

4. This line of argument is to be found in English, "What Do Grown Children Owe?" It is found again in Daniel Callahan, "What Do Children Owe Elderly Parents?" *Hastings Center Report* 15 (2), April, 1985; in Norman Daniels, *Am I My Parents' Keeper?* (New York: Oxford University Press, 1988); and in David Archard, "Filial Morality," *Pacific Philosophical Quarterly* 77 (1996). The argument would entail that you would owe no gratitude to a fireman who saved your life by pulling you out of a burning house, since firemen have an obligation to do that. Rather, on this view, you should take what he did as no more than what you ought to expect, as if a clerk had given you proper change. But the fireman *saved your life*, quite possibly at considerable personal risk—surely you should be very grateful to him for doing so, even if it is his job to do such things and thus his obligation to do them.

5. Keller, "Filial Duty," 257.

6. Keller, "Filial Duty," 257.

7. Keller, "Filial Duty," 259.

8. Keller, "Filial Duty," 259.

9. Keller, "Filial Duty," 259.

10. Keller, "Filial Duty," 260.

11. I think Keller's third objection to gratitude theories makes this mistake: "Thirdly…Filial duties are ongoing and open-ended, and can be very demanding. Gratitude does not require ongoing commitments or significant sacrifices" (260); "Thinking of filial duties in terms of special goods makes it easy to see why they are ongoing and open-ended rather than being the sorts of duties that can be discharged once and for all" (268).

12. For arguments that it is illegitimate for parents to control their children's choices, see "Down with Childhood," in Shulamith Firestone, *The Dialectic of Sex, The Case for a Feminist Revolution* (London: Jonathan Cape, 1971); Richard Farson, *Birthrights* (London: Collier MacMillan, 1974); and John Holt, *Escape from Childhood, The Needs and Rights of Children* (Harmondsworth, UK: Penguin, 1974). For telling arguments against this position, see David Archard, *Children, Rights and Childhood* (London: Routledge, 1993).

13. It also follows that someone whose parents never conveyed the rudimentary idea that love is to be reciprocated would not have this obligation to love them and look after them in their old age. That idea does not seem counterintuitive, however.

14. Keller, "Filial Duty," esp. 260ff.

15. Keller, "Filial Duty," 269.

16. Keller, "Filial Duty," 269.

17. For a somewhat different view about a grown child's obligations to a parent who "no longer even knows who she is," see Claudia Mills, "Duties to Aging Parents," *Care of the Aged: Biomedical Ethics Reviews*, ed. James Humber (Totowa, NJ: Humana Press, 2003). The topic requires a far fuller discussion than can be given here.

Notes to Chapter 12

1. John Hardwig, "Is There a Duty to Die?" in *Is There a Duty to Die? And Other Essays in Bioethics*, ed. John Hardwig(New York: Routledge, 2000), 120.

2. Hardwig, "Duty to Die?" 120.

3. Hardwig, "Duty to Die?" 121.

4. Hardwig, "Duty to Die?" 121.
5. Hardwig, "Duty to Die?" 129.
6. Hardwig, "Duty to Die?" 126.
7. Hardwig, "Duty to Die?" 126.
8. I thank Frances Kamm for calling my attention to the third point when I presented a version of this chapter to the James Rachels Memorial Conference (Birmingham, Alabama, September 24, 2004). As I have noted, it is objectionably selfish to use someone else's resources rather than your own when that is all you are doing and the cost to that person is very high. In contrast, consider a case in which a son wants to give his father a gift and has far fewer resources than his father has. Suppose the gift is something the father could obtain for himself, perhaps even at a cheaper cost through his "connections." However, he allows his son to give this to him as a gift. Is he being selfish in an objectionable way? I would say he is not, as long the gift isn't ruinous for the son. To think otherwise makes it wrong ever to accept gifts from someone who is not as well off as you are, and that is surely mistaken.
9. I thank Rick Kaufman for showing me the need to address this point.
10. "Even if death were the greatest burden... serious questions would remain about the moral justifiability of choosing to impose crushing burdens on loved ones in order to avoid having to bear this burden oneself. The fact that I suffer greater burdens than others in my family does not... necessarily release me from a responsibility to try to protect the quality of their lives." (Hardwig, "Duty to Die?" 127.)

Notes to Conclusion

1. I owe the remark that creating a child is "so easy that even a child can do it" to Donald C. Hubin. He used it in "Procreator's Duties," his contribution to a conference on the ethics of bearing and rearing children held at the University of Cape Town in May 2008.
2. Joel Feinberg, "The Child's Right to an Open Future," in *Whose Child?* ed. William Aiken and Hugh LaFollette (Totowa, NJ: Littlefield Adams, 1980), 124–153.
3. Simon Keller, "Four Theories of Filial Duty," *Philosophical Quarterly* (April 2006): 254.
4. John Hardwig, "Is There a Duty to Die?" in *Is There a Duty to Die? And Other Essays in Bioethics*, ed. John Hardwig (New York: Routledge, 2000), 119–136.

Bibliography

Abrams, Natalie. "Problems in Defining Child Abuse and Neglect." In *Whose Child?* ed. William Aiken and Hugh LaFollette, 289–303. Totowa, NJ: Littlefield Adams, 1980.

In re Adoption of Baby E. A. W., 658 So.2d 961 (Fla., 1995).

Aiken, William, and Hugh LaFollette, eds. *Whose Child?* Totowa, NJ: Littlefield Adams, 1980.

Anderson, Elizabeth A. "Is Women's Labor a Commodity?" *Philosophy and Public Affairs* 18 (1990): 71–92.

Archard, David. *Children: Rights and Childhood*. London: Routledge, 1993.

———. *Children, Family and the State*. Aldershot, Hampshire: Ashgate, 2003.

———, and Colin M. Macleod, eds. *The Moral and Political Status of Children*. New York: Oxford University Press, 2002.

Aristotle. *Nicomachean Ethics*, trans. J. A. K Thompson. New York: Penguin Books, 1965.

Balzac, Honoré de. *Père Goriot*, trans. Jane Minot Sedgwick. New York: Holt, Rinehart, Winston, 1950.

Batey, Robert. "The Rights of Adolescents." *William and Mary Law Review* 23 (Spring 1982): 363–384.

Bellotti v. Baird, 428 U.S. 132 (1976).

Benatar, David. "Corporal Punishment." *Social Theory and Practice* 24 (Summer 1995): 237–260.

Berger, Fred R. "Gratitude." *Ethics* 85 (1975): 298–309.

In the Interest of B. G. C., a Child, 496 NW 2d 239 (Iowa 1992).

Blustein, Jeffrey. *Parents and Children: The Ethics of the Family*. New York: Oxford University Press, 1982.

———, Carol Levine, and Nancy Neveloff Dubler, eds. *The Adolescent Alone*. Cambridge: Cambridge University Press, 1999.

———, and Jonathan D. Moreno, "Valid Consent to Treatment and the Unsupervised Adolescent." In *The Adolescent Alone*, ed. Jeffrey Blustein, Carol Levine, and Nancy Neveloff Dubler, 100–110. Cambridge: Cambridge University Press, 1999.

Braithwaite, John, and Stephen Mugford. "Conditions of Successful Reintegration Ceremonies." *British Journal of Criminology* 34 (Spring 1994): 139–171.

Brennan, Samantha. "Children's Choices or Children's Interests: Which Do Their Rights Protect?" In *The Moral and Political Status of Children*, ed. David Archard and Colin M. Macleod, 53–69. New York: Oxford University Press, 2002.

Brighouse, Harry. "What Rights (If Any) Do Children Have?" In *The Moral and Political Status of Children*, ed. David Archard and Colin M. Macleod, 31–52. New York: Oxford University Press, 2002.

Brotherhood Shipping Company, LTD. v. St. Paul Fire and Marine Insurance Company and City of Milwaukee, 985 F.2d 323 (1992).

Callahan, Daniel. "What Do Children Owe Elderly Parents?" *Hastings Center Report* 15 (April 1985): 32–37.

Callan, Eamonn. *Creating Citizens: Political Education and Liberal Democracy*. Oxford: Clarendon Press, 1997.

Centers for Disease Control and Prevention. *2003 Assisted Reproductive Technology Report*. Atlanta: Centers for Disease Control and Prevention, 2003.

Conly, Sarah. "Seduction, Rape, and Coercion." *Ethics* 115 (Oct. 2004): 96–121.

C.V. v. J.M.J. and T.F.J. (In re Baby Boy G.), 810 So. 2d 629.

Ex parte C.V., 810 So.2d 700.

Damon, William. *The Moral Child*. New York: The Free Press, 1988.

Daniels, Norman. *Am I My Parents' Keeper?* New York: Oxford University Press, 1988.

Darby, Andrew. "Opposition May Force Inquiry." *The Age* (June 15, 1996): A 24.

Department of Health and Rehabilitative Services v. Privette, 617 So.2d 305.

Dodds, Susan, and Karen Jones. "Surrogacy and Autonomy." *Bioethics* 3 (Jan. 1989): 1–17.

———. "A Response to Purdy." *Bioethics* 3 (Jan. 1989): 35–39.

Dworkin, Andrea. *Intercourse*. New York: Free Press, 1987.

Dzeich, Billie Wright, and Linda Weiner, eds., *The Lecherous Professor: Sexual Harassment on Campus*. Boston: Beacon Press, 1984.

Dzeich, Billie Wright, and Linda Weiner, eds. *The Lecherous Professor: Sexual Harassment on Campus*, 2nd ed. (Champaign-Urbana: University of Illinois Press, 1991).

Dzeich, Billie Wright, and Michael W. Hawkins, eds. *Sexual Harassment in Higher Education: Reflections and New Perspectives* (New York: Garland Publishing, 1998).

English, Jane. "What Do Grown Children Owe Their Parents?" In *Having Children*, ed. Onora O'Neill and William Ruddick, 351–356. Oxford: Oxford University Press, 1979.

Ex parte C. V., Petition for Certiorari, Supreme Court of Alabama (2000).

Farson, Richard. *Birthrights*. London: Collier Macmillan, 1974.

Feinberg, Joel. "The Child's Right to an Open Future." In *Whose Child?* ed. William Aiken and Hugh LaFollette, 124–153. Totowa, NJ: Littlefield Adams, 1980.

———. *Harm to Others*. New York: Oxford University Press, 1984.

Firestone, Shulamith. *The Dialectic of Sex: The Case for Feminist Revolution*. London: Jonathan Cape, 1971.

Firth, Marilyn. "The Stolen Generation." *The Age* (June 15, 1996): A 24.

Fitzgerald, Louise F. "Sexual Harassment: The Definition and Measurement of a Construct." In *Sexual Harassment on College Campuses: Abusing the Ivory Power*, ed. Michele A. Paludi, 25–47. Albany, NY: SUNY Press, 1996.

Fitzgerald, Louise F., and Lauren M. Weitzman. "Men Who Harass: Speculation and Data." In *Ivory Power: Sexual Harassment on Campus*, ed. Michele A. Paludi, 125–140. Albany, NY: SUNY Press, 1990.

Frankfurt, Harry. "Autonomy, Necessity, and Love." In *Necessity, Volition and Love*, 129–141. Cambridge: Cambridge University Press, 1999.

Franks, Lucinda. "The War for Baby Clausen." *The New Yorker* (March 22, 1993): 56–73.

Freund, Kurt, Robert Watson, and Douglas Rienzo. "Heterosexuality, Homosexuality and Erotic Age Preference." *Journal of Sex Research* 26 (1989).

Galston, William. *Liberal Purposes*. Cambridge: Cambridge University Press, 1991.

———. *Liberal Pluralism*. Cambridge: Cambridge University Press, 2002.

Garbarino, James. *Lost Boys*. New York: Free Press, 1999.

Garrod, Andrew. *Approaches to Moral Development: New Research and Emerging Themes.* New York: Teachers College Press of Columbia University, 1993.

Goldstein, Joseph, Albert J. Solnit, Sonja Goldstein, and Anna Freud. *The Best Interests of the Child.* New York: The Free Press, 1996.

Grisso, Thomas. "Society's Retributive Response to Juvenile Violence: A Developmental Perspective." *Law and Human Behavior* 20 (April 1996): 229–247.

Guggenheim, Martin. *What's Wrong with Children's Rights?* Cambridge, MA: Harvard University Press, 2005.

H. L. v. Matheson, 450 U.S. 398 (1981).

Hardwig, John. "Is There a Duty to Die?" In *Is There a Duty to Die? And Other Essays in Bioethics,* ed. John Hardwig, 119–136. New York: Routledge, 2000.

———, ed. *Is There a Duty to Die? And Other Essays in Bioethics.* New York: Routledge, 2000.

Herek, Gregory M. "Gender Gaps in Public Opinion about Lesbians and Gay Men," *Public Opinion Quarterly* 66 (Spring 2002): 40–66.

Hoffman, Martin L. "Empathy, Social Cognition, and Moral Education." In *Approaches to Moral Development: New Research and Emerging Themes,* ed. Andrew Garrod, 157–179. New York: Teachers College Press of Columbia University, 1993.

Holt, John. *Escape from Childhood, The Needs and Rights of Children.* Harmondsworth, UK: Penguin, 1975.

Houlgate, Laurence. "What Is Legal Intervention in the Family? Family Law and Family Privacy." *Law and Philosophy* 17 (March 1998): 141–158.

———, ed. *Morals, Marriage and Parenthood.* Belmont, CA: Wadsworth, 1999.

Irvine, Leslie. "A 'Consensual' Relationship." In *Sexual Harassment on Campus,* ed. Bernice R. Sandler and Robert J. Shoop, 234–247. Needham Heights, MA: Allyn and Bacon, 1997.

Irvine, William B. *Doing Right By Children.* St. Paul, MN: Paragon House, 2001.

Ivanhoe, P. J. "Filial Piety as a Virtue." In Rebecca Walker and Philip J. Ivanhoe, eds., *Working Virtue: Virtue Ethics and Contemporary Moral Problems:* 297–312. New York: Oxford University Press, 2006.

Jecker, Nancy. "Are Filial Duties Unfounded?" *American Philosophical Quarterly* 26 (1989): 73–80.

Jenny, Carole, Thomas A. Roesler, and Kimberly L. Poyer. "Are Children at Risk for Sexual Abuse by Homosexuals?" *Pediatrics* 94 (July 1994): 41–43.

Keller, Simon. "Four Theories of Filial Duty." *Philosophical Quarterly* 56 (April 2006): 254–274.

In re Petition of Kirchner, 649 NE 2d 324 (Ill., 1995).

LaFollette, Hugh. "Licensing Parents." *Philosophy and Public Affairs* 9 (1980): 183–197.

Lamb, Sharon. *The Secret Lives of Girls.* New York: The Free Press, 2001.

Larzerlere, Robert E. "A Review of the Outcomes of Parental Use of Nonabusive or Customary Physical Punishment," *Pediatrics* 98 (Oct. 1996): 824–828.

Locke, John. *Two Treatises on Government.*, ed. P. Laslett. New York: New American Library, 1965.

Lomasky, Loren A. *Persons, Rights, and the Moral Community.* New York: Oxford University Press, 1987.

McConnell, Terrance. *Gratitude.* Philadelphia: Temple University Press, 1993.

MacCormick, Neil. "Children's Rights: A Test-Case for Theories of Right." In *Legal Right and Social Democracy,* 154–166 Oxford: Clarendon Press, 1982.

MacKinnon, Catherine. *Feminism Unfolded: Discourses on Life and Law.* Cambridge, MA: Harvard University Press, 1987.

Maynard, R. A., ed. *Kids Having Kids: A Robin Hood Foundation Special Report on the Costs of Adolescent Childbearing. New York: Robin Hood Foundation, 1996.* [Online] Rev. June 2004. Available: http://www.healthyteennetwork.org [Accessed July 13, 2009].

Meyers, Diana Tietjens, Kenneth Kipnis, and Cornelius F. Murphy, Jr., eds. *Kindred Matters: Rethinking the Philosophy of the Family.* Ithaca, NY: Cornell University Press, 1993.

Mill, John Stuart. *On Liberty,* ed. Currin v. Shields. New York: Liberal Arts Press, 1956.

Mills, Claudia. "Duties to Aging Parents." In *Care of the Aged: Biomedical Ethics Reviews,* ed. James Humber, 147–166. Totowa, NJ: Humana Press, 2003.

Minow, Martha. "Forming Underneath Everything that Grows: Toward a History of Family Law." *Wisconsin Law Review* 1985 (1985): 819–898.

Narayan, Uma, "Family Ties: Rethinking Parental Claims in the Light of Surrogacy and Custody." In *Having and Raising Children,* ed. Uma Narayan and Julia J. Bartkowiak, 65–86. University Park: Pennsylvania State University Press, 1999.

———, and Julia J. Bartkowiak, eds., *Having and Raising Children.* University Park: Pennsylvania State University Press, 1999.

Noggle, Robert. "Special Agents: Children's Autonomy and Parental Authority." In *The Moral and Political Status of Children,* ed. David Archard and Colin M. Macleod, 97–117. New York: Oxford University Press, 2002.

Olsen, Frances E. "The Politics of Family Law." *Law and Inequality* 2 (Feb. 1984): 1–20.

———. "The Myth of State Intervention in the Family." *University of Michigan Journal of Law Reform* 18 (Summer 1985): 835–864.

O'Neill, Onora, and William Ruddick, eds. *Having Children.* Oxford: Oxford University Press, 1979.

Paludi, Michele A., ed. *Ivory Power: Sexual Harassment on Campus.* Albany, NY: SUNY Press, 1990.

———, ed. *Sexual Harassment on College Campuses: Abusing the Ivory Power.* Albany, NY: SUNY Press, 1996.

Parfit, Derek. *Reasons and Persons.* Oxford: Oxford University Press, 1984.

Pateman, Carole. *The Sexual Contract.* Cambridge: Polity Press, 1988.

———. *The Disorder of Women: Democracy, Feminism and Political Theory.* Cambridge: Cambridge University Press, 1989.

Patterson, Charlotte J. *Lesbian and Gay Parenting.* Rev. July 2007. [Online.] Available: http://www.apa.org/pi/parent.html [Accessed July 13, 2009].

Planned Parenthood v. Danforth, 428 U.S. 52 (1976).

Pritchard, Michael S. *On Becoming Responsible.* Lawrence: University Press of Kansas, 1991.

———. *Reasonable Children.* Lawrence: University Press of Kansas, 1996.

Purdy, Laura M. "Surrogate Mothering: Exploitation or Empowerment?" *Bioethics* 3 (Jan. 1989): 18–34.

———. "A Response to Dodds and Jones," *Bioethics* 3 (Jan. 1989): 40–44.

———. "Should Children Be Able to Divorce Their Parents?" In *Having and Raising Children,* ed. Uma Narayan and Julia J. Bartkowiak, 153–162. University Park: Pennsylvania State University Press, 1999.

R.S. v. State of Utah, 940 P.2d 527 (Utah App. 1997).

Robertson, John A. "Assisted Reproductive Technology and the Family." *Hastings Law Journal* (April 1996): 911–934.

Rush, Sharon. "Breaking with Tradition: Surrogacy and Gay Fathers." In *Kindred Matters: Rethinking the Philosophy of the Family,* ed. Diana Tietjens Meyers, Kenneth Kipnis, and Cornelius F. Murphy Jr., 102–142. Ithaca, NY: Cornell University Press, 1993.

Rutter, P. *Sex in the Forbidden Zone*. New York: Fawcett Crest, 1989.

Sandler, Bernice R., and Robert J. Shoop, eds. *Sexual Harassment on Campus*. Needham Heights, MA: Allyn and Bacon, 1997.

Schapiro, Tamar. "What Is a Child?" *Ethics* 109 (July 1999): 715–738.

Schoeman, Ferdinand. "Rights of Children, Rights of Parents, and the Moral Basis of the Family." In *Morals, Marriage and Parenthood*, ed. Laurence D. Houlgate, 220–227. Belmont, CA: Wadsworth, 1999.

Smith, Greg. "Baby Jessica Takes to New Life, New Name," *L.A. Times* (August 7, 1994), A 10.

Smith, Patricia. "Out of Focus, a Child Is Lost." *The Tuscaloosa News* (June 4, 1997).

Snodgrass, Teresa. "Minor's Right to Privacy: Bypass Procedures to Notification Statutes." *Journal of Juvenile Law* 10 (1989): 251–259.

Society for Assisted Reproductive Technology Registry and the American Society for Reproductive Medicine. "Assisted Reproductive Technology in the United States: 2,000 results generated from the American Society for Reproductive Medicine/ Society for Assisted Reproductive Technology Registry." *Fertility and Sterility* 81 (May 2004): 1207–1220.

Sommers, Christina Hoff. "Filial Morality." *Journal of Philosophy* 83 (July 1986): 439–456.

Stanford v. Kentucky 492 U.S. 361 (1989).

Stone, Andrea. "Drives to Ban Gay Adoption Heat Up in 16 States." *USA-Today*, Feb. 21, 2006, 1A.

Tadros, Victor. *Criminal Responsibility*. Oxford: Oxford University Press, 2005.

Thompson v. Oklahoma, 487 U.S. 815 (1988).

Tittle, Peg, ed. *Should Parents Be Licensed?* Amherst, NY: Prometheus Books, 2004.

Wardle, Lynn D. "A Critical Analysis of Interstate Recognition of Lesbigay Adoptions." *Ave Maria Law Review* 3 (2005): 561–616.

Watkins, Sian. "Single Mothers Were Told Their Babies Had Died." *The Age* (June 12, 1996): A4.

Weir, Robert. *Selective Nontreatment of Handicapped Newborns*. New York: Oxford University Press, 1984.

Wicclair, Mark. "Caring for Frail Elderly Parents: Past Parental Sacrifices and the Obligations of Adult Children." *Social Theory and Practice* 16 (Summer 1990): 163–189.

Young, Iris Marion. "Mothers, Citizenship, and Independence: A Critique of Family Values." In *Having and Raising Children*, ed. Uma Narayan and Julia K. Bartkowiak, 15–38. University Park.: Pennsylvania State University Press, 1999.

Young, Robert. "In the Interests of Children and Adolescents." In *Whose Child?* ed. William Aiken and Hugh LaFollette, 177–198. Totowa, NJ: Littlefield Adams, 1980.

Zalk, Sue Rosenberg. "Men in the Academy: A Psychological Profile of Harassment." In *Ivory Power: Sexual Harassment on Campus*, ed. Michele A. Paludi, 141–175. Albany, NY: SUNY Press, 1990.

Index